People

who live

in the dark

' *I think the obsession with the media and the focus groups is making us look as if we want power at any price and that we don't stand for anything. And the people who think Tony has got to look very strong are making him less attractive than he is. This is a very stupid thing to do. He came along as a fresh, young, principled and decent man and some people are trying to turn him into macho man, not seeming decent and principled. I know they are doing it because they think it's the way to win, but I think they're making the wrong judgement and they endanger our victory . . . I sometimes call them the* **PEOPLE WHO LIVE IN THE DARK.** *Everything they do is in hiding. We go to the shadow cabinet, we go to the National Executive Committee. Everything we do is in the light. They live in the dark.* '

Clare Short in an interview with Steve Richards,
New Statesman, 9 August 1996

People
who live
in the dark

ANDREW BLICK

POLITICO'S

First published in Great Britain 2004 by
Politico's Publishing, an imprint of
Methuen Publishing Limited
215 Vauxhall Bridge Road
London SW1V 1EJ

10 9 8 7 6 5 4 3 2 1

A CIP catalogue record for this book is available from the British Library

ISBN 1 84275 062 3

Printed and bound in Great Britain by
Mackays of Chatham

Contents

Preface   vii

Acknowledgements   xi

Prologue: 'The sand in the machine'   xiii

1   Pernicious growth or valuable resource?   1

2   Precedents and precursors   30

3   Enter the special adviser: the Wilson experiment   63

4   Key figures of the Wilson years   90

5   Aides to a thwarted administration: the Heath government   123

6   Expertise and politics: Labour in the 1970s   148

7   'One of my people': Thatcher and the heroic mould   185

8   Storm troops, peacemakers and 'bastards': advisers under Major   223

9   Proliferation and control since 1997   251

10   Trends and achievements   297

Appendix. Special advisers: names and figures   315

A note on historiography and sources   324

Notes   328

Bibliography   351

Index   359

Preface

The main text of this book takes the story of special advisers up to mid-2003. No developments since then have served to contradict the theories which I have advanced, but some occurrences certainly merit attention. In August 2003, Alastair Campbell announced his (long-planned) imminent departure from post as the Prime Minister's Director of Communications and Strategy. The tributes that were consequently paid to his achievements served to suggest that his effectiveness was demonstrable, and may have been one motive for attacks upon him by political opponents. Campbell's replacement was David Hill. Born in 1948 and Oxford educated, Hill worked for Roy Hattersley for two decades from the early 1970s, including a stint as his special adviser from 1976 to 1979. Hattersley writes that 'Hill saved me from far more catastrophes than he created and managed, with remarkable aplomb, to minimise the effect of the fiascos that were unavoidable.' Hill did not enjoy the exemption that Campbell had from the Order in Council stipulation that special advisers were appointed only to supply counsel, and was therefore not officially empowered with executive responsibility for permanent civil servants.

In allowing that formal authority to lapse, the government was acting upon a recommendation contained in the interim findings of the Independent Review of Government Communications chaired by Bob Phillis, Chief Executive of the Guardian Media Group. Phillis's final report appeared in January 2004. It warned against the danger that special advisers might 'become an independent "gateway", channelling instructions out and government work back into the Minister'. In such circumstances, they might wield considerable power within a department. Similar issues had arisen from the government response, in September 2003, to the Committee on Standards in Public Life inquiry into relations between special advisers, ministers and permanent civil servants. An

official commitment was made to providing 'greater clarity on [special advisers']
status' in the next edition of the Code of Conduct for Special Advisers. Additions
to the Code were proposed which would signify an increase of influence on the
part of aides, as compared with the description of their functions in the existing
version, though they were possibly an acknowledgement of arrangements as they
were working. It was intended to state that special advisers could 'convey to
officials Ministers' views, instructions and work priorities', 'seek information and
data from officials', 'commission internal analyses and papers' and 'hold meetings
with officials to discuss the advice being put to Ministers'. They could also
'comment on advice being prepared for Ministers by officials'. The Committee
on Standards in Public Life consequently expressed concern that the provision
for the conveyance of instructions 'seems to enhance the position of Special
Advisers and confuses accountability within the Department'. In late 2003, the
Prime Minister, after 'reflecting on the wording . . . decided to delete "instructions" from the amendment to the Code'.

Two of the dominant political issues from mid-2003 into early 2004 involved
special advisers. Andrew Adonis, an aide at No. 10, is credited as an instigator of
the plan to introduce variable tuition fees for universities, which met with much
resistance, including from the government side of the House. The Hutton
Inquiry into the circumstances surrounding the death of Dr David Kelly took
evidence from Tony Blair's then two senior special advisers, Campbell and
Jonathan Powell, as well as Richard Taylor, a counsellor to Geoff Hoon, the
Secretary of State for Defence. While the findings were disputed by some, it
might be argued that, as has often been the case, a thorough examination of the
facts of the activities of aides, such as Hutton conducted, did not substantiate
allegations and insinuations made in the media. It was also apparent that
permanent officials were capable of the inappropriate disclosure of confidential
information to journalists, an activity more often attributed to special advisers.
Hutton's criticisms of the BBC prompted Gavyn Davies, the Chairman of its
Board of Governors (and a Labour prime ministerial special adviser in the
1970s), to resign. Had Hutton's conclusions been less favourable to the government, or the Higher Education Bill not (narrowly) passed through the
Commons on its Second Reading, Blair's position might well have become
extremely precarious. Perhaps historians would have one day examined the role
of special advisers in his downfall as I have done for some of his predecessors at

Downing Street. They may yet, possibly concluding that an extreme centralisation of government led to a backlash against him. However, on 3 February 2004, to the Commons Liaison Committee, Blair expressed the view that, while he was portrayed by some as a domineering Prime Minister, his No. 10 did not interact with the rest of the government in a manner radically different to that of previous premiers.

Finally, there was increased momentum for the campaign to introduce a Civil Service Act, which would cover aides as well as regular staff, although it was not a foregone conclusion. The Public Administration Committee published a draft Bill in January 2004 and the government reiterated the fact that it intended to bring one forward, something which the Conservative Party also now advocated. Such public commitments were prompted in part by a level of concern over the condition of the state machinery, to which the controversy surrounding special advisers had contributed. The initial chief architect of the permanent Civil Service, Charles Trevelyan, had advocated the enshrinement of its values in an Act of Parliament, but for the following one hundred and fifty years – at least – this did not come about. The employment of special advisers during the late twentieth and early twenty-first century has challenged central principles of career Whitehall. If their continued use indirectly contributes to the creation of the sort of legislation which Trevelyan desired, that would be a perverse outcome indeed.

Acknowledgements

First I would like to thank Professor Peter Hennessy, whose guidance and advice over a number of years has made my research and writing possible. Sean Magee, Iain Dale, John Schwartz, Emma Musgrave and everyone else at Politico's have my gratitude for their efforts in publishing the book. My study of special advisers began in the summer of 1998 as a research project for the Communication Group. Following some work carried out on the subject in conjunction with Steve John and Scott Kelly, I began a PhD in the autumn of 1999.

In the interim, I served an internship at No. 10 Downing Street. I have not used any confidential information that might have been acquired in the course of my (largely functional) duties there. However, my work was informed, and my understanding broadened, by my experiences. I ensured that all those I worked with were aware of my research interest, and am grateful for their tolerating my presence.

My PhD was funded by a three-year Studentship from Queen Mary, University of London. Amongst those in the history department who helped me are Professor John Miller, Professor Miri Rubin, James Ellison, Mark White, Mark Glancy and Professor John Ramsden, as wel as fellow students including Helen Parr.

June Morris and Professor Anthony Thirlwall read parts of my PhD and made valuable suggestions, as did my examiners, Professor Paul Addison and Professor Ben Pimlott.

Professor George Jones, Professor Frances Stewart, Michael Stewart, Karen Blick and Robin Blick read and commented on sections of or the entire book. Gillian Somerscales meticulously copy-edited it. All conclusions and errors of fact or omission are my own.

The staff of the British Library, University of London Library at Senate House, London School of Economics Library and Archive, Public Record Office at Kew, and King's College Archive, Cambridge helped greatly. The Fabian Society and Centre for Policy Studies gave me permission to use their files. Sir Samuel Brittan allowed me to quote from his diary, Lord Lipsey from correspondence produced by him in the Crosland Collection, and Professor Anthony Thirlwall from the Kaldor Collection. Stuart Holland supplied me with a selection of his personal papers.

A number of people have provided me with employment while working on the book. They are: Graham Allen MP, Harriet Jones and the Institute of Contemporary British History, Illumina Productions, Lord Radice, and King's College, London.

Finally, I am grateful to Nicola Brookanks and my family members for their support.

Prologue
'The sand in the machine'

On 25 June 2003 Alastair Campbell appeared before the Foreign
Affairs Select Committee during the course of its investigation of the government's decision to go to war against Iraq the previous March. The occasion
attracted extensive media attention – to the extent of being broadcast live on
news channels – not only because of interest in the substantive policy issue under
debate, but because of a widespread fascination with Campbell himself. Here was
further confirmation, if any were needed, of the significance attached within and
beyond political circles to Tony Blair's Director of Communications and
Strategy, and to the role of special advisers within the Labour administration.

The committee was concerned in this session with the contribution made by
the Prime Minister's office to the production of dossiers on Saddam Hussein's
regime, and in particular its military capabilities, in the lead-up to war. Some
sections of the media had seemed to suggest that partisan aides had overridden
and compromised the professional integrity of the security services in order to
serve presentational ends. A Conservative committee member, John Maples, put
it to Campbell that 'there are more politically appointed specialist [sic] advisers
in Downing Street under this administration than there have ever been in the
past and their fingerprints are awfully close to all these documents.' In particular,
one document compiled in September 2002 and another from February 2003
were both alleged to have been altered by No. 10 to the extent of being
misleading, exaggerating the threat posed by Iraq's alleged illicit weapons
programme in order to add force to the case for war. In the case of the latter,
Campbell explained that the staff who had introduced changes had not realised
that they were altering material produced outside the government. As far as the
former was concerned, Campbell appeared particularly angry at a story by a BBC

correspondent, supposedly based on the views of a well-placed source, that he had himself insisted on the 'sexing up' of a report compiled by the Joint Intelligence Committee to make the Iraqi threat appear more grave. The allegation against him, said Campbell, was that he had

> *helped the Prime Minister persuade Parliament and the country to go into conflict on the basis of a lie. I think that is a pretty serious allegation. It has been denied by the Prime Minister, it has been denied by the Chairman of the Joint Intelligence Committee, it has been denied by the Security and Intelligence Co-ordinator and it has been denied by the heads of the intelligence agencies involved, and yet the BBC continue to stand by that story . . . It is completely and totally untrue . . . It is actually a lie.*

He insisted that the BBC should apologise.[1]

Not only his particular actions, but Campbell's personal authority, and that of other senior aides, were under the microscope. He was the chair of the Iraq Communications Group, which included senior representatives from the Secret Intelligence Service (SIS, commonly known as MI6), the Foreign Office, the Ministry of Defence and the Department for International Development.[2] The Coalition Information Centre, first established during the Kosovo conflict in 1999, was based at the Foreign Office; however, the committee concluded that it 'appears to have operated as an autonomous unit, within the FCO, chaired by a senior FCO official but reporting to Alastair Campbell'.[3] Campbell's influence over the conduct of public relations, then, was great. Did it extend further, into the determination of actual policy decisions?

Just over a week earlier Clare Short, Secretary of State for International Development until her resignation the previous month, had told the committee that she believed Campbell to be responsible for more than communication. 'Alastair Campbell,' she had said, 'is responsible for the presentation of government policy, and that soon becomes propaganda and there is a place for that. Once proper decisions have been made, then the government should put forward what it is trying to do as well as it can and communicate to the public, *but the two often conflate*' (emphasis added). Short referred to a 'close entourage' surrounding the Prime Minister, comprising three special advisers – Campbell, Jonathan Powell and Baroness (Sally) Morgan – as well as Blair's foreign affairs adviser, the career official Sir David Manning. In Short's words, 'That was the team, they were the ones who moved together all the time. They attended the daily "War Cabinet". That was the in group, that was the group that was in charge of policy.' The consequence of such a *modus operandi*, Short argued, was the bypassing of Cabinet, where there was 'no kind of collective decision-making'. She broadened the argument, saying that the tendency existed 'not just in relation to Iraq, but ... more generally'. Short believed that 'this is our political system, this is our country's decision-making system and it is not good enough ... I think your Committee has to take this seriously for the sake of our country's good governance.'[4]

Pursuing the theme with Campbell, Maples asked whether, approaching the conflict, 'there were meetings which the Prime Minister called at which his special advisers were present and his foreign policy adviser but no other minister ... at which decisions were made'. Campbell's response was that it depended

what sort of decisions you mean. If I were having a meeting with the Prime Minister about whether he should do Newsnight *with Jeremy Paxman or ITV with Trevor McDonald . . . whether the Prime Minister might go to see President Bush on a Tuesday or a Thursday, that is the sort of decision we might take in that group. If you are talking about a decision about whether the Prime Minister was going to commit British forces into action, the idea something like that is going to be taken without full consultation of his ministerial colleagues in the Cabinet is nonsense.*

Campbell defended the right of the Prime Minister to 'have a support team around him, whether [or not] they happen to be special advisers', and argued that 'the aim of the Conservative Party is somehow to contaminate the concept of special advisers.' Maples argued that Campbell and Powell's 'great positions of power', which were not derived from 'having ... been elected or gone through the Civil Service selection and reporting and career procedure', were 'a novelty', and drew attention to their formal empowerment with executive authority by a 1997 Order in Council. Campbell said that, on the contrary, 'the Order in Council is the novelty.'[5]

Two days later, the Director of Communications and Strategy made an unusual appearance on *Channel Four News* in which he referred to the media perception of 'the evil spin doctors in the dark'.[6] He also took the opportunity to drive home his complaint about the BBC, and shortly thereafter his confrontation with the corporation became a major news story. Within a month of Campbell's appearance before the committee, Dr David Kelly, a Ministry of Defence weapons expert, confessed to having spoken about the Iraq dossiers to the BBC journalist, Andrew Gilligan, who had made the allegation about the September dossier's having been 'sexed up'. Dr Kelly appeared before the Foreign Affairs Select Committee, which judged that he was not the main source for Gilligan's allegation. By this time Kelly was at the centre of the whirlpool of media attention generated by the conflict between Campbell and the BBC. Following Kelly's apparent suicide, the BBC confirmed that he had indeed been Gilligan's main supplier of information.

Those embroiled in these events included not only serving aides, but a number of their predecessors. Jack Straw, the Foreign Secretary, had been a special adviser to Barbara Castle when she was the Secretary of State for Social Services from 1974 to 1976 and to Peter Shore at Environment from 1976 to 1977. Gavyn Davies (whose partner, Sue Nye, was an assistant to Gordon Brown, the Chancellor of the Exchequer), chairman of the BBC, had served as a Policy Unit member during the premierships of Harold Wilson and James Callaghan. Robert Jackson MP, who as Dr Kelly's constituency representative demanded Davies's resignation, was from 1973 to 1974 a political adviser to Maurice Macmillan, Edward Heath's Secretary of State for Employment. Earlier in the year he had told me that he felt the use of temporary civil servants had got out of hand. 'They're not the grit in the oyster,' he said, 'they're the sand in the machine.'[7]

Even the briefest of glimpses of this episode reveals that the use of special advisers in government has become an embedded part of British public life, significant in its own right as well as in having provided apprenticeships for some of the great and the good. It requires illumination. Much controversy has surrounded the use of political appointments to the Civil Service. As Campbell suggested, there has been a tendency for media treatment of the topic to resort to caricature and exaggeration. Nevertheless, the attention was merited: the advisers' positions were significant, their proximity to power a reality, albeit difficult to quantify. Collectively, they were a well-known, even notorious breed. Individually, some aides were celebrities – the extreme case being Campbell himself, whose fame rivalled or exceeded that of many Cabinet members. The darkness I have sought to dispel in writing this book, then, is not the obscurity associated with a lack of publicity or media attention; rather, I have set out to investigate and explain the historical origins, development and significance of the 'special advisers', with a view to arriving at a better understanding of their current nature and functions, and the extent to which they represent discontinuity with past practice.

Chapter 1 considers the various perspectives from which the phenomenon of the special adviser is of relevance and interest. It describes the pronounced level of interest in special advisers which had emerged by the early twenty-first century. It also defines the formal framework within which they currently operate. In Chapter 2 the long-term background is explained and precedents for the use of aides of this type sought; and the circumstances and motives lying behind the introduction of the special adviser are described. In Chapters 3 and 4, a study of the experiment which followed during the 1964–70 Labour administrations of Harold Wilson is conducted.[8] Extended space is devoted to the period for a number of reasons, among them that it was the crucial, formative period for the special adviser; that it has, so far, been largely overlooked; and that a rich archive of primary evidence, including Public Record Office (PRO) files, is available. Chapter 3 provides an overview of Wilson's introduction of aides into government, while Chapter 4 is concerned with biographical studies of selected individuals. The rise of the special adviser in the years following the fall of Wilson's government in 1970 is then depicted, divided according to prime ministerial terms, in Chapters 5–9. A conclusion is drawn in Chapter 10.

One

Pernicious growth
or valuable resource?

Special advisers are a firmly established but not widely understood element in British government. Temporary civil servants, very often associated with the party in office, they are drawn from beyond the Whitehall career structure, their appointments subject to the patronage of individual ministers to whom they are attached and for whom they work. They may be in possession of specialist knowledge or skills or particular experience, acquired in fields such as academia or business. Variously, they provide services including political counsel, expert guidance, the maintenance of contact with outside groups and the media, and personal assistance. Changes in the party of government are accompanied by wholesale clear-outs of special advisers. If their ministers are sacked or shifted to new portfolios, they may serve the successors, follow their employers to different offices of government, or leave Whitehall. Since the advent in 1997 of a Labour administration under the premiership of Tony Blair, the role of the special adviser has received a high level of, often disapproving, public attention.[1] There has, however, been no specific attempt to investigate the historical origins and development of the phenomenon – which is what this book sets out to do, examining the period from 1964 onwards.

Who are special advisers and why do they matter?

In selecting subjects for detailed consideration I have confined myself to aides attached to central government, not including, for example, those appointed to serve the Scottish Executive. In determining whether a particular individual should be considered a special adviser, a listing as such in official publications, particularly the *Civil Service Yearbook* and *Hansard*, is taken as a strong, though not infallible, indicator; for this reason, members of the Prime Minister's Policy Unit not drawn from the career Civil Service are included for study, a choice with which some might quibble. Where subjects do not quite fit into the category – for example, if they are not paid from public funds – but are deemed to merit investigation anyway, the fact is indicated.

I have set out to establish who these counsellors were, what they did and why, how they functioned and how many of them there were. What were their official positions, in terms of matters such as job titles, pay, access to information and particularly rules governing conduct? How did they deal with one another, with career civil servants and with ministers? How was their role debated, in public and in private? I have examined the relationships between special advisers and the major political and administrative developments of their periods of office, and also the cultural resonance they have had beyond the proximate world of politics. Through all these lines of investigation I have sought to arrive at an explanation of their collective and individual significance and to determine whether their fundamental characteristics have changed over time.

A number of themes emerge from these deliberations. First, there is the relationship between special advisers and their particular appointing ministers. Aides depended for their employment upon the patronage of individual politicians. Their first loyalties, therefore, were arguably owed to those they served. The political interests of both were synonymous. The furtherance of the minister's career, even at the expense of others, was likely to be desirable to the counsellor. Politicians who employed aides could become reliant upon them. Special advisers and their ministers sometimes belonged to the same party faction and shared a similar ideological outlook. They frequently worked together in pursuit of key policy objectives. In some cases, ministers and aides were long-standing associates. Sometimes, they moved in the same social circles and were friends. Special advisers might be members of the informal 'courts' which sometimes coalesced around politicians.[2] The members of such groups, which were frequently marked by internal rivalries, achieved influence through their individual relationships with the person upon whom they centred. Where there was no pre-existing close personal connection between aide and politician, it could develop in office. Bonds of the type described here could override other commitments, including those to party and to the government as a whole. At times, for example, special advisers acted against their employers' rivals within the Cabinet.

Special advisers can also be assessed in terms of their partisanship. Sympathetic aides were recruited partly as a means of ensuring the implementation of programmes by parties entering government after periods of opposition. Special advisers tended to be supporters of the administrations they served. Their employment resulted from electoral success and was dependent upon the governing party's continuation in office. Most were active in party circles prior to their appointment as aides. Some participated in the implementation of policies they had helped develop in opposition. Special advisers often concerned themselves with the ideological content of policy. They also took a particular interest in the party political implications of decisions, for example their potential impact upon the popularity of the government. Aides could perform the function of maintaining links between ministers who, having worked closely together in opposition, were now spread out across the various departments of government. They also served to preserve ministers' contacts with both their party organisations and backbench MPs.

Some special advisers were recruited from media or public relations backgrounds to bring their skills to bear on behalf of ministers. Many were occupied largely or partly in presentational activities such as the development of public relations strategy and speech-writing; even those who were not primarily charged with such duties nevertheless often took an interest in the area. One facet of this work was the cultivation of relations with journalists, extending in some cases to the controversial practice of giving anonymous briefings, whether in the attempt to secure a favourable public reception for the government and its policies or in the pursuance of internal rivalries within the government relating to personal ambitions, factional disputes and ideological disagreements. On occasions, aides themselves became the subject of press interest.

The recruitment of aides could be portrayed as a response to political and economic malaise. From the late 1950s a pronounced perception of national decline emerged in British political circles, prompted by such factors as a rapid deterioration in international status and relatively low economic growth rates. Associated with this perception was an erosion of social deference, expressed among other ways through criticism of traditional institutions, including the career Civil Service, which in turn led to demands for measures leading to the instigation of the special adviser. Subsequently, particularly from the late 1960s, other difficulties, including poor industrial relations, soaring inflation, rising unemployment and a weak currency came to the fore. Aides developed major policies aimed, in various ways, at the reversal of national fortunes. Successive crises with which government had to contend contributed to a phenomenon which has been labelled 'overload', entailing the subjection of administrators to demands which could not possibly be fully, effectively, met by any individual. Aides arguably helped ease the burden, for example by scrutinising papers being channelled to the offices of secretaries of state and briefing them on significant issues.

The perception of national decline arguably encouraged greater polarisation in politics. From the late 1960s a number of historians began to argue that, at some point during the 1940s or early 1950s, a 'broad agreement' emerged at elite political level 'over certain fundamentals of government policy' including 'Britain's world role, the welfare state, the mixed economy, and the goal of full employment'. This consensus, according to those who believe it existed, broke down in the 1970s, conclusively following the establishment of Margaret Thatcher's Conservative administration in 1979. Since the late 1980s the very idea of the 'postwar consensus' has been portrayed by some as a myth.[3] Nevertheless, the appearance of and proliferation in special advisers coincided with the crisis in the supposed political settlement.

It is possible to argue that the special adviser was not a genuine innovation at all. At various stages in British history administrations have used temporary civil servants, some of whom bore similarities to those employed from 1964. There have been, for example, individual personal aides and teams of prime ministerial advisers, as during the career of David Lloyd George. The conclusion could be drawn that, rather than signifying the emergence of something new, special advisers were simply the latest in a long line of outsiders to be introduced to Whitehall. This is not a view I take; nevertheless, this book will investigate earlier experiments with the use of outside aides and the changes already under way in 1964.

The introduction of the special adviser can also be explained in terms of a desire to incorporate into administration qualities absent from government. From the late 1950s onwards a number of observers called for the correction of a perceived weakness in the Civil Service, which, it was argued, overvalued abstract intelligence at the expense of particular skills and knowledge. One of the functions of special advisers, in particular those recruited as experts in various fields, including economics, was to provide ministers with advice of a type that would otherwise be lacking. Their skills were brought to bear in the development of a number of policy packages. Businessmen have also been recruited, who have applied private sector methods and values to government.

It may be possible, for analytical purposes, to divide aides into two groups, namely those who were specialists and those who were not. Within the latter category, there are arguably subdivisions, for example between media handlers and others. Possibly, over time, the proportion of specialists among those employed as temporary civil servants declined. However, this is only one way of distinguishing between types of adviser, for other characteristics, such as partisanship and an interest in the effective presentation of policy, can be detected in specialist and non-specialist alike.

Special advisers can be regarded as political actors in their own right. Some of them were already substantial figures, for example in the intellectual field, and carried that weight with them into office; some possessed skills and contributed ideas which might otherwise have been absent from the administration; some were motivating forces behind a number of policy initiatives that bore their distinctive personal imprints. Attempts were made by special advisers both to bring about the implementation of particular schemes and to influence the overall direction of government policy, in accordance with their own preferences. Their personalities, which were in some cases characterised by pronounced eccentricities, became important factors in the environment where they worked. Special advisers could become embroiled in political intrigue. The importance of the individual in the role might suggest that the qualities of particular aides could be more significant than the total number in employment.

The subject must also be examined from the perspective of the governmental centre. The Prime Minister has nearly always had a larger number of special advisers than any other minister, and has had the power of veto over the appointment of ministers' advisers. Both factors could be interpreted as associated with the ability of premiers to exert control over their administrations. Aides were involved in activities such as the scrutiny of policy and implementation chasing on behalf of the Prime Minister, whom they also helped to develop ideological approaches. Special advisers could facilitate policy interventions from No. 10. It could also be argued that the appearance of special advisers attached to the premier signified a stage in the emergence of a prime ministerial department, albeit on an informal basis. The attachment of a staff directly to the Prime Minister can be associated with the growth of a leadership cult in British politics. The use of aides across administrations as a whole has to some extent reflected the personal style of each individual premier.

There is potential for comparison between foreign arrangements and the use of special advisers in British government. The continental bureaucratic model, particularly the use of *cabinets* – mixed teams of career officials and outsiders – was a direct influence. Similarities could also be identified with the approach taken in the United States, where the 'spoils' system, entailing a blanket replacement of senior staff upon changes of administration, prevailed. Throughout the history of the special adviser analogies of this sort have been drawn, in the course of both approving and critical comment. Certain international tendencies in the changing types of aides recruited by ministers – from the extensive use of outside experts by John F. Kennedy in the United States in the 1960s and Gough Whitlam's recruits in Australia in the 1970s to Mitterrand's expansion of presidential appointments in the 1980s – can be identified and observed in the British case.

Another perspective from which to view special advisers is that of their contributions to policy. They have been associated with the implementation of numerous significant proposals across a variety of fields. A number of these might not have appeared at all were it not for the input of aides, including detailed formulation, preparing the ground inside the government and public presentation. Many of the conflicts in which special advisers became embroiled related to policy objectives. Aides have often provided counsel on the approaches to be taken in relation to the most important developments during their periods in office.

Since the subjects of this work were employed as civil servants, albeit on a temporary basis, they should also be considered in terms of their relationship with the permanent machine. The appointment of special advisers challenged certain entrenched Whitehall customs, many of which could be traced to the mid-nineteenth century. Traditionally, senior civil servants were neutral in party politics, recruited on a basis of open competitive examination, rather than personal patronage; their tenure was not dependent upon the fortunes of individual ministers or election results. Normally, they entered the Civil Service shortly after graduation from university and stayed there throughout their working lives. Movement in and out of the Civil Service during the course of a single career was abnormal. So, too, was the temporary recruitment of outsiders into Whitehall. The philosophy of generalism, which valued abstract intelligence over specialist knowledge, prevailed. Typically, senior bureaucrats were educated in subjects such as Classics or mathematics at Oxford or Cambridge. The most influential office of government within Whitehall, in terms of both personnel decisions and policy formation, was the Treasury.

The introduction of the special adviser followed a period of public questioning of many of these traditions, and was partially intended as a corrective to them. Aides have often been critics of existing Whitehall arrangements and proponents of reforms to them. Particular opposition has been shown to the Treasury dominance of the Civil Service. One motive for the use of political appointments has been the desire to ensure that party policy programmes were not obstructed by permanent civil servants, intentionally or otherwise. Antagonism has developed between career officials and special advisers, centring on issues such as status, propriety and access to ministers, committees and official papers. There have been concerns regarding the potential for corruption. For example, knowledge and influence obtained inside Whitehall might have commercial value, which outsiders would be both more likely and more able to exploit.

Finally, the emergence of the special adviser as a constant element in government had implications for the British constitution, within which a neutral body of permanent officials was traditionally regarded as an essential element. Critics have attacked the use of overtly partisan aides on the grounds that it undermined this settlement, through threatening to politicise the Civil Service. An informal understanding that special advisers were employed only to supply counsel to ministers, and not to manage career staff, existed from the outset and in 1991 was embodied in an Order in Council. However, in some cases aides arguably took on effective executive authority; and indeed, from 1997 a small number at Downing Street were officially empowered to do so.

In this book, phrases such as 'executive powers' and 'management functions' are used to describe integration into the bureaucratic hierarchy and therefore the possession of some sort of authority over others within the Civil Service. It is argued here that such a status can be acquired unofficially as well as officially, and that its exercise can take overt forms, particularly issuing instructions, as well as more subtle ones. The latter include suggestions, requests and the expression of viewpoints during discussions, which acquire weight through the fact that the person from whom they emanate is known to be close to a minister (or Prime Minister). Whatever roles special advisers were supposed to be confined to, they could become powerful within Whitehall. In the British constitutional tradition, a divergence between strict official descriptions and realities is common. For example, the Prime Minister only formally 'advises' the monarch on a variety of matters. It is possible to cloud the issue, through second-order debates over matters such as whether certain functions can strictly be classified as 'line management', or if someone determines expenditure from budgets, or is involved in recruitment, promotions, rewards, discipline or appraisals. What is most important is the extent to which a political appointee is in some respect able to influence, or even control, the activities of career officials. This is relevant because, for special advisers, while working directly with the minister has been important to achieving effectiveness, so too was dealing with representatives of the machine, which they did continuously. There is also a semantic discrepancy between the term 'advice' and tasks including press briefing, although it is not as significant a matter as the exercise of *de facto* or *de jure* executive authority by aides.

The growth in numbers of special advisers which took place over the period as a whole might be seen as overwhelming permanent Whitehall. As with many constitutional developments in Britain, the appearance of special advisers took place in an informal, ad hoc fashion. As Sir Richard Wilson, the outgoing Cabinet Secretary, remarked to the Committee on Standards in Public Life in July 2002, 'it seems to me that we have, over the last 20 or 30 years – and this is not a criticism of anybody – been fairly casual in our approach to some of these issues and they have developed in a fairly low-key way.'[4] The introduction of rules and regulations to govern these incomers was similarly gradual and piecemeal. Even at the time of writing, guidance had yet to become comprehensive and demands were being made for a Civil Service Act. Special advisers possibly challenged other constitutional understandings. Their attachment to the Prime Minister assisted an erosion of Cabinet government. Furthermore, they were arguably not subject to appropriate parliamentary scrutiny, and facilitated the direct communication of the government with the public, circumventing the legislature.

'A blight on the government and public life'

'Why have special advisers come to be ranked somewhere alongside paedophiles in the lexicon of media opprobium?'[5] This was a question posed by Tony Wright, a Labour MP and chairman of the Commons Select Committee on Public Administration in February 2002. He was writing in the *Guardian* in the midst of a protracted scandal involving Jo Moore, a political appointee to the Department of Transport, Local Government and the Regions (DTLR). The 1997 return of a Labour administration saw heightened interest in such temporary recruits to Whitehall, from a wide range of sources and, as Wright suggested, of an increasingly critical nature. This interest reached a peak around the time of the Jo Moore affair.

Even before Tony Blair took office, his use of aides, some of whom went onto serve as special advisers in the new administration, was subject to public criticism from within his own shadow Cabinet. In a *New Statesman* interview in August 1996 Clare Short, following her demotion from the transport to the international development brief, cautioned that the leadership's 'obsession with the media' was endangering the party's chances of election success. Labour's traditional values, Short claimed, were being abandoned and Blair presented as a 'macho man' in an attempt to win over the Conservative press. She identified the culprits as Blair's inner circle of personal counsellors, whom she referred to as 'the people who live in the dark'. Distinguishing between them and shadow ministers such as herself, she said, 'We go to the Shadow Cabinet. We go to the NEC. Everything we do is in the light. They live in the dark. It is a good place for them.' *The Times* noted that Short was 'known to be resentful about the way Mr Blair's media advisers privately criticised her after a series of controversial statements'. One of those she had in mind was believed to be Blair's press secretary, Alastair Campbell.[6]

Right from the inauguration of the new administration in May 1997, the press displayed an interest in the use of temporary civil servants under Blair. Initially, some of the coverage was positive. On 5 May 1997 the *Financial Times* referred to an 'expanded network of special advisers' who were 'some of the people destined to shape Labour government policy'. It suggested that, in contrast to the use of special advisers during the previous Conservative administration, when 'the stress was on "spinning" . . . under Labour the balance is expected to shift towards policy development'.[7] Even at this early stage, however, prime ministerial appointments were portrayed as manifestations of Blair's supposed intention, in the words of John Deans in the *Daily Mail* on 6 May, to 'impose a tight presidential-style grip on his government right from the start'.[8] There were also suggestions that temporary civil servants were members of an incestuous, closed circle of individuals which had now been elevated to a position of power. Kamal Ahmed, writing in the *Guardian* on 21 May, referred to 'the "new network" – that intricate, sometimes obscure amalgam of friends and advisers of Tony Blair that now make up the most important grouping of contacts and dinner table guests in Britain'.[9] Collective profiles of the expanding group of aides began regularly appearing in the press.[10] A further suggestion that special advisers had 'arrived' was provided by the increased attention they began to receive from lobbyists.[11]

Increasingly, the mood turned sour. The media started to question the probity of a government which had initially been widely portrayed as signalling a new, scrupulous approach. Campbell, now appointed as the Prime Minister's official spokesman, became a particular target. It was argued by some that, where controversial subjects were concerned, he was, as one observer put it, 'likely . . . to rely on those facts that suit his case'.[12] In July 1998 allegations were made regarding government links with certain lobbying organisations. Attention was drawn to the fact that Roger Liddle, a Blair aide, was a co-founder of the Prima Europe public affairs company, although his financial association with it had ceased.[13] Further negative publicity was generated when the patronage nature of special adviser appointments was subjected to legal challenge in 1998. The Lord Chancellor, Lord Irvine, was taken to an industrial tribunal by a female solicitor on grounds of sexual discrimination, since (following the standard practice) he had appointed an aide, Garry Hart, without advertising the post.[14] Had Irvine lost the case, some argued, the method by which special advisers were recruited might have been called into doubt. The argument offered in his defence, which eventually won through, was that, since the vacancy was not publicised, all potential applicants, regardless of gender or race, were excluded. Personal knowledge, it was held, was a vital and legitimate requirement for the Lord Chancellor when selecting an aide.[15] The case provided fuel for those who sought to accuse the Blair administration of 'cronyism'.

A secondary literature noting the importance of special advisers was generated. The BBC political correspondent Nicholas Jones was the most detailed, persistent analyst of aides under Blair, taking a particular interest in those engaged in presentational activities – 'spin doctors', as they were commonly known. Since 1997 he has published two books on the subject, *Sultans of Spin* and *The Control Freaks*.[16] It was Jones's contention that Labour, in applying to government the same centralised news management techniques that apparently transformed its fortunes in opposition, undermined Civil Service neutrality and, through advance press briefing, the role of Parliament as the official outlet for government announcements. It also encouraged a further lowering in the overall quality of political coverage in the media. Special advisers, Jones argued, were integral to these developments. He believed, furthermore, that the 'spin doctors' failed to operate within guidelines restricting the partisan nature of their activity. In 1999 Peter Oborne published his biography of Blair's chief press secretary, Alastair Campbell, emphasising Campbell's extensive influence upon the Prime Minister.[17] James Naughtie's *The Rivals*, which described the relationship between Blair and his long-time friend and competitor, Gordon Brown, the Chancellor of the Exchequer, portrayed the two politicians as surrounded by largely mutually exclusive entourages, within which aides were senior figures.[18] Graham Allen, a Labour MP and government whip from 1997 to 2001, produced a book entitled *The Last Prime Minister*, which appeared in 2001. Although not critical of the trend, he suggested that a de facto presidential system had emerged, with prime ministerial special advisers comprising a significant proportion of the 'Presidential staff'.[19] Cabinet government, he believed, was now a fiction. Allen wished to see the strong centre complemented by a genuinely separate, enhanced legislature, arguing that MPs were currently under-powered.

Criticism was also directed at special advisers from within the Conservative Party. In the 2000 paperback addition of his autobiography, John Major suggested that the use of increasing numbers of special advisers under Blair, paid for by public funds, threatened to compromise Whitehall impartiality. In Major's view, political appointees were an undesirable element in an excessive concentration of power in the hands of the Prime Minister, to the detriment of collective Cabinet government. He argued, like Jones, that the practice of unattributable briefing of journalists by ministerial counsellors had encouraged a tendency towards sensationalism and speculation rather than more sober discussion on the part of the press. Furthermore, presentation 'became an obsession:

spin and soundbite became more important than argument and fact – in the process, turning the public ratchet a little more towards cynicism'.[20]

In January 2001, referring to aides who were not in possession of specialist knowledge, the former senior Conservative Cabinet minister Michael Heseltine told the Public Administration Committee that 'all these special advisers, the political ones, are going to be the Achilles heel about this government's neck before long. I would get rid of all those. One of the worst things that has happened has been the politicisation . . . of government. I would get them all out.'[21] The notoriety of special advisers was confirmed by a reference in the 2001 Conservative election manifesto. Here, it was claimed that 'Our constitution is being perverted, and faith in politics and politicians is at an all-time low.' In order to help remedy such supposed disillusionment, the Conservatives promised to 'cut the number of political advisers and spin doctors employed, at the taxpayer's expense, to serve government ministers'.[22]

In July 2000 Ken Follett, the novelist and husband of the Labour MP Barbara, and formerly a public supporter of Blair, attacked No. 10's supposed use of unattributable briefings to inspire press articles suggesting that ministers were due to be removed from their posts. Blair, he cautioned, was in danger of being remembered as 'the Prime Minister who made malicious gossip an everyday tool of modern British government'. Before the 1980s, Follett wrote, 'it would have been highly unusual for a Prime Minister, or his messengers, to calumniate members of his own government to the press.' Thatcher's press secretary, Bernard Ingham, had pioneered the practice, Follett argued, but it had not been continued under Major. Campbell was named as a chief offender, but ultimately, Follett believed, Blair himself was both aware of what was happening and ultimately responsible for it. Memorably, Follett went on to state that the 'people who do the briefing, who whisper the words of poison into the ears of journalists, are of no consequence. They are the rent boys of politics, and we shudder with disgust when they brush past us in the lobby'.[23]

Both the Committee on Standards in Public Life and the Public Administration Committee took an interest in the subject. In January 2000 the former drew attention to the fact that the number of special advisers had increased from thirty-eight in early 1997 to seventy-four in late 1999, and called for a cap to be placed on the permissible total. It envisaged this rule as forming part of a Civil Service Act, which would establish a single legal framework for Whitehall. The committee also proposed the introduction of a separate code of conduct for politically appointed special advisers, including a section covering contact with the media.[24] The government agreed in principle to act on both the latter suggestions.[25] In March 2001 the Public Administration Committee, which in 1998 had sought clarification and codification of the activities of aides in the public relations field,[26] produced a report entitled *Special Advisers: Boon or Bane?*[27] One of its most important proposals was that 'special adviser posts should be publicly advertised and the Minister given the final choice between suitably qualified candidates'. This step would have undermined the central principle underpinning the use of special advisers, that of appointment on a purely patronage basis. The proposal was rejected.

By the autumn of 2001, then, special advisers had already become the subject of great interest and controversy. In some quarters they were being held at least partly to blame for many of the perceived woes of modern politics. Then, on 9 October, reports appeared in the media that Jo Moore, an aide to Stephen Byers, Secretary of State at the DTLR, had sent an e-mail to officials on 11 September suggesting that the terrorist attacks which had taken place that day in the United States meant that it was 'a very good day' to 'get out anything we want to bury'. A discontented element inside the department was the probable source of the leak. In the midst of predictably moralistic press demands that she be removed, Moore remained in her post, although she did receive a personal reprimand from Byers and an official warning from Sir Richard Mottram, Permanent Secretary at the DTLR. Then on 11 and 12 October stories began to emerge that Moore had asked one or more permanent civil servants to provide journalists with negative briefings regarding Bob Kiley, Transport Commissioner for London, who was at that point locked in a dispute with central government regarding the financing of London Underground. Any such request would have tested Whitehall impartiality regulations applying to career officials, to whom, moreover, Moore was not formally empowered to issue instructions. At this time Alun Evans, the DTLR Director of Communications, left his post, moving elsewhere in Whitehall.

Setting aside the electronic media, the quantity of press coverage which was generated – most of it hostile to Moore, special advisers in general, Byers and Blair – was immense, in broadsheets and tabloids alike. On 13 October the *Daily Star* suggested that Byers did not want to remove Moore because 'she was only doing what he pays her for – with OUR money, mind'. Its verdict was that Byers should give Moore 'the boot' and 'sack himself while he's at it'. If necessary, Blair, whose 'own integrity is at stake', should force such an outcome.[28] It was a very similar line to the one taken at the other end of the market by the *Independent*, which argued on the same day that if Byers 'cannot see that Ms Moore has committed a sackable offence, then he is unfit to remain in government'. Furthermore, it was 'worrying that Mr Blair . . . did not recognise Mr Byers' stance as an insult to his allegedly elevated view of the moral purpose of politics'.[29]

The *Mirror* (pro-Labour, although not necessarily entirely supportive of Blair) argued that Moore, who had displayed a 'horrible heartlessness' and 'ordered a senior civil servant to breach Whitehall rules', was 'damaging the government and the Labour Party'.[30] Writing in the *Express* under the headline 'This twisted spin is just as hideous as terrorism', Martin Samuel went so far as to state that he found it easier to understand the actions of the 11 September terrorists than those of Moore, 'who looked at the horror and misery within the World Trade Centre and saw only a PR opportunity'.[31] On 14 October the *Mail on Sunday* reported comparisons drawn by a representative of the Public Relations Standards Council between Moore and Adolf Hitler.[32]

A number of public figures and celebrities not normally associated with political commentary voiced opinions. On 13 October both the Archbishop of York, Dr David Hope, and the Board of Deputies of British Jews were referred to in the *Daily Mail* as expressing concern at Moore's e-mail.[33] Writing in the *Sun*, the breakfast television presenter Lorraine Kelly described Moore as a 'sneaky spider . . . spinning her web of lies and half truths' and went on to ponder whether Moore was a 'cold-hearted one-off, or [whether] all of the government's special advisors have this warped view of the world?'. If they did, in Kelly's view, 'then not only should she be shown the door, but the whole sad and sorry bunch of spinning spiders should be firmly crushed under foot.'[34] That a form of Whitehall appointment should be the subject of news headlines was, in itself, unusual. The extension of coverage to columns such as Kelly's was even more so.

Alun Evans's replacement as Director of Information at the DTLR, Martin Sixsmith, took up office on 19 November. On 14 February 2002, claims appeared in the press that Moore had encouraged the release of unfavourable statistics relating to the rail industry on the day of Princess Margaret's funeral. The following day, Moore's and Sixsmith's resignations were announced; but on 24 February Sixsmith denied that he had left his post. In May the DTLR, Byers and Sixsmith publicly agreed that the resignation statement had been based on 'an incorrect misunderstanding'. Byers, whose position was undermined by these events, stepped down from his Cabinet post later that month. The DTLR itself was then abolished and its functions reapportioned elsewhere.

Leaving aside the particular personality clashes involved, all of this suggested that there were considerable difficulties associated with the use of politically appointed aides. The idea that special advisers were little more than unscrupulous, partisan propagandists was reinforced. There was also a lack of clarity as to how, and by whom, they were to be disciplined if they behaved in a questionable manner. While aides possessed the confidence of ministers, permanent secretaries – the official heads of departments – were hampered in their ability to act. The Prime Minister had the authority to remove advisers but, in the case of Moore, had not exercised it. Problems involving spin doctors could themselves become media events. Moreover, the fates of, among others, Moore, Sixsmith, Byers and the DTLR demonstrated how grave the outcomes could be. It could be inferred that the DTLR was not an isolated case, and that widespread internal administrative warfare was taking place.

The Public Administration Committee's inquiry into the affair, which reported in July 2002, concluded that 'Ms Moore took on a series of executive and, in effect, managerial tasks without reference to proper procedures. In addition, a number of civil servants abandoned professional standards by leaking information and misinformation in a way intended to undermine Ms Moore. Management found itself unable to prevent a catastrophic taking of sides at senior level in the department.'[35] Given the level of criticism being directed at aides, it was timely that, in March 2002, the Committee on Standards in Public Life, chaired by Sir Nigel Wicks, a former career official, announced its decision to conduct an investigation into the boundaries between ministers, civil servants and special advisers within the executive.

Special advisers, then, had moved yet further up the media and political agenda. In the words of Tony Wright, referring to the level of interest in a group who were eighty-one in number, rarely 'has so much been said about so few'.[36] Criticism was intense, frequent and widespread, with many serious charges being levelled at aides and those who used them. In February 2002 Peter Oborne raised questions relating to impropriety and personal resentment within Whitehall. While most special advisers were not formally permitted to manage permanent officials, he argued, in practice many of them did. 'In some departments,' Oborne went on, 'this army of advisers and spin-doctors is known as "Hitler Youth".'[37] Two months later Oborne published an open letter to the incoming Cabinet Secretary, Sir Andrew Turnbull. In it, he suggested that the 'independence of the civil service' had, over the preceding decade, been 'subverted', and pointed at special advisers as an important element in the process. Oborne referred to the use of high-powered aides inside Downing Street and the large increase in numbers from 1997. He argued that Blair's approach amounted to 'a thoroughly corrupting merger of political party and state' and accused senior officials of falling short in their duty to prevent such a development.[38]

The political commentator Hugo Young also drew attention to the increase in numbers of special advisers following Blair's election victory in 1997, suggesting that it was the product of a mistaken view on the part of the Prime Minister and his colleagues that permanent Whitehall, after eighteen years of Conservative government, was not disposed towards co-operation with Labour. Political appointments to No. 10 in particular 'prodigiously multiplied to form, in effect, a para-government, second guessing departmental civil servants at every turn'. Young also argued that, whereas in earlier periods special advisers had tended to be policy experts, they were now overwhelmingly 'information peddlers', dedicated to presentation of the government in the most politically convenient light. Such tendencies, taken together, meant that 'the ethic and the structure of the civil service have been gravely damaged'; and, according to Young's contacts, morale among senior officials 'has never been lower'.[39]

Unsurprisingly, the opposition persisted in its attempts to involve itself in the issue. On 3 March 2002 the Conservative leader, Iain Duncan Smith, wrote in the *Sunday Telegraph* that 'Political appointees are wielding excessive power over career civil servants.' His proposals for a future Conservative administration were partly presented as a bid to reduce supposed public cynicism regarding politicians. Duncan Smith conceded that it might prove necessary to employ a partisan spokesman to act on behalf of the Prime Minister. He also acknowledged that the administrations of the two most recent Conservative prime ministers, Thatcher and Major, had employed aides, and that it was likely any administration headed by himself would do the same. However, he argued for the abolition of the Order in Council which granted up to three of Blair's special advisers the managerial functions normally available only to permanent officials and made a commitment to 'tackle the Hydra-like mass of over-mighty special advisers created by this government'. Their current number, which was 'costing the taxpayer more than £2 million a year', would be reduced by at least 25 per cent. Rules governing conduct would be passed into law, in particular preventing them from giving instructions to career officials. The problem of special advisers who 'have reportedly bullied, intimidated and insulted their way around Whitehall' would, he claimed, thereby be ended.[40]

On 1 May the Lords debated the question of relations between different elements within the executive. Concern that the role of special advisers was moving beyond that of merely supplying counsel to ministers was expressed by Baroness Prashar, head of the Civil Service Commission, the body responsible for the regulation of Whitehall recruitment. Examples of such transgression included briefing the press and writing papers intended to stimulate activity within departments. Moreover, Prashar argued, special advisers were now regularly assuming de facto management functions over career officials, whether formally permitted to or not. 'Such lack of clarity,' she went on, 'over the role and powers of special advisers leads not only to speculation about whether there is increased politicisation of the Civil Service but also confuses the rights and obligations of civil servants.'

During the same debate, Lord Campbell of Croy complained that 'special advisers are not accountable to Parliament . . . they cannot be summoned to give evidence to Select Committees.' He also argued that, although these aides were relatively few in number, their importance was increased by the fact that they 'work directly for Ministers – mostly on political subjects', while 'The large majority of the civil servants are engaged in work which does not involve dealing with Ministers directly on political subjects.' Lord Bridges suggested that 'We should remind ourselves of what the Northcote–Trevelyan report was up to,' referring to Sir Charles Trevelyan's 1854 recommendation that civil servants should be recruited on a basis of competitive examination, and went on, 'something is happening to the unwritten constitution. It is changing in front of our eyes . . . Any tendency to revert to political patronage in the service of the state should be carefully controlled.'[41]

Criticism of the use of special advisers also came from Labour veterans. In June 2002 allegations surfaced that another former DTLR aide, Dan Corry, had sought to run background information checks on individual members of the Paddington rail crash survivors' group who were causing political embarrassment for Byers. Leaked e-mails showed that Corry had contacted the Labour Party, asking, 'Basically, are they Tories?'[42] This revelation prompted Joe Haines, press secretary to Harold Wilson from 1969 to 1976, to weigh into the debate. In an article for the *Mail on Sunday*, Haines warned that political appointments were proving damaging both to Labour and, more broadly, to democracy itself, undermining the impartiality of the Civil Service and the supremacy of Parliament. Haines bemoaned the fact that 'one ministerial assistant after another is exposed as a conniving, unprincipled zealot in pursuit of doing down the imagined enemies of their masters.' Special advisers, according to Haines, were 'often youthful and mainly inexperienced' opportunists, many of whom had only recently attached themselves to Labour, 'some after a spell as Communists or Liberal Democrats'.

Haines raised the familiar objections regarding excessive numbers and the valuing of presentation over substance, making that point that under Wilson, by contrast, 'special advisers were brought in to advise the government because they had special skills.' Such aides, according to Haines, while often challenging the views of the permanent machine, worked with, rather than against the Civil Service. Now, Haines argued, the main qualification required in a special adviser was loyalty and willingness to do what was required, unhindered by scruples, to further the ambition of the employing minister. Haines proposed that Blair should 'wield the axe' and dispose of aides whose ministers could not provide a satisfactory description of the qualifications they brought to their jobs. Special advisers, Haines went on, 'have been a blight on the government and public life almost from the day it was first elected in 1997' and in particular had poisoned the 'atmosphere between Blair and Gordon Brown, his Chancellor'.[43] The same month, celebrating forty years as an MP, the Labour left-winger and Father of the House of Commons, Tam Dalyell, expressed the view to journalists that he regarded Blair as the worst Labour Prime Minister he had encountered, singling out for particular criticism the premier's tendency to value the views of personal aides above those of ministers, and his supposed reluctance to remove Moore. 'Special advisers are a huge menace to democracy,' he stated.[44]

A particular problem, from the point of view of the government, was that identified by *The Economist* in June. The Labour administration had '[f]or much of its life . . . enjoyed a remarkably harmonious relationship with the press'. However, 'the ceaseless courtship of the owners and editors of newspapers, the calculated pandering to the BBC and, above all, the sophisticated use of spin with favoured journalists – are no longer working.'[45] Moreover, as has been shown, special advisers, a number of whom had been appointed with the very aim of obtaining favourable media portrayal of the administration, had now become the subject of extremely negative press coverage and popular perceptions.

Some support was voiced for special advisers. For example, writing in March 2002, the former aide to Robin Cook during his period as Foreign Secretary from 1997 to 2001, David Clark, cautioned that 'The demonising of special advisers has reached ridiculous proportions. Anyone following recent events could be forgiven for thinking that it was Jo Moore, rather than Slobodan Milosevic, that had just gone on trial for crimes against humanity.' Clark argued that the assault on partisan aides was driven by a coalition of journalists obsessed with their own immediate surroundings, civil servants 'seeking to resist the intrusion of influences they cannot control', an opportunistic Conservative Party and disgruntled Labour MPs. In Clark's words, 'Big tent politics doesn't get much bigger than this.' He argued that the current debate was characterised by an absence of 'any appreciation of what special advisers do or how they came into being.'[46] Tony Wright, too, argued that 'Part of the problem stems from the fact that we know so little about what these 80-odd individuals actually do.'[47]

There was also a robust official defence. On 26 March 2002 the outgoing Cabinet Secretary, Sir Richard Wilson, gave a speech on the Civil Service at the Centre for Management and Policy Studies. One of the subjects he addressed was that of special advisers, 'about whom all sorts of concerns have been expressed'. He acknowledged his awareness that, in the prevailing climate, 'anything I say – or do not say – on this subject is liable to be misinterpreted, either as an attack on the government, or a rearguard action to protect Civil Service interests, or a mouthing of words given to me by somebody else.' Wilson emphasised that special advisers were an established constitutional fixture with a legitimate contribution to make to the work of the government. While welcoming a debate about them, he was concerned that 'it needs to address the facts'.

Wilson pointed out that, when compared to the 3,429 senior civil servants, the 81 aides were relatively few in number. Rather than threatening the politicisation of Whitehall, they protected the impartiality of career officials by carrying out activities in which it would be inappropriate for permanent civil servants to engage. Furthermore, on the question of presentational activities, 'Most special advisers are not "spin doctors". There are 11 out of the 81 who are employed primarily in the field of communications and perhaps another 30 who, as well as policy development, deal with presentation and speeches without necessarily talking to the press themselves. But most contribute behind the scenes in ways that could by no stretch of the imagination be called spin.'[48]

The Prime Minister himself defended the practices of his administration when appearing before the Commons Liaison Committee on 16 July 2002. On the question of whether an extensive concentration of prime ministerial power had taken place during his premiership, in which a growth in the number of special advisers at No. 10 was a factor, Blair argued that a strong centre was a necessity. But he added that 'my Number 10 office has roughly the same or perhaps even fewer people working for it than the Irish Taoiseach's . . . there are far fewer than either the French Prime Minister . . . or the German Chancellor [has].' Blair rejected the suggestion put to him that his personal aides wielded more influence than Cabinet members. Regarding the number of special advisers across the whole administration, Blair remarked that in the United States there were '3,500 or even 4,000 political appointments; we have 80 special advisers for the whole of government. There are 3,500 senior civil servants; there are 80 special advisers; there are 400,000 civil servants as a whole. I think we need to get this in context'. He also argued that 'their role is sometimes a bit misunderstood . . . there is often talk of them being simply media people. Actually few of them are media people; the vast bulk of them are policy people.'[49]

It is clear from this review of recent commentary that the argument over special advisers, which this work will investigate from an historical perspective, involves a number of points of contention. It has been suggested that, since 1997, the number of such aides has become excessive, constituting a drain on the public purse in order to serve partisan ends. The fact of their presence in Whitehall, it is argued, collectively constitutes a threat to the political neutrality of the career Civil Service. It challenges long-term Whitehall traditions associated with the Northcote–Trevelyan report, a touchstone for the values of career officialdom, and therefore has great constitutional implications. There has been conflict, sometimes open warfare, between career officials and outsiders. It has been claimed that too much personal power has accrued to certain individual special advisers. There is a suggestion that the quality of special advisers has generally declined, with fewer in possession of genuine expertise and more – whether political aides or media handlers – who are characterised by their unscrupulousness rather than by any genuinely 'special' qualities. Allegations of opportunism have also included a questioning of their genuine commitment to

Labour. Some within the party feel undervalued in relation to special advisers.

Aides have been associated with a supposed central failing of the Blair administrations, namely the overvaluation of presentation. Special advisers, it is suggested, are predominantly concerned with media briefing, or 'spin'. This, it is argued, has led to greater public cynicism: the opposite of the desired effect. Such activities have entailed the bypassing of Parliament, the official conduit for government announcements. Taken together with the lack of accountability of aides to Parliament, this could be construed as a devaluation of that institution, an anti-democratic tendency. It has been argued that Blair has conducted prime ministerial government, to which his use of special advisers has been central, at the expense of collective Cabinet deliberation. There is a view, too, that aides have become a political liability. First, they are the subject of intense public interest in their own right, thus negating the value of those concerned with the conduct of public relations. Second, owing to their very personal connections with the ministers who employed them, they were liable to become engaged in power struggles between government members. Their activities in this field may have served to worsen tensions within the Cabinet, particularly between Blair and Brown, and their respective entourages.

There are countervailing arguments. It has been suggested that the debate surrounding special advisers was near-hysterical, distorting, driven by ulterior motives and ill-informed. Special advisers, it is pointed out, have been an established feature of government life for some time; they did not appear out of nowhere in 1997. Theirs was a valuable contribution, the bulk of it relating to policy rather than presentation. The neutrality of career officials could be protected by the presence of outsiders with acknowledged party political affiliations. While much has been made of the proliferation of special advisers under Blair, it ought to be put in perspective. Relative to the totality of senior civil servants, they were few in number. Moreover, in other countries, there were greater quantities of political appointments. The concentration of power in the hands of the Prime Minister was a necessity. Again, compared with foreign arrangements, the number of staff at the centre was not immense.

Orders, codes and contracts

Some of the more unfavourable depictions of special advisers have related to the appropriateness of their activities in the context of their status as public employees.

For this reason, and as an antidote to the sometimes melodramatic tone of their detractors, the full official framework within which these aides operate must be outlined and analysed. It is formally defined by Orders in Council, the Ministerial Code, the Civil Service Code and the Special Adviser Model Contract, each of which will be examined below. It is notable that no Act of Parliament exists to demarcate such activity within Whitehall. While the introduction of a Civil Service Act is official Labour policy, the government has yet to make the parliamentary time to bring one forward, suggesting a lack of political will. Traditionally, Whitehall has been regulated through Orders in Council: decrees issued on the advice of the Privy Council, drawing on the royal prerogative for their authority.

The Civil Service Order in Council 1995 reiterates the long-standing and fundamental Whitehall principle that 'no person shall be appointed to a situation in the Service unless ... the selection for appointment is made on merit on the basis of fair and open competition.' An exception applies 'where the holder is appointed by a Minister of the Crown for the purpose only of providing advice to any Minister, and [where] the period for which the situation is to be held terminates at the end of an Administration'.[50] This part of the Order in Council, then, which first appeared in complete form in a 1991 Order, allows for the temporary appointment of aides, on a basis of personal ministerial patronage, who are formally allowed only to supply their employers with counsel, and are therefore not integrated into the bureaucratic hierarchy; in other words, special advisers.

The 'purpose only of providing advice' clause was waived by a 1997 amendment 'in the case of up to three situations in the Prime Minister's Office which are designated by him'.[51] Only two posts have been so designated: they were held by Jonathan Powell, Blair's Chief of Staff, and Campbell, who were accordingly officially permitted to perform management functions.

These two Orders in Council provide the legal basis for the special adviser. Taking, as they do, the form of exemptions from other rules, they provide only a negative definition, offering very little guidance as to what can and cannot be done by individuals who are appointed under their provisions. For this is it necessary to look elsewhere, to an assortment of other documents whose status is more ambiguous.

The Ministerial Code provides guidance to ministers on conduct and procedure; its exact constitutional position, however, is a matter of some debate. It states that the 'employment of Special Advisers on the one hand adds a political dimension to the advice available to Ministers, and on the other provides Ministers with the direct advice of distinguished "experts" in their professional field, while reinforcing the political impartiality of the permanent Civil Service by distinguishing the source of political advice and support'. Each Cabinet minister, the Code stipulates, can employ up to two special advisers. The written approval of the Prime Minister is required in advance of all such appointments.

Ministers who regularly attend Cabinet without being members of it may also appoint one or two aides, subject again to the authorisation of the Prime Minister. The recruitment of individuals in possession of 'outstanding skills or experience of a non-political kind', in addition to the normal ceiling of two, can also be approved by the Prime Minister. A public explanation must be given whenever the limit is exceeded. The numerical restrictions do not apply to the Prime Minister, a fact which could be taken as clear evidence of a bias towards power at the centre. The presence of politically appointed staff within Whitehall raises the possibility that the influence of career officials might be eclipsed. In the Ministerial Code, however, it is stipulated that 'Ministers have a duty to give fair consideration and due weight to informed and impartial advice from civil servants, as well as to other considerations and advice, in reaching policy decisions.' The inference can be drawn that decisions should not be taken solely in closed circles comprising only ministers and special advisers.

To assess the value of aides, it is necessary to understand the activities not considered appropriate for permanent civil servants. Ministers are given instructions regarding Whitehall neutrality by the Ministerial Code. It is their 'duty to uphold the political impartiality of the Civil Service, and not to ask civil servants to act in any way which would conflict with the Civil Service Code'. They are also required 'to ensure that influence over appointments is not abused for partisan purposes'. Civil servants, the Ministerial Code also cautions, 'should not be asked to engage in activities likely to call in question their political impartiality, or to give rise to the criticism that people paid from public funds are being used for Party political purposes'. To give one example, while permanent officials may provide factual briefs for speeches made by ministers at party political events, they should not be asked to participate in them, or in 'meetings of policy or subject groups of any of the Parliamentary parties'. Career civil servants can attend conferences in a formal capacity only if 'their presence is required for carrying through essential Departmental business unconnected with the conference'. Special advisers, on the other hand, although not permitted to speak publicly, can go to such occasions 'and maintain contact with Party members'.[52]

As with regular civil servants, special advisers' contracts of employment are with the Crown, with their ministers acting as the appointing authority, countersigning the contract. The Model Contract for special advisers stipulates that they are engaged 'for the purpose of providing advice to the Minister' and are required 'to serve the objectives of the government and the Department in which [they] are employed'. Their salaries are transferred monthly, in arrears, into a bank or building society account, and reviewed annually from 1 April. Increases are determined by the Special Advisers' Remuneration Committee, on the recommendation of their ministers. Overtime is not paid. Special advisers are subject to regular performance reviews, which they can discuss with their ministers. Formally, they are required to work a minimum of forty-one or forty-two hours, over a five-day week, 'including daily meal breaks of one hour'. Ominously, the Model Contract notes that the special adviser 'will be required to work additional hours as may from time to time be reasonable and necessary for the efficient performance of your duties'. They have an annual leave allowance of thirty days, as well as being entitled to all public holidays and two and a half 'privilege days' (extra days' leave granted to civil servants courtesy of the Queen). Payment for absence resulting from sickness or injury is also provided.

The Crown is empowered to dismiss special advisers 'at will'. Their employment terminates 'at the end of the present Administration', when the minister 'leaves the government or moves to another appointment', or 'in the event of a General Election, on the day after Polling Day'. If employment ceases for one of these reasons, or because of 'disciplinary proceedings, inefficiency or grounds justifying summary dismissal at common law', there is no 'period of notice'. However, if none of these conditions apply, then they 'will in practice normally be given not less than 3 months' notice in writing'. Severance payments are provided, calculated on a sliding scale according to length of service. Special advisers must give five weeks' written notice to their employer if terminating their own employment.

Aides are informed by their contracts that they 'owe duties of confidentiality and loyal service to the Crown'. Bound by the Official Secrets Act 1989, they are also required to abide both by departmental rules and by the Civil Service Code, excepting those aspects of them which relate to 'political activities', 'impartiality and objectivity' and the need to be able to serve 'a future Administration and potential future Ministers'. Before taking part in outside activities where experience or knowledge gained in the course of their work might be relevant, special advisers 'must first seek permission from the Official Head of Department'. They may have, at their ministers' discretion, 'access to all papers submitted to Ministers', except those for which their security clearance is insufficient, or which relate to civil servants personally. Special advisers are subject to the rules which apply to ministers restricting access to the papers of previous administrations. Departmental discipline, but not inefficiency procedure, applies to them. Complaints on their part can be addressed, in writing, either to their minister or to the official head of their department. Whitehall rules regarding the acceptance of outside employment within two years of departure apply.[53] If privileged information acquired during service may be of benefit to the new employer, a waiting period can be imposed.

Attached to the 2001 Model Contract is the Code of Conduct for Special Advisers. This states that the special adviser's function is to 'help Ministers on matters where the work of government and the work of the government Party overlap', and where the involvement of career officials would consequently not be appropriate. Use of the term 'overlap' in describing the area of operation is significant, suggestive of the hybrid nature of these aides, as well as the desire to prevent them from straying into purely partisan activities. An 'additional resource' for the employing minister, they provide 'advice from a standpoint that is more politically committed and politically aware' than that supplied by permanent civil servants. The Code goes on to list the types of work that ministers may entrust to special advisers. One is 'reviewing papers going to the Minister' from a party political perspective, ensuring that any relevant points are raised and acted upon accordingly. They can also 'give advice on any aspect of departmental business'. This includes counselling ministers when they are 'taking part in Party political activities'. Another task is described as '"deviling"', which entails 'checking facts and research findings from a Party political viewpoint'.

One activity referred to in the Code which is particularly suggestive of the influence that special advisers can wield is 'preparing speculative policy papers which can generate long-term policy thinking within the Department', and might 'reflect the political viewpoint of the Minister's Party'. Aides can contribute to 'policy planning within the Department, including ideas which extend the existing range of options available to the Minister with a political viewpoint in mind'. An important area in which special advisers add value is that of 'liaising with the Party', ensuring that departmental policy processes take 'full

advantage of ideas from the Party'. They can also encourage 'presentational activities by the Party', contributing to the objectives of the government; participate
in briefing party MPs and staff 'on issues of government policy'; and liaise 'with
outside interest groups', in order to obtain their contributions to policy debate.

Other possible tasks of special advisers include 'speechwriting', in the course of
which they can add 'Party political content to material prepared by permanent civil
servants'. They may represent 'the views of their Minister to the media including a
Party viewpoint'; but they must be 'authorised by the Minister to do so'. They may
'provid[e] expert advice as a specialist in a particular field'. As stipulated in the
Ministerial Code, they may attend party functions, although they may not speak
publicly at conferences. Contact can be maintained with party members. Finally,
they may participate in 'policy reviews organised by the Party', ensuring that the
views of their minister and the government as a whole are taken into account.

Special advisers are required to 'conduct themselves with integrity and
honesty' and not to 'deceive or knowingly mislead Parliament or the public'.
Significantly, in the context of the activity of briefing journalists, they are
forbidden from disclosing, without authority, 'official information which has
been communicated in confidence in government or received in confidence from
others'. Special advisers 'should not use official resources for Party political
activity' and should maintain 'the political impartiality of civil servants', not
behaving in a manner which conflicts with the Civil Service Code. It is important
that they 'avoid anything which might reasonably lead to the criticism that
people paid from public funds are being used for Party political purposes'. The
Code of Conduct provides more detail regarding the Order in Council stipulation that aides are employed only to advise. It states that they 'stand outside the
departmental hierarchy' and should not be responsible for 'budgets or for the
line management of permanent civil servants including their recruitment and
matters covered by their contract of employment such as their appraisal, reward,
discipline and promotion'. Attention is also drawn to the fact that up to three
prime ministerial appointments are exempted from this rule.

Under the heading 'Contacts with the media', the Code of Conduct for Special
Advisers states that, while special advisers are permitted to 'represent Ministers' views
on government policy to the media with a degree of political commitment that
would not be possible for the permanent Civil Service', briefing on 'purely Party
political matters should however be handled by the Party machine'. It is stipulated

that all such interaction 'should be authorised by the appointing Minister and be conducted in accordance with the *Guidance on the Work of the Government Information Service*. Departmental heads of information are also to be kept informed, in order to ensure that consistent lines are taken, and that 'contacts are recorded'. Furthermore, aides are not supposed to 'take public part in political controversy', in the form of speeches, letters to the press, books, articles or leaflets. Moreover, they 'must observe discretion and express comment with moderation, avoiding personal attacks; and would not normally speak in public for their Minister or the Department'. *Guidance on the Work of the Government Information Service* was published in July 1997. It stipulates that it is 'right and proper for governments to use Civil Service Information Officers and public funds and resources' to inform the public of the full range of government activities and public services. However, 'resources may not . . . be used to support publicity for Party political purposes.'[54]

In a section entitled 'Relations with the Government Party', the Code emphasises the fact that the Civil Service does not have a 'monopoly of policy analysis and advice'. There are a number of sources whose contributions are to be taken into account, including the government party. Special advisers are not allowed to support the contribution of its views, but may participate in obtaining them – perhaps a fine distinction. Furthermore, aides can liaise with their party, briefing MPs and officials where necessary, in order to ensure that its publicity is consistent with that of the government. It would, after all, be 'damaging to the government's objectives if the Party took a different approach to that of the government'.

If special advisers wish to 'undertake work for a political Party' they may do so only 'in their own time, outside office hours, or under a separate contract with the Party, working part-time for the government'. National political activities, including holding office in a national party organisation, are forbidden. The Code states clearly that when publicly identified as a candidate, or prospective candidate, for Parliament, the Scottish Parliament, the National Assembly for Wales, the Northern Ireland Assembly or the European Parliament, a special adviser must resign. Resignation is also required prior to participation in a 'General, European or by-election campaign, or to help in a Party headquarters or research unit during such a campaign'. Special advisers who remain in post must be careful 'not to take any active part in the campaign'. Attendance at public meetings, for example, is ruled out.

Aides are informed that, with the approval of their minister, they may participate in other party political activities, 'such as a leadership campaign', but only 'while on paid or unpaid leave or at times which do not interfere with their normal duties, for example, out of office hours'. Subject to ministerial approval, they may engage in 'all forms of local political activity', but not in support of national politics. They cannot speak publicly, or in councils, or vote, on matters for which their minister has responsibility. Taking part in deputations to ministers is not allowed, and when a matter in which their department is involved comes before the council, they must declare an interest. They should not criticise the policies of other ministers or disclose privileged information to which they have access. Finally, the Code states that a 'civil servant who believes that the action of a special adviser goes beyond that adviser's authority or breaches the Civil Service Code should raise the matter immediately with the Secretary of the Cabinet or the First Civil Service Commissioner, directly or through a senior civil servant'.[55]

The Civil Service Code, which came into force on 1 January 1996, 'sets out the constitutional framework within which all civil servants work and the values they are expected to uphold'. It constitutes part of the terms and conditions of employment for both regular civil servants and special advisers, although with some exemptions in the case of the latter. The 'constitutional and practical role of the Civil Service' is described as being 'with integrity, honesty, impartiality and objectivity, to assist the duly constituted government of the United Kingdom ... whatever their political complexion, in formulating their policies, carrying out decisions and in administering public services for which they are responsible'. Since they are 'servants of the Crown', and constitutionally 'all the Administrations form part of the Crown', civil servants, according to their Code, 'owe their loyalty to the Administrations in which they serve'. An 'Administration', for the purposes of the document, is defined as 'Her Majesty's government of the United Kingdom, the Scottish Executive or the National Assembly for Wales'. How, then, are civil servants to maintain impartiality and objectivity while also serving the government of the day? It is stated that they 'should give honest and impartial advice to the Minister . . . without fear or favour . . . [and] conduct themselves in such a way as to deserve and retain the confidence of Ministers' while ensuring that they will be able 'to establish the same relationship with those whom they may be required to serve in some future Administration'. Presumably, special advisers are supposed to be 'honest', and they certainly need to maintain 'confidence' on the part of their employers. However, it might be argued that 'fear and favour' come into play, given the personal dependency involved and the other requirements described here do not seem to apply to aides, a fact which should be regarded as a central distinction between them and career officials.

The framework within which special advisers operate is a complex one, not without ambiguities, backed up by no Act of Parliament. The fundamental basis for the role of special adviser is provided by the two Orders in Council of 1995 and 1997. The first defines the role as solely advisory. However, some activities seem to exceed this. In 2002, appearing before the Committee on Standards in Public Life, Sir Robin Mountfield, the former Cabinet Office Permanent Secretary, questioned whether press briefing was 'really an advice function'. He suggested that there was a disjunction between the 1995 Order in Council and the description of the advisers' activities in the Code of Conduct, as well as actual practice.[56] It might be argued that certain references in the Code, including that to 'preparing speculative policy papers which can generate long-term policy thinking within the Department', also go beyond the advice remit. Judged by the 1997 Order in Council, the extent of the powers of the executive special advisers in No. 10 is unclear, and no more extensive guidance is offered elsewhere. Such uncertainties are in keeping with the gradual, informal emergence of the special adviser, a process which will be described in the following chapters.

The overall picture provided by the documents discussed above is one of politically committed outsiders temporarily incorporated into an institution with historical traditions of career-long employment and non-partisanship. Such an operation is inevitably a delicate one, likely to cause a variety of tensions. This theme, which has run throughout the existence of the special adviser, is an important one. Issues relating to pay, status and conduct are significant, as are numbers in employment. Generally speaking, ministers are technically limited to two, while the Prime Minister is not. This leads on to the question of the power of the premiership. The types of activity engaged in by aides, suggested in the Code of Conduct for Special Advisers, are also a central concern. In particular, the accuracy of official descriptions of their roles will be examined, as will the possibility that their tasks now are different from those undertaken in earlier periods. A particularly significant feature that will emerge from an examination of the rules governing the use of aides is the close link to the minister who makes the appointment, subject to prime ministerial approval. The importance of the relationship will become clear.

Two

Precedents and precursors

There is a long history in Britain, within which special advisers can be located, of political leaders appointing aides from beyond established circles of influence. One advantage of the practice is that such recruits owe primary loyalty to the individual who has selected them. Outsiders of this kind have often been associated with significant policy developments and changes in administrative methods. A tendency for conflict to arise between entrenched groups, seeking to preserve their importance, and incomers can also be identified. The incomers themselves, many of them colourful characters, have sometimes become prominent figures in their own right, although always dependent upon retaining the confidence of their patrons.

In the sixteenth century, Henry VIII used the services of Thomas Wolsey. Of humble origin,[1] Wolsey owed his social elevation, and therefore allegiance, to the King. Regardless of the wealth, status and offices he had accumulated, when he incurred Henry's displeasure, Wolsey fell.[2] More than a century later, in 1667, Charles II, faced with a financial crisis, put the Treasury into commission and appointed Sir George Downing as its secretary. The upwardly mobile Downing proved very effective in applying modern accounting techniques, based on his knowledge of Dutch methods; however, his personal traits earned him almost universal dislike, and the commission was undermined by intrigue on the part of members of the aristocratic class with whom power had traditionally resided.[3]

Special advisers, then, represent in some respects a very old and often recurring phenomenon. Yet they must also be explained as a particular manifestation of that enduring tendency within a specific context. Essential to an appreciation of the special adviser is an understanding of the emergence, during the nineteenth and twentieth centuries, of a politically neutral, generalist, career Civil Service, dominated by the Treasury. The Northcote–Trevelyan report of 1854 has long been regarded by career officials as the foundation of their profession and values.[4] It requires examination. There were various occasions during the twentieth century, especially under the Liberals from 1906 and during both world wars, when outsiders were incorporated into Whitehall. Arguably they were forerunners to the experiment which began in 1964. Despite certain challenges, however, permanent Whitehall's near-monopoly on both advice to ministers and the responsibility for the implementation of policy was generally maintained, or, when interrupted, subsequently reasserted.

This chapter will review the circumstances leading to the introduction of the special adviser by Harold Wilson's first government.

Victorian reform of the Civil Service

From the mid-eighteenth century, a body of permanent staff, without seats in Parliament, performing executive functions, began to emerge in Britain.[5] The appearance at the head of a government department of a single official, later known as the permanent secretary, can be traced to the early nineteenth century.[6] Nearly all appointments to the embryonic institution were made on a basis of personal patronage. As a mode of recruitment, it had both advantages and drawbacks. In some cases, it meant that the right man was chosen for the right post. However, nepotism and jobbery were rife. By the mid-nineteenth century, the Civil Service, as Peter Hennessy puts it, 'sagged under the weight of family, patronage and obligation'.[7]

Charles Edward Trevelyan was appointed to the most senior Treasury post of Assistant Secretary in 1840, at the very young age of thirty-two. He was a fierce campaigner for reorganisation of the Civil Service,[8] and throughout his career used the press as a means of obtaining his objectives, both encouraging editors to promote certain views and writing letters and articles under pseudonyms.[9] What, then, did he want to achieve? The Treasury already lay at the centre of government, as the office responsible for overseeing spending – a role conferred upon it by Parliament, partly in the quest for accountable administration.[10] Primarily, Theakston argues, Trevelyan sought to strengthen the Treasury and increase its status, installing it as the chief office of government.[11]

Most famously, Trevelyan is credited with being the motivating force behind the Northcote–Trevelyan report, commissioned by the then Chancellor of the Exchequer and future Prime Minister, William Gladstone, and published in early 1854.[12] Trevelyan's co-author (allegedly in name only; clearly a subordinate partner) was Sir Stafford Northcote. It has been argued that the report misrepresented the existing administrative machine;[13] indeed, it has been described as not so much a balanced appraisal of the evidence as 'a manifesto of Civil Service reform' based on preconceived ideas.[14] It advocated a division of labour within the Civil Service between mechanical and intellectual functions, with corresponding classes of employee. Much of the report was concerned with the means by which the members of the two groups should be selected, particularly the elite intellectual, policy advisory group, which is of most interest for the purposes of this book.

Throughout Trevelyan's 1854 recommendations ran the principle that Whitehall should be staffed by individuals of the highest calibre. As a result of initial recruitment being conducted on a basis of patronage, the report contended, the Civil Service had become ridden with 'the unambitious, and the indolent or incapable'. As a consequence, when senior posts had to be filled, it was difficult to find a suitable candidate from inside the service; often, there was no option but to 'go out of the office, and to appoint someone of high standing in an open profession, or someone distinguished in other walks of life, over the heads of men who have been for many years in the public service'. Such a practice, it was argued, had a detrimental effect upon morale within the service. Moreover, it was often abused. There were 'numerous instances . . . in which personal or political considerations have led to the appointment of men of very slender ability, and perhaps of questionable character, to situations of considerable emolument'. The idea of personally selected ministerial aides, was, therefore, opposed.

Northcote–Trevelyan suggested that young entrants were more suitable recruits to a life in public service than older individuals with more experience in the outside world, and proposed the recruitment of recent graduates through competitive written examination. These young recruits could be more easily infused with the appropriate corporate spirit (and could also be paid lower salaries). The blueprint was for a Civil Service closed to the outside world; by implication the employment of outsiders was undesirable and to be avoided.

Regardless of changes in the political mastery of departments, a job in the Civil Service was permanent – a career. The recruitment process, the report recommended, ought to be carried out for the whole service by a central board. This was an attempt to rectify the perceived problem of a 'fragmentary' service, where each 'man's experience, interests, hopes and fears are limited to the special branch of services in which he himself is engaged'. The examinations which were ultimately introduced arguably tested intellect more than abilities directly relevant to state service. Northcote–Trevelyan, then, put the case for a centralised service headed by an intellectual elite of permanent officials. The members of this group were to be recruited directly from university on a basis of academic ability rather than personal qualities or experience. Here can be detected the philosophy of generalism: the belief that the faculty for abstract thought can be applied to any practical duty. In the Civil Service which developed in the era following the Northcote–Trevelyan report, 'technical expertise tended to be frowned upon.'[15]

The call for the introduction of examinations was a manifestation of the intention on the part of the reformers that the senior Civil Service should become an exclusive haven for graduates from Oxford and Cambridge (until 1827, the only universities in England).[16] This view had specific social implications. At the time, in order to qualify for classification as a gentleman, an individual not of unquestionably noble birth or established in one of the professions had to have attended a university.[17] Gladstone's political programme has been portrayed as directed towards the preservation of the existing social order. He seems to have believed that the Northcote–Trevelyan recruitment methods would favour those from the upper echelons, maintaining their grip on political power. A little over a century later, one advocate of the special adviser, the economist Thomas Balogh, regarded the permanent Civil Service as an element of a social establishment he sought to overturn.

Another factor important to an understanding of the Trevelyan programme was the nature of the Victorian state. Government did, and was expected to do, far less than would be the case in the following century; *laissez-faire* principles held sway, particularly within the Treasury.[18] As Balogh put it, the Victorians 'conceived the role of the state in purely negative terms' and sought simply to ensure that its '"night-watchman" functions should be ably, efficiently and cheaply performed'.[19] But though the state was small, it was about to grow very rapidly. Employees of the Civil Service in the 1850s numbered around 40,000. That figure would double within forty years.[20] Here was an important source of post-1945 criticism of the Civil Service. The generalist, it was argued, was redundant within a state the many and varied tasks of which required specialist skills. Moreover, Treasury control, which entailed emphasis upon *laissez-faire* principles and minimising expenditure, became inappropriate.[21]

Despite the best efforts of its political sponsor, Gladstone, the Northcote–Trevelyan report was not immediately implemented.[22] However, in 1855 – albeit through Order in Council rather than, as Trevelyan had sought, Act of Parliament – a Civil Service Commission of three members, answerable to the Crown, not the Prime Minister, was established. Its certification was required for appointments, although the shortlist of candidates from which it chose was drawn up by individual departments, leaving open the possibility for manipulation of outcomes.[23] In 1870, as a result of the exertions of the Chancellor of the Exchequer, Robert Lowe, and Gladstone, now Prime Minister, more progress was made towards the attainment of Trevelyan's objectives. A further Order in Council provided for those political heads of department who wished to do so to open up their ministries to competitive entrance.[24] Trevelyan's objectives in another area were gradually realised during the second half of the nineteenth century, with the tightening of the Treasury's grip on government as it obtained greater powers of scrutiny and control over departmental expenditure, nominally as a response to political demands for retrenchment.[25]

A distinctive Civil Service ethos of party political neutrality began to take shape. From 1870, the practice of appointing experts to administrative posts declined. Generalist career officials were less readily associated with particular policies than the outsiders they replaced. The tendency was connected with the rise of the doctrine of ministerial responsibility. Political heads of departments were accountable to the legislature, while officials, in theory, were answerable to ministers, and required to carry out instructions once decisions had been reached. Such principles, combined with the waning of patronage-based recruitment, meant that reform had guided the developing Civil Service away from the arena of party politics.[26] In 1884 the rule was established that a civil servant who accepted candidature in a parliamentary election should thereupon resign his position.[27] Moreover, in the view of one very senior twentieth-century career official, the personal commitment of officials to the particular minister they served declined, to be gradually replaced by loyalty to the Civil Service itself.[28]

Whitehall outsiders in the early twentieth century

In 1901, the Fabian social reformer Sidney Webb stated that the country was 'ripe . . . for a policy of National Efficiency'.[29] This was one contemporary label used to describe the fairly heterogeneous modernisation movement that emerged in Britain during the late nineteenth and early twentieth centuries. Another general term, subsequently attached to the tendency by academics, is 'social-imperialism'. Ideas from left and right were synthesised into a brand of welfarism which, it was intended, would be founded upon a revitalised empire. The varied members of this cross-party movement, who included in their number the Unionist politician Joseph Chamberlain, believed in reform designed to appease the potentially revolutionary working classes.[30] As well as providing assistance for the lower orders, the social-imperialist programme was intended to facilitate the more efficient deployment of national resources. Leading figures within the tendency, such as the journalist J. L. Garvin, feared that, relative in particular to the United States and Germany, Britain was a declining power.[31] Japan was also regarded as an increasingly formidable rival.[32] One of the social-imperialists' many demands was for the greater utilisation of expertise within government. For example, during 1902 the Co-efficients – a turn-of-the-century cross-party discussion group, the members of which included Sidney Webb, the philosopher Bertrand Russell, and the writer H. G. Wells – debated the question: 'By what methods is it possible to increase the thinking element in the administrative departments?'[33]

The Liberal Party took power late in 1905 and the following year won a crushing general election victory over the Conservatives. The return of the Liberals to office occurred in a political context which social-imperialism had helped generate. The administrations of the Liberal Prime Ministers Henry Campbell-Bannerman and Herbert Asquith introduced ambitious public welfare programmes, including measures such as the establishment of old age pensions and unemployment insurance, influenced by schemes developed in Germany during the 1880s. Such innovations 'placed new demands on the state that were beyond the scope of the existing machine and its minders to meet'.

Outsiders had to be recruited. For example, in 1908 Winston Churchill, the President of the Board of Trade, set up the first labour exchanges. In order to do so, he had to import experts into Whitehall, including the academic William Beveridge.[34]

The Liberal David Lloyd George held high government office from 1906 to 1922. His political technique involved encircling himself with customised institutions and chosen allies. Lloyd George's tendency to make personal appointments was interpreted by some contemporaries as a 'predilection for surrounding himself with a bunch of second-rate cronies'.[35] However, Balogh referred approvingly to his use of 'men of great ability and expertise advising him directly – a method . . . of bypassing bureaucratic obstacles'.[36] Some of Lloyd George's selections were political aides, others were primarily policy experts. The former included John Rowland, one of many of Lloyd George's allies who shared the politician's Welsh origins. Rowland worked in Lloyd George's private office alongside permanent civil servants. He helped bring about such achievements as the introduction of national insurance, which passed into law late in 1911.[37] Sir George Paish, who falls into the latter category, was Lloyd George's economics expert in the early stages of the First World War.[38] During the conflict Lloyd George oversaw the introduction of a number of outsiders into Whitehall, for example the businessmen who were recruited to the Ministry of Munitions, which was established under his leadership in 1915.[39]

Another of Lloyd George's innovations, from his time as premier, was the Prime Minister's Secretariat, established during the First World War, in early 1917. Labelled the 'Garden Suburb' because it was housed in huts on the lawn behind Downing Street, its members were temporary appointments made personally by the Prime Minister. As well as dealing with specific contingencies as they arose, the Garden Suburb was responsible for interdepartmental co-ordination. For most of its existence the Prime Minister's Secretariat had a staff of five, each of whom was allotted specific policy areas. Their tasks included chasing the implementation of decisions, speech-writing and research work.[40] It seems that they also engaged in the calculated leaking of information to the press, 'what in a later day became known as "spin doctoring"'.[41] The historian John Turner describes the Garden Suburb as arising from a 'presidential concept of war-leadership'. He argues that, rather than providing policy guidance to the wartime coalition government as a whole, the Prime Minister's

Secretariat primarily served the individual, short-term political interests of Lloyd George.[42]

Interwar Treasury dominance

During the course of the nineteenth century the Treasury became ever more markedly the dominant office of government. By the early twentieth century, the Permanent Secretary to the Treasury was often the first port of call for a Prime Minister seeking advice, receiving a salary higher than that of other departmental chiefs; but he was not the official head of the service, no such post existing at that stage. Then, on 15 September 1919, a Treasury minute announcing Treasury control over the Civil Service was distributed around Whitehall. It declared that the Permanent Secretary to the Treasury was now also the Permanent Head of the Civil Service and adviser to the First Lord of the Treasury (a post almost always held by the Prime Minister) on Civil Service appointments and patronage. Another circular, of 12 March 1920, further strengthened the Permanent Secretary to the Treasury by stipulating that prime ministerial approval was needed for all senior Civil Service appointments. As the premier's pre-eminent consultant in such matters, the Permanent Head of the Civil Service would naturally have great influence. An Order in Council of July 1920 completed the process by giving the Treasury complete control over personnel and staffing.[43]

The man Lloyd George chose to head the Civil Service in 1919 was Warren Fisher, who was then aged just forty and remained in the top job for twenty years. Early on in his tenure, Fisher saw to it that elite civil servants were conceived of, and viewed themselves, as a single group throughout almost all departments. Collectively, they were termed the 'administrative class'.[44] Freely admitting that he had little knowledge of economics, Fisher was a conscious opponent of the notion of the rule of the specialist in Whitehall. He advocated the movement of administrators through a number of different offices of government during the course of their careers,[45] and was hostile to the admission of outsiders into the service.[46]

To Fisher, the belief that the Civil Service should exist as an entity in and for itself was vital.[47] Unification of the Home Civil Service was later seen by one special adviser as having contributed to the creation of an independent power base, collectively seeking to maximise its influence.[48] Administrators tended to take more interest in glamorous policy-formation matters than in their other functions such as internal management.[49] During the 1920s the grip of permanent Whitehall on government tightened when Ramsay MacDonald was installed as the first Labour Prime Minister in January 1924. In a break with convention, there was no clear-out of Downing Street private secretaries upon a change of resident. The principle that the employment of private office staff in No. 10 is not wholly dependent upon the premier can be traced to this event.[50] Another development during this period led to the existence of institutions from which partisan, temporary aides could be drawn. This was the emergence of party research bodies, such as the Conservative Research Department (CRD), which was formed in the late 1920s.[51]

A rare interwar attempt to introduce greater expertise into the Civil Service took place when in January 1930 MacDonald, returned to office the previous year, created the Economic Advisory Council (EAC). The EAC was intended to help tackle the problem of unemployment, which had become severe. Its membership of economists, industrialists and trades unionists, among others, included some eminent individuals, such as the trades union leader Ernest Bevin and the economist John Maynard Keynes.[52] However, this collection of specialist opinion was not properly integrated with the government machinery, and its role was poorly defined.[53] As one EAC member, the future Labour Prime Minister Clement Attlee, put it, there were 'interesting discussions but nothing constructive ever emerged'.[54] Special advisers, by contrast with the EAC, were deliberately located within the Whitehall loop.

Outsiders and total war

During the Second World War, in its bid to direct an effective struggle against the Axis powers, the British government engaged in domestic economic and social intervention on an unprecedented scale.[55] The advent of total national mobilisation held certain implications for the administration. Large numbers of additional staff were needed, many of whom had to be in possession of particular skills. Accordingly, a specifically established Central Register supplied the various Whitehall departments with thousands of temporary civil servants.[56] In May 1940, following the German surge through the Low Countries into France,

Winston Churchill supplanted Neville Chamberlain as Prime Minister. The new premier instigated major changes in the way government was advised, entailing the use of many expert outsiders.

Churchill was hostile towards the Treasury, partly because its permanent secretary, Sir Horace Wilson, was associated with Chamberlain's appeasement of Nazism.[57] In place of Treasury control, economic co-ordination was carried out by the Lord President of the Council and his committee.[58] A ministerial Cabinet body, this committee was advised by the temporary civil servants who comprised the Economic Section of the War Cabinet. The first Director of the Economic Section was Professor John Jewkes, an economist from a research department attached to Manchester University. His staff supplied briefs and papers for the Lord President's Committee and provided secretaries and members for a number of its subcommittees.[59] The Economic Section consisted of ten to twelve members, and never more than twelve. A variety of statisticians and economists of academic origin were recruited. They included one James Harold Wilson, previously an Oxford don, who was transferred from the Anglo-French Co-ordinating Committee. Wilson's account of his service in the Economic Section shows that, as well as applying their specialist skills, members engaged in 'more general duties'.[60] One aspiring politician who found employment inside the Economic Section was Evan Durbin, an economist associated with the Labour Party. He was said to have 'adopted a role more like that of a junior minister than a civil servant ... [he] was in touch with Labour ministers, and concentrated on large, general issues, particularly those involving social reform.'[61] Durbin could be seen as a precursor of the special adviser, in so far as he was a partisan, temporary civil servant.

Another organisation, the Prime Minister's Statistical Section, was attached specifically to Churchill. It consisted of six economists, most of whom were temporary appointments,[62] and its central task was to keep the Prime Minister informed of matters relating to the allocation of resources in the context of the conduct of the war.[63] According to one of its staff, Donald MacDougall, it was 'essentially personal to the Prime Minister; it worked continuously for him; it had some idea of what was in his mind; it knew the sort of thing he wanted to know and how he liked to have it presented; its loyalty was to him and no one else'.[64] Another member of the Statistical Section stated that it was created because 'Churchill wished ... to have around him a band of critics, who, precisely because they were not fully merged into the general machinery of government, would give him an independent judgement on how things were going forward'.[65] It was led by Professor Frederick Alexander Lindemann, a physicist nicknamed 'the Prof', whom Churchill described as 'my friend and confidant of so many years'.[66] 'The Prof' was soon given the ministerial post of Paymaster General and raised to the peerage as Viscount Cherwell.[67] Despite his many successes, 'the Prof' has been stigmatised for his influence upon the strategy of bombing civilian targets in Germany. Both the morality and the effectiveness of the approach have been questioned.

Outsiders were also introduced into longer-established areas of government. In the summer of 1940 Keynes was recalled to the Treasury, where he had previously served during and immediately after the First World War, subsequently becoming a leading critic of its *laissez-faire* tendencies. By then in his late fifties, he remained there until his death in 1946. He had no formal position and was unpaid; but his influence was considerable. From 1940 onwards the government began to assume responsibility for the whole economy, rather than merely setting out to balance its own books.[68] Budgets had previously been little more than annual public sector statements of account. From April 1941 they became tools designed to maintain equilibrium between demand and supply.[69] Henceforth, such statements included estimates of the total national income and expenditure.[70] Keynes's input was crucial to this development.[71] He was also entrusted with obtaining foreign loans, in particular from the US government.[72] Keynes was the key British figure in the negotiation of the Bretton Woods Agreement of 1944, which provided for fixed, but adjustable, exchange rates.[73] Experts, Keynes believed, had a part to play in postwar government. In 1943 he suggested the 'grouping of the principal economic departments under a single super-Minister', to whom a staff of economists could be attached.[74]

In 1940, once war had begun in earnest, normal methods of administration went into abeyance. This state of affairs presented an opportunity to those members of the intelligentsia who sought a radicalisation in the functions of government, for example the novelist, playwright and broadcaster J. B. Priestley. Priestley made the case for an egalitarian society as a war aim. Groups such as the 1941 Committee, which met in the home of the *Picture Post* proprietor, Edward Hulton, and included among its members a young Thomas Balogh, campaigned to such an end.[75] Their efforts did not go unrewarded. Considerable official time and attention were devoted to planning the society that would be created after hostilities had ceased.[76]

Many individuals who forced the pace of the reconstruction project were temporary civil servants. One such significant outsider was the social scientist William Beveridge. Beveridge had long sought to implement his ideas through association with politicians, for example Lloyd George.[77] During the late 1930s, while working at Oxford, Beveridge became increasingly convinced of the need for economic planning combined with an ambitious social welfare programme, both during the coming war and beyond.[78] Like Keynes, he had worked in the Civil Service during the First World War, reaching the level of permanent secretary at the Ministry of Food. From the autumn of 1939 Keynes, Beveridge and other such 'Old Dogs' held regular meetings at 46 Gordon Square, Keynes's Bloomsbury residence.[79] All awaited the call to duty, which, one by one, they received. Beveridge certainly possessed the difficult personality often associated with individualistic outside policy specialists. Harold Wilson, who served Beveridge as a research assistant before the war, described him as 'inspiring and constructive in research, impossible in personal relations'.[80] Presumably it was partly because of such tendencies that Beveridge was one of the last advisers to be admitted from academia into Whitehall during the Second World War. Even then, his insufferable traits led to his being shunted around various departments of government.[81]

In June 1941 a committee on 'Social Insurance and Allied Services' was established under Beveridge. He took the initiative, conducting investigations which extended far beyond his apparent initial brief, which was to evaluate existing social insurance provisions. The White Paper published in December 1942 laid out a blueprint for the welfare state, advocating universal benefits, health care and education, as well as the maintenance of high employment levels.[82] Wilson wrote that Beveridge 'certainly was not guilty of underselling his achievement'.[83] Taking on a life of their own in the public imagination, partly as a result of Beveridge's calculated priming of the press, the Beveridge Report recommendations were forced upon a reluctant but distracted Churchill. During 1943 Beveridge conducted his own unofficial inquiry into methods of ensuring full employment. His assistants in the endeavour included a young Hungarian economist, Nicholas Kaldor.[84]

Essential to effective conduct of the war was the maintenance of morale. To this end, the Ministry of Information (MoI) co-ordinated government propaganda. In 1935 a subcommittee of the Committee of Imperial Defence prepared guidelines for the establishment of the MoI in the event of conflict, almost certainly taking as its main inspiration the Nazi Ministry of Propaganda. Ultimate responsibility for planning the ministry was handed to Sir Stephen Tallents. Tallents possessed practical experience of the job he was required to do, having worked at the Empire Marketing Board, Post Office and British Broadcasting Corporation. However, his appointment as Britain's answer to Josef Goebbels did not find favour within the permanent Civil Service, and, partly as a result of the consequent hostility, Tallents was dismissed in 1939. Indeed, the nascent MoI in general was 'subject to highly disruptive Whitehall intrigue'.[85] As a new organisation the MoI recruited in part from beyond permanent officialdom.[86]

A sinister aspect to the MoI was detected by some, for example the novelist George Orwell. His dystopian novel *1984* was set in a British totalitarian society of the future. The office of state propaganda featured in *1984*, the Ministry of Truth, was inspired in part by the MoI. Its headquarters were reminiscent of Senate House, the Bloomsbury MoI headquarters building acquired from the University of London.[87] Orwell himself fell foul of MoI informal censorship arrangements. During June 1944 the publishing firm Jonathan Cape received strong warnings from the MoI that Orwell's anti-Bolshevik novel *Animal Farm* would sour Anglo-Soviet relations were it to appear in print.[88]

Interaction between temporary and permanent officials during the Second World War generated certain tensions. Durbin experienced numerous difficulties relating to his status and pay.[89] Experts such as Keynes were often confronted with the problem of 'the inability or unwillingness of some senior officials to understand the issues under discussion'.[90] The Economic Section engendered a certain amount of resentment among the departments, when proposals produced by the latter were subjected to criticism or amendment by the former.[91] Obstruction was encountered by Churchill's Statistical Section when attempting to obtain information from Whitehall officials.[92] As might be expected, certain policies developed by temporaries did not find favour among permanent civil servants. For example, established elements within the Treasury offered considerable resistance to the more radical approaches proposed by the Economic Section to the possible problem of postwar unemployment.[93] Nevertheless, most temporaries were full of praise for the co-operation they received from career Whitehall.[94]

The question of the applicability of outsiders to peacetime conditions was examined during the war. The official inquiry into the future machinery of government, conducted by the Treasury official Sir Alan Barlow, concluded in November 1943 that 'the expert economist has an important contribution to make to the future business of Government', but cautioned against the establishment of a central economic general staff, on the grounds that it might usurp the power of the permanent Civil Service.[95]

Re-establishment of bureaucratic normality

Allied victory signalled a return to business as usual in Whitehall. The Statistical Section was dissolved following Churchill's defeat in the 1945 general election. Although it remained in existence, by 1953 the Economic Section had been officially absorbed by the Treasury, an acknowledgement of the fact that it had become largely an advisory body to the Chancellor of the Exchequer.[96] The vast majority of temporaries, including, for example, MacDougall, found their way back to their previous occupations. One reason for this trend was the fact that Civil Service salaries were not sufficiently high;[97] another, that employment as a wartime adviser was often particularly arduous. It is not surprising, therefore, that a return to academia or business appeared attractive to many. The traditional Whitehall strictures on conduct and free speech also encouraged the exodus.[98] A note produced by Keynes in 1943, which correctly anticipated many of these problems, demonstrated that they were foreseeable.[99] However, little effort was made to overcome them.

The Ministry of Production was abolished after the war, 'when it might conceivably have been built up into a major co-ordinating department or even a Ministry of Economic Planning'.[100] The way was open for a comeback by the career officials of the Treasury. Hugh Dalton, Chancellor of the Exchequer from 1945 to 1947, was a trained economist. He persuaded Keynes, who was formerly his teacher at Cambridge, to stay on 'as my personal adviser, outside the establishment'. Keynes, wrote Dalton, 'became my most trusted counsellor at the Treasury for the last nine months of his life'.[101] However, it has been suggested that, generally, because of his economics background, Dalton resisted the appointment of experts to the Treasury, feeling that he did not need such help.[102]

With Keynes's death in April 1946, the Treasury lost its sole and irreplaceable expert; but it soon regained its prewar administrative hegemony, which had temporarily been lost to the Ministry of Labour and the Lord President's Committee. Sir Stafford Cripps, who became Chancellor of the Exchequer in 1947, took with him to the Treasury the responsibilities for economic policy co-ordination which he had held as the Minister for Economic Affairs.[103] Such developments constituted a pendulum swing back towards generalist, permanent administrators and Treasury control. Ironically, at the same time that the principle of non-specialism was being reasserted, the role of the state was expanding in ways which suggested a need for more expertise, in greater quantities, than ever before.

In July 1945 the first general election held in ten years produced a shock result. A Labour government was returned, with 393 seats in the Commons, as opposed to the Conservatives' 210. The victory arguably represented a capitalisation on the mood for social change which had crystallised around the Beveridge report.[104] The Labour manifesto had laid out a radical programme which the government, led by the Prime Minister Clement Attlee, set about implementing. Policies included the creation of a universal benefits system, state-funded health care for all and the nationalisation of a number of industries, for example coal mining.[105] Labour held power until 1951. By then, it has been argued, the peacetime functions of government had altered fundamentally. In the words of Addison, 'the new collectivist state was set in concrete.'[106]

Government was now involved in a vast array of new activities, which surely called for a stronger presence of expertise within the bureaucracy.[107] It was not brought about to any great extent. Attlee was not averse to administrative modernisation per se, as his use of a complex Cabinet committee system demonstrated.[108] Furthermore – importantly from the perspective of this work – personal aides were used by the 1945–51 Labour administration. During 1945 and 1946 Attlee employed Douglas Jay, a rising star within Labour, in his late thirties, as his personal economic adviser.[109] Jay was experienced in the role. From 1943, while he was President of the Board of Trade, Dalton had employed Jay as 'my Personal Assistant on post-war problems'.[110] In his capacity as an adviser to Attlee, Jay took an interest in 'economics and the press'. After initial opposition from the permanent machine, Jay was granted access to Cabinet minutes. He also sat on 'Cabinet committees on major subjects such as food and coal'.[111] As will be shown, Jay's role and experiences are comparable to those of special advisers in later decades. Attlee was not the only member of his government to appoint a temporary aide. Herbert Morrison, as Lord President, was advised by Max Nicholson, formerly the director of the research body Political and Economic Planning.[112]

One attempt at administrative innovation which involved the employment of temporary civil servants was the establishment of the Central Economic Planning Staff (CEPS) in March 1947, under the industrialist Edwin Plowden. Plowden's team contained a mixture of outsiders and permanent staff. From September 1947 the CEPS was attached to Sir Stafford Cripps as Minister for Economic Affairs. However, it was absorbed into the Treasury upon Cripps's appointment as Chancellor of the Exchequer compromising its independence.[113] Moreover, the body never fulfilled its supposed long-term planning role, instead addressing problems on an ad hoc basis.[114] Neither the CEPS nor any of Attlee's other measures amounted to far-reaching administrative change. The qualities associated with senior officialdom remained unaltered.

Aside from introducing greater expertise, Labour might have been expected to bring in outsiders committed to its political objectives. Whitehall was often portrayed in internal Labour mythology as dominated by public-school-educated enemies of the workers' movement.[115] On a more sophisticated level, in 1938 the socialist theorist Harold Laski argued that the narrow outlook of civil servants made them incapable of implementing radical legislation.[116] Balogh later argued that Attlee should have made patronage-based appointments to senior posts, since, as he put it, certain 'key positions of power need for success to be held by sympathisers'. In Balogh's view, Attlee's failure to displace the existing elites, particularly those based in Whitehall, amounted to squandering the advantages he possessed in 1945. It was a mistake Balogh was determined should not be repeated by a future Labour administration.[117] The views of Laski and Balogh, however, were seemingly not shared by participants in the Attlee governments.

Civil Service reform in the immediate postwar period is a non-event in need of an explanation. Attlee, as well as other members of his Cabinet, had served in Churchill's wartime coalition. As a result, he and his colleagues were far more comfortable in dealing with the personnel and mechanisms of the Civil Service than they might have been coming fresh to Whitehall, in the manner of the incoming Labour administrations of 1964 and 1997. Furthermore, the ministers who had already operated within the existing system generally felt it was effective. In the words of Hennessy, they 'had seen the recent administrative past and it had worked'.[118] By 1945, too, the Civil Service itself was practised in the implementation of economic planning and welfare policies, thanks to the experience of total war;[119] and the left-wing academic Ralph Miliband contended that the Labour leadership never contemplated 'a fundamental transformation of the social order on the basis of common ownership'.[120] From such a perspective, it could be argued that the Attlee government had no need to overturn Trevelyan's regulatory Civil Service. Theakston, moreover, draws attention to the fact that Labour has never worked out a proper theory of the state.[121]

The Civil Service which emerged from the Second World War was epitomised by Sir Edward Bridges, Secretary of the Cabinet from 1938 to 1946 and Permanent Secretary to the Treasury and Head of the Civil Service from 1945 to 1956. Bridges' power was undeniably great. Peter Barberis writes that while Bridges 'deliberately soft-pedalled the use of the term "Head of the Home Civil Service" . . . he did not soft-pedal his exercise of the role'.[122] Bridges was, however, virtually unknown to the general public.[123] According to Balogh, an official in Bridges' position was able to 'determine the tone of the whole of the Establishment'.[124] Consciously taking his cue from Northcote–Trevelyan, he was a repository for many of the characteristics associated with the permanent civil servant. Sir Derek Mitchell, his private secretary from 1954 to 1956, agrees that Bridges was the embodiment of the Victorian ideal, who saw his job as a quest for 'truth which could be expressed in the form of a minute'.[125] Though a product of the past, Bridges' long-term influence was great. Upon becoming Head of the Home Civil Service in 1977, Sir Ian Bancroft let it be known that he wanted to set a tone as Bridges had done.[126] In 2002 the outgoing Cabinet Secretary, Sir Richard Wilson, delivered a public lecture addressing himself specifically to Bridges' legacy, the title of which, 'Portrait of a Profession Revisited', was a reference to a talk given by Bridges half a century previously.[127]

Bridges was a supreme generalist. The text of a speech he gave to a London University audience in November 1950 contains his description of himself as 'neither an economist nor a statistician'.[128] The rapid movement of staff within and between departments was, in his view, a 'healthy practice', since 'when a man has done five jobs in fifteen years . . . he is afraid of nothing and welcomes change'.[129] Bridges preferred on-the-job learning to the training of administrators in colleges. In his most famous lecture, 'Portrait of a Profession' (delivered in 1950),[130] as well as in his 1964 book *The Treasury*,[131] Bridges described Treasury control of Civil Service organisation and economic policy in uncritical terms. He approved of the idea that each department should have its own particular philosophy built up over a long period of time. Critics would come to regard these as agendas which were imposed on ministers. Non-partisanship was also highly important to Bridges. As he put it, 'a Civil Servant . . . is perhaps the least political of all animals.' Furthermore, he conceived of officials as owing loyalty to the Civil Service as an institution rather than to particular ministers.[132] The introduction of the special adviser was, in part, a reaction against the type of ideas this distinguished civil servant espoused.

Decline and administration

The Fabian Society's *The Reform of the Higher Civil Service*, which appeared in 1947, described the British Civil Service as 'probably the best . . . in the world'.[133] The fact that even reform campaigners could be so generous in their appraisal of the Civil Service was indicative of the high level of complacency concerning the administrative machine in British political circles at the time.[134] It was part of a 'general tendency' of contentment,[135] in the face of a vanishing Empire, that did not survive the 1950s. Seventeen years later the Fabian Civil Service Group, composed of economists, Labour politicians and Whitehall insiders, chaired by the economist Robert Neild, produced *The Administrators* – foreshadowing the major committee of inquiry into the Civil Service which Wilson was to announce in February 1966, under the chairmanship of Lord Fulton. It stated that for 'many years it has been customary to say that Britain has the best civil service in the world. The depth of this conviction has perhaps deflected people from considering what they mean.'[136] While Whitehall had previously been the subject of relatively gentle criticism, as the 1960s approached the 'mood became nastier, more anguished, more recriminatory'.[137] Just as satisfaction with the Civil Service had been related to a general sense of national well-being, so condemnation of it was the product of a feeling of crisis. As will be shown, from late 1956 onwards members of the intelligentsia began to urge the declaration of an unofficial countrywide state of emergency.

The first series of events to encourage this tendency were associated with the actions of the Conservative Prime Minister, Anthony Eden, during the Suez crisis. Eden participated in a military intervention in Egypt intended to prevent nationalisation of the Suez Canal. The US opposed the action and a sterling crisis ensued, forcing British withdrawal. Britain's loss, not only of its colonial possessions but of its ability to pursue an independent foreign policy, was made painfully apparent.[138] Feelings of inferiority were compounded by a number of other developments. From 1945 onwards the rate of economic growth in Britain was consistently lower than that of significant other countries including France, Germany and Japan. Such a disparity was an increasing source of concern to many domestic commentators. Britain also suffered from a confused approach to the developing European unification project. The European Economic Community (EEC) was formally created on 1 January 1958. It included France, Germany, Italy and the Benelux nations as member states and, after a few years of existence, was generally judged in Britain to be a success. Britain declined to involve itself with the EEC at the outset, but in 1961 the Cabinet decided to seek membership. The resulting application was vetoed by the French in 1963. This chain of events was widely interpreted as indicative of national weakness.[139] By the early 1960s, then, it was becoming clear that Britain's global role had been considerably diminished, but its European one was yet to be found. The worst fears of the 'National Efficiency' campaigners of six decades previously had become reality. Britain was now a second-rate power.

British observers drew dramatic comparisons with the demise of the Spanish Empire.[140] Domestic scapegoats were sought and one was found in the form of 'the establishment'. The use of the word 'establishment' as a socially descriptive term may have had its origins in the early nineteenth century. It was applied to the Anglican Church, the 'established' church, to distinguish it from nonconformism.[141] In 1959 Hugh Thomas, a former Foreign Office official who had left the Civil Service two years previously, attempted to define the establishment as a collection of institutions which together governed the country. Thomas characterised it as possessing an attachment to ideas and practices associated with the period 1830–70, when Britain was unchallenged as an international power.[142]

During the late 1950s, conspiracy theorising in various forms was prevalent throughout the Western world, including the United States.[143] In Britain, establishment-bashing, initiated by the journalist Henry Fairlie of *The Spectator* in 1955,[144] took on a particular ferocity. A 1959 book entitled *The Establishment*, edited by Thomas, investigated various aspects of the supposed entity, including the public school system, the armed forces, the City of London, Parliament and the BBC.[145] It also included a chapter on the Civil Service, entitled 'The Apotheosis of the Dilettante', written by Thomas Balogh – later to be a key member of the Fabian Civil Service Group that produced *The Administrators*.

Those who sought to evaluate bureaucratic arrangements in Britain in these years did not constitute a homogeneous group. Nevertheless, certain ideas did recur in the reform literature published between Suez and Harold Wilson's 1964 election victory. A consensus developed among many intellectuals regarding the shortcomings of the Civil Service. Areas of agreement were that Whitehall suffered from Oxbridge domination and was an environment in which specialist skills were undervalued and 'amateurism' prevailed. Such criticisms had a basis in fact. Between 1937 and 1968, 75 per cent of entrants to the administrative class were Oxbridge graduates, of whom 59 per cent had studied humanities, 29 per cent social sciences and only 7 per cent technical subjects.[146] There was also said to be excessive secrecy and a lack of movement in and out by staff. Furthermore, the power of the Treasury was felt to be too great. More broadly, observers felt that the Civil Service was a product of the nineteenth century, which might benefit if it took a modernising cue from its foreign counterparts. A related idea was that economic policy should move away from the *laissez-faire* approach associated with the Treasury and towards greater interventionism.

Balogh was particularly vehement in his criticism, although, in the view of Robert Neild, an economist and colleague, he contributed little by way of original analysis.[147] As an institution, Balogh argued in 'The Apotheosis of the Dilettante', the Civil Service, and in particular the Treasury, was guilty both of technical incompetence and conspiracy to enforce its own liberal economic policy agenda upon ministers. The typical senior career official, he wrote, was a 'smooth, extrovert conformist with good connexions and no knowledge of modern problems, or of up-to-date techniques of getting that information'. He believed that Treasury staff ensured the continued pre-eminence of non-interventionist policy approaches, undisturbed by election results.[148]

What changes did the reformers propose? There was agreement over the need for increased specialist knowledge and the recruitment of experts. Better training was advocated for civil servants. A model frequently cited as an example to be followed in this respect was the French one. The French tradition of technocracy, that is the rule of experts, dates back at least as far as the foundation in 1794 of the Ecole Polytechnique ('school of many skills'), also known as the 'X'.[149] 'Les X', as its students were known, often went on to serve the French state as engineers and technicians. The Ecole Nationale d'Administration (ENA), created immediately after the Second World War, turned out students with specialist administrative training which could be applied in the field of government. It was also argued that mid-career movement, in both directions, between the service and the outside world, should be encouraged.

Drastic changes were envisaged for the Treasury. A suggestion common to many proposals was that Establishments (that is, personnel policy) should be removed from the Treasury to a separate Civil Service Commission. In the context of the traditional function of the Treasury, namely the control of spending, it is interesting to note that none of the reform texts analysed here called for retrenchment or a reduction in waste; in fact *The Administrators* specifically ruled this out.[150] Plans for a new approach to economic policy formation were at the radical core of the proposals made by Balogh, the Fabians and others. Increasingly, the idea emerged that a new economics ministry should be created.

A need for temporary civil servants, appointed on a patronage basis, was frequently identified. The economics journalist Samuel Brittan, for example, argued for the creation of 'a new class of adviser' whose 'job would be both political and technical. They would be selected in accordance with the personal preferences of ministers and move freely in or out from the academic world, industry, the professions, and elsewhere'.[151] Similarly, the Fabian Society's *The Administrators* also proposed 'political appointments'. The Fabians suggested that there should be two types of temporary adviser: 'experts who are called in to help implement the particular policies of the government of the day, and personal aides to provide general help to Ministers in their private office'.[152]

As will be shown, ideas of this type took concrete form in the shape of the special adviser. Again, foreign influences were at play. The US 'spoils system' of patronage-based appointments was admired at the time. However, the complete clear-outs upon changes of administration it entailed were seen by some as too extreme and chaotic.[153] An even more favoured model, associated in particular with France, was the *cabinet*, the hand-picked team of ministerial advisers composed of both outsiders and seconded career officials.[154] In July 1962, at the first meeting of the Fabian Civil Service Group which produced *The Administrators*, there was 'some support in the discussion for a modified chef de cabinet system'.[155] The proposal had great implications for the Civil Service as it was constituted at the time. As Simon James notes, in countries where the *cabinet* is used, the minister's private office as constituted in Britain typically has no place, and the equivalent to the permanent secretary, if there is one at all, is responsible for little more than logistical support. Policy formation is in the hands of the ministerial team.[156] Moreover, the clear distinction between a career as a party politician and a career as a bureaucrat which has existed in Britain does not exist. For example, the French presidents Georges Pompidou, Valéry Giscard d'Estaing and Jacques Chirac all previously served as *cabinet* members.[157] There have been instances in Britain of civil servants becoming senior politicians – Douglas Hurd is a prominent example – but such cases are the exceptions that prove the rule rather than instances of an established pattern. Certainly, in the postwar period such transition was not the norm; and those engaged as civil servants were expected to comport themselves in strict accordance with the principles of neutrality and not to attach themselves to particular parties, individuals, viewpoints or policies. With the advent of the special adviser this clear distinction would begin to blur.

Some reform campaigners wanted to introduce greater political control over the bureaucracy. Balogh in particular argued from such a standpoint. He saw the recruitment of 'expert opinion from outside, sharing the point of view of the Government of the day . . . at senior levels' as vital.[158] There was certainly a distinction between the kind of explicitly partisan advisers advocated by Balogh and those envisaged by, for example, Brittan. Brittan's temporaries 'would tend to change with governments, but this would not be a rigid rule'.[159] As already shown, perceptions of relative national decline prompted many intellectuals to turn their fire upon what they described as the establishment. Balogh's solution to the problem of the establishment was to replace it with a new socialist one, since 'So long as Labour hankers after being accepted by the old "Establishment", instead of creating its own, so long will it be in an awkward position, forced mainly on the defensive.'[160]

In Balogh's view, a Labour administration had to be led by the correct individual and the correct faction. In his 1963 pamphlet *Planning for Progress*, Balogh noted that 'Mr Harold Wilson's election to leadership has made a coherent planning of future Labour strategy easier.' Balogh subjected Wilson's less *dirigiste* opponents inside Labour to even greater derision than he did the Conservatives.[161] Conceiving of the special adviser as more than mere technician or indeed partisan, he stressed the requirement of personal loyalty to the employing minister. In a memorandum he drafted for the Fabian Civil Service Group during 1963, he described how 'each Minister responsible for an important department should have men at his disposal who are not merely technically able, who are not merely in sympathy with the political party in power, but who are personally devoted to the Minister himself'. Such aides would be expected to enter and leave office with the politician they served.[162]

Many of the arguments for administrative reform described above rested, to some extent, on a belief in economic planning. The sign of British economic weakness considered most significant from the late 1950s was that of relatively slow expansion. It led to demands for the introduction of planning.[163] In *Planning for Progress*, Balogh produced a table detailing annual rates of growth of gross domestic product and output in various capitalist countries between 1950 and 1960. At the bottom of the pile was Britain, at 2.7 per cent; at the top, with 9.5 per cent, stood Japan. France, in the top half, had managed 4.3 per cent.[164] The perceived postwar success of the French economy cast a long shadow. In contrast to Britain's Treasury-led *laissez-faire* tradition, the French state had long taken a *dirigiste* approach. After 1945 this took the form of indicative planning: that is, aiming at the achievement of certain targets within given time-frames, under the aegis of highly trained technocrats. Under this influence, by the beginning of the 1960s in Britain attempts were being made within government to replace the central negative objective of minimum unemployment with the positive one of maximum growth.[165] In addition to the French, another influence upon members of Wilson's circle, and those further to the left within Labour,166 was the State Planning Committee (Gosplan) of the Soviet Union, instituted in 1921.[167] Balogh, demonstrating the extent of his faith in state intervention, went so far as to warn that the command economy of the Soviet Union 'with its vast output of technicians and ever increasing production' might 'overwhelm us'.[168] According to Balogh, as a result of their generalist tendencies permanent civil servants were naturally inclined to adopt *laissez-faire* principles. As he put it, in a 'planned economy, the crossword-puzzle mind, reared on mathematics at Cambridge or Greats at Oxford, has only a limited outlet'.[169] The implication was that outside recruits would be vital to a successful adoption of planning.

Even before Labour returned to power in 1964, there had already been significant government activity related to the concerns described above. The Conservative governments of 1951 to 1964 drew on outside expertise, even before the 'decline' vogue began. Churchill, at the beginning of his second and final spell as Prime Minister from 1951 to 1955, recalled Cherwell (as a Cabinet member)[170] and MacDougall. Their team was smaller than the wartime Statistical Section had been, but was housed in 11 Downing Street, allowing easy access to the Prime Minister.[171]

Harold Macmillan, Prime Minister from 1957 to 1963, had an affinity for counsellors drawn from beyond Whitehall, some of whom served on a basis of personal loyalty as much as specialist expertise. John Wyndham, for example, served, unpaid, in the Prime Minister's office from May 1957, handling politically sensitive issues. As Macmillan put it, 'On and off he [Wyndham] has helped me with his friendship and advice for a period of over twenty years.'[172] Sir Derek Mitchell, the Prime Minister's principal private secretary from 1964 to 1966, recalls that Wyndham was able to work alongside permanent bureaucrats effectively and amicably.[173] Macmillan's outlook was informally influenced by the Cambridge economist Sir Roy Harrod, whom he considered to be a 'man of considerable genius. He is often wrong; but then he is often right'.[174]

Macmillan and the Chancellor he appointed in 1960, Selwyn Lloyd, oversaw a number of significant administrative innovations. One of them was the establishment of the National Economic Development Council (NEDC). Its tripartite approach, involving government, trades unions and management, was modelled on that of the French four-year plan.[175] 'Neddy', as it became known, concerned itself with planning for growth.[176] The NEDC was headed by the Chancellor and therefore did not constitute a direct threat to the Treasury. However, it was staffed by professional economists drawn from outside Whitehall. The man recruited as the NEDC's economic director was Sir Donald MacDougall, who had been back at Oxford since 1953. Perceived relative national decline was certainly an influence on the development of the NEDC.[177] Wilson later argued that the NEDC provided a precedent for his use of temporary advisers. Questioned by the academic Norman Hunt shortly before becoming Prime Minister regarding his intentions to recruit from beyond Whitehall, Wilson said, 'Well, they had to bring in people from outside to staff Neddy, didn't they?'[178]

Labour and technocracy

The Labour Party has a long technocratic tradition, associated in particular with its intellectual wing, the Fabian Society. The Fabians began in 1884 as a splinter from a religious social reform group established the previous year, the Fellowship of the New Life. Significant figures in the development of Fabianism included the playwright George Bernard Shaw, the novelist H. G. Wells and the social reformers Beatrice and Sidney Webb. The Webbs were particularly important to the technocratic aspects of Fabian influence upon Labour. As Theakston states, their socialism 'had an unmistakable centralist and bureaucratic flavour. A major role in bringing about and then governing a socialist society would be played by a selfless, dedicated, unassuming and public-spirited elite of expert bureaucrats'.[179]

In their 1920 work *A Constitution for the Socialist Commonwealth of Great Britain*, the Webbs suggested that, following the nationalisation of key industries, it would 'clearly be necessary to train, for the control departments, a Civil Service of a new kind; to set these officers to develop a new administrative technique; and to enable them to study on the spot, the various devices by which other nations, and other forms of organisation in our own country, are coping with analogous problems'.[180] Another prominent Fabian, Harold Laski, was an agitator for bureaucratic change, suggesting in 1925 that government should 'develop the habit of special appointments to a small number of technical posts'.[181]

During 1932 the New Fabian Research Bureau, a branch of the Fabian Society, investigated the Civil Service. The trades union leader and future Labour Foreign Secretary, Ernest Bevin, and his colleague Colin G. Clark produced a memorandum proposing that 'an administrative Department should be built up consisting of Civil Servants directly responsible to the Prime Minister for the purpose of assisting him in his own special tasks', usurping the authority of the overmighty Treasury. Such an innovation, they argued, should be combined with the establishment of a 'National Economic Planning Department . . . staffed by full-time experts whose function it would be to prepare, revise, and advise on the execution of a general plan for the whole country'.[182] Kingsley B. Smellie, a political scientist, also made proposals. A critic of the generalism fostered by the competitive examination, he advocated greater post-recruitment training. With a particularly interesting choice of words, he also called for 'a special advisory body within the Treasury' to provide the administration with technical expertise.[183] It will be shown that such notions were central to the Wilson programme which included the creation of the special adviser.

Fabian proposals for bureaucratic reform, however, were tempered by a genuine respect for the calibre of existing civil servants and drew back from a full embrace of the concept of technocracy. In 1931 Laski wrote a Fabian pamphlet entitled *The Limitations of the Expert*, stressing the fact that 'it is one thing to urge the need for expert consultation at every stage in making policy; it is another thing, and a very different thing, to insist that the expert's judgement must be final.'[184] A similar admiration for permanent civil servants has also been ascribed to a later would-be reformer, Harold Wilson.[185] Moreover, Laski was concerned that the 'special appointments' he called for should not become 'merely a reservoir of ministerial patronage' and should be subject to approval by the official machine.[186]

It is possible to detect the recurrence of ideas associated with the Fabians in the approach adopted by Harold Wilson following his 1963 attainment of the Labour leadership. In a prophetic novel, *The Shape of Things to Come*, written during 1932–3, the former Fabian and Co-efficient H. G. Wells predicted a socialist revolutionary movement founded on an emergent new class of worker. Wells wrote that

> by the third decade of the twentieth century two-thirds of the technicians, scientific workers and able business organisers were talking active revolution . . . [a] revolution in revolutionary ideas had occurred. The protean spirit of Revolution had cut its hair, put on blue overalls, made blue prints for itself, created a New Model, and settled down to work in a systematic fashion.

Wells labelled his new type of socialist the 'Technical Revolutionary'.[187] Three decades later, Wilson concerned himself with similar ideas. Famously, at the 1963

Labour Party conference in Scarborough, he described how 'we are re-defining and we are re-stating our Socialism in terms of the scientific revolution' and referred to the 'Britain that is going to be forged in the white heat of this revolution'.[188] Wilson seems to have used the term 'scientific' in a broad sense, taking in the discipline of economics. The following year – still in opposition – he made it clear in a BBC interview that in order to achieve his modernising agenda, he would recruit outsiders into the Civil Service.[189]

Wilson's own background as a 'sparkling temporary civil servant in wartime Whitehall' was an influence on his plans to use advisers from beyond Whitehall.[190] Shortly before becoming Prime Minister, when discussing his intentions with Hunt, Wilson referred to the time 'when I was a member of the Cabinet Secretariat'.[191] The left-wing Labour intellectual Richard Crossman, a close ally of Wilson, held Cabinet posts throughout the period 1964–70. As leader of the opposition, Wilson gave Crossman the science brief. In an article entitled 'Scientists in Whitehall', based on a Fabian lecture given in the autumn of 1963, Crossman asserted that between '1940 and 1945, Britain was probably the best-governed country in the world', with a successful 'centrally planned economy'. This had been made possible through the introduction into Whitehall of 'an army of outsiders, uninhibited by civil service procedures'. Therefore, suggested Crossman, in the 'technological revolution to which we are now committed . . . we shall permanently need the marriage of established civil service and outside expertise that we developed as a temporary expedient in World War I and perfected in World War II.'[192]

Technocratic ideals were, therefore, an element in the genesis of the special adviser. However, there were other motivating factors. Nicholas Kaldor, an economist imported to the Treasury in 1964, later stated that 'Tommy Balogh and myself . . . were brought in under the ticket . . . that it would be a good idea to move towards the French system in which ministers should have a *Chef du Cabinet*, or their own advisers.'[193] The influence of the US spoils system has also been mentioned. To some, the resemblance between the use of special advisers and the US approach, in particular that of 1961–3 Democrat President John F. Kennedy, was clear. Wilson himself felt it to be the case.[194] Cairncross described Robert Neild's post as Economic Adviser to the Treasury as similar to that of Walter Heller, who was Chairman of the Council of Economic Advisers in the US from 1961 to 1964.[195]

The fact that Labour had been in opposition for a long time was also important. Between 1959 and 1964 the task of the co-ordination of Labour policy fell to Peter Shore (later Lord Shore), head of the Labour Party Research Department. In Shore's view, the creation of the special adviser was attributable to the feeling within Labour that, after thirteen years of Conservative government, the Civil Service might have difficulty adjusting to a change in approach. Special advisers were to be 'guardians of the manifesto'. It was their task, he remembered, to ensure that 'habits of mind and surmountable obstacles [within Whitehall] should not prevent the working out' of Labour policy pledges.[196] Conservatism with a small 'c', then, was an enemy. Kaldor subsequently stated that special advisers were introduced in order to conduct Labour ministers' 'battles with the Civil Service', a necessity since 'the Civil Service gradually develops its own set of views and is an autonomous body, which is on the whole naturally conservative'.[197]

Neild emphasises the prevalence of the idea that ministers should have their own aides, of Labour persuasion, in order to avoid being 'run by the Treasury'. Moreover, members of the Labour government wished to be seen to have outside advisers 'so as to protect themselves against the accusation of being too much in the hands of the regulars'.[198] Inside Labour, there was a long-term view that partisan aides were required to implement the party's programme. For example, following the experience of office in 1924, there was pressure from within the party for a large clear-out of Foreign Office staff by a future administration, designed to enable the pursuance of a socialist foreign policy. However, a wary Ramsay MacDonald saw to it that this did not take place.[199]

George Lansbury, who officially became Labour leader in 1932, argued that 'when a Labour government comes to power it will need as its leading men in all departments men who accept Labour's policy and are wholeheartedly determined to make it successful.' For Lansbury, partisan commitment was more important than expertise, which, he felt, the 'early Fabians' had overrated.[200] Lansbury was writing shortly after the political crisis of 1931, which resulted in MacDonald's formation of a National Government. Treasury officials were no doubt among the villains in Labour interpretations of this chain of events. There was also a belief within Labour that career officials were not suited to the proactive presentation of policy. At a Fabian conference in February 1948, held to discuss 'The British Government's Public Relations Information Services', the view emerged that temporary civil servants 'who were formerly journalists are much better as Press Officers than permanent civil servants'.[201] This was not an entirely new concept. Both major parties had found employment inside the administration for professional media handlers as far back as the 1850s, when the Liberal journalist Albany de Fonblanque was rewarded with a post at the Board of Trade, and Emerson Tennent, also at the Board of Trade, wrote for the Conservatives.[202]

Certain individuals who participated in the development and presentation of Labour policy in the period leading up to the 1964 election went on to become special advisers. Owing to the limited financial resources available to Shore, he was the grateful recipient of intellectual assistance offered on a voluntary basis. This was one reason why the likes of Balogh were able to exert considerable influence over Labour's plans.[203] Furthermore, Balogh had long been close to Wilson. As Theakston states, 'Balogh's access to the Labour leadership gave his ideas a special importance.'[204] In a 1963 Fabian pamphlet, Balogh advocated a centrally planned 'increase in the rate of ... economic growth' in order to achieve greater social equality at home, and provide assistance to nations within the developing world. He suggested that it should be brought about by a 'central office of control – though not necessarily within the Treasury'.[205] In May 1963 Balogh produced a document for Wilson, at the Labour leader's request, which laid out his proposals for such an economic planning ministry in the context of a radically restructured Civil Service.[206]

Immediately after Labour's 1964 election victory Wilson established the Department of Economic Affairs (DEA), deliberately conceived as a rival to the Treasury and charged with the coordination of economic expansion. Should the DEA be attributed to Balogh? Brittan is not convinced, pointing out that at the time of its creation many claimed credit for the DEA, but that upon its demise no one was disposed to accept the blame.[207] Shore, close to Wilson at the time, would only go so far as to say that Balogh was 'important' to the genesis of the DEA.[208] George Brown, Secretary of State at the DEA from 1964 to 1966, suggested that the department was the product of a broad movement within Labour, rather than the work of one individual. Nevertheless, in Brown's account Balogh's close intellectual association with the instigation of the DEA is clear.[209] Even before his appointment as a special adviser, then, Balogh's influence was great.

Balogh used every means at his disposal to force other aspects of his bureaucratic reform programme firmly on to the agenda of his party while it was in opposition. As with the DEA, Balogh's views on the appointment of temporary civil servants were not unique within Labour, but there is no doubt he was a forceful advocate.

Another future special adviser, Nicholas Kaldor, had been involved in party policy formation for many years,[210] and his influence can be detected in the 1964 Labour manifesto, in the form of its promises of major tax reforms.[211] Labour's bid for power in 1964 also required assistance of a non-academic type, for example in writing speeches and formulating campaign strategy. To this end, two more future special advisers, John Allen and John Harris, proved useful.[212] It is arguably possible here to discern distinctions between types of adviser: namely, the policy expert (Balogh and Kaldor), the political counsellor (Allen) and the presentational aide (Harris). However, as will be shown later, these categories were not completely watertight.

Wilson's embrace of administrative reform was not as wholehearted as some would have wished. Benn described an animated conversation which took place between himself and Balogh in May 1963. The topic of discussion was the political/scientific takeover of the Civil Service which both men believed would follow a Labour election victory. As mentioned above, later that month Wilson solicited a document from Balogh laying out the latter's conception of a reformed Civil Service. Two proposals were central to Balogh's plan. First, a department for economic planning was to be instigated and the functions of the Treasury cut back to those of a finance ministry. Second, the Prime Minister's office would be given an enhanced role, absorbing the NEDC and assuming responsibility for the resolution of disputes between the Treasury and the new economics department. Over the summer of 1963, Balogh, Shore and Crossman discussed floating various ideas to Wilson, including Balogh's proposal that ministers of state responsible for home, foreign and information policy should be installed at No. 10.[213] If implemented, this would have meant the emergence of something resembling a Prime Minister's department. As will be shown, Balogh envisaged special advisers playing an important role within such a body.

In his speech to the Labour Party conference in September that year, Wilson publicly indicated that while he was in agreement with the first aspect of Balogh's programme, the second had not found favour with him.[214] Additionally, Wilson rejected the notion that the ministerial *cabinet* should be introduced to British government. As he told Hunt,

> *I'm rather hesitant about this . . . There is a danger that you get a false division between his [the minister's] political cabinet . . . and the civil servants. My own experience, having tried as a minister to bring in one or two outside experts with the right political approach, was that I did far better when I relied on loyal civil servants who knew what I wanted, in my private office, and who saw to it that the rest of the department knew what I wanted.*[215]

The rejection of the formal *cabinet* was a crucial decision. *The Administrators* recommended the instigation of 'something akin to the Continental system of ministerial *cabinets* . . . a Minister would be able to make a number of appointments in his private office – up to, say, three or four – as assistants in his private office'.[216] This was not done, and permanent Whitehall maintained its grip on one of its most important instruments of power. Brittan, who served inside the DEA from 1964 to 1966, noted in his diary on 9 November 1964: 'Reflection. Machine works through Private Office.'[217] The Fabian scheme would have posed a greater challenge to the Civil Service machine than the one ultimately put into place.

Wilson did, however, tell Hunt that he would bring in 'a small number' of specialists to the 'Cabinet Secretariat'.[218] As his statement suggested, Wilson initially 'considered that perhaps he should concentrate his senior advisers in the Cabinet office'.[219] Had he done so, it would have represented a considerable bolstering of the prime ministerial centre. Ultimately, however, the first wave of special advisers was split between the Cabinet Office and the Treasury (with one at the Foreign Office).

Wilson's rejection of certain administrative reform proposals before Labour came to power may have resulted, at least in part, from a brief consultation he had as leader of the opposition with the former Head of the Home Civil Service, Lord Normanbrook (Norman Brook). Naturally, Normanbrook was opposed to reform.[220]

Wilson's plans for administrative change, then, were in certain respects fairly mild – but this did not prevent elements on the political right from engaging in scaremongering. Aims of Industry was a pressure group dedicated to opposing what its supporters saw as the scourges of organised labour and state intervention in society. In the run-up to the 1964 election, it published a pamphlet, entitled *Advice – And Dissent, Two Men of Influence*, dealing with the subject of Balogh and Kaldor as senior Labour advisers. *Advice – And Dissent* suggested that Wilson's takeover of Labour had brought to the fore its already existing 'enthusiasm for controls'. The pamphlet also drew attention to proposals for the creation of a planning department and Civil Service reform. It insinuated, incorrectly, that a Wilson government might embark upon a massive Balogh-inspired nationalisation programme.[221]

Representatives of permanent officialdom were apprehensive. In 1964 Edward Bridges, now in retirement but still acting as an unofficial spokesman for career Whitehall, revealed his thoughts on possible Civil Service reform. Of the *cabinet*, Bridges argued that it 'is significant that one wants to use the French pronunciation here. It is an idea foreign to us, with political overtones. I dislike the idea a good deal. It implies that a department is unable or unwilling to serve all ministers loyally and effectively, irrespective of party'. He was also concerned that Wilson's planned introduction of outsiders into the Cabinet Office 'could make for difficulties'. While not opposed to the use of temporary civil servants per se, he did not favour their being 'charged with executive duties'.[222] The significance of his views will become apparent in subsequent chapters.

* * *

A number of conclusions can be drawn regarding the long- and short-term background to the introduction of the special adviser in 1964. The modern Civil Service was established as a response to the undoubted shortcomings of a system of patronage-based appointment. Consequently, the growth in numbers of special advisers from 1997 has been portrayed as a reversion to the arrangements with which the Northcote–Trevelyan report found fault. Since this document, and the protracted administrative changes with which it was associated, have often been held as central to Civil Service integrity, its contents merit critical scrutiny. It is interesting to note that the objectives of the Victorian reformers seem to have included the extension of Treasury power and the shoring up of the existing social elite. Their innovations, therefore, should not be seen as democratic in motivation. Moreover, they were to some extent founded in Trevelyan's prejudices and misrepresentations, and the requirements of a state which had changed considerably by the early twentieth century. This partly explains the recruitment of outside advisers which took place under various administrations thereafter. Particularly in wartime, temporary civil servants were vital to certain concerted policy efforts. However, career Whitehall generally maintained its high level of influence. Its merits, moreover, were considerable, and it made significant contributions when working in conjunction with outsiders, notably during the Second World War.

The perception of national decline which became widespread from the late 1950s had a profound impact upon British political culture. There followed an erosion in the status of traditional institutions, including the Civil Service. The generalist values of Whitehall were subjected to particular criticism and unfavourable comparisons were drawn with foreign approaches. Such attitudes chimed particularly strongly within the Labour Party, with its Fabian-tinged, technocratic approach. While the Conservatives had used outsiders, Labour was more ideologically disposed towards a conscious overhaul of existing arrangements – a tendency further encouraged by the implications of its long period in opposition. The party also had a radical policy programme, the implementation of which, it was felt, required aides possessed of not only technical skill but also political commitment, and, especially in Balogh's view, loyalty to individual ministers.

Three

Enter the special adviser: the Wilson experiment

This chapter relates the circumstances surrounding the appointment in 1964 of five special advisers to the Cabinet Office and the Treasury – John Allen, Thomas Balogh, Nicholas Kaldor, Robert Neild and Michael Stewart – and describes public and parliamentary responses to Harold Wilson's experiment. It goes on to examine the implications of the 1968 Fulton Report on the Civil Service, some of whose recommendations related to the use by ministers of counsel drawn from outside Whitehall, and the extent to which it was acted upon. Wilson's premiership has been criticised, both for the policy failures over which he presided and for alleged shortcomings in his leadership style. In respect of the former, the role of special advisers in the ill-fated attempt to preserve the dollar–sterling exchange rate at $2.80 will be identified; in respect of the latter, the association of aides with Wilson's supposed flaws and the presence of special advisers within Wilson's personal inner circle are discussed.

The first wave

The international origins of 'special adviser' as a governmental term are not entirely clear, but it certainly gained prominence in the United States during the first half of the twentieth century. A search of the British Library's computerised catalogue reveals that it was already in use there by 1924.[1] The Library of Congress Online Catalogue contains references to presidential special advisers dating back to the 1930s.[2] The title occurs in British Public Record Office files pre-dating October 1964, where it is often used to describe aides to foreign diplomats.[3] In May 1957 Harold Macmillan appointed Admiral Sir Matthew Slattery as a 'special adviser on the transport of Middle East oil'.[4] From 1964, however, the designation took on a new and distinctive meaning.

The five special advisers examined in this chapter, all of whom were appointed immediately upon Labour's 1964 election victory, were temporary civil servants of party political association, drawn from beyond the Civil Service but employed within it, subject to the patronage of individual ministers. Other possible candidates for examination have been passed over for various reasons. Since he was already a long-serving formal supplier of counsel on defence matters, the official 1964 listing of Solly Zuckerman as a special adviser must be taken as anomalous. A number of new ministries were created during the first Wilson administration, inevitably resulting in a large influx of outsiders to Whitehall. In order to avoid dilution of the topic, only newcomers employed temporarily in already existing offices of government have been selected for discussion here. Four of the five individuals chosen are listed in the 1965 *Imperial Calendar* (the name of the *Civil Service Yearbook* in a less politically correct past) as special advisers; one, Robert Neild, was labelled differently, for reasons which will be explained. A sixth aide, John Harris, appointed to the Foreign Office in 1964, will be considered in the next chapter.

On the first day of the Labour administration, Thomas Balogh told Derek Mitchell, the Prime Minister's principal private secretary, that he did not have a title yet. In his own account Mitchell's quick-witted response, not appreciated by Balogh, was that such things were not bestowed until departure from government.[5] In the 1965 edition of the *Imperial Calendar* Balogh, John Allen and Michael Stewart were grouped as Cabinet Office temporaries under the general heading of 'Special Advisers'. Balogh was described as 'Adviser on Economic Affairs'. Nicholas Kaldor and Robert Neild were recruited to the Treasury. The *Imperial Calendar* described Kaldor as 'Special Adviser (part-time) to the Chancellor of the Exchequer on the Social and Economic Aspects of Taxation Policy'. His convoluted job title came about as a result of concern within Whitehall that his description should not appear to 'usurp' the Treasury and the Boards of Inland Revenue and Customs and Excise, who were the 'official advisers of the Chancellor on taxation policy'.[6] It was an early indication of concern among career officials that special advisers posed a threat.

Neild was referred to in the *Imperial Calendar* not as a special adviser but as 'Economic Adviser to the Treasury'. A probable reason for this anomaly was the fact that Sir Laurence Helsby, Joint Permanent Secretary to the Treasury and Head of the Home Civil Service, was anxious to present Neild's appointment as non-party-political.[7] While Neild had previously served a Conservative administration as a member of the Economic Section from 1951 to 1956, his links to Labour and the Chancellor of the Exchequer, James Callaghan, were clear.[8] Initially, it was anticipated that Neild's appointment might entail his wresting control of the Economic Section from its existing Director, Alec Cairncross.[9] In Kaldor's account, a chance series of events led to Callaghan's acquisition of Neild as an adviser and the development of the misunderstanding that Cairncross was ready to leave Whitehall and become the senior Treasury representative in Washington.[10] The problem of placing a political appointee in charge of neutral civil servants was intractable. Brittan recorded Cairncross's stating that 'the Labour Party would have to make up its mind whether to sack him and introduce the spoil system.'[11]

A resolution, however, first proposed to Callaghan by William Armstrong, Joint Permanent Secretary of the Treasury, on 23 October 1964, was eventually reached. Armstrong's suggestion was that

> Broadly speaking Mr. Cairncross would be in charge of the economic analysis of forecasting operations and also the Treasury's man on the recruitment, training and posting of career economists in the Government service. Mr. Neild will . . . have a remit which will be somewhat wider and also more personal to you. He will be particularly useful in keeping in touch with you about how your mind is working on policy.[12]

Neild and Cairncross achieved a mutually harmonious division of responsibilities whereby the former provided advice while the latter ran the machine.[13] Nevertheless, files indicate that Neild sat with Cairncross on the Management Committee for the newly established Government Economic Service (GES). So, too, did Balogh.[14] Aside from the threat to his own position, Cairncross was concerned that he was not being consulted over temporary appointments and that their exact status in relation to the career machine was unclear.[15] This failure to provide advance notice was replicated in other cases. The decision to appoint special advisers to the Cabinet Office was taken without prior discussion with the Treasury Establishment Officer, Elsie Abbot.[16]

The question of remuneration was a contentious one. In the Commons, on 10 November 1964, the Conservative MP Simon Wingfield Digby asked how the salaries of incoming advisers, including Balogh, Kaldor and Neild, were worked out.[17] In fact, there was no precise formula. Matching special advisers to Civil Service grades was extremely difficult, as the examples of Allen and Stewart, both of whom worked under Balogh, demonstrated. Allen (thirty-two years old at the time) requested payment at principal scale – at the beginning of 1965, between £1,951 and £2,725 a year.[18] Stewart (aged thirty-one), who, like Neild, had previously served in the Economic Section (from 1957 to 1962) suggested that the calculation of his salary should take into account the fact that he had less job security than during his previous spell as a bureaucrat.[19] In October 1964 Andrew Collier, a Treasury assistant secretary, remarked to David Heaton, the Principal Establishment Officer at the Cabinet Office, in relation to attempts to fix the level of Allen's and Stewart's salaries, 'I fear we may run into difficulties in the long run if we try to equate either of these people to any particular point in an existing scale; it doesn't really fit.'[20] Allen's and Stewart's grades, were, therefore, officially deemed as ones for which 'no national scale or rate exists'. The figure arrived at for both was £2,500 a year.

Sir Burke Trend, the Cabinet Secretary, wrote to both the Vice-Chancellor at Oxford and the Master of Balliol College in order to secure unpaid leave of absence for Balogh (aged fifty-eight).[21] As with Allen and Stewart, there was officially 'no national scale or rate' for Balogh's salary. Balogh's position upon joining the Civil Service on 17 October 1964 was described as 'Special Adviser to the Prime Minister'.[22] Balogh told Heaton that he was not 'concerned with money as such, but with the status a salary implies and confers',[23] and suggested 'a salary . . . somewhere between Cairncross and Sir Donald MacDougall [i.e. above Cairncross and below MacDougall, the Economic Director of the Department of Economic Affairs]'.[24] Heaton initially proposed to Trend that Balogh receive £7,200.[25] Ultimately, Balogh's starting salary was fixed at £6,500, compared to Cairncross's £6,750. This episode was a curtain-raiser to much skirmishing between the two economists. In April 1966 Balogh requested an increase in his salary, drawing attention to the disparity between his and Cairncross's respective levels.[26] Wilson was prompted to issue a 'dictat that Mr. Balogh should be on a salary £100 less than Mr. Cairncross's'.[27] Nor was Balogh concerned only with his own remuneration: he regularly lobbied for the salaries of his staff to be increased. Indeed, the matter was one of many sources of resentment towards the permanent Civil Service on his part. As he wrote to Louis Petch, a Treasury second secretary, in February 1967, 'I am not at all satisfied with the way in which my staff is being treated from the point of view of pay.'[28]

In July 1966 Balogh asked to be docked an increase in his salary, which he believed amounted to £315, following a general review.[29] It was a principled stance, taking into account government retrenchment measures which were introduced at the time. Two months later, he wrote to Heaton explaining that he

> had hoped in July to persuade Ministers to forgo part of their increase in remuneration and ask senior Civil Servants to do the same. It seemed to me that it was wrong to ask other people to do what one was not prepared to do myself . . . It has become clear that I was not successful. I do not usually go in for such gestures. I believe in changing the rules of the game but also to profit by them fully so long as they remain unchanged . . . I therefore ask you to tell the Treasury to pay my salary in full as from 1 November.[30]

Neild (aged forty) initially received £6,100. Kaldor (fifty-six), as a part-time employee, was awarded £4,000.[31] Kaldor somehow managed to compress his weekly duties at Cambridge into the whole of Monday and Tuesday morning, making himself available to the government from Tuesday afternoon onwards.[32] When Kaldor became full-time in November 1965, his salary was pitched at £6,300: lower than that paid to Balogh and Neild by that point. Kaldor complained at the disparity, remarking to Abbot that 'he was a Cambridge Professor and neither Mr. Balogh nor Mr. Neild would get anywhere near such eminence in the University World'.[33] In comparison, in 1964 the Joint Permanent Secretaries to the Treasury, Sir Laurence Helsby and Sir William Armstrong, were paid £8,800, as was Sir Burke Trend, Secretary of the Cabinet.

Special advisers were entitled to certain Civil Service benefits. Balogh, for example, was employed by the Cabinet Office as a 'temporary adviser', receiving 'sick and annual leave allowances', superannuation and a pay review after two years. Resignation or removal from office required one month's written notice on either side;[34] beyond this there was no security of tenure. In the run-up to the

1966 election Balogh gave advance notice of his immediate departure from the Civil Service in the event of a Labour defeat.[35] Lord Croham, who, as Douglas Allen, was Permanent Secretary to the Treasury from 1968 to 1974, recalls that the five special advisers discussed here were recruited on terms already in place for the temporary employment of economists.[36]

Shortly after the appointment of the first group of aides, the First Division Association (FDA), the union representing senior career officials, approached the Treasury in order to voice its concerns about the development. On 2 March 1965 Collier wrote to Abbot summarising FDA anxieties, which centred on 'the way the Treasury has seemed to acquiesce in a rush of appointments, at high salaries, of people with political connections'. The union felt that this trend had negative implications for the career prospects of neutral officials. Such fears were very difficult to placate. The FDA was also disturbed by the possibility that special advisers might be allowed to see the papers of previous administrations, the implication being that politically appointed officials might not exercise discretion in the public discussion of advice tendered by FDA members in the past. Following a request for a ruling from the Cabinet Office, Wilson determined that Balogh should not have such access. The position of Kaldor in this respect is not clear. Neild, however, was granted the right. In the words of Collier, Neild 'can more reasonably be regarded as a civil servant, albeit temporary' – a judgement possibly inspired by the fact of his previous employment in the Economic Section.[37]

On 19 October 1964, in a letter to Trend, Heaton referred to 'general principles which the Treasury may be formulating for temporary Civil Servants brought in at the instance of the new Government'.[38] He may have been alluding purely to a method of determining pay, rather than a broader set of rules relating to matters such as propriety; in any event, no clear guidelines of any type seem to have materialised. As far as Croham recalls knowing, no official code governing the conduct of special advisers existed during 1964–70.[39] None was found in the PRO during the course of research for this work.

Although formal regulation was lacking, there was an understanding that special advisers would not compromise the neutrality of permanent officials or involve themselves in exclusively party political activities. However, this understanding seems to have been honoured as much in the breach as in the observance. In June 1965 Mitchell cautioned Balogh against habitually approaching Peter Jay, a principal in the Treasury, when making Treasury-related enquiries. Jay, the son of Douglas and son-in-law of Callaghan, was concerned that he should not come to be regarded as partisan.[40] Kaldor's personal papers show that not only did he devote a substantial quantity of his own time to activities such as drafting Labour pamphlets, but he also enlisted career officials in them.[41]

When the 1966 general election loomed, Wilson, prompted by Trend, reminded Balogh that 'he is a temporary civil servant and should so comport himself during the period of the Election'. Cabinet Office staff were warned that if 'there is any reason to suppose that he is failing to heed this injunction, Sir Burke Trend should be informed at once'.[42] In the 1966 poll Stewart unsuccessfully contested Croydon North West – a safe Conservative seat – for Labour. An agreement was arrived at before the election that, were he unsuccessful in his bid to enter Parliament, he would be re-employed as a civil servant. However, in a meeting with Wilson, Trend emphasised the 'difficulty of so doing'. The decision caused 'quite a bit of anguish' for career bureaucrats. Furthermore, Balogh, to the disgust of career Whitehall, suggested that Stewart should come back at a higher salary. As Collier put it to Abbot at the time, 'if we are to avoid the impression of the Civil Service providing a convenience for political candidates between Elections, it is particularly important that the individuals concerned should at least not benefit financially from their resignation and re-employment.'[43]

Further questions of propriety related to the outside business contacts, additional occupations and financial activities of special advisers. Upon his recruitment, Kaldor decided to leave the Investment Advisory Board of his college, since inside Treasury knowledge would make his position awkward.[44] He also had to relinquish his directorship of four investment trusts, worth £2,000 a year in total, as well as 'odd jobs with U.N., B.B.C., and journalism'.[45] Balogh, Crossman and Paul Streeten, an economist whom Balogh had helped place at the Ministry of Overseas Development, were trustees of family funds for their various children; as holders of positions in government, their making changes in trust investments was potentially awkward. Balogh wrote to Trend in April 1965 to enquire whether it would be satisfactory to hand over decision-making responsibilities to a broker. Trend raised the point with Mitchell, who in turn approached Wilson. Wilson's handwritten response was: 'Yes, can't stop these fellows' tax dodging activities.'[46]

In November 1964 attempts were made on the Conservative benches in the Commons to raise security concerns related to Labour's administrative innovation.[47] Balogh and Kaldor were both required to sign the Official Secrets Act, as all special advisers must have been. The two aides were both subject to positive security vetting, a process which entailed active enquiry into an individual's past and personal details.[48] A form from Balogh's Cabinet Office personal file has a tick next to 'M.I.5' (i.e. the internal security service), although 'Yard' (presumably meaning the Special Branch of the police) has a line through it. Balogh's referees for the personal vetting process were George Wigg and Donald MacDougall. The latter had to be chased to return the relevant form. 'Field investigations' were also a requirement.[49] It seems there were well-founded concerns regarding the sexual conduct of at least one of Balogh and Kaldor.[50]

Employment as a permanent civil servant was permitted for anyone who was a British subject and had resided in the country for five of the previous eight years. Balogh and Kaldor, both born in Hungary, fulfilled these requirements. However, the Cabinet Office, but not the Treasury, normally required its staff to be of Commonwealth origin, along with both parents, although ministers could overrule this stipulation. In any event, such regulations did not apply to temporary staff.[51] As well as Balogh and Kaldor, John Allen and Michael Stewart received basic, negative security clearance immediately upon their appointment, followed by positive vetting;[52] and it can be assumed that Neild did, too. The first wave of special advisers also received a 'memorandum which sets out the policy of H.M. Government on membership of the Communist Party', which was given to all civil servants, permanent or temporary, upon their appointment.[53]

Balogh was regarded by some as being reckless regarding the acquisition and dissemination of restricted information. Fears of indiscretion seem to have motivated Heaton in writing to Balogh in April 1967, shortly before the special adviser was due to visit Moscow, to caution that 'it is prudent to assume that any conversation (in or near a building or in a car), save in a "safe" room at the Embassy, is liable to be overheard by one sophisticated technical device or another'.[54] There were scares. In March 1966 Trend wrote to Mitchell regarding an unnamed Hungarian defector whose statement to a US congressional committee 'refers to a Mr. Balogh who, he alleges, was an Hungarian émigré, working for the Hungarian Embassy in London'. However, Trend went on, 'We have confirmed that this Mr Balogh is in no way related to, or connected with, our Economic Adviser.'[55]

Channels of communication and physical access to ministers were of great importance to special advisers. Throughout his time in Whitehall, Balogh sent Wilson a large amount of written material and saw him regularly. Senior officials in Downing Street, horrified by Balogh's assumption that he could call on the Prime Minister in the Cabinet room at any time, saw to it that Balogh was housed in 70 Whitehall.[56] Balogh was not given a key to the permanently locked connecting door and therefore faced the indignity of having to ring a bell every time he wished to visit Wilson. He was unhappy with the accommodation he had been given, which he probably saw as the product of malice on the part of career Whitehall. Aside from restricted access to Wilson, Balogh experienced more petty difficulties. In March 1966 he complained that he was 'increasingly dissatisfied with the lavatory arrangements in this building. On investigation I have found that there is a private lavatory at the end of the corridor on the 2nd Floor which is kept locked . . . I would be much obliged if you would send me a key for private use'.[57] A colleague recalls that Balogh was euphoric upon moving into an office in No. 10 proper following the 1966 election, believing it would allow him to attain increased influence,[58] although he was ultimately disappointed.

Cairncross's diaries indicate that Neild had a direct line of contact with the Chancellor, enabling him to fulfil the role of personal aide to a greater extent than Kaldor.[59] Following the initial confusion regarding Neild's role, Armstrong found him an office, next to his own, on the second floor on the inner circle of the Treasury building in Great George Street. Thus he could call in on Callaghan or Armstrong in effect whenever he wanted. However, Neild recollects that ultimately he spent less time with Callaghan than Kaldor did, since the Chancellor of the Exchequer devoted so much attention to taxation policy.[60]

Like Balogh, Kaldor was not initially accommodated where he wanted to be. From the outset, according to Abbot, Kaldor was 'very anxious' to have a room in the main Treasury building. However, there was supposedly no space, and he was housed instead in the Inland Revenue premises at Somerset House. He did not find the arrangement satisfactory, and in November 1964 complained to Armstrong that it was 'very difficult' to provide effective general advice 'without having a room in the Treasury'.[61] Eventually, in the autumn of 1965, when he became a full-time employee of the Treasury, he got his wish. According to his biographer, Kaldor had immediate access to Armstrong, but not to Callaghan.[62] However, as will be shown, he did send numerous papers directly to the Chancellor of the Exchequer. Inside Balogh's small team, Allen had 'direct access to the Prime Minister', a privilege not afforded to Stewart at first.[63]

To gain an adequate picture of the position of special advisers in relation to the centres of decision-making and policy formation, it is necessary to examine the extent of their inclusion on Whitehall circulation lists and their attendance at official committees. It is an indication of how seriously the matter was taken at a high level that on 22 October 1964 a 'meeting of [Permanent] Secretaries' was held in Trend's office. They determined that Balogh should receive all papers and minutes of economic committees, social committees (with the exception of the Home Affairs Committee) and the Queen's Speech Committee.[64] According to Shore, Balogh saw inclusion on key circulation lists as the most important prerequisite for the effective performance of special advisory duties. He coveted, but seemingly was never formally granted, access to the Prime Minister's box *before* it was sent to Wilson, in order that he could insert his own comments on the papers it contained.[65] Balogh continually struggled to ensure that he received copies of all Wilson's instructions 'on the economic side' as well as of all Trend's similar minutes to the Prime Minister. In March 1967 Balogh complained to Wilson that this was not happening.[66]

At the October 1964 meeting in Trend's room, the decision was also taken that Balogh was to receive 'top secret' papers only when permission was given by the relevant permanent secretary. Defence-related papers, which in any case he had said he did not want, would not be available. Requests for Treasury or DEA materials were to be made by Balogh himself. It was assumed that Allen and Stewart would see all the papers received by Balogh, but they would not automatically be sent their own copies.[67] Balogh was never content with these arrangements, suspecting that, as a result of permanent Civil Service conspiracy, he was not being made privy to all the information he needed.[68] Mitchell suggests that repeated failures to supply Balogh with certain papers may have been a product as much of the desire of ministers associated with the policy area concerned to keep Balogh at bay as of Whitehall subterfuge.[69]

In particular, Balogh sought to expand his access rights to include papers produced within the Treasury and intended for restricted internal circulation only. In November 1964 Armstrong resisted Balogh's demands to be sent materials normally seen exclusively within the circle of the Chancellor of the Exchequer, on the grounds that that the Prime Minister was happy to deal with the subject matter orally.[70] In February 1966 Balogh requested access to materials produced by Treasury committees dealing with 'capital balance . . . export incentives . . . [and] new taxes'. The Treasury's response was to deny that the committees existed.[71] The scenario was sometimes reversed, with permanent civil servants feeling that they were being kept in the dark as to the activities of special advisers. Cairncross did not appreciate Kaldor's habit of initiating discussions on tables and papers which had not been circulated in advance.[72]

Balogh sat on a variety of official committees. When an Official Steering Committee on Prices and Incomes Policy was established in May 1966, Balogh was placed on the circulation list and asked to attend. However, he still complained of being excluded from committees held under Treasury auspices. A document from March 1967 described Balogh as being 'free to roam around Cabinet Office Economic Committees' as he saw fit, even those he did not formally belong to.[73] Balogh and his staff, it seems, among them either attended or were members of 'the whole field of Official Committees dealing with economic policy'. At this point Kaldor was a member of the Statistical Policy Committee and, along with Neild, the Official Committee on the Economic Implications of Entering Europe. Kaldor occasionally appeared at the Export Policy Committee. Neild attended meetings on 'Possible International Economic Arrangements'.[74] Balogh and Kaldor were both, however, excluded from one very important, highly secret Treasury committee, which will be discussed later.

The Economic Advisers, according to MacDougall, was an unofficial body, initially consisting of Balogh, Neild, Kaldor, John Jukes (MacDougall's deputy at the DEA), Cairncross and MacDougall himself, who normally took the chair. A formal status for the entity would have posed a greater challenge to the influence of the permanent machine, but was never conferred. No doubt with this in mind, in an April 1966 submission to Wilson, Balogh proposed the establishment of a 'committee . . . under the Chancellor's chairmanship, and containing the Economic Advisers apart from the Permanent Secretaries'.[75] While the Economic Advisers were often consulted by ministers on important macroeconomic issues such as forecasts and assessments, MacDougall subsequently wrote that they were sometimes sidelined into 'specific questions like state pension schemes and even fisheries . . . to keep us too busy to have mischievous thoughts about things like the exchange rate'.[76]

MacDougall, Balogh, Kaldor and Neild also met, even more informally, without Cairncross present. Balogh, Kaldor and Neild sometimes participated in bilateral discussions held between the Chancellor of the Exchequer and other ministers or officials, such as Sir Alexander Johnston, chairman of the board of the Inland Revenue. They also attended, in an ex officio capacity, informal suppers that Wilson held at No. 10 for senior ministers and advisers. In such company, special advisers tended to be more vocal and assertive than permanent officials. Temporaries often dominated discussion at meetings held in conjunction with regular civil servants, sometimes, at least in Cairncross's account, to the irritation of the latter. Of course, it did not necessarily mean they were more influential than their less outspoken colleagues.[77]

There was much contemporary media interest in the special adviser experiment, focusing in particular on Balogh and Kaldor, whose appointments were front-page news. It extended beyond the broadsheets to include newspapers not generally associated with the in-depth treatment of bureaucratic matters. For example, the pro-Conservative *Daily Express* found space for the two 'experts from Budapest' alongside its more typical society profiles and human interest stories.[78] The high level of attention was felt by some insiders to be out of all proportion with the actual influence exercised on ministers by Balogh and Kaldor.[79] Victims of thinly veiled racial abuse in the press, which dwelt on their foreign origins and left-wing views, Balogh and Kaldor were frequently referred to by journalists as the 'terrible twins', the 'Hungarian Mafia', 'B and K' (after Bulganin and Khrushchev, the Soviet leaders), and 'Buda and Pest'. Hungarian (and, by implication, Jewish) origins were portrayed by some press commentators as indicative of an intention to implement Soviet-style communism in Britain.

The level of negative press attention the two economists received may have undermined their positions inside the government. Journalists from the Express Group pursued a particular vendetta against the pair.[80] The fact that two Hungarians, who were born within a street of each other in Budapest and had attended the same school (the Minta Gymnasium, founded by Balogh's great-uncle), had simultaneously become senior advisers to a British government was certainly remarkable. However, the portrayal of Balogh and Kaldor as of a piece was facile. They 'were the closest of friends . . . but equally the greatest of competitors'.[81] There were clear personal and theoretical distinctions between them.[82] As the *Financial Times* put it, 'Balogh . . . is often shaky on theory and woolly on statistics: his interests are essentially worldly and political . . . Kaldor . . . essentially unworldly . . . is happiest in the remoter reaches of theoretical abstraction.'[83] Wilfred Beckerman, an economist and colleague of both men in academia and government, suggests that, as an economist, Kaldor was a great believer in models, which Balogh mistrusted, preferring to rely on his instincts. In Beckerman's view, however, Balogh's judgements, although arrived at by obscure means, were often more sound than Kaldor's theoretical deductions.[84]

Both men had long been regularly on the receiving end of prejudiced hostility. Keynes, enraged by their opposition to the Bretton Woods agreement, once expressed the view, privately, that they, 'like many Jews, are either Nazi or Communist at heart'.[85] The Labour leader, Hugh Gaitskell, recorded Alan Lennox-Boyd, the Conservative Colonial Secretary from 1954 to 1959, referring disparagingly to Balogh as 'that Hungarian Jew'.[86] As Prime Minister, in March 1963, provoked by Kaldor's public support for floating sterling, Macmillan sent his Chancellor of the Exchequer, Reginald Maudling, a minute which stated that 'I am afraid that the Budapest Group – B. and K. – Balogh and Kaldor are not valuable immigrants.' Maudling's reply was, 'I am afraid B. and K. does not appear to be a happy combination of initials.'[87] In November 1964, Wingfield Digby asked in the Commons whether it was 'wise . . . to pay outside economists of foreign extraction to create chaos in Britain?'[88] Shortly after his appointment as a special adviser, Balogh claimed to have received a letter from a man he considered a friend, Lord Boothby, recommending that he 'should go back to Hungary "where there was much work to be done"'.[89]

Reforming Whitehall

The Fulton Committee on the Civil Service, which reported in 1968, is crucial to any examination of the special adviser. As noted in the previous chapter, domestic criticism of British administrative arrangements had become widespread since the late 1950s. In February 1966, responding to a recommendation from the House of Commons Select Committee on Estimates, Wilson announced that he was appointing his fellow wartime temporary civil servant,

Lord Fulton, now the Vice-Chancellor of the University of Sussex, to examine the 'structure, recruitment and management, including training, of the Home Civil Service'. Fulton's committee of twelve (counting himself in the chair) comprised four officials (including, notably, Neild), three academics, two MPs, two industrialists and a trades unionist.

In Fulton's report,[90] specific criticism was made of the 'philosophy of the amateur' – that is, generalism – the Treasury's role in 'central management' and the sealed-off nature of Whitehall. The removal of pay and management responsibilities from the Treasury and their combination with the Civil Service Commission in a new department, under the control of the Prime Minister, was recommended. This was enacted in October 1968, when the Civil Service Department was established, with William Armstrong as its permanent secretary. Preference for relevant qualifications in the selection of civil servants, also called for by Fulton, was not implemented, however.[91] A number of Fulton proposals dealt specifically with the subject of the special adviser and related matters. More interchange between employment inside and beyond the bureaucracy was presented as desirable. Moreover, the establishment of departmental planning units was advocated. It was recommended that they should in many cases be headed by senior policy advisers, appointed to 'assist the Minister', to whom they would enjoy 'direct and unrestricted access'. The title 'senior policy adviser' was given to the head of the No. 10 Policy Unit from 1974. Planning units would be composed of both outsiders and insiders, although senior policy advisers would normally, but not always, be career officials. In addition, in certain 'big technical departments' a 'chief scientist, engineer or other specialist' might be appropriate.

Specific reference was made in the Fulton Report to the special adviser experiment, which was welcomed 'as a means of bringing new men and ideas into the service of the State'. The report suggested that ministers ought to 'be able to employ on a temporary basis such small numbers of experts' as they saw fit, who should be 'of standing and experience'. While desiring that the 'practice should be put on to a regular and clearly understood basis', Fulton did not attempt to recommend 'any precise limitation of the numbers of these appointments or any defined procedures'. The temporary nature of the employment of these aides, as well as the personal link with the minister, was emphasised. So too was the need for close association with official committees. No specific allowance was made for the use of general political aides or public relations advisers.

Fulton, then, endorsed the temporary employment of experts inside Whitehall and even the use of teams of specialists. The report did not, however, advocate a violent dislodgement of permanent officialdom, insisting that 'the great majority of those who come to occupy top jobs will in practice be career civil servants'. Permanent secretaries ought to retain 'overall responsibility under the Minister for all the affairs of the Department', and the senior policy adviser and chief specialist, it was emphasised, should not between them 'constitute a formal board'. Moreover, while it should be possible in extreme circumstances for a minister to replace a permanent secretary, this event ought to be 'exceptional'. Even senior policy advisers were expected, normally, to enjoy security of tenure. However, ministers should, if they wished, be able to choose private secretaries suited to their way of working, whether from within the department, or perhaps on secondment from elsewhere in the Civil Service. Combined with the use of special advisers, the suggestion represented support for a limited increase in ministerial patronage.

Finally, there were foreign influences. Members of Fulton's group made visits to France, Sweden and the United States. In Sweden, Fulton noted, the senior ministerial policy adviser 'is very close to the minister and is generally a semi-political appointment'. Attention was also given to the US use of 'political appointees'. The adoption of a French-style *cabinet* system would have been ominous for the future of both the permanent secretary and the private office. Fulton remarked that the '*directeur du cabinet* is . . . the official in a French ministry who exercises some of the functions of a Permanent Secretary'. While normally a career official, 'that his appointment is made by the Minister is a very important difference'. Moreover, the 'staff of a *cabinet* are normally changed when a new minister comes in'. The authors of Fulton expressed admiration for such foreign methods, which, in their view, 'could be used to strengthen the Minister's control of the departmental policy-making process and to increase the sensitiveness with which the department responds to the needs of Parliament and the public'. However, they argued that measures such as the introduction of planning units would ensure that there was 'no need for ministerial *cabinets* or for political appointments on a large scale'.

Many aspects of the Fulton Report, including the planning unit proposal, were not implemented during the remaining two years of the second Wilson administration. No doubt one reason for this was the fact that the government had numerous more immediately pressing difficulties to contend with. Also, as Theakston argues, it may be the case that 'with ministers' short-term political horizons and with *detailed* involvement in civil service reform (as opposed to the creation of a general modernising image) offering only limited political returns, the outcome was virtually inevitable'.[92] Nevertheless, a marker had been put down. Wilson remained personally attached to the Fulton recommendations, and his considerable expansion in the use of special advisers on returning to office in 1974 was presented as based on the report.

Wilson: style and substance

Labour took office in October 1964 with a parliamentary majority of four. Few retrospective judgements of Harold Wilson's subsequent approach to the premiership, from across the political spectrum or by academics, have been generous, save for tributes that have been paid to his undeniable tactical skill and manoeuvrability, talents directed most effectively towards significant electoral success and the preservation of Labour Party unity. The central criticism levelled at Wilson is that he was an opportunist, lacking in long-term strategy. According to Theakston, Labour under Wilson, for all its sloganeering, had little idea how such measures as economic planning were to be implemented. Its difficulties in office after 1964, Theakston argues, were attributable to this shortcoming, rather than to obstruction on the part of the permanent Civil Service.[93]

We should consider, then, the extent to which the special adviser experiment can be associated with Wilson's supposed flaws as Prime Minister. The accusation of lack of preparedness is supported by the suggestion that Balogh knew little of the Whitehall official committee system prior to his appointment to the Civil Service.[94] Kaldor, a taxation specialist, was unaware that Sir Alexander Johnston was chairman of the board of the Inland Revenue.[95] Balogh, furthermore, had long displayed a degree of naïveté regarding the ease with which permanent civil servants could be replaced.[96]

Confusion surrounded the exact nature of the role of the new temporaries, in particular Neild, in relation to the existing Treasury Economic Section staff. According to George Brown, First Secretary of State and Minister of Economic Affairs, 'there were too many of us advising and counter-advising one another.' Brown's memoir suggests that he was slightly surprised that, when appointed to the Civil Service, Balogh was attached not to the DEA but to the Prime Minister.[97] Wilson's active involvement in the DEA's development of the National Plan was minimal; and so, as Wilson's adviser, Balogh was cut off from the department he helped instigate and the economic plan he had long advocated. Moreover, he did not, in his own expression, 'click' with Sir Eric Roll, Permanent Secretary to the DEA. Roll, perhaps wisely, made himself scarce. On 9 May 1966 Balogh wrote to Roll, complaining that 'you have not answered my letters of April 20th, 26th, 29th, two letters of May 4th and one letter of May 5th . . . If you could spare a minute, perhaps you might telephone at least.'[98] In the light of these circumstances it is harder to blame Balogh for the excessively optimistic growth targets set by the DEA, projected at 25 per cent over the period 1964–70 (an average annual rate of 3.8 per cent). In fact, he wrote to Wilson on 3 February 1965 warning that 'I should be very surprised if we got more than 3 to 3½ per cent this year,' although he believed that, after a slow start, expansion would accelerate.[99]

Nevertheless, it could be argued that on occasion Balogh encouraged Wilson towards blind optimism. In a 1965 note to the Prime Minister, Balogh stated, rather prematurely, that 'your decision to bring in outside experts and to partition the Treasury has proven a brilliant success. The monolithic supremacy of the Treasury is now balanced inter-departmentally (as it should be) by an organisation dedicated to expansion.'[100] However, in May 1966 the Prime Minister's senior special adviser did warn him that 'we might get into difficulties in the summer'.[101] As will be shown, he was correct. Moreover, Balogh also attempted to impress upon Wilson the view that Britain's continued posturing as a global military power could not be reconciled with economic realities. As he wrote in August 1966, 'the whole level of [defence] expenditure both in Germany and East of Suez is of an ostentatious standard not at all in keeping with our present problems.'[102]

Closely related to Wilson's supposed shortcomings in terms of style were his administrations' policy failures. Ironically, they were concentrated in the realm of economics, the area in which both Wilson and most special advisers during 1964–70 were expert. Arguably, Wilson's greatest mistake was made immediately following Labour's narrow election victory, on 17 October 1964. The 'economic triumvirate' of Wilson, Brown and Callaghan took the decision, in the face of a balance of payments crisis, not to devalue sterling from its existing fixed rate of $2.80.[103] The economist and future special adviser Wilfred Beckerman was not alone among Labour supporters in his consequent dismay. In his view, attainment of the objective of higher growth was dependent upon increased exports, for which a correction in what he saw as the overvaluation of sterling was a prerequisite.[104]

In the words of Hennessy, 'Thereafter, until the rate finally went three years and one month later, the Wilson governments were locked in a titanic and near continuous struggle to reconcile the three incompatible aims of economic growth, a balance of payments surplus and a currency worth $2.80 to the pound.'[105] MacDougall, who was appointed Director General of the DEA in 1964, later argued that the 'first great mistake of the new Government was not to devalue at once. In my view this dominated – and distorted – economic policy for the next four years'.[106] In July 1966, crucially, the desperate defence of sterling entailed the introduction of deflationary measures which killed off the notion of planned growth. Richard Pryke, a special adviser recruited in May 1966 and working under Balogh, resigned from the government in protest over the failure to abandon the fixed rate at this point.[107] MacDougall subsequently suggested that the adjustment in the exchange rate which finally took place on 18 November 1967 came 'at least three years too late'.[108] In 1969 the DEA was finally abolished. The futility of the course pursued by the Wilson administration suggests that the appointment of special advisers certainly did not result in better policy formation in this area.

Wilson's determination not to devalue was probably initially influenced, in part at least, by Balogh, who wrote in 1963 that devaluation 'or a (downward) floating exchange rate do[es] not provide a panacea'.[109] According to MacDougall, Balogh convinced Wilson that socialist planning was the means of overcoming current difficulties and would render the sterling question irrelevant.[110] If such was the case, then it was, unfortunately, one of Balogh's most significant policy contributions as a special adviser. Kaldor and Neild, on the other hand, had already made it clear to Callaghan that they favoured an immediate devaluation.[111] Balogh rapidly came to agree with his two fellow special advisers.[112] On 9 December 1964 Brittan recorded that 'Dr. B. now believes in devaluation.'[113] This change of outlook was probably brought about by a realisation of the enormity of the balance of payments problems and the 'ferocious . . . reconsideration of policies' which defence of the rate would therefore entail.[114] Balogh was, however, never as enthusiastic about abandonment of the parity as Kaldor, seeing it as a necessary evil if success were to be achieved, rather than a positive step towards achieving that success.

A question raised by support for abandonment of the existing parity was whether it should be replaced by a floating rate or a new, lower, fixed rate. While the term 'devaluation' was generally used to cover both options, the former, theoretically at least, could result in an appreciation in the value of the pound. Kaldor, who had favoured floating at least as far back as 1952,[115] sent Armstrong a note to this effect in July 1965.[116] Entitled 'Fixed or Flexible Rates', it was a particularly full expression of his important alternative approach to the one ultimately taken.[117] To Kaldor, the economic benefits which would accrue from floating were clear. Britain's share of world trade was too small. In order to achieve a sufficient increase, a considerable sterling depreciation was required. If this were enacted in a one-off move, it would raise the possibility of a threat to the gold parities of other currencies. There might also be problems in maintaining the new fixed rate. The economy could not respond to a shock of this nature, and potential gains would be lost, in the form of inflation. Preferable was 'a gradual downward drift in the rate over a longer period'.

Kaldor advocated floating 'for a temporary period' in order that the pound could find a new equilibrium rate, whereupon a new parity would be fixed. He did not, then, favour floating 'of indefinite or permanent duration'. On the other hand, he gave no specific deadline for the return to fixed parity, or indeed any indication of timescale. Importantly, Kaldor dismissed the idea that '"price-destabilising" speculation' could lead to a plunge in the value of sterling, rejecting this major argument against floating as 'a mirage'. Kaldor argued that 'Sooner or later any speculative trend reverses itself: prices do not fall to zero, or rise to infinity.'

In an undated paper from 1966, possibly March, Balogh wrote, 'I favour a floating exchange,' although he was not as optimistic as Kaldor about its potential benefits.[118] Neild says that he was uncertain about whether floating was the best option at the time, and remains so.[119] Wilson himself subsequently stated that on 'the technique of devaluation, I favoured floating, rather than a cut to a lower fixed parity'.[120] If he did take this view, he did not act upon it at the time.

Once the decision had been taken to defend the rate, Wilson banned reference to any other course of action in official circles. Cairncross's diary entry from 25 November 1964 described a paper produced by Balogh, Neild and MacDougall that pronounced abandonment of the existing parity inevitable, merely discussing the relative merits of floating and fixed rates.[121] Mitchell says he was entrusted with ensuring that all copies of it were destroyed.[122] In December 1964, when, as part of a more general prime ministerial brief, Balogh referred to the need for an adjustment, Wilson noted that the offending section should 'be extracted & destroyed'.[123] Neither Balogh nor his colleagues were daunted, and their lobbying became incessant.

Special advisers, then – special advisers hired as experts in economics – spent three years being ignored and even silenced over the question of sterling. Furthermore, all but one of them were excluded from planning for the possibility of a forced abandonment of the exchange rate. The Forever Unmentionable Committee (comically abbreviated to FU), probably established early in 1965, met under Armstrong to review developments and prepare a 'war book' for the contingency of ministers deciding to devalue. Neild recollects that the formation of FU was a response to his warning to Armstrong that 'devaluation is going to happen one day and I trust the Treasury has a contingency plan for it.' Many of the FU papers are missing and some are still classified. The earliest set still in existence in the PRO is the sixth batch, dating from March 1965. While Neild, along with Cairncross and various permanent Treasury officials, was present on the circulation list, Balogh and Kaldor were not. Neild says that, willingly, he never attended FU meetings and did not look at the papers.[124]

Matters discussed in FU files included what the new parity should be and the timetable for devaluation. Cairncross described how the question of the required size of the accompanying retrenchment package was also addressed.[125] Given Kaldor's absence from FU, the consideration of whether to adopt a fixed or flexible rate is of particular interest, since he firmly favoured the latter. At an April 1965 meeting of the committee Armstrong framed the question in terms of 'whether it was desired to make a significant break with the present international monetary system'; Cairncross suggested that such a move 'was inevitably a gamble which it was hard to contemplate taking'.[126]

One FU report, undated but certainly from mid-1965, stated that 'we cannot recommend the adoption of a floating rate, either as a temporary expedient or as a more permanent arrangement.'[127] Such was certainly the view of the Bank of England, which was understandably protective of the value of sterling and sent two representatives to FU. The Bank produced a paper for FU 'recommending that any move should be straight to a new fixed rate'.[128] On 16 June 1965, FU concluded that 'the considerations against flexible rates were felt to override those in their favour.' At a meeting of FU in September 1966, Armstrong referred to the 'risk . . . that . . . the rate itself would . . . spiral downwards out of control, producing very serious dislocation of our overseas trading activities and within the home economy'.[129] The view was probably the main motive for opposition to a float; and, as we have seen, Kaldor believed it to be fallacious.

Having pronounced on the matter, officials then had to ensure that, when the moment arrived, ministers would heed their advice. At the time, this did not seem inevitable to those inside FU. On 29 July 1965 Armstrong told FU that Wilson 'was understood to have a firm preference for floating if the need for devaluation arose and several ministers were known to share this view. The Chancellor veered towards it though he was certainly not completely committed'. It was a cause of concern for Maurice Parsons, the Deputy Governor of the Bank of England and an FU member, who wished to ensure that 'the Governor and the Bank should have ample opportunity to present their advice to Ministers before precipitate decisions were taken without full consideration'.[130] Officials, then, had decided to close off floating as a policy option, although the Cabinet, a significant portion of which favoured, or was inclined towards, flexible rates, did not yet know this.

For FU, secrecy was paramount. Frequent references were made in FU papers to those 'within the circle'. Members were reminded of the need for 'complete discretion at all times'. MacDougall does not recall knowing anything of FU, the existence of which was of great interest to him when interviewed in 2001.[131] Mitchell, too, says he was unaware of FU, although he is not surprised by the level of secrecy which surrounded it.[132] When Kaldor got wind of its existence and sought to attend in July 1965 he was not permitted to do so, on the grounds that, as Cairncross put it, 'we couldn't have him without Tommy [Balogh] and all.'[133] He was allowed, however, to produce a paper for the committee, advocating flexible rates.[134] The objection to Kaldor, in Neild's view, was not his support for floating in itself, but the unrelenting way in which he would have driven his point home.[135] The desire to exclude Balogh was probably motivated by his difficult personality and a widely held feeling that he was prone to gossip.[136]

Ministers were 'not informed of the existence of' FU, although Callaghan was shown some papers. Rather shockingly, it appears that even Wilson was kept in the dark, at least initially. In a diary entry for 29 July 1965, Cairncross recorded

Armstrong saying that he would 'put to the Chancellor the need to let the P.M. (and perhaps T.B. [Balogh]) see some of the papers on devaluation'.[137] It is likely that Wilson was informed verbally of the existence of the contingency plans at some point. However, he probably made no effort to bring Balogh 'within the circle' and showed a serious interest in FU materials only when he needed them, at the actual time of devaluation. Michael Posner, an economist, joined the Treasury in 1967 and became a member of FU. Confidentially, he informed Balogh, a patron from Oxford, of its existence.[138] Balogh did not acknowledge his awareness of FU's existence until after devaluation had taken place. He had probably seen none of its papers.[139] Following devaluation, the government pursued a policy of deflation to which Balogh objected because of its *laissez-faire* nature. No doubt, had he been a member of FU, he would have proposed a different course. On 16 November 1967, now aware that devaluation was imminent, Balogh urged Wilson to 'strengthen the social content of the announcement'.[140]

The Chancellor of the Exchequer had not accepted the advice of his politically appointed aides; but, early in November 1967, when, in the economist's own account, Cairncross advised him that an immediate devaluation of sterling was necessary, Callaghan finally snapped.[141] The defence of sterling was resumed at a new rate. In her memoir, Barbara Castle described it as 'merely putting ourselves into a different strait-jacket'.[142] Kaldor continued lobbying for flexibility.[143]

Certain aides were members of the Prime Minister's personal entourage. In September 1965, writing of the group surrounding Wilson, Benn employed the phrase 'the court of King Harold'.[144] Wilson was far too skilful a politician to rely on one single counsellor. Rather, he had a 'most extraordinary unconventional collection of personal advisers'.[145] They were all kept, again in the words of Benn, 'at arm's length',[146] and could be played off against one another.[147] In a diary entry from September 1965, Benn referred to Balogh as being one of Wilson's 'three favourites', the other two being George Wigg and Marcia Williams.[148] Wigg was given the post of Paymaster General following Wilson's 1964 election success and was responsible for security and intelligence matters, as well performing the role of all-round aide. Williams was Wilson's private and political secretary – a post newly created in 1964, and maintained by successive administrations thereafter. Political secretaries, however, do not fit the definition of the special adviser, since they are paid from party, rather than public, funds. Another figure who should

not be overlooked as a key Wilson adviser was a representative of career
Whitehall: Sir Burke Trend, Secretary of the Cabinet. Trend's influence increased
as Wilson lost touch with what Crossman called the 'vague leftism which he
[Wilson] brought with him to the job', and Crossman recounts how in spring
1967 Trend and Balogh engaged in a 'terrible struggle for . . . the ear of the P.M.'.[149]

Balogh enjoyed close personal proximity to the Prime Minister, bolstered by
his membership (along with other temporary civil servants) of the informal
group of political allies which surrounded Wilson, popularly known as the
'Kitchen Cabinet'. In the words of Pimlott, 'Such a body never existed, but there
was certainly a group of advisers who were closer to Wilson, much of the time,
than many of his officials or Cabinet ministers.'[150] A nebulous entity, the
Kitchen Cabinet was frequently referred to by Crossman as the 'little group' or
the 'old gang'.[151] Its key members included Shore, Balogh, Crossman and Benn;
future Paymaster General Judith Hart; Barbara Castle, who was made Minister
for Overseas Development in 1964; Gerald Kaufman, who became Wilson's
political press officer in 1965; and, at the centre, Williams. The Kitchen
Cabinet's ancestry lay in the early 1950s and the associates of Aneurin Bevan,
then the leader of the Labour left. Within this grouping, Crossman and Wilson
came to comprise 'a left-of-centre sub-group, well to the right of the
devotees'.[152] Other Bevanites who went on to become members of the Kitchen
Cabinet included Castle and Balogh.

Owing to these origins the Kitchen Cabinet was, in part, an ideological entity,
which served, in theory, to 'keep Harold in contact with his left-wingers' once he
became Prime Minister.[153] The group began to crystallise around Wilson while he
was leader of the opposition. Balogh, along with Crossman, Benn and Shore,
planned the Labour leader's approach to the 1964 election, occasionally
discussing matters with Wilson himself. As the poll approached, meetings
expanded to include Wigg, Williams and, significantly, two future special
advisers, John Allen and John Harris, although the latter was from the Labour
right and never a Kitchen Cabinet member.

The use of personal aides suited Wilson's penchant for maintaining a close
circle of allies. It also fitted, to some extent, with his public image. In his
evocative book *The Neophiliacs*, the journalist Christopher Booker attempts to
relate radical cultural developments of the 1960s to postwar trends such as the
growth of affluence and consumerism, the decline of British status as a world

power and the erosion of deference. He suggests that, by the mid-1960s, social, economic and political upheaval during the preceding decade had engendered a mood of 'frantic euphoria' among large sections of the British populace. Influenced by hysterical news media, the electorate, Booker argues, was susceptible to the presentational skills possessed by Wilson. To Booker, the appointment of special advisers was one of a series of administrative gimmicks in which Wilson indulged upon taking office.[154]

Booker and those who share his view of Wilson would no doubt find further confirmation of this assessment in a scheme the Prime Minister devised in July 1965. Wilson intended to flush the perpetrators of the notorious 1963 Great Train Robbery into the open by removing all pound notes from circulation and issuing ones of a new design.[155] The robbery and its sequels were great media events in their own right, a fact which surely encouraged Wilson's interest.[156] He instructed one of his special advisers, Michael Stewart, to contact the Treasury regarding the viability of the proposal. In so doing, Stewart managed to contravene Whitehall etiquette, prompting the Prime Minister's principal private secretary, Derek Mitchell, to write to him pointing out that 'if any information is sought from a Department "on behalf of the Prime Minister" we prefer that the Prime Minister's Office should be the channel; failing that we would at least like to know that the request has been made.' By November, Callaghan had become convinced that Wilson's scheme was impracticable. Even Wilson, it seems, was not certain of its viability, since he failed to raise the matter at two meetings with the Chancellor in early December. The idea appears to have then been dropped.[157]

Such notions are arguably supportive of Booker's assessment of Wilson as deliberately projecting an often shallow image of himself as the dynamic leader of a modern administration. However, the creation of the special adviser was more than a mere novelty, and had lasting constitutional implications. And in fact, Wilson was not entirely comfortable with the possibility that he might be perceived as surrounded by a team of advisers. As Tony Benn, who was at the time a close ally of Wilson, noted in his diary during the 1964 election campaign, the 'fact is that Harold doesn't want any people to know that anyone helps him at all. He wants it all to be his show and Dick [Crossman] and Tommy [Balogh] and I have to pretend we don't exist. Kennedy never minded it being known that he had speech writers and advisers, but Harold does'.[158]

An important theme here is that of prime ministerial authority. During the 1960s a high-profile academic debate was taking place as to whether the Prime Minister was becoming increasingly powerful in relation to the rest of the Cabinet.[159] One participant, who believed that the dominant premier was already a reality, was Crossman.[160] It has been shown that Wilson resisted the creation of what would have amounted to a prime minister's department. Nevertheless, from 1964 a small personal team of temporary aides was attached to the premier. Balogh, as head of the group, persisted in his efforts to persuade Wilson to bolster the centre. In a 1965 note to Wilson, Balogh proposed the creation of a 'high-level and very small Cabinet Committee, chaired by the Prime Minister' to 'initiate and carry through decision-making on questions of intricate economic planning'. In order to make it work, Balogh argued, 'the Cabinet Secretariat needs further strengthening', possibly with additions to Balogh's own team.[161] There was a suggestion, then, that political appointments might usurp certain functions previously performed by career officials, possibly even communicating instructions across Whitehall, once ministerial decisions had been taken. During late 1967, continuing in the centralising vein, Balogh and Crossman tried to persuade Wilson of the need to create an inner Cabinet to provide the government with central direction.[162]

Shortly before his 1964 election victory, in his interview with Hunt, Wilson said, 'I am very worried about what I feel is the amateurism of the central direction of Government.' Bringing in aides 'from outside', Wilson said, was intended as one means of correcting the problem. The Cabinet Office was to be expanded, partly through recruitment from beyond Whitehall, in order to enable it to

> *do much more in the way of briefing the Prime Minister, not only briefing him on the machinery of Government and briefing him on the work of any cabinet committee, but also providing a briefing agency, so that he is right up to date and on top of the job in respect of all [the] major departments of state. My conception of the Prime Minister is that if he's not managing director, he is at any rate and should be very much a full-time executive chairman.*

Wilson drew presidential analogies, saying, 'I think one can learn from the Kennedy experience . . . he [brought] into the White House a number of top people from universities, one or two top scientists, top administrators.'[163]

For Wilson, then, special advisers were, to some extent, a means of leading from the centre. They engaged in activities related to the implementation of election programmes. Writing in 1965, Crossman described how Wilson 'is always getting . . . Balogh to try and convince him that of the seventy-three promises in the manifesto, fifty-two are already being carried out'.[164] As the next chapter will show, Wilson used John Allen, a special adviser, to scrutinise departmental proposals from the party political perspective and follow up on prime ministerial policy recommendations. Balogh redrafted departmental White Papers.[165] He also lobbied for the establishment of 'a form of possible machinery for chasing up progress on important decisions made by the Cabinet and Ministerial meetings'.[166] All of these were activities which became increasingly prominent in subsequent decades, as aides based at Downing Street proliferated.

* * *

The year of 1964, then, marked the beginning of the special adviser experiment. It saw the introduction of five outsiders to posts, three of them at a high level, at the centre of the administration. Incorporating political appointments into the Whitehall machine was a delicate process and it appears that there was a degree of obstruction from career officialdom, presumably motivated by a desire to preserve the position of the Civil Service. It is hard to believe that, given a will to do so, a room could not have been found for Kaldor in the Treasury building. There was also a definite, and successful, attempt to exclude Balogh and Kaldor from devaluation contingency planning. On the part of the newcomers, the struggle for status and influence centred on matters such as job titles, salaries and access to papers and committees. As Stewart discovered when contacting the Treasury directly over Wilson's banknotes scheme, Whitehall private offices were intent upon guarding their status as the formal channels of official communication. Strong resistance was offered to the idea that Neild might take on management responsibilities; hence the dual arrangement between him and Cairncross. Nevertheless, both Neild and Balogh sat on a committee responsible for running the GES. Media interest in and parliamentary criticism of the appointments were present from the outset. Because of the policy difficulties experienced by the Wilson administrations, momentum for Whitehall reform had been lost by the time the Fulton Report appeared, and recommendations with implications for the use of aides were not implemented. Wilson's special advisers encouraged the administration to take different courses from the ones eventually adopted, particularly in relation to sterling – which leads one to question the value of appointing economists whose counsel on matters of economics was then ignored, or even suppressed. Nevertheless, Wilson should be credited as the premier who brought about a significant constitutional innovation in the form of the modern special adviser.

Four

Key figures of the Wilson years

Throughout the period under examination here, special advisers were distinguished from one another and from those among whom they worked by the individual qualities they contributed. A biographical approach, discussing their backgrounds as well as their functions and accomplishments in office, is therefore of value. There is an especially wide variety of sources available for the years 1964–70, enabling the conduct of detailed personal studies. They will contribute to an understanding of Wilson's administrative experiment, as well as, more broadly, the character of his first two administrations. Furthermore, once identified, the various roles of aides at this time can be used both to establish models for their successors in subsequent administrations, and for the purpose of examining the extent to which, over time, the special adviser has changed in nature.

The first individual profiled in this chapter is John Allen, a political aide to Wilson. Allen will be followed by Nicholas Kaldor, the distinguished economist who served at the Treasury, and the assistants he recruited. Thomas Balogh, the Prime Minister's senior special adviser, must be portrayed, along with the small advisory body he established. One member of Balogh's team, Stuart Holland, is particularly interesting both from the perspective of his policy work and from that of his experience of Whitehall vetting procedures. John Harris, who became very closely attached to the minister he served at the Home Office and Treasury, Roy Jenkins, took an especial interest in the cultivation of journalists, generating much suspicion among Jenkins's Cabinet colleagues in the process. Two departmental experts, Brian Abel-Smith and Christopher Foster, worked at, respectively, the Department of Health and Social Security (DHSS) and the

Ministry of Transport. Finally, brief descriptions will be provided of other aides during 1964–70.

John Allen

John Allen's significance was a consequence not so much of great personal achievement on his part as of the fact that he was an early example of a non-expert, political special adviser, the type of which became more common in later years. He has been described as 'one of the outstanding casualties of modern British politics'.[1] The nature of both his role in post and his departure from it related to his involvement in the group of allies centring on the person of Wilson. Although he had studied economics at Cambridge, Allen worked 'in association with Mr. Balogh, but not, essentially, on economic matters', possessing direct access to the Prime Minister.[2] The son of Sidney Scholefield Allen QC, the Labour MP for Crewe from 1945 to 1974, he was close to Shore, for whom he worked at the Labour Research Department for five years prior to 1964. Friendly with both Balogh and Kaldor, Allen has been credited with inventing the joke, 'Wilson's first Budget may have sounded complicated, but "you should have heard it in the original Hungarian."' He 'enjoyed both the company of reporters and the drinks they bought him'.[3] Involved at leadership level in the organisation of the Labour bid for power, Allen travelled with Wilson during the 1964 election campaign.[4] When Labour took office, he remained a member of Wilson's inner circle – the 'Kitchen Cabinet'. Indeed, he took it upon himself to ensure that regular meetings of the group took place.[5]

According to Mitchell, Allen's precise role was unclear to all concerned, except in so far as he was supposed to 'help Marcia [Williams]'.[6] One of his functions was to facilitate communication between the party political components of the administration. Following his 1964 appointment as Postmaster General, Benn felt isolated from Wilson's inner circle. In Allen he saw 'an excellent channel . . . to the P.M.'. As he had done before the election, Allen contributed to the development of general political strategy. Wilson used Allen to scrutinise the party political implications of policy proposals, and to follow up prime ministerial suggestions to departments. This could be awkward for Allen when it involved dealing with Labour colleagues from his new vantage point of proximity to power. As a partisan figure within Whitehall, Allen was suspicious of representatives of the permanent Civil Service. In Benn's account, he felt that the women employed in the No. 10 secretarial pool 'were deb types and he wouldn't trust any of them'.[7] Allen's professed distaste for the secretarial staff did not stop him from becoming particularly close to some of them.

Allen, regarded by some within Wilson's circle as a lightweight, was not a great success as a special adviser; and his career was not aided by his personal entanglements. According to Pimlott, during 1964 Allen engaged in a 'brief, doomed, affair' with Marcia Williams.[8] Williams refers hardly at all to Allen in her own memoir of the 1964–70 administrations, beyond the statement, made twice, that he 'had been with us in 1964'.[9] According to some sources, pressure was applied to him to divorce his wife and marry Williams. Ultimately, 'accused of trifling with her affections', he was forced to depart from Downing Street, and left his post in 1965.[10] Reportedly with the assistance of Barbara Castle at Overseas Development, 'in the finest Victorian tradition Allen was banished to Africa to purge and purify his soul', where he spent 'a year surveying conditions in Bechuanaland and Swaziland on HMG's behalf'.[11] Although he returned to the Wilson camp for the 1970 election campaign, Allen's career never fulfilled its early promise. He 'settled down in his early forties to a premature retirement, mainly devoted to eating and drinking (his size became gargantuan)'. In 1998, aged sixty-six, he died of a heart attack.[12]

Nicholas Kaldor

In October 1964 Robert Neild wrote to Callaghan proposing a 'Teenage Compulsory Saving Scheme', which the two apparently discussed in opposition, for inclusion in the forthcoming Budget. The 'very high spending income' enjoyed by individuals in their teens, Neild argued, had led to 'a strong sense of unfairness amongst older people' and possibly added 'to [juvenile] delinquency'. He went on to say that this disposable income 'is of such a size that it has attracted a lot of attention amongst market research organisations and business', leading to the emergence of goods for '"the teenage market", comprising records, motorbikes, clothing, cosmetics, etc.' Neild sought a charge that would be levied on teenagers, to be 'repaid in whole or part, upon marriage or, say, at the age of 25'. Callaghan's response was: 'I think this is political dynamite. Let us leave it for the moment.'[13] The idea, although it came to nothing, illustrates the fact that the desire to effect fiscal innovation was a defining characteristic of the Labour government returned in 1964. Within such a tendency, Nicholas Kaldor was the central figure.

Born in Budapest in 1908, Kaldor came to London in 1927 to study at the London School of Economics (LSE). In 1940, along with the rest of the LSE, he was evacuated to Cambridge, and in 1945 elected to stay there, accepting a fellowship at King's College in 1949. He was a long-term friend of Hugh Gaitskell and, in appointing Kaldor as a special adviser, Callaghan was fulfilling the deceased Labour leader's pledge to employ the economist in a future administration.[14] In doing so he was probably acknowledging Kaldor's key role in formulating (and, by extension, implementing) central elements of Labour economic policy as well as honouring a moral obligation. Cairncross described Kaldor as 'a highly ingenious, fertile and knowledgeable economist with great faith in the power of taxation to make the economy work better; entertaining but rarely stopped talking'.[15] His party affiliations were clear, and his wife, Clarissa, was an active Labour member in Cambridge. As an aide, he devoted considerable attention to drafting Labour pamphlets and briefing ministers for public debates with Conservative politicians, and he continued to participate in party policy committees.[16] According to Thirlwall, Kaldor was 'a professed and committed Socialist' who sought to achieve his ends not through revolution but through fiscal innovation.[17] Kaldor's particular role was to advise the Chancellor of the Exchequer on taxation, although he expanded his brief far beyond this. During his time as a special adviser in the 1960s, Kaldor held the view that fiscal measures could provide a solution to almost any problem.[18]

In Brittan's opinion, of all the special advisers appointed during 1964–70, Kaldor was clearly *the* intellectual heavyweight.[19] Sir Douglas Wass, who was Permanent Secretary to the Treasury during Kaldor's second spell as a special adviser, in 1974–6, was personally and professionally close to Kaldor, whom he describes as a fervent Keynesian, with his own particular slant on the doctrine. For as well as believing in broad macroeconomic demand management, Kaldor held that certain particular forms of beneficial economic behaviour could be strongly encouraged by the state, particularly through the use of fiscal innovation.[20] Similarly, Neild describes Kaldor as an inventor of 'gadgets' designed to achieve ends deemed desirable, such as the more equal distribution of wealth, or accelerated economic growth. Intended to deliver the latter, selective employment tax (SET) was perhaps the best example of such an endeavour.[21]

From the outset of the first Wilson administration Kaldor's contribution to policy was considerable. He was closely involved with the taxation aspects of the 1965 Budget, which introduced two major new measures, corporation tax and capital gains tax.[22] But of all the contributions made by special advisers to the 1964–70 Wilson administrations in Shore's view the most significant was SET;[23] and Kaldor was the driving force behind it. Unlike capital gains tax and corporation tax, it was not the product of years of debate within the Labour movement, springing more from his own mind.[24] The measure was based on theoretical considerations. At a lecture given at Cambridge in November 1966 in which he explained the ideas underpinning the scheme, Kaldor concerned himself with the problem of relatively slow British growth rates. On a basis of international comparisons, he argued, there was a 'highly significant relationship between the rate of growth of the G.D.P. and the rate of growth of manufacturing production'. This empirical association formed the basis for what became known as 'Verdoorn's Law', named after P. J. Verdoorn, whose investigations on this subject first appeared in print in 1949.[25]

Introduced in September 1966, SET was 'a tax on all labour, but rebatable in the public sector and transport, and rebatable with a subsidy to labour in manufacturing industries'. Kaldor intended SET to transfer labour from the tertiary (service) to the secondary (manufacturing) sector of the economy, where returns to scale were far greater and more dynamic, triggering higher levels of national growth. As well as the benefits which would accrue to the latter grouping, he felt that the former would gain through the greater efficiency consequently forced upon it.[26] The adoption of his idea was dependent upon political expediency. In the light of favourable balance of payments forecasts, Callaghan suggested during the March 1966 election campaign that his next budget would not contain 'severe' tax increases.[27] Following Labour's victory, the trade position rapidly worsened and a deflationary tax hike was needed. However, 'To the Chancellor's rescue . . . came Nicholas Kaldor' – with the payroll levy idea he and Callaghan had discussed in opposition. Stewart criticises Callaghan for using a measure 'designed to bring about long-term structural changes in the economy as if it was a weapon suitable for coping with a short-term crisis'.[28] SET was also attractive to politicians since it was seen as a 'bypass for devaluation', subsidising exports without contravening international regulations.[29]

Kaldor's powerful presence probably resulted in an overrepresentation of fiscal innovation in government policy, a fact which had political and cultural resonance. Wigg felt that the 1965 Budget was overcomplicated.[30] The 1966 Conservative manifesto complained of how complicated 'tax penalties are sapping individual enterprise'.[31] The policies Kaldor helped develop received the ultimate backhanded compliment when in 1966 they became the subject of a (critical) song written by George Harrison of The Beatles.[32]

Kaldor's relations with his ministerial employer were not always good. A former Inland Revenue officer, Callaghan may have shared with Kaldor an interest in fiscal matters, but the Chancellor was not very patient with his special adviser – to whom a certain stigma attached as an adviser with a track record for 'getting governments overthrown'.[33] Critics from the right gleefully drew attention to the fact that in 1961 severe rioting had erupted in Ghana following the introduction of a budget on whose taxation aspects he had advised. There were supposedly other examples, internationally, of Kaldor provoking civil unrest. In April 1965, when Kaldor attempted to suggest to Callaghan how public opinion might be affected by the forthcoming Budget, Callaghan replied: '"Well we haven't had a revolution yet! And if we do, I'll see to it that you get pushed in front of the crowd."'[34]

Following the devaluation of sterling in late 1967, Callaghan resigned and Roy Jenkins replaced him as Chancellor of the Exchequer. One of Jenkins's immediate concerns was the production of a deflationary package which would reduce domestic demand, thereby increasing export capacity. His attempts in this direction have been criticised by Edmund Dell, among others, partly on the grounds that the £923 million of tax increases Jenkins introduced were not sufficient to bring about the required redirection of resources to exports.[35] There is evidence that Kaldor lobbied for greater deflationary measures than those ultimately introduced in March 1968. Michael Posner, a Treasury economist at the time, recalls Armstrong remarking to him that 'the good thing about Nicky is that he isn't afraid of large numbers',[36] Kaldor proposed that the hike be achieved through an increase in SET. However, Jenkins was 'antipathetic to' SET,[37] and wanted to increase only indirect taxation. In this the Chancellor was opposed by advisers including Kaldor on the grounds that it would be 'regressive', depriving the worse-off of a disproportionately large share of their income,[38] and possibly eroding the goodwill that would be required from the trades union movement in coming months in order to achieve pay restraint. In Cairncross's account, at a meeting between the Chancellor of the Exchequer and aides, Kaldor told Jenkins that the Chancellor's proposals 'would be regarded as a Tory budget'.[39]

Kaldor's defensive advocacy of SET was a source of friction between Jenkins and himself, and there seems to have been something of a personality clash between adviser and minister. It is also possible that Jenkins, whose dislike of SET was founded in the fact that he saw it as 'a symbol of Callaghan's Treasury',[40] may have harboured similar feelings towards the aide most closely associated with the tax. Whatever the reasons, by 1968 Kaldor, deprived of his minister's confidence, was a spent force at the Treasury. Douglas Allen took over from William Armstrong as official head of the Treasury shortly after the 1968 Budget, and Jenkins informed his new permanent secretary that Kaldor was an irritant he could do without. While Kaldor did not leave the Treasury altogether, Allen saw to it that he was removed from key policy areas, and out of the way of the Chancellor of the Exchequer.[41] From March 1969 onwards Crossman, at the Department of Health and Social Security, engaged in a sustained attempt to acquire to services of Kaldor, as his 'main economic consultant', on a part-time basis.[42] While Treasury permanent officials were content to release Kaldor, Jenkins, who believed that 'SET damaged our image and is ashamed of Nicky as an adviser' was not.[43] Maybe he preferred to have Kaldor within his own *demesne* rather than elsewhere, arming another department with economic arguments against the Treasury (particularly during spending rounds). Finally, however, Jenkins gave way, relinquishing 'all claim on Professor Kaldor's services'.[44]

Upon Kaldor's recruitment in 1964, Sir Alexander Johnston, chairman of the board of the Inland Revenue, attempted to ensure that 'there is no question of his [Kaldor] endeavouring to build up a staff to help him'. Subsequently, Kaldor decided to appoint a small number of assistants.[45] In August 1966 Christopher Allsopp, an economist from the Ministry of Overseas Development, was obtained as a temporary economic assistant. Formally he was employed by the Economic Section, presumably in an attempt to avoid criticisms arising from attitudes such as Johnston's. One of Allsopp's most substantial pieces of work inside the Treasury was a report on economic growth, based on international comparisons.[46] When Allsopp was elected to a Fellowship at New College, Oxford, which he took up in October 1967, he was replaced by Francis Cripps, a

Cambridge economist born in 1943. Cripps's work for Kaldor included studies of wages, expenditure and growth.[47]

Thomas Balogh

Thomas Balogh was born in Budapest in 1905. Having studied at Budapest, Berlin and Harvard, he arrived in Great Britain in 1930 and began lecturing at Balliol College, Oxford in 1940. Prior to 1964 he provided economic advice to a number of governments including those of India, Malta, Mauritius and Greece. He was a Fellow of Balliol College, Oxford from 1945 to 1973. Balogh's private conduct was colourful. Among his numerous lovers was the novelist Iris Murdoch.[48] Taking place during 1943–4, the entanglement, which involved both a close friend of Murdoch's and her existing partner, is said to have created strong feelings which she 'revisited in several novels'.[49]

Balogh, as discussed in the preceding chapter, made a significant contribution to Labour's official policy objectives after the 1964 election. While Kaldor was a Keynesian, Balogh rejected the macroeconomic methods advocated by disciples of this school, favouring *dirigiste*, hands-on intervention. In February 1965 he wrote that one 'of the great failures of economic policy in recent years was the belief that changes in taxes and interest rates could secure economic objectives. We must deal in a much more direct and physical way with particular variables'.[50]

During the 1920s Hungary battled against financial, budgetary and balance of payments difficulties. This may help explain why Balogh's initial views as an economist, dating from the late 1920s, were – like Kaldor's – conventional for their time, conditioned by the belief that the restraint of inflation ought to be the primary concern of policy-makers. However, the worldwide slump of the early 1930s prompted a change in his outlook,[51] marking the beginning of Balogh's conversion to socialism. In the late 1920s he was awarded a series of traineeships at central banks, including the US Federal Reserve and the German Reichsbank. At the latter Balogh worked under the bank's president, Hjalmar Schacht, a man of whom Balogh was already an admirer and who was to serve as Hitler's minister of economic affairs from 1934 to 1937. While at the time neither Balogh nor Schacht subscribed to the unorthodoxies with which they later became associated, the intellectual development of the former was influenced by the practical activities of the latter. Balogh later wrote that by the mid-1930s 'it was obvious to all who did not want to be blind that the economic systems of the West, based on decentralised decision-making, were confronted with a planned giant [Nazi Germany] dedicated to destructive dominance and of increasingly superior economic and military strength.[52] Denis Healey recalls that at Oxford in the late 1930s Balogh 'warned us not to imagine that the Nazis' economic policies would fail in their objectives'.[53]

Resident in Britain from 1930, Balogh was taken under the wing of the leading radical economist of the time, Keynes.[54] Balogh's relationship with his mentor was to end in acrimony. During the course of the Second World War, Balogh became a leading opponent of the emergent postwar settlement between Britain and the United States, as encapsulated in accords such as the Bretton Woods agreement. His motive was an objection to the US agenda for 'making trade and payments as free as possible and . . . restoring currency convertibility at an early date' on the grounds that these aims did not serve Britain's interests.[55] Here again his belief related to the perceived successes of Schacht, who had built up a system of bilateral trade with a group of mainly Balkan and Latin American states during the 1930s. Through it, Germany was able to achieve full employment without balance of payments problems.[56] Moreover, the countries with which Germany traded, Balogh argued, also benefited from the arrangement. He was not, of course, a supporter of the objectives and warlike tendencies of the Nazis. In the 1940s Balogh was united in his bilateralist views with the Oxford economist and estranged former colleague of Keynes, Hubert Henderson, in opposition to fellow professionals Lionel Robbins, James Meade of the Economic Section and, most significantly, Keynes himself. As a result Balogh, who was, as he put it, 'under no illusions about the vigour of the wrath to come' – he had, after all, experienced Keynes's vicious hostility towards the protégé turned heretic once before, in the 1930s – was permanently ostracised by his former patron.[57]

At a rare social engagement between the two men in 1965, Balogh told Cairncross that his 'hero was [Hubert] Henderson'.[58] Although Henderson was not a socialist, some of his activities and ideas prefigured Balogh's. As Assistant Secretary and then Joint Secretary to the Economic Advisory Council from 1930 to 1934, he was '[Ramsay] MacDonald's personal economic adviser . . . for the first time in British history, the prime minister had an economic adviser, working within the Government machine yet independently of the Treasury.'[59] The parallels with Balogh's career are clear. As a temporary Treasury recruit during the Second World War, Henderson participated in discussions regarding the form that expert advice might take in peacetime. He argued that politicians required not neutral technicians but partisan aides; but he was not necessarily enthusiastic about the inevitable corollary of wholesale changes of administrative personnel upon changes of governing party.[60] It is likely that Balogh's demands for measures which resulted in the introduction of the special adviser were influenced by Henderson's outlook. While it is not clear when he formed the view that a Whitehall purge was needed, he had certainly arrived at this opinion by the late 1950s.[61]

Balogh's objectives in the 1960s reflected the long-held ideas described above. As a socialist, he sought the 'supremacy of social over private interest'.[62] He saw the Soviet Union of the 1960s as a threat to the democratic world of an even greater magnitude than that formerly posed by the Nazis, for the same reason: namely, the superiority of centralised organisation. The only way to meet its menace, Balogh argued, was to concentrate more economic power in the centre, without adopting the brutality which often characterised communism.[63] Hence his advocacy of indicative planning, to be carried out by a department created for the specific purpose, the DEA. Balogh was by the 1960s a leading representative of what was known as the structuralist view of British economic weakness. He argued that the attainment of growth without inflation required the successful implementation of an incomes policy, to be conducted in the broader context of a national economic plan. Balogh had been convinced of the need for an 'incomes policy based on social consensus' at least as far back as 1941.[64]

Another important theme for Balogh throughout much of his career was the problem of lack of international liquidity, which he felt hampered the pursuance of full employment policies. As a prime ministerial aide, he ensured that Wilson was briefed to raise the matter at meetings with international leaders.[65] An important element in the balance of payments problem was, he considered, the long-term British tendency towards 'large investment overseas'. During his time as a special adviser he regularly sought 'tightening of the existing exchange control machinery' as well as use of 'the tax system to affect the relative attractiveness of domestic and foreign investment'. Such measures, at least initially, would not apply to the sterling area[66] – the group of countries, based largely on the Commonwealth but excluding Canada – which held their reserves in sterling, in London; he had other plans for them, which will be discussed later.

Balogh was frequently referred to as 'Economic Adviser to the Cabinet'; however, despite all protestations to the contrary, he was first and foremost a prime ministerial aide. He had acted as an informal adviser to Wilson for a long time before 1964. The two men were friends and had first met as early as 1937, at Oxford.[67] Balogh helped organise Wilson's 1963 election to the Labour leadership.[68] In his capacity as an aide to Wilson, Balogh often provided advice which was very much of a short-term, presentational nature and useful to Wilson individually, rather than to the government as a whole. Following deflationary measures to protect sterling, Balogh wrote to Wilson on 28 July 1965 suggesting that 'you should try to put a distance between yourself and these measures, for which after all the Chancellor is responsible. It is essential that you should build up your image as one who is determined to safeguard full employment.'[69] Cairncross recalled his predecessor as head of the Economic Section, Robert Hall, describing Balogh as '"the Prime Minister's spy"'.[70]

There is no doubt that Balogh was extremely partisan. In February 1965 he encouraged Wilson to use organised heckling as a tactic in parliamentary debates.[71] He was concerned with the way in which policy was presented and sought to bring about interdepartmental coordination of government policy statements, claiming in November 1964 that this was the reason he sought access to Treasury papers.[72] Official 'press releases should be co-ordinated and directed by a high level committee', he believed.[73] Balogh also engaged in such propaganda activities as the costing of the 1966 Conservative manifesto.[74] He and Wigg sometimes collaborated on press rebuttal exercises and discussed presentational strategy.[75] Balogh was involved in the drafting of key Wilson speeches, such as that given by the Prime Minister on the EEC in November 1966 at the Guildhall.[76]

Balogh was shameless when arguing for an expansion of his own role. In early 1965 he suggested that a prime ministerial economic committee should be created and that his team should be extended in order to service it.[77] The proposal represented a challenge to the Cabinet Secretary, Trend, whose staff had previously monopolised such bodies. And a year later, as noted in Chapter 3, he sought to establish an economic policy body under the Chancellor, excluding the permanent secretaries. However, Balogh's personality could get in the way of his ambition. Long regarded as a 'bad collaborator',[78] he was notoriously troublesome. In a 1964 discussion of the use of temporary economists, the '*Observer*' column in the *Financial Times* noted of Balogh that 'however many advisers there are he is likely to have the last word. As another Oxford don observed: "There are three kinds of conversation: Dialogue, monologue and Balogh."'[79] The *Observer* wrote that he 'is reputed to be incapable of taking yes for an answer'.[80] Balogh was also regarded as possessing paranoid tendencies (a characteristic he shared with Wilson). Often, if not always, outspoken and abrasive, he was willing to direct criticism and abuse at both officials and ministers, in their presence or otherwise. Crossman suggested that the reason why the Prime Minister employed a 'jarring element' such as Balogh was that 'he feels a need to have unconventional people close to him because he knows his own extremely conventional nature'.[81] For permanent civil servants, who valued a smoothly running machine, this was not welcome. In this respect Balogh stands in sharp contrast to Neild, who displayed a marked ability to work with the machine.

Balogh's commitment to his work was definitely not in doubt – even though he suffered from heart problems and took seriously the possibility that he might die during his period of service as a special adviser.[82] His devotion was reflected in the phenomenal quantities of memos, notes and papers he produced on a vast range of subjects during his time in Whitehall – documents which, in one ungenerous description, defied 'filing just as much as comprehension'.[83] He became involved in the policy areas of a number of government ministers, attention which not all of them welcomed. He took a keen interest in personnel matters, too, and often recommended individuals for advisory jobs (eventually building up a network of individuals across government in whose employment he had had a hand).[84] According to Crossman, in 1964 Balogh went so far as to urge that Wilson should remove Helsby from his position as Head of the Home Civil Service.[85] Balogh also sought to involve himself in decisions over ministerial appointments.[86] He was obsessed with what he saw as the skulduggery and incompetence of the permanent Civil Service. Andrew Graham notes a certain contradiction in the fact that 'he denounced administrators in general (and the British Civil Service in particular) with the same passion that he advocated administrative controls'.[87]

A formidable, but not always reliable gossip, Balogh was long practised in the art of priming journalists.[88] He acquired a reputation for being a source of leaks. Greatly skilled at ferreting out information, Balogh was willing to go further than most to this end. In April 1967 Burke Trend presented Wilson with a dossier of his adviser's misdemeanours. According to Crossman, Balogh was accused of 'going into the Cabinet offices and reading documents. In particular . . . Thomas makes a practice of looking into the box prepared for the Prime Minister late at night and seeing what briefing Burke Trend has provided so that he, Thomas, can insert a memorandum giving a reply to it'.[89] There was substance to Trend's complaints. During his time at the Treasury, Neild instructed his secretary not to leave Balogh on his own in Neild's office while any papers were visible.[90] On the subject of Balogh's reading documents not intended for his eyes, Sir Michael Palliser, Wilson's foreign affairs private secretary from 1966 to 1969, remarks that 'he used to do these things surreptitiously, but everyone knew he was doing them.' In Palliser's account, Balogh sometimes referred to materials he was not supposed to have seen in his own circulated papers.[91]

Having received Trend's dossier on Balogh in April 1967, Wilson finally decided that the problems created by his aide could no longer be tolerated and took steps to persuade him that it was time to return to academia, talking at length not only to Balogh himself but also to Balogh's wife, Pen.[92] There was also pressure from Oxford, where it was felt by some that he had been absent for long enough. The process of departure was extremely protracted. In July 1968, just after he had finally given up his post, Balogh was reportedly 'miserable', despite the fact that he was entering the Lords and being taken on as part-time aide to Crossman at the Department of Health and Social Security.[93] His entry to the Lords was announced as part of the Queen's Birthday List on Saturday 15 June; upon arriving at No. 10 the following Monday, he was informed that he had to leave by midday. According to Crossman, in 'those two hours everything was closed down, his security pass handed in and his cupboards emptied. Finally he unsigned himself from the Official Secrets Act . . . he was out on his ear, leaving Burke [Trend] and the rest of the civil servants rejoicing'.[94]

How should Balogh's contribution be assessed? Arguable successes were the introduction of exchange controls in the 1965 Budget, which he probably influenced,[95] and – probably his greatest victory of the period – a complete revision of pricing arrangements for the exploitation of gas in the North Sea fields.[96] Indicative planning, his core policy objective, was abandoned in July 1966, however. As his colleague Andrew Graham suggests, with his interventionist economic programme Balogh was, 'in many ways, running against the whole [Whitehall] grain of thought – "pissing into the wind" as he would have described it'. It is also possible that he engaged in 'too much activity'.[97] Moreover, although at times Wilson relied upon him as a trusted ally, there is doubt as to the extent of the Prime Minister's faith in Balogh, particularly when it came to the latter's proposals for action. However, Robert Hall, who knew both Balogh and Wilson, was probably going too far when he told Cairncross that Balogh was 'not somebody the PM felt any need to turn to for advice'.[98] From the point of view of this study Balogh was significant both as an advocate of the special adviser and as a practitioner of the role. He was also the head of a prime minis-terial team that was both a descendant of bodies such as Lloyd George's Garden Suburb and Churchill's Statistical Section and a forerunner of the No. 10 Policy Unit. This group deserves consideration on its own account.

First, personnel.[99] The initial members of Balogh's team were Michael Stewart and John Allen. Allen's ignominious exit from Whitehall in May 1965 has been discussed above. He was replaced in June 1965 by an economist from St Hugh's College, Oxford, Theo Cooper: the first female special adviser. Born in 1934, Cooper specialised in wages, working conditions and social security, and remained in post until late 1968, though in September 1966 she changed from full- to part-time service. Another later arrival to the team, appointed to augment it rather than to fill a gap left by a departure, Stuart Holland began working for Balogh part-time in January 1966. Born in 1940, he was also writing a thesis on 'Growth and Output'.

In April 1966 Wilson informed Balogh that he wanted 'a reinforcement of [Balogh's] . . . staff', with a particular view to the examination of European issues and foreign policy decisions which related to international economic commit-ments.[100] To this end Richard Pryke, aged thirty-two, was recruited from the Cambridge Department of Applied Economics in May 1966. Only a couple of months later Pryke, who had previously worked for the Labour Research Department, resigned in protest at the direction of government policy following the July 1966 deflationary measures. His place was filled in October 1966 by Andrew Graham, an economist from the DEA. During 1967 Stewart left, having successfully applied for the post of economic adviser to the Treasury in Kenya. Crossman believed that the 'difficulties' then being experienced by the govern-ment were influential upon his decision to leave.[101] He presumably had the sterling question in mind. Stewart was a supporter of devaluation, but had not made a snap decision to go; the last straw for him had in fact been the measures of July 1966. Following Stewart's departure in October 1967, Margaret Joan

Anstee was employed as Senior Economic Adviser. Forty-one years old at the time, she was a development expert most recently employed by the United Nations in Ethiopia. She stayed for twelve months.

When Balogh left Wilson's service in June 1968, Graham was promoted to become Economic Adviser, remaining in the post until July 1969. Graham did not possess the same authority as his predecessor, nor did his behaviour suggest he was a political actor in the Balogh mould. Wilson regarded Graham as 'quite first-class', partly for his ability to produce work at short notice.[102] One particular concern for Graham was prices and incomes policy, the pressing issue of the time.[103] Some of the difficulties previously experienced by Balogh continued to cause friction. In October 1968 Graham complained to Michael Halls that following Balogh's departure Cabinet papers and minutes on economic matters were no longer being circulated to his office.[104]

As to *modus operandi*, it seems that Balogh passed most analytical work on to subordinate staff: in the first instance, Stewart.[105] Stewart functioned as the deputy head of the team, monitoring 'the whole field of economic policy' and producing 'memoranda on major issues of economic policy at the request of the Prime Minister or Mr. Balogh, and sometimes of other Ministers'. He also gave oral advice to ministers 'on economic issues of particular concern to their own Departments'. Stewart was responsible for supervising work within Balogh's unit and 'keeping the office running as smoothly as possible'.[106] When Balogh suffered a heart attack in March 1965, Stewart, following some resistance from career Whitehall, temporarily took over as head, with Balogh's rights of access both to papers and to the Prime Minister. The files suggest that Balogh's team members worked very much according to his requirements, producing largely technical analysis. Individual departments or policy areas were not systematically shadowed by particular staff; rather, work was divided on an ad hoc basis. Holland says that this was not a weakness since team members were equipped to cope with varied tasks.[107] Palliser, for one, found Balogh's team to be stimulating and original colleagues.[108]

Stuart Holland

Stuart Holland worked for Balogh, based in an office in 70 Whitehall, from January 1966 until October 1967. He then moved into No. 10, no longer employed as a special adviser but working personally for Wilson, handling correspondence with the party outside Parliament, trades unions and members of the public declaring themselves to be Labour supporters. Holland returned to academia in June 1968, taking up a research fellowship at Sussex, having, in the words of Marcia Williams, 'proved his value'.[109] His case is particularly interesting, both from the point of view of his own activities, and for the light it throws on Whitehall security procedures. In the first instance there was the matter of his support for positive engagement with the EEC, which brought him into conflict with his own superior, Balogh.

The question of Britain's policy towards European integration was 'one of Tommy's manias'.[110] According to Williams, Balogh 'never disguised his personal dislike of the European project'.[111] The EEC was in part the product of US sponsorship, and fitted with the US multilateral agenda. A customs union as opposed to a free-trade area, the EEC did not permit its member states to conduct individual trade policies. Balogh was a long-term opponent of the 'general drive towards non-discrimination and a unilateral lowering of preferences' that it represented. Membership would involve Britain surrendering some of its rights to use economic controls, which were very important for him. Balogh lobbied Wilson to focus on the expansion of Commonwealth trade, at the expense of European integration and in resistance to the US drive for multilateralism. He argued that 'the preferences still enjoyed by Britain in the Commonwealth are of substantial value' and that British industry, 'behind a protective screen based on a larger trading area, could be re-organised and made fit to compete'.[112] Here, it could be argued, the influence of Schacht's New Plan, discussed above, was present. Balogh's ideas can also be placed in a tradition traceable at least as far back as the early twentieth-century National Efficiency movement, led by figures such as Joseph Chamberlain.[113]

Dissent from Balogh's view of the EEC was voiced from within his own team by Holland. At the time, the more conventional Labour left attitude towards the EEC was that it was an institution founded on *laissez-faire* economic principles and therefore to be opposed. However, Holland felt that the EEC was developing more interventionist tendencies and now presented a possible means of bringing about economic planning co-ordinated among European states. Here he was following the lead of Robert Marjolin, a vice-president of the European Commission from 1958. In October 1966 Holland produced a paper, which Balogh forwarded to Wilson, suggesting that secret negotiations directly between the Prime Minister and the immediate circle of the French President, Charles de Gaulle, therefore bypassing the Foreign Office, might be the best means of beginning an approach to the EEC.[114] The following year Holland was able to put this idea into practice.

During 1967 Holland's views led to his falling out of favour with Balogh, thereby losing his formal line of communication with the Prime Minister. However, Holland was already known to Wilson, and in April 1967, in Holland's account, the Prime Minister 'put his head round my door' to enquire why he had seen none of his work for three weeks. There followed a meeting between the two in the flat above No. 10, at which Holland presented his view to Wilson of how the bid for EEC membership should be conducted. He argued that, as well as being framed in terms of economic co-operation between members, Britain's application strategy should be supportive of the intergovernmentalism then advocated by de Gaulle, as opposed to the supranationalism believed to be favoured by the West Germans. West German agreement to the approach, Holland suggested, could be obtained by offering the possibility of associate status for East Germany.[115]

Although very much taken with the idea, Holland recalls, Wilson lamented that he could not reach de Gaulle directly. The French President had long been the main obstacle to British membership of the EEC. Holland then suggested that he might be able to put the new agenda to Louis Joxe, minister of justice in de Gaulle's administration, through Joxe's son, Pierre, a friend of his. Wilson agreed, confidentially dispatching Holland, who paid his own fare, to Paris.[116] Holland saw Joxe senior alone on 19 May 1967. At the meeting, Holland attempted to minimise many of the barriers to British entry previously outlined by de Gaulle. From de Gaulle's point of view, the main objection to Wilson's bid for EEC membership was that, as the junior partner in the so-called 'special relationship' with the United States, Britain was a 'Trojan horse' for US foreign policy objectives. Holland suggested to Joxe that the exceptionally close bond between the United States and Britain no longer existed and that Britain 'would prefer to be one among equals in Europe'.[117] Holland felt that the proposals were given a positive reception by Joxe,[118] and returned to Paris for further discussions with various ministers and advisers on 15 and 16 June 1967.[119]

Holland's activities were remarkable. They involved the conduct of informal diplomacy on behalf of the Prime Minister without reference to the Foreign Office. Moreover, the policy approach Holland advocated entailed a break with traditional Commonwealth ties and a rejection of the 'special relationship' with America. Furthermore, his conception of EEC membership as a vehicle for economic planning was, among the British left at the time, novel. The idea was never implemented. Again in Holland's account, Wilson wanted to appoint him as an economist at the Foreign Office for the EEC entry negotiations. However, the Prime Minister met with strong objections from senior officials and backed down. Wilson then decided to move Holland directly into the No. 10 Political Office.

Holland's route to employment as a special adviser was an unorthodox one and aroused concerned interest in certain quarters. He became personally acquainted with Mary Wilson during his time at Balliol College, Oxford. Holland was staying in a room in the house of the university organist John Webster, an old friend of the Wilsons. When Holland joined Balogh in the Cabinet Office there were no evident problems with his vetting. When he moved to No. 10 his security status had to be upgraded. During late 1967 he was interviewed, in his first-floor Downing Street office, twice weekly, by the same operative, for three weeks in a row. Questioning was detailed and lasted for up to two hours on each occasion.

During the sessions, Holland says, it was alleged that while at Oxford he had been involved in ultra-left-wing activities. It was also claimed that there were photographs showing him participating in demonstrations organised by the Campaign for Nuclear Disarmament (CND). Holland, who insists there was no basis for this, says he protested at what he saw as ridiculous fabrications. Irritated by what he considered to be a waste of his time, Holland complained to Wilson. To Holland's surprise, Wilson said that he would prefer Holland to continue co-operating with the process.[120]

The prime cause of concern, as far as Holland could tell, was the way in which he had appeared inside the Prime Minister's circle, apparently from nowhere. The security service knew hardly anything about him, and saw this as a problem in itself; perhaps he was, as far as his investigators were concerned, too clean. Holland recalls being told, 'We have a problem with you, you know. We know nothing about you and have nothing against you and then, suddenly, you are in Number Ten with direct access to the Prime Minister.' Holland says he replied that if they saw having nothing as a problem then they certainly were in trouble. The security officer then suggested that 'you might be another Philby, for all we know'. Holland was incredulous at what he was being subjected to. In his view, it was obvious that the security service had nothing against him but was not going to clear him. Immediately after the session when Philby was mentioned, Holland recalls, he met Sir Dick White walking along Downing Street towards St James's Park. White was Director General of the Secret Intelligence Service (SIS, responsible for external intelligence; commonly known as MI6) and a personal acquaintance. Holland described what he calls the 'crude fabrications and smears'. White was embarrassed but protested he did not know anything about it; a plausible response, given that the agency he headed was not responsible for vetting.[121]

Echoes of the investigation, and associated activities involving other special advisers, can be found in the PRO. In November 1967 Kaldor informed Andrew Collier, a Treasury under-secretary, that he wanted to recruit Henry Neuberger, an economist then serving in the Ministry of Transport, as an assistant. Neuberger's name had come to Collier's attention shortly before 'in relation to the case of S. K. Holland'.[122] This was presumably a result of the fact that Neuberger had recently moved into a flat shared with Holland and Christopher Allsopp, already an adviser to Kaldor.[123] Collier informed Kaldor that he 'was quite confident that we would not be able to clear Neuberger for PV purposes'. The reason, undisclosed to Kaldor, was 'the strong indication that he [Neuberger] either took drugs himself or gave parties at which drugs were taken – or both'.[124] There seems to have been an insinuation that Holland was also involved in these activities.

Holland states, 'I did not smoke pot or take any drugs other than tobacco and alcohol.'[125] Furthermore, although they lived in the same accommodation, he and Neuberger were not close friends. Holland plausibly dismisses as ludicrous the notion that the two were running a narcotics den.[126] The subject of Neuberger and drugs, he adds, was broached only very briefly, in one of the interviews. To the question, 'What about Neuberger? Does he take drugs?' Holland, disliking this and sensing he was being used, responded, 'Not that I know.' He was then asked, 'Does he have friends for dinner parties . . . and do they take drugs?' This prompted Holland to respond, 'Look, how should I know – I'm not Henry's keeper – he has his own friends and leads his own life.' Having been shown the PRO file referred to above, Holland believes that 'some construction' may have been put on the exchange that contributed to Neuberger being denied clearance.[127]

How is the matter to be interpreted? The only accusation available in the official papers relates to drugs. If Holland, Neuberger and others genuinely were associated with the use of controlled substances, there was legitimate concern regarding the risk of blackmail. It should be noted that there is no indication to be found of evidence for these, or any other, allegations. The security service, Holland says, did not clear him, but Wilson ignored them and continued to employ him anyway. Holland remained at No. 10 for eight months after the investigations, leaving at the time of his choosing.[128] Neuberger became the head of domestic economic forecasting in the Treasury in 1971, for which he must have been cleared. In 1979 he left the Civil Service to become an adviser to the Labour Party. He was close to the Labour leader Michael Foot, and also counselled Neil Kinnock, Foot's successor, until 1987. Neuberger died in 1999, aged fifty-five.[129]

A degree of hostility towards Wilson existed within the intelligence community, stemming from suspicions, long harboured by some on both sides of the Atlantic, that Wilson had at some point become an asset of the Soviet security organisation, the KGB (Committee of State Security).[130] Nevertheless, in retirement, Sir John Hunt, Cabinet Secretary during Wilson's 1974–6 term of office, told Peter Hennessy, 'I don't think that there was anything to smear him with.'[131] Moreover, the illicitly compiled archive of Vasili Nikitich Mitrokhin, a former KGB officer who defected to Britain in 1992, containing details of Soviet intelligence operations covering the period 1918–84, does not support such suspicions.[132] It is widely accepted among analysts of the period that elements within the security service who regarded Wilson as a risk may have attempted to destabilise his governments during his second and final term as Prime Minister.[133] The beginnings of such activity are traceable to 1964–70, when the security service, it seems, continuously investigated Wilson and those associated with him.[134] It may explain Holland's experience.

In Holland's view, what he describes as 'a sustained effort to discredit me' resulted from the fact that 'the mavericks in MI5 were trying to discredit Wilson, playing with the thesis that he was a Soviet agent'. However, he stresses, 'This is hindsight: none of us knew of the MI5 mavericks' Wilson-as-agent fantasies at the time.'[135] If, as Holland's account suggests, the security service's political line of enquiry drew a blank, the implication of narcotics use could be seen as an alternative attempt to smear him and thereby remove him from Downing Street. Holland speculates that rogue elements within the security service chose to represent his refusal to give information about Neuberger as an attempt to conceal illegal activities.

While much of this account is dependent upon Holland's personal recollections, the PRO file provides some corroboration. Moreover, Sir Christopher Foster, under whom Neuberger was working at the Ministry of Transport when Kaldor made his approach, says that he was told that there were problems with Neuberger's clearance, but that they related to left-wing activism as a student. No mention was made of drugs, and Foster insisted on employing Neuberger despite security service reservations.[136] It may be that, to some extent, the investigators' activities were impelled by incompetence rather than conspiracy. A senior Downing Street permanent official from the period of the first two Wilson administrations describes security service officers as tending to behave 'like plodding policemen',[137] not over-endowed with either intelligence or a sense of proportion. Holland, however, distinguishes the interview he received from a 'plodder' when he first joined the Cabinet Office with the 'spymaster' grilling to which he was later subjected.[138]

John Harris

Writing in July 1969, Crossman referred to 'Roy Jenkins and his boon companion John Harris, who is a kind of American character, a real "kitchen cabinet" in one. He steers Roy a great deal and represents him to the press'.[139] Wilson's personal standing suffered from devaluation in 1967, and increasingly Roy Jenkins, the new Chancellor of the Exchequer, emerged as a possible successor to the Labour leadership. At Jenkins's side was a special adviser, John Harris. Born in 1931, Harris first found employment as a journalist. By 1956 he was working on the Labour paper *Forward*, which was orientated towards the Labour right, with Gaitskell and Douglas Jay both closely involved, and remained firmly associated with this wing of the party. He was appointed as Gaitskell's 'political adviser' for the 1959 election campaign.[140] His work entailed involvement in presentational, strategic and tactical decisions, and no doubt more menial duties as well. Although no specific arrangement was made, Harris believed that, had Labour won that election, the new Prime Minister would have employed him as an aide.[141] It seems that Gaitskell rated Harris highly, and he was kept on as 'Hugh's adviser' after the poll.[142]

Although regarding Harris as a 'pleasant young P.R.O. [public relations officer]', Crossman came to resent his role as 'nothing more than Gaitskell's personal pressman',[143] as opposed to being a party representative. Significantly, at the time Crossman began to suspect that Harris was deliberately furnishing journalists with confidential information in order to further the interests of Gaitskell at the expense of other Labour politicians.[144] Gaitskell was grooming Harris for a parliamentary career,[145] and during his time as a special adviser Harris sought selection as a Labour candidate;[146] but he was unsuccessful, and entered Parliament only in 1974 – and then in the Lords. He became Labour's Director of Publicity in January 1962, and was a key figure in Labour's 1964 election campaign, collaborating with Kitchen Cabinet members.

Upon Labour's victory in 1964 Harris resigned his party post and within a month was employed as a temporary civil servant, working for the Foreign Secretary, Patrick Gordon Walker, to whom he was close personally and politically. The move had been discussed by and agreed between Gordon Walker and Harris in advance of the poll.[147] During his time as a temporary civil servant Harris's job title was 'special assistant' rather than 'adviser' – perhaps because of the non-technical nature of his role. Like 'special adviser', the term had an American flavour to it, having become prominent in the United States before the Second World War.[148] Gordon Walker was in a peculiar position. He held a place in the Cabinet despite having lost his Smethwick parliamentary seat in October 1964, against the national trend, in the face of an anti-immigration campaign conducted by his Conservative rival. A new constituency, Leyton, in East London, was found for him to contest; but he was defeated again, and in January 1965 was obliged to resign his Cabinet post, to be replaced by Michael Stewart (not to be confused with the economist), who retained Harris's services. However, Harris was 'not equally at home with Michael Stewart as he had been with Gordon Walker and before that, in opposition, with Gaitskell'.[149]

Harris, however, was in demand. In June 1965, in the face of perceived problems with the press, 'an abortive attempt' was made to obtain the services of Harris for Wilson. Why was the appointment never made? According to Marcia Williams, 'not only were there objections from the civil servants, but . . . one of Mr Gaitskell's closest friends . . . raised the strongest outcry possible at the thought of installing one of Hugh's closest confidants in Downing Street working for Harold.' While Williams believed that he was 'keen',[150] Harris, who shared with other Gaitskellites a low opinion of Wilson, recalled that at the time he was determined not to work for the Prime Minister.[151] This being the case, the proposal was a non-starter.

Nevertheless, the prospect of Harris's appointment was clearly taken seriously inside the Prime Minister's office. The Downing Street principal private secretary, Derek Mitchell, was apprehensive regarding the incorporation of another political appointee. He wrote to Wilson that as

> *a temporary civil servant John Harris has been used to all the facilities of the Foreign Office, including very free access to official papers . . . it will avoid upsets if it is made clear from the outset that this is not possible [at No. 10]. This links closely with the question of whether he should have a room here . . . it would be a mistake (as well as wrong on grounds of propriety) for him to have anything beyond a peg on which to hang his coat when he calls.*

Mitchell felt that Harris should work at the Labour Party's Transport House headquarters. Helsby agreed that Harris was 'the sort of active political animal . . . for whom there is no safe place in No. 10 or the adjacent buildings'.[152]

In the same year the possibility emerged that Roy Jenkins, a friend and ally of Harris's in the government, might be promoted from the post of Minister of Aviation to replace Frank Soskice as the Home Secretary. Harris made it clear to Jenkins that, should this happen, he found the idea of a move to the Home Office agreeable. Wilson appointed Jenkins as the Home Secretary in December 1965. Michael Stewart was seemingly reluctant to lose Harris, and until Stewart left for the DEA, swapping jobs with Brown in July 1966, Harris divided his time between the Home and Foreign Offices.[153] Harris then became a full-time adviser to Jenkins, who 'took to him very strongly'.[154] Jenkins writes that his special adviser was 'concerned primarily but not exclusively with public relations'.[155] When Jenkins replaced Callaghan as Chancellor of the Exchequer in November 1967, Harris moved with him to the Treasury, where he remained until Labour's June 1970 election defeat. As well as Harris, Jenkins retained his Home Office private secretary, David Dowler, a career civil servant, whom he insisted on being appointed at the Treasury. The existence of a clique composed of Jenkins, Harris and Dowler led to resentment among certain Treasury officials at the supposed tendency for decisions to be taken in a closed 'court'.[156]

Harris helped write party political speeches for Jenkins, for instance the one delivered at the 1969 Labour conference. He also accompanied his minister on official visits, sometimes abroad. Jenkins used Harris as a conduit for personal messages to and from fellow Cabinet members, and the aide seems to have been generally regarded as able to speak for his minister. On occasion Harris accompanied Jenkins to party political engagements which it was more awkward for career officials to attend in a professional capacity. However, there were difficulties with this, since Harris, too, was 'on the public payroll'.[157] Croham regards Harris as the first true special adviser, since his contract (probably drawn up in 1964 by the Foreign Office), Croham remembers, was the standard one for permanent civil servants, modified with provisions for temporary status; other aides in the period were recruited on terms already laid down for the employment of outsiders prior to 1964.[158] At Cabinet in March 1968, Callaghan complained that 'some Ministers seemed to have political press officers to protect them – looking hard at Roy.' Wilson's response was if 'you are thinking of John Harris . . . he is a civil servant'. Callaghan then enquired, if this was the case, 'why Harris had been moved from his job at the Home Office without consulting Roy's successor [i.e. Callaghan] and what was he doing now at the Treasury?' Jenkins's comment was: 'It's none of your business, Home Secretary.'[159]

Just as Balogh was part of a group descended from the Bevanite left which crystallised around Wilson, Harris was one of a clique of Gaitskellite loyalists, who during the course of the 1960s began to centre on the personality of Jenkins. Shore suggested that, following Gaitskell's sudden death in 1963, Harris was a 'deeply disappointed man'. In Shore's view, Harris sought another suitable politician to attach himself to in place of Gaitskell and eventually found one in Jenkins. Shore was certain that it was Harris's intention to promote Jenkins publicly as a future Prime Minister, at the expense of Wilson.[160] Wilson, for his part, suspected that Jenkins, among others, was plotting against him, with the assistance of Harris.[161]

Kitchen Cabinet members took concerned note of Harris. Writing in June 1967 with particular reference to Harris, Crossman expressed the view that personal public relations advisers should be forbidden to ministers.[162] Nor was mistrust of Harris confined to the Labour left; Jenkins's use of a political aide engendered suspicion among supposed allies on the right of the party, such as Crosland.[163] According to Benn's diary entry from 9 August 1966, Crosland believed that Harris, encouraged by Jenkins, was briefing journalists as to which Cabinet post Jenkins wanted to move to next, presumably that of Chancellor of the Exchequer,[164] which Crosland himself coveted. Crossman was deputed to ask Crosland whether he could persuade Jenkins that 'John Harris's press campaign was poisoning relationships and would in the end do Roy no good'. Crosland felt there was little he could do, since his contact with Jenkins had become minimal.[165] Castle suggested that disagreements over the position of Harris undermined the potential for an anti-Wilson alliance between Callaghan and Jenkins.[166] Indeed, Crossman described a Cabinet meeting in November 1968 at which there was a 'universal conviction . . . that John Harris had become Roy's evil genius'.[167]

Suspicion focused particularly strongly on Harris's use of the press. In the first place, it was felt that Harris was dedicated to obtaining newspaper articles calling for the furthest possible advancement of Jenkins, even to the level of Prime Minister, and generally building his image. In January 1968 the *Daily Mirror* ran a series of stories drawing attention to Wilson's supposed failures and portraying Jenkins as a Renaissance man and potential national saviour.[168] Crossman noted his view that they were inspired by Harris.[169] Second, some believed that Harris deliberately tried to undermine the position of Wilson and others, to Jenkins's benefit. Benn suggested that Jenkins used 'John Harris, his press adviser, quite ruthlessly against anyone who [stood] in his way', citing as an example during 1968 Peter Shore, secretary of state at a rival economics ministry, the DEA as a supposed victim of such attacks.[170] Castle recorded being told by Wilson in July 1968 that Harris was responsible for press attacks on her.[171] Third, Harris was suspected by some of attempting to use the press in order to force policy decisions upon Cabinet, by informing journalists of Jenkins's views.[172] Similar means were used to suggest which concessions Jenkins might be willing to make on certain issues.[173] Harris's method of getting articles slanted in the way he wanted seems to have involved furnishing journalists with confidential official information relating to matters such as Jenkins's personal attitudes, the opinions of other ministers and developments inside the administration.[174] Susan Crosland writes that 'Cabinet Ministers took no great pleasure in reading newspaper versions of private meetings and events gone slightly askew in the telling.'[175]

Was Harris guilty as charged? Shore, one of his supposed victims, remained convinced to the end that he was.[176] Harris did not deny the use of inside knowledge in order to obtain favourable press coverage, but argues that such activities were commonplace across the government.[177] Lord (Richard) Marsh, a Wilson Cabinet member, agrees. 'I don't doubt that he [Harris] was doing it,' he states, 'but so was everyone.'[178] Certainly, ministers such as Crossman record sharing internal government knowledge with journalists and, while there were no other special advisers with Harris's precise role, there were political press officers, for example Gerald Kaufman at No. 10.[179] Croham, who also notes that Harris was far from being the only culprit, states that press priming 'was a safety valve for collective Cabinet responsibility'. Through such means, Croham suggests, ministers were able to signal to their party supporters disagreement with government policies that they were obliged publicly to support.[180] Harris was obviously good at his job; perhaps too good for some. Balogh, who, predictably, shared the conspiracy theorists' view of Harris, was uncertain of the extent to which Jenkins was complicit in his aide's alleged machinations. On the subject of hostile briefing, Balogh remarked to Castle in June 1968, "I just don't think he [Jenkins] knows what is done in his name."[181]

When pressed on whether his primary loyalty was to Jenkins or the Labour administration as a whole, Harris said that the one entailed the other. While he was a supporter of the government, he was not, he stated, one of Wilson. Harris maintained that both he and Jenkins were mainly concerned with averting the possibility of Britain 'going down the plug-hole', possibly dragging the world economy with it. They were, he argued, not interested in such matters as political conspiracy. However, his protestations of innocence did not fully accord with Gordon Walker's description of a plot against Wilson by the Labour right that brewed during 1968–9 – a plot of which, Harris conceded, he and Jenkins were aware, but which, he claimed, they did not condone.[182]

Harris had maintained contact with Gordon Walker, who returned to the Cabinet as minister without portfolio in January 1967.[183] Gordon Walker became active in a scheme to oust Wilson as premier and replace him with Jenkins. In his diary Gordon Walker recorded informing Jenkins, on the evening of 27 May 1968, of an 'inner group of 9 or 10' MPs ready to mobilise support for an anti-Wilson coup. Gordon Walker then suggested that Harris should find the text of a 1957 Labour Parliamentary Committee document dealing with the removal of leaders, for leaking to the press at an appropriate moment.[184] On 3 July, in his account, Gordon Walker went to the Chancellor's room in the House of Commons, at Jenkins's request. John Harris was also there. Jenkins made it clear that he 'did not want to say, at any time, that we should move. He wanted to be consulted and might advise against action – but, otherwise, would leave it to us. He clearly did not want to be implicated in actually launching an action'.[185]

Gordon Walker's diary entry for 7 May 1969 described how the conspirators, including Bill Rodgers, David Marquand and Robert Maclennan, finally decided to launch a strike against Wilson.[186] However, the following day John Harris, described by Gordon Walker as 'Roy's press man and a very good friend of ours', sent word to Christopher Mayhew, a co-conspirator, that 'Roy Jenkins did not want us to move'.[187] The reason for Jenkins's hesitance was that the passage of the Industrial Relations Bill had reached a critical point, likely to rally the support of moderate Labour MPs to Wilson.[188] The excitable tone of Gordon Walker's accounts of the putsch-that-never-was may lead the reader to doubt the serious-ness of the participants. Nevertheless, it seems that Harris and Jenkins were not averse to benefiting from a successful move against Wilson, and were willing to co-operate with the attempt up to a point, merely wishing to avoid association with a bid that failed.

Given that there was no effective attempt to oust Wilson by Jenkins or his followers,[189] the Chancellor of the Exchequer and the Prime Minister were mutually dependent for political success. When suggesting to Castle that Harris was guilty of intrigue in July 1968, Wilson added, 'Mind you, I like Roy and work well with him. After all, I appointed him and I was right.'[190] Harris nearly performed the ultimate service for Wilson and the Labour administration as a whole. Labour's defeat on 18 June 1970 followed a late dip in the party's aggre-gated opinion poll standing, which began on 12 June.[191] Harris had lobbied for the election date to be set for 11 June, pushing the issue so hard that Jenkins arranged an audience for him with Wilson. Harris's primary motivation was the possibility of violent demonstrations at a forthcoming test match against the South African cricket team at Lord's, which could damage the government's image. Ultimately, it was a false fear. However, Harris also suspected that the trade figures due to be published on 15 June, might, after a long run of good results, be unfavourable; and in this he turned out to be correct. As Jenkins later noted, 'Had he [Harris] carried his point, who can tell what changes in the pattern of British politics over the years which have since gone by might not have followed?'[192]

Brian Abel-Smith

Brian Abel-Smith was employed as Crossman's senior adviser at the nascent Department of Health and Social Security (DHSS) from September 1968 until Labour's election defeat in June 1970. Towards the end of his time as Secretary of State for Social Services, Crossman remarked in a diary entry that Abel-Smith 'has been my closest personal friend and without him I could have done very little in the past two years'.[193] Castle, who employed him as a special adviser when she was Secretary of State for Social Services from 1974 to 1976, writes of Abel-Smith that 'His incomparable knowledge of the whole field of health and social security and his Socialist sympathies made him an invaluable asset to Labour Ministers'.[194] He was, therefore, a special adviser in possession of technical expertise as well as party political and personal attachments.

Abel-Smith was an embodiment of the ideals which had inspired the London School of Economics, the educational establishment with which he was associated for most of his working life. The Webbs, the driving force behind the LSE, had envisaged it from its formation as an intellectual stable rearing an elite breed of humane technocrats, of which Abel-Smith was a fine example. Born in London in 1926, 'said to be thirty-eighth in succession to the Throne',[195] from a 'military-cum-City' background, Abel-Smith attended Haileybury and completed postwar military service before studying economics at Clare College, Cambridge.[196] An association with Labour was clear from early on. While at Cambridge, Abel-Smith came to the attention of Dalton, who met him in March 1951 on one of his regular scouting missions to the university. Dalton viewed Abel-Smith as a 'very promising young man . . . good socialist, intelligent, good presence and personality'.[197] As a research student at Cambridge in the 1950s under the distinguished left-wing Keynesian economist Joan Robinson, Abel-Smith already harboured radical intentions and initially contemplated a career as an elected Labour politician; but it never materialised. The reason seems to have been his concern over the prejudice his sexual orientation, beyond the legal and moral pale of the time, might attract. A colleague and friend writes that Abel-Smith 'refused to apply for safe seats, more because of the risk of public humiliation if he was discovered to be homosexual than anything else'.[198] From 1955 he was employed by the LSE as a lecturer under Richard Titmuss, Professor of Social Administration since 1950 and a dynamic force within the school. In 1961 Abel-Smith became a Reader and, in 1965, Professor of Social Administration himself.

The DHSS was formally established, with Crossman as its ministerial head, on 1 November 1968, following the announcement of its creation the previous spring. Rather than an entirely new department, it was an amalgam of already existing ones, and therefore suitable for investigation here. Crossman decided to employ Abel-Smith, on a part-time basis, after a discussion with Titmuss in April 1968. Crossman felt that the appointment would 'be very important for our organisation of the Intelligence side'. Abel-Smith began work in September 1968. Given the title of 'senior adviser', he was eventually allocated a room in the departmental building in John Adam Street and, according to Crossman, was 'very happy there'. Initially 'anxious whether there would be enough for him to do', Abel-Smith soon discovered that there was 'plenty on his plate'.[199]

Abel-Smith and Crossman had frequent contact and their relationship was personal as well as professional. To Crossman, Abel-Smith's value derived in part from his appetite for such activities as 'inventing devices for improving contributions'. The aide possessed great skill and originality in the area of the application of statistics to problems of social administration. It was put to good use inside the government. Abel-Smith's functions included, in conjunction with ministers, assessing the departmental workload and planning its execution. Crossman's special adviser helped devise public speeches for him, as well as assisting with the preparation of his representations to Jenkins on departmental spending and supplying Crossman with gossip from within the DHSS.[200] Abel-Smith was assisted by David Piachaud, a lecturer in social administration from the LSE.

Abel-Smith played an important part in Crossman's attempt in 1969–70 to restructure the regional hierarchy of the National Health Service.[201] Also during 1970 he produced a White Paper on the subject of better care for the mentally handicapped which was adopted virtually unchanged by the Conservative administration formed that June.[202] Abel-Smith was also a driving force behind the National Superannuation pension scheme. In conjunction with Titmuss and

Peter Townsend, another LSE academic, Abel-Smith originated National Superannuation in the mid-1950s, and its underlying principles remained unaltered. Founded in a critique of the flat-rate system, which, it was argued, had never provided benefits reaching the subsistence levels defined by Beveridge,[203] it was a differentiated state pension. Lower contributions would ultimately lead to smaller benefit entitlements. However, the sums retired lower-wage earners were to receive would considerably outstrip those they could expect under existing arrangements, subsidised, as they would be, by the greater payments made by the better-off.[204] Importantly, benefits would be 'dynamised', that is, altered in order to keep pace with inflation and rising average earnings.[205] National Superannuation was lost as a result of Labour's June 1970 election defeat, though it was revived in simplified form by Barbara Castle and eventually came into effect as SERPS.

Christopher Foster

When Castle arrived at the Ministry of Transport in 1965 her 'first step was to set up an Economic Planning Unit', as she had done at the Ministry for Overseas Development. At its head she appointed Christopher Foster, a thirty-five-year-old economist from Jesus College, Oxford who specialised in transport policy. Foster's unit, the Directorate-General of Economic Planning, consisted of around twelve economists, including both seconded permanent officials and outsiders. From his university base, Foster had assisted the previous administration, co-ordinating research projects and allotting work to academic colleagues.[206] Achievements already to his credit included the production of statistical information suggesting the economic and social viability of what became the London Underground Victoria Line.[207] Despite his prior co-operation with a Conservative government, Foster was personally inclined towards Labour. While not strongly attached to a particular faction, he generally regarded himself as belonging to the right of the party. In 1964 he became a part-time adviser at the DEA.

The challenge Foster faced at Transport was considerable. Labour had made the grandiose promise of a 'national plan for transport' in its 1964 manifesto, and again in 1966.[208] Unfortunately, what precisely this meant was unclear. It was, therefore, the task of Foster and his team to turn Labour's vague commitment into a concrete package of policies.[209] Castle wanted to bring about greater co-ordination of transport policy and preserve the railway network in the face of competition from road vehicles, without resorting to a full nationalisation programme.[210] The ultimate result was the vast and complex 1968 Transport Act, described by Wilson as 'the biggest and most far-reaching Transport Bill in our history'.[211] Foster and his unit were closely involved in the development of many aspects of the Act, for example, the creation of the National Freight Corporation (NFC), intended as a clearing house directing the most efficient possible trans-portation of goods.[212] During 1966–9 Foster was also associated with the introduction of the 70 m.p.h speed limit for cars and the use of the breathalyser by traffic police. Aside from his role as a policy expert, Foster also undertook political work. He and Stephen Swingler, a junior transport minister, held regular informal consultations with groups of Labour backbenchers in the House of Commons.[213]

Castle's appointment of Foster coincided with her attempt to remove the permanent secretary at Transport, Sir Thomas Padmore. A *Guardian* front-page story from 6 January 1966 revealed Castle's intention of replacing Padmore, preferably with 'a younger civil servant ready for promotion'.[214] The source of the story was Foster, who naïvely spoke too freely to his journalist friend Peter Jenkins – thus incurring Castle's wrath. While Castle was not successful in her attempt to displace Padmore, the permanent secretary was left gravely weakened and Foster became, in his words, 'the de facto permanent secretary'.[215] Castle portrays Foster as an influential ally.[216] Like other special advisers, however, Foster depended on the confidence of his minister, and this was eroded late in 1967. Castle came to suspect him of intriguing to have himself appointed as chairman of British Rail, skewing some of his advice to this end.[217] Foster was not aware of Castle's doubts at the time and plausibly claims that he would never have considered himself a candidate for the post in question. Other matters aside, he was surely too young to have been in contention. Foster suspects that since he was then tainted in her eyes, Castle opted not to take him with her when she became Secretary of State for Employment and Productivity in April 1968.[218]

Castle's replacement at Transport, Richard Marsh, not numbered among her admirers, decided to introduce changes at the ministry. He insisted that Padmore, who, according to Marsh, was spending time on interests including playing the violin, be replaced.[219] The new permanent secretary, David Serpell, was not likely to be as docile. Indeed, in Castle's words, he possessed 'the reputation of being a bastard'.[220] Foster was removed from office in early 1969, to be replaced by John Jukes, formerly MacDougall's deputy at the DEA. According to Foster, what prompted this was his minuting Marsh over the head of Serpell, an act which enraged the permanent secretary. The development suggests the difficulties associated with combining the introduction of greater expertise into Whitehall with patronage-based recruitment. Nevertheless, as Foster points out, the Directorate-General survived his departure and, indeed, the advent of a Conservative administration in 1970.[221]

Additional appointments

Neild left his post at the Treasury, dispirited by the failure to devalue sterling, in May 1967. Eventually Callaghan alighted upon Michael Posner, Economic Director at the Ministry of Power since 1966, as a replacement. Posner, born in 1931, came from Pembroke College, Cambridge and was yet another economist in whose appointment to a government post Balogh had a hand.[222] Appointed Economic Adviser to the Treasury, Posner went on to engage in important work such as helping to draft Callaghan's November 1967 statement to the House on sterling devaluation.[223] That he was not as senior as Neild is suggested by the fact that he saw himself as subordinate to Cairncross. He was, however, a member of FU.[224] Posner's was intended to be a fairly personal role, 'guided to some extent by the kind of things on which the Chancellor seeks his help'. In policy terms, he was initially charged with contributing in the areas of international liquidity and finance, industrial problems and demand management.[225] Though Posner's sympathies were with the political left, his was not a partisan appointment, and he stayed on beyond Labour's 1970 election defeat until the following year. He does not, therefore, entirely fit the definition of the special adviser used here.

Kenneth Berrill, an economist from King's College, Cambridge, who held the post of special adviser to the Treasury from 1967 to 1969, was also appointed following Neild's departure. However, Berrill's job title was anomalous since he was not party political.[226] His main concern was intended to be public expenditure; in particular, specific items rather than the overall level. Following his appointment as President of the Board of Trade at the end of August 1967, Tony Crosland recruited the Balliol economist Wilfred Beckerman, aged forty-two, as an economic adviser. Although he developed a close personal relationship with his minister, Beckerman seems to have regarded his period of service as fairly futile. He writes, 'My job as a top-level economic advisor at the Board of Trade consisted mainly of dashing off brief and succinct comments on the economic aspects of the various files . . . that arrived in my "In Tray" every day. It was like sitting one's final examinations in economics every day, the only difference being that it did not matter so much whether or not one got the answers right for nobody was going to take much notice of them anyway.'[227]

A number of conclusions can be drawn from individual studies of special advisers between 1964 and 1970. Although not successful in achieving all their objectives, together they comprised a substantial, radical force within government. Great influence was wielded by Kaldor at the Treasury and Abel-Smith at the DHSS. On occasions, they achieved the implementation of long-held Labour movement objectives. At other times, temporary civil servants were acting on their own account. Inevitably, there were tensions between outsiders and representatives of the permanent machine. Personality was important, particularly in the case of Balogh, whose flaws served to undermine his effectiveness. The relationship with the employing minister was crucial. Balogh's position, for example, resulted from his closeness to Wilson. The absence of such a bond, as the cases of Foster and Kaldor showed, could be fatal. Often aides were extremely useful to their employers, as Crossman's references to Abel-Smith demonstrate. There was a tendency for special advisers to become involved in disputes between Cabinet members, possibly aggravating them in the process.

Most of the aides recruited were economists, and should, therefore, be categorised as experts. However, Allen may be seen as a prototype for the political aide; and Harris was a 'spin doctor' before the term was in use. Roles, including press briefing, extended beyond the mere provision of counsel. Indeed, special advisers, especially Foster, seem to have acquired executive authority over both outsiders and career officials. There was an overlap of roles and characteristics. Balogh, for example, took an interest in presentation, while Foster helped maintain contact between government and backbench MPs. Kaldor and Abel-Smith, although in possession of expertise, were not neutral technocrats. Their commitment to the Labour cause was as great as that of special advisers who might be defined as 'political'.

Five

Aides to a thwarted administration: the Heath government

The aides appointed under Edward Heath's administration, from 1970 to 1974, were a subject of some, largely internal, controversy. In addition to this political presence within Whitehall. other outsiders, not truly special advisers, were introduced into the administration. Reform of the machinery of government was an important aspect of Heath's agenda, and certain aides made proposals of their own as to how this might be achieved. One aspect of the administrative overhaul which took place was the significant innovation of the Central Policy Review Staff. As to policy formation, while the Conservatives initially appeared to be committed to a free-market programme, which some aides had helped develop, it was abandoned in the face of economic difficulties. An assessment will be made of the extent to which special advisers influenced decisions taken in office.

Conservative aides

Kavanagh and Seldon state that the 'structure of ministerial "special advisers" was beginning to develop during the Heath government. Drawn from party ranks, or from business, they were short-term appointments, designed to give the minister political or policy advice'.[1] The use of temporary civil servants with the job title 'special adviser' persisted. One such was Brian Reading, an economic counsellor to the Prime Minister from 1970, formally located in the Cabinet Office as a 'special adviser'. Another was Michael Wolff, a political import into the Prime Minister's office, seemingly with the job title 'Special Adviser to the Government'. A handful of aides was scattered across the departments: Brendon Sewill on the Chancellor of the Exchequer's staff, Miles Hudson at the Foreign Office and Mark Schreiber at the Cabinet Office. Despite the changeover in party government, then, the special adviser was maintained. The roles performed were similar enough to those of 1964–70 to be classed as a continuation of Wilson's experiment.

As John Ramsden notes, during his premiership Heath came to be perceived as neglectful of his party and overly reliant on 'civil service advice'; this in turn motivated the appointment of more outsiders, in order to 'break down this impression'.[2] During 1972–3 Douglas Hurd, the Prime Minister's political secretary, endeavoured with Heath's approval to persuade ministers to recruit more aides. Hurd notes that some 'had them already . . . Others did not see the point. Others saw the point, but could not find the right person. The choice must be personal. I could suggest names, but only the Minister could say whether the face fitted'. Slowly progress was made, with Robert Jackson being appointed to serve Maurice Macmillan at Employment and John Cope joining Peter Walker at Trade and Industry.[3]

Towards the end of the Heath administration, Hurd began convening meetings of the counsellors, 'to share problems and help impart a common purpose'.[4] Yet despite Hurd's efforts, the collective impact of special advisers during 1970–4 has been judged as minimal. Heath's biographer, John Campbell, writes that 'as a group they quickly sank without trace'. The reason, Campbell argues, was that they were 'too few and too isolated'.[5] Certainly their potential effectiveness was vitiated by the successive and worsening crises which the Heath administration endured. According to Hurd, by the time he began bringing aides together for discussions at No. 10, circumstances were already 'desperate'. Hurd's account also suggests that the expansion in the number of aides, as well as the attempt to galvanise them into a collective entity, came too late. He writes that it 'would be absurd to claim that we made much difference, though we would have made more difference if as a team we had come into being earlier'.[6] Jackson, the last of the recruits, notes that by the time he arrived at Employment in 1973, both the department and the secretary of state were already overwhelmed by industrial relations problems.[7]

The total in service does not seem to have exceeded ten; and none of them had the public profile of, for example, Balogh. Probably for this reason, in part at least, corresponding levels of public interest in the phenomenon of the special adviser were not as great as they were during 1964–70. The imbalance of media scrutiny prompted Wilson, writing in 1976, to complain that, while the Conservatives had brought in outsiders, 'unremitting press comments . . . have been addressed, uniquely, to my appointees.'[8] Nevertheless, Heath's use of counsel drawn from beyond Whitehall in general was noted in the press, as were individual recruits including Sewill.[9]

Not all recruits were employed as civil servants and therefore some cannot be classified as special advisers according to the definition used here. Jackson and Wolff, to give two examples, were not paid from official funds; and Hudson, in a letter to *The Times* in 2002, noted that 'I was paid by the Conservative Party'. That arrangement, in his view, was preferable to drawing on the taxpayer, since it clarified the relationship between aides and career civil servants, kept numbers low and meant that the party in power did not receive an unfair 'hidden subsidy'.[10] For those on the public payroll, who included Schreiber, around £6,000 per annum was a standard salary in 1970. It exceeded that of MPs, who were paid £3,250 in 1970, rising to £4,500 in 1972. The salary of a minister of state rose from £5,625 to £7,500 in the same year, and the parliamentary salary for ministers in the Commons increased from £1,250 to £3,000. A permanent secretary's maximum was £14,000. In terms of age range, Cope, born in 1946, was at the younger end of the scale, Sewill, born in 1929, at the older. There was not always a personal link with an individual minister: Schreiber, for example, operating within the Civil Service Department, was not directly answerable to any one government member.[11]

What were these special advisers recruited to do? In 1970, shortly after Heath's arrival at Downing Street, *The Economist* proposed that the government 'should . . . try to attract some fairly young economists as temporary civil servants, injecting some bright ideas'.[12] Certain aides did perform the role referred to in *The Economist*. Reading was a PPE graduate from Wadham College, Oxford, who had been awarded a studentship at Nuffield College from 1958 to 1960 and then lectured in economics at Christ Church from 1960 to 1963. He was also closely linked to the Conservatives as a member of the Conservative Research Department (CRD) and a personal adviser to Heath in opposition. Indeed, political affiliation was at least as prominent a feature of special advisers during 1970–4 as expertise.

The means by which channels of communication between party and government could be maintained was a concern from the outset of the Heath administration. In June 1970 the Lord President, William Whitelaw, established a ministerial 'Liaison Committee', the purpose of which was to 'give guidance to Members of Parliament, candidates and others on the interpretation of Government policy and to take such action as, in their opinion, is necessary to sustain public confidence in the Conservative administration'. Modelled on a similar body which operated from 1951 to 1964, it met weekly on Tuesday mornings. Its existence and proceedings were to be kept secret. In order to assist the Liaison Committee, various ministers were requested by Whitelaw to ensure that their private secretaries kept the CRD informed of 'any particular matters which are likely to have political reactions'. In other words, presentation was to be co-ordinated between party and government in order to ensure maximum effectiveness, a responsibility which in later years was specifically entrusted to special advisers rather than permanent civil servants. There was unease in Whitehall about the proposed arrangement, which entailed career officials dealing directly with a political party. Agreement was obtained from William Armstrong, Head of the Home Civil Service, on the proviso that all reports to the CRD by private secretaries were specifically instructed by ministers, with civil servants not being required to act on their own initiative.[13]

The recruitment of aides was a means of establishing a staff more suited than permanent civil servants to the performance of party political duties. Hurd refers to the need of a Cabinet minister for

> *political advisers to help with that side of their life. It is easy for a Minister to be swallowed up in the engrossing work of his own department. He can lose touch with colleagues, with his Party, with the political strategy of the Government. If questioned, he will deny this indignantly. 'What nonsense! I see them all the time.' So he does, on formal or purely social occasions, but he has lost real contact, he is drifting out of sight.*[14]

Heath subsequently told the House of Commons Treasury and Civil Service Select Committee that he brought

> *into the Minister's personal staff people from outside . . . who can maintain contact with his party organisation . . . It is a means of trying to keep a minister in contact with his party when he is extremely busy and overworked and also*

of trying to keep his feet on the ground as far as party opinion is concerned. Both of these things can be useful.[15]

A previous direct involvement in the party machine was common to all special advisers. Sewill, for example, was the director of the CRD from 1965–70, having first joined it in 1952. Better funded and with a larger staff than its Labour equivalent, the CRD went on to supply successive Conservative administrations with temporary civil servants. Special advisers' submissions were often party political in content, for example considering the Conservative Party's chances of obtaining a second term. In a pessimistic economic assessment of autumn 1971, Reading stated that as 'things are going . . . this Government has little if any chance of winning the next Election'.[16] Among the Heath intake of aides, both Cope and Jackson became Conservative MPs.

Partisanship was likely to entail a keen interest in public relations. Lord (David) Howell, appointed Minister for the Civil Service in 1970, says that the briefing of journalists by special advisers did not occur on the scale it did in subsequent periods, but contact, for example over lunch, took place nonetheless.[17] In a letter of January 1972 to Robert Armstrong, the Prime Minister's principal private secretary, Reading stated that 'the presentation of policy is of equal importance to its contents'.[18] Of the view that public confidence was essential to a successful economy, Reading argued it was 'imperative that we devote a much greater proportion of our time and effort to communicating with the public'.[19] He attempted to ensure that the Prime Minister's office was kept abreast of possible announcements regarding positive economic developments.[20] Many of Heath's party political public relations requirements were catered for by Wolff, whom he described as an 'an excellent speech-writer'. During the build-up to the February 1974 poll, Wolff was one of those who briefed Heath in advance of his 11 a.m. press conferences.[21]

On 11 February 1971 questions were raised in the House by Labour members regarding the partisan activities of civil servants. Wilson suggested, in an exchange with Heath, that 'a very considerable deterioration in . . . standards' might be taking place.[22] The accusation was interpreted within Whitehall as a reference to Schreiber, who, as well as being a special adviser, was a Conservative councillor. In response – probably in order to avoid political embarrassment, or piqued by the criticism he had received – Heath took a line tougher than the one which William Armstrong wished to pursue.

Robert Armstrong wrote to William Armstrong on 12 February stating that the 'rule is, I understand, that civil servants of the grade of executive officer and above may take part in local political activities with the permission of their Departments . . . Mark Schreiber . . . sought and obtained his Department's permission to continue to serve as an elected member of the East Suffolk County Council'. Sewill, too, had 'sought and obtained his Department's permission to continue to serve as Chairman of his local Conservative Association'. Heath, Robert Armstrong stated, was of the opinion 'that senior members of the civil and diplomatic services should not be office-holders in party political organisations and associations or members of local councils on a party political ticket'. The enforcement of the premier's view, in the form of new guidance issued across Whitehall, would mean 'revoking the permission given to Mark Schreiber and Brendon Sewill and asking them to resign their positions forthwith'. Robert Armstrong added that 'this should be done, and should be seen to be done' in the context of 'a general review and tightening up of existing procedure and practice in this matter'. There might, he added, turn out to be other cases to which the new regulation would have to be applied.[23]

In his reply, dated 25 March 1971, William Armstrong informed Robert Armstrong that he had 'asked the Heads of all the main Departments whether . . . permission had been given to any officers at Assistant Secretary level and above to serve on local councils on a party political label or to hold office in party political organisations mainly concerned with supporting candidates for local government' and whether 'any special advisers appointed by their Minister had been given permission to take part in local political activities'. The only special advisers to have been granted such authorisation were Schreiber and Sewill. In both cases, a careful weighing up of 'the risk . . . of conflict with the individual's official duties or the interests of his Department' had been carried out. As far as William Armstrong was aware, 'no actual difficulty or misunderstanding' had occurred. Moreover, he added, the introduction of 'people of known political views and activities' into government service was not an entirely new practice, and he doubted 'whether they need necessarily be treated with greater restriction than would a permanent civil servant'. However, Sewill had already resigned his office, and Schreiber was 'ready to resign if asked to do so'. William Armstrong suggested that 'the Prime Minister may wish to reconsider the position of Mr Schreiber – in my view, unless there is a change of circumstances, this permission . . . could be allowed to stand.'[24]

Heath, however, was firmly convinced that the external party political roles of both special advisers had to cease. Schreiber was loath to relinquish his council membership, proposing that he be permitted to continue as an Independent. Robert Armstrong expressed the view to Heath that 'I myself doubt whether this compromise will convince anybody, and I should have thought that your previous instruction that he should resign should stand.' The Prime Minister's principal private secretary had also investigated the position of Joe Haines, Wilson's press secretary at No. 10 from 1969, which had been raised by Wilson himself in the Commons in order to draw a contrast with political appointments under his successor. Armstrong was able to confirm Wilson's claim that Haines had 'resigned his position as councillor immediately upon appointment and was not allowed even to attend the next meeting of the Council in order to tender his resignation'.[25] Ultimately, Heath ruled that Schreiber should resign from East Suffolk County Council.[26]

Machinery of government

As distinct and autonomous elements within Whitehall, special advisers took upon themselves the task of supplying independent advice. Reading saw himself as fulfilling 'the need for some kind of general economic comment at the centre, independent of both the Treasury and other main economics departments and of involvement in the day to day business of Government'.[27] He regarded it as one of his advantages that, in producing papers, 'I do not have to worry about the protocol of trespassing on Treasury territory.'[28] Nevertheless, although in some instances aides were critical of Whitehall's *modus operandi*, interactions between outsiders and the permanent machine were seemingly not as problematic as they had been in certain cases during 1964–70. Sewill, for one, found career officials in the Treasury to be collaborative. This was, in his view, 'partly because it is a small and high calibre Department, partly because in seeking to keep down public expenditure and reform taxation we were working "with the grain"'. Sewill noted that more resistance to Conservative policies was offered, 'for example, in the Department of Trade and Industry where Conservative Ministers were working against the whole interventionist purpose of the Department'.[29]

Schreiber, similarly, on the whole found the Whitehall machine co-operative. He was allowed to attend the committees he wanted to, although discovering their existence in the first place sometimes entailed a degree of detective work on his part.[30]

The existence of generally good relations between political appointees and civil servants, however, did not mean an uncritical acceptance of the status quo. When Heath took office, there was an expectation that significant administrative reorganisation would follow. In July 1970 *The Economist* predicted that a 'wind of change is due to blow through the length of Whitehall'.[31] Special advisers could be critical of the methods and structures of the Civil Service, and see themselves as agents for change, seeking to rectify the shortcomings they had identified. This tendency, in the propitious environment of a political leadership inclined towards reform led to far-reaching proposals.

Reading had previous experience working inside policy-forming institutions. From 1962 to 1963 he was seconded from Christ Church, Oxford, to the Bank of England. He then went on to work for the National Economic Development Council (NEDC) in 1964 and then the DEA (1964–6) before joining the CRD. Heath describes Reading as, on one occasion, 'scathing' about the Treasury.[32] His opinion, expressed in a letter to Robert Armstrong in December 1970, was that Britain's poor economic performance since 1945 was attributable to 'the mistakes and failures of economic policy'. Successive governments, he noted, had 'questioned the institutional arrangements for policy formulation and execution and have tried to challenge and change them in various ways'. All modern societies experienced economic problems, but in Britain they were pronounced, partly as a consequence of 'accidents of history' leading to 'a uniquely powerful and privileged Treasury (and Bank)'. To overcome this, Reading proposed the development of 'a centre outside the bounds of Whitehall'. A means of achieving it would be 'to hive off certain activities'. The new bodies formed might include a 'council of economic advisers . . . reporting directly to the Prime Minister', which could be achieved through a regrouping of the NEDC. Such an institution 'would have the advantage of calling upon a basic staff and structure which already exists and creating an expertise and authority with a power base of its own capable of challenging the Treasury direct'. The Prime Minister would thereby be provided with 'the machine he lacks today without any great extra cost in resources'.[33] Therefore, as well as proposing a reduction in the influence of the Treasury and the Civil Service in general, Reading was advocating a centralisation of power in the hands of the Prime Minister.

Responding to Reading's proposal for 'a separate source of advice to the Government from the Treasury and the Bank of England', Robert Armstrong wrote, 'I do not think that your analysis is wholly fair to the existing institution,' on the grounds that economic policy mistakes were more properly attributed to ministers than to the officials they instructed. While being

> *very much a believer in having properly thought out strategies, and for in-depth study of alternative strategies . . . I would myself stop short of your 'second force' solution . . . because I think that conflicting streams of public official advice would make it more difficult rather than easier for the Government to arrive at a sensible and coherent strategy.*

In place of Reading's proposal, Armstrong preferred 'a more systematic organisation of the economic advisers. I should like to see the Government's Chief Economic Adviser heading a formally constituted group of economic advisers, meeting and reporting regularly to Ministers'.[34]

Schreiber, too, was an advocate of a thorough overhaul of administrative structures and methods of policy formation. He was described by Howell as 'an unsettling original – a classic example of the kind of character who refuses to toe the line and march in step with the rest'.[35] As he indicated in a note to the Prime Minister's office in October 1971, Schreiber was troubled by 'the lack of imagination and creative thought' he observed in several government departments. Correcting the problem was a considerable task, since 'changes proposed to anyone's territory in Whitehall will be strongly resisted. The more inadequate those affected, the weaker the case against change, the more it is seen as a threat'. Moreover, departmental ministers often 'allowed themselves to be put forward in defence of the Departmental interest when they should be supporting the attack'. One of Schreiber's main proposals was that 'economic strategy, which is at the heart of the success or failure of the Government, needs to be brought into the policy formulation of each Department' rather than being monopolised by the Treasury. He also believed that 'the creation of the CSD [Civil Service Department] was a major administrative error' and wanted to see the combination of the 'expenditure side of the Treasury and the manpower and management side of the CSD' in a single, newly created unit. The remainder of the CSD's responsibilities, including recruitment, 'training, pay, personnel management' could be 'hived off'. In order to achieve more effective 'Treasury cuts exercises', Schreiber suggested the establishment of a 'small full-time task force', which would prepare a package 'at least double in size that which is thought to be required' prior to Cabinet discussion of the subject.[36]

None of the above proposals produced by Reading and Schreiber were adopted – which is perhaps not surprising, given their radical nature. They challenged long traditions within Whitehall, in particular the Treasury dominance of economic policy and control of expenditure. Furthermore, the increasing difficulties encountered by the Heath governments as time passed rendered administrative reform a lower priority. Nevertheless, the fact that ideas of this type were floated was significant. It has been written that, as Prime Minister, Heath was mistrustful of the Treasury as an institution.[37] Certainly some of his political aides were, and they may have influenced, or at least reinforced, his outlook. It is possible to detect a tendency among special advisers, regardless of which party they serve in government, to find fault with, and seek to reform, the Civil Service.

Beyond the immediate realm of the special adviser, the bureaucratic programme embarked upon from 1970 merits examination. When Heath took office, detailed Conservative plans for administrative reform were already prepared. From 1964, before becoming Conservative leader, Heath was chair of the party's policy group, which took a particular interest in the subject. When he succeeded Home in 1965 his former responsibility passed to Sir Edward Boyle, who also became a member of the Fulton Committee. A Public Sector Research Unit was established under the former transport minister, Ernest Marples, who sent Howell and Schreiber, respectively a junior minister and a special adviser at the Civil Service Department from 1970, to foreign countries including the United States to study management techniques. Heath himself conducted consultations with former civil servants; he also obtained the services of various businessmen, who helped develop ideas in their spare time during the Conservatives' spell in opposition, and later accompanied them into government. These included David Cruikshank from Bovis, Tim Sainsbury from Sainsbury's and Derek Rayner from Marks and Spencer.[38] Sainsbury subsequently became a Conservative MP. However, such recruits should not be classified as special advisers. Confined to business-related activities including procurement, most of them were not possessed of the partisanship associated with other aides under examination here. Nevertheless, their appointments were representative of a desire to incorporate outside knowledge and skills into Whitehall. Their recruitment also reflects a Conservative affinity for counsellors drawn from the private sector, which became more pronounced under Thatcher's leadership.

In October 1970, following 'much haggling between the regulars and irregulars',[39] a White Paper entitled *The Reorganisation of Central Government* appeared.[40] It propounded the view, associated with the early stages of the Heath administration, that 'government has been attempting to do too much. This has placed an excessive burden on industry, and on the people of the country as a whole, and has also overloaded the government machine itself'. *The Reorganisation of Central Government* was concerned with tackling the latter manifestation of overreach, with a view to attaining 'a new and better balance between the individual and the modern State . . . less government, and better government, carried out by fewer people'. One of the intended means of achieving this end was the establishment of 'a small multi-disciplinary central policy review staff in the Cabinet Office . . . at the disposal of the Government as a whole. Under the supervision of the Prime Minister, it will work for Ministers collectively'. The Central Policy Review Staff (CPRS) came into being in 1971.

In opposition, Schreiber and Howell had helped originate the idea of a 'Crown Consultancy Unit', and it was this which eventually became the CPRS. It was part of a broader concept called the 'Central Capability': a means of co-ordinating and reviewing administration from the centre. Schreiber and Howell both wanted the institution to be personal to the Prime Minister.[41] Howell sought to establish a fully fledged Prime Minister's department, with himself as its minister of state. He regards arrangements at the outset of the Blair administration in 1997, with an expanded staff of special advisers at No. 10, and Peter Mandelson appointed the minister without portfolio, as close to what he had in mind. Howell sought to emulate the structures surrounding the US President (in particular the Bureau of the Budget) and the (West) German Chancellor.[42] Historically, he writes, the Central Capability was influenced by favourable observations of the wartime support systems attached to Lloyd George and Churchill.[43]

In a note to the Lord Privy Seal, Lord Jellicoe, in August 1970, Schreiber referred to a body which would fulfil 'the need to provide Mr Heath with the means of making a success of what we identified would be his particular "style of government"'. It was intended, Schreiber maintained, to be 'very political and rather personal' to Heath. He argued that it would not necessarily survive a change in administration. The motive lying behind its design was the attainment of a particular policy objective, namely a thorough assessment of public expenditure in the contexts of political strategy and cost-effectiveness. As well as being technically skilled and adept in the conduct of personal relations, its head would need to be 'a committed Conservative. He would be appointed personally by the Prime Minister and hold office at the pleasure of the Prime Minister'. Regular personal access to the premier would be essential for the person concerned, who, Schreiber suggested, should not be an MP, unless, possibly, a minister, but could be a Lord.[44]

Perhaps because of the difficulty of finding an individual who fulfilled all the requirements Schreiber envisaged, and presumably also because of Civil Service pressure, the eventual appointment to the head of the CPRS was not a partisan one. Moreover, the idea that the group be a specifically prime ministerial body was defeated by resistance from Burke Trend, the Cabinet Secretary. Instead, as indicated in *The Reorganisation of Central Government*, the decision was taken to create a team of specialists to counsel the Cabinet as a whole.[45] What were the Cabinet Secretary's motives in pressing for this broader focus? Perhaps, valuing Cabinet government, he sought to reinforce it (and preserve the position of the Cabinet Office), rather than facilitating a move towards a more centre-driven model. Memories of Balogh were no doubt still fresh, discouraging any endorsement of a larger influx of advisers into No. 10. Schreiber subsequently came to the view that Trend was correct. A body too closely linked to the premier, he suspects, would have been resented elsewhere in the government, limiting its effectiveness.[46] Nevertheless, although not an exclusively prime ministerial entity, the CPRS, which was supervised by the premier, ultimately became dependent upon him for its effectiveness. Had the model advocated by Schreiber won through, a team of special advisers, comparable to that established in 1974 under Wilson, would have been created.

Perhaps a high-ranking policy aide, personal to himself and overtly political, backed up by a full support staff, was what Heath needed. Hurd writes that 'a Prime Minister . . . needs more powerful help than I could provide in 1970–4 . . . Maybe Mr Wilson's innovation in 1974, when he installed Bernard Donoughue in Number Ten at the head of a policy unit, is the right answer.'[47] As the crises of his premiership intensified, it is notable that Heath grew increasingly reliant upon William Armstrong, to the point where the official was in some quarters referred to informally as the 'Deputy Prime Minister'. Armstrong became personally and publicly associated with the activities of Heath and his Conservative governments, such as the attempt to implement an incomes policy from 1972.[48] Such a tendency ran counter to Whitehall tradition, and was subject to criticism from Labour. Shortly after the fall of the Heath administration, Brian Sedgemore, a Labour MP and former civil servant, suggested that 'the use of the head of the home Civil Service as deputy Prime Minister . . . constitutes a serious constitutional impropriety, and is conduct which might threaten the integrity and impartiality of the Civil Service'.[49] Lord (Robert) Sheldon, who became the Labour Minister for the Civil Service in 1974, says that the association that developed between Armstrong and certain aspects of Heath's premiership was 'very bad, very bad'.[50] Armstrong's Whitehall career ended prematurely in 1974, shortly after a mental breakdown. Consequently, the question as to how, having become so embroiled in a Conservative government, he could have served its Labour successor, never had to be answered.[51]

The CPRS became popularly known as the 'Think Tank'. Its youthful, mixed-gender staff of around sixteen was composed of both outsiders and seconded career officials. The parallels with the continental *cabinet* were clear. In the words of Heath, the CPRS

had three main functions. The first was to keep under review the country's economic performance, and to tell ministers how well or badly the government was doing in terms of its objectives. The second was to undertake studies in depth of major long-term issues which transcended departmental boundaries. The third function was to provide collective briefs for the Cabinet, or sometimes personal briefs for the Prime Minister, on specific issues being submitted to Cabinet or Cabinet committees for ministerial approval.[52]

Its first head was Lord (Victor) Rothschild, 'research scientist, ex-MI5 bomb disposal expert during the Second World War, don and banker'.[53] In Rothschild's view, the role of the Think Tank was to provide 'advice independent of Government Departments . . . and of particular political beliefs'.[54] An extremely numerous and wide range of issues was covered.

Officially, the CPRS was a non-party-political body. In his memoir, Heath refers to those members drawn from beyond Whitehall as 'selected from the universities [and] business'.[55] However, during 1970–4 it contained certain staff who were Conservative in their loyalties. William Waldegrave, aged only twenty-five in 1971 'was an active and political Conservative, who had been working in the Conservative Research Department'. A Fellow of All Souls College, Oxford, Waldegrave functioned 'as Rothschild's trusted emissary and channel of communication with the wider world' and 'in particular as a link with the Conservative party organisation, including the Research Department, and with individual Conservative politicians'.[56] Waldegrave was involved in the drafting of CPRS reviews of government strategy, for presentation to gatherings of government ministers.[57] He subsequently became Heath's political secretary and, in the 1980s, a Conservative minister. Another CPRS partisan was Reading who, having served as an aide to Heath, joined in November 1971.[58] Reading maintained his personal link with Heath.

Individuals such as Waldegrave and Reading were not clear-cut special advisers during their spells at the CPRS, but the similarities were plain. Adam Ridley's case is an interesting one, which casts some light on the nature of the 1970–4 CPRS. A career civil servant, he was seconded from the Treasury to the CPRS. While his family background was as much Liberal as Conservative (his second cousin, Mathew Ridley, was an active Conservative member of the House of Lords, whose younger brother, Nicholas, became a Conservative minister; yet he was a great-grandson of Asquith), he developed personal contacts with some Conservatives during his spell in the CPRS. Following the fall of the Heath government, Ridley joined the CRD, eventually becoming a prominent special adviser to Conservative Chancellors of the Exchequer from 1979 to 1984.[59] More generally, the CPRS 'had fairly close contacts not only with Conservative Ministers but also political advisers, whether in departments (Mark Schreiber, John Cope) or in the research department'. Much of Schreiber's work was carried out on behalf of Rothschild.[60]

Permanent officials expressed unease regarding the possibility of the presence of a special adviser at a CPRS presentation to ministers held at Chequers in October 1971. In September, through Hurd, Schreiber sought to attend, in a non-speaking capacity. Robert Armstrong resisted, initially on the grounds that it was intended to be 'a meeting of the Cabinet, and I should have thought official attendance (beyond secretariat) should be confined to CPRS members, really'.[61] When Trend expressed his preference that the event should not be a formal Cabinet, different objections to Schreiber's presence were raised. Heath's principal private secretary informed him that Trend took the view that if Schreiber was invited, then there were 'a number of other people', for instance Howell, who might consequently feel unfairly excluded.[62] Ultimately, Heath decided that both Schreiber and Howell should attend.[63] Questions of propriety and ministerial sensibilities may have genuinely been a factor here. However, it is also possible that there was concern regarding the presence of a radical bureaucratic reformer at a high-powered government meeting over which, since the CPRS was setting the agenda, the regular machine had little control. Supported by the Prime Minister, Schreiber also went to subsequent similar events.[64]

Special advisers and policy

Upon his election, Heath appeared to be committed to free-market, 'small government' principles. A significant contribution to his programme was made by CRD staff, some of whom, such as Sewill, became special advisers from 1970. The 1970 Conservative manifesto, entitled *A Better Tomorrow*, set out objectives including 'greater freedom of choice [and] greater freedom from government regulation and interference'. It suggested that, under the Conservatives, 'the need to curb inflation will come first' and that 'unnecessary Government spending' would be eliminated. Also proposed were 'fair, up-to-date rules for industrial relations' and 'a climate for free enterprise to expand'.[65] In the words of Dell, the approach 'emphasised "disengagement" from government intervention in the economy'.[66] The inference could be drawn that the Conservative administration would not step in to support failing companies, was willing to let unemployment rise in order to control inflation and intended to reduce public expenditure. Positive regulation of industrial relations, it was believed, would remove the need for an incomes policy. There has been discussion among historians over whether Heath's apparent initial approach constituted a break with the supposed postwar political settlement.[67] Certainly Schreiber both believed that 'there was a consensus' and was motivated by a desire to overturn it.[68]

The extent to which Heath was ever personally committed to free-market principles has been questioned. Lord Marlesford (Schreiber), for one, doubts Heath's radicalism.[69] Sewill has sought to clarify the programme the Conservatives devised prior to June 1970. As Director of the CRD, he played an important part in opposition policy-making. For him, the Conservative intention in 1970 was 'no less than . . . to change the whole attitude of mind of the British people to create a more dynamic, thrusting, "go-getting" economy on the American or German model'. The three main elements, Sewill believed, were the attainment of EEC entry; the reduction, reform and simplification of taxation; and industrial relations changes designed to create stronger, more responsible trades unions. He has argued that one aspect of the Heath agenda was widely misunderstood. While 'the programme was one of economic liberalisation', in his view the ending of government intervention to support failing companies was not as central an objective as has often been thought.[70] Howell believes that Heath was genuine in his commitments.[71] It seems that the CRD acted as a force for moderation, resisting bold ideas, including the transfer of state-owned concerns into private ownership, that emanated from the Public Sector Research Unit.

Sewill has expressed certain reservations regarding Conservative policy under Heath. In his view, the need to defeat inflation was not given enough attention. He argues that much of the 1970 Conservative programme was fixed before the 1966 election; therefore, 'by 1968 and 1969, when I proposed that price stability should be made the main priority, the mould had set too hard for any fundamental change.'[72] Failure in this respect became a defining shortcoming of Heath's premiership. Whether the government as a whole was ever likely to hold its nerve when faced with a choice between high inflation and rising job losses is debatable. Reading subsequently referred to 'a strong aversion to controlling inflation by creating unemployment, which characterised all postwar economic policy until the generation change marked by Mrs Thatcher's arrival in Downing Street'.[73]

However, in the manifesto and elsewhere, Heath appeared to commit himself to stable prices. 'On the Sunday before polling,' Reading wrote in 1997, 'I drafted the most famous speech Heath never made. It promised to cut the increase in prices "at a stroke". Reading showed this to Heath the following Tuesday.[74] Heath claims he did not have time to check the text personally.[75] According to Reading, Heath said, 'I'm not saying that, but you can put it out as background briefing if it keeps you happy.' Reading did so, but 'forgot to tell Conservative Central Office to change the heading from "Speech by the Rt Hon Edward Heath" to background briefing'.[76] The phrase 'at a stroke' was later used by the opposition as a stick with which to beat Heath.[77]

Disengagement was abandoned by stages. Moreover, the approach that replaced it was unsuccessful. By November 1971, faced with rising unemployment, Heath decided to embark on a programme of large-scale investment in industry. In the March 1972 Budget the Chancellor, Anthony Barber, encouraged what became known as the 'Barber boom', revising growth targets upwards to 5 per cent per annum. While unemployment was successfully reduced, the balance of payments, which had moved into surplus since the 1967 devaluation, returned to deficit. Dell argues that the decision to reflate indicated complacency about inflation, which subsequently soared.[78] There were some mitigating circumstances. Reading has noted that the 'Barber boom, as we all know, presaged unprecedented inflation. But in fairness, Barber's boom coincided with the world oil and commodity price explosions of 1973–4, and the worst inflation occurred under the following Labour government'. Moreover, money 'stock growth rocketed to 30 per cent, but there were excuses. The financial system was being restructured'.[79]

The 1971 Industrial Relations Act, which contained provision for cooling-off periods and compulsory arbitration in trades disputes, failed in the face of the trades unions' refusal to participate. In early 1972 the National Union of Mineworkers defeated the government with strike action in support of a pay claim. Heath decided to resort to an incomes policy. Failing to secure agreement from union leaders for voluntary measures, on 6 November 1972 the Prime Minister announced a statutory standstill on wages and prices, to be followed by the phasing in of greater flexibility. Faced with another miners' strike, this time in support of a 35 per cent pay increase, Heath called a general election in February 1974 and was removed from office.

The fact that commitments made in opposition were discarded in power may be attributable in part to the declining influence of some of those who had helped devise them. Certainly, Lord Marlesford argues that, once the

Conservatives had taken office, the influence of Conservative staff who were appointed as special advisers was eclipsed by that of permanent officials. On the career Whitehall side, Lord (Robert) Armstrong shares this view.[80] Howell describes the bureaucratic blueprint he and Schreiber developed as intended to enable the Prime Minister to direct a reduction in the role of the state from the centre. The dilution and alteration of the Central Capability concept, he argues, was a setback for the free-market agenda, to which there was resistance from permanent Whitehall.[81] Special advisers cannot, therefore, be entirely blamed either for the failure to implement the initial programme or for the new course that was adopted in its place. However, certain aides, particularly Reading, came to advocate the pursuance of higher economic growth, which, as discussed, seems to have taken precedence over the control of inflation in the Heath administration's priorities. While they were not necessarily decisive influences, their voices were presumably heard. Moreover, the policy, once adopted, led on to further re-engagement, in particular the use of a statutory incomes policy.

Reading began to support expansion at least as early as July 1971.[82] In October 1971, writing in advance of the first CPRS review meeting at Chequers, he still appeared to support the disengagement agenda, for example, insisting on the value of a 'cut-back . . . in the share of resources going to the public sector'. However, he thought that Conservative prospects for re-election were poor, presumably because of the rise in unemployment, and that as a result Heath's programme might be defeated before it had had a chance to take effect.[83] To preserve the administration in office, Reading suggested, the government should consider being 'much bolder in its management of the economy'. Instead of pursuing its existing growth targets of 4¾ per cent for the following year and a little over 3 per cent for the one after that, it could 'go for 5 per cent a year for the next three years'. Contrary arguments, Reading stated, would be founded in the belief that the so-called 'Phillips Curve' relationship between demand and wage inflation had, since the 1960s, permanently broken down, and that higher growth would lead to severe inflationary and balance of payments difficulties. Reading emphasised that 'this is only an assumption' and proposed the alternative interpretation that 'the [Phillips Curve] breakdown . . . was caused by slow growth and the excessive re-allocation of resources away from the consumer'. If that were the case, the 'pace of inflation would be reduced rather than accelerated by faster growth', which would bring about 'steadily increasing competitiveness'.[84]

In recommending such a course, Reading saw himself as being in opposition to the view of the Treasury. Heath apparently agreed, writing that, regarding the prospect of a drive for growth, the Chancellor of the Exchequer, Tony Barber, was 'relatively cautious . . . I . . . had to overcome too great a degree of traditional Treasury caution on his part'.[85] However, Sewill suggests that he and Treasury officials shared the view that 'there seemed a real chance to get the economy on the path of sustained growth that had eluded Britain through so many stop-go cycles. The Treasury forecasts showed the possibility, without strain on the economy, of 5 per cent growth for some time, thereafter declining to a long-term rate of about 3½ per cent'.[86] Similar advice was proffered by Schreiber. Like Reading, he saw 'economic growth which is fast enough to allow market forces to continue' as a potential success.[87]

At the October 1971 Chequers policy review, the idea that there was 'spare capacity' in the economy was discussed. The theory was that the relatively high level of unemployment, which rose to 900,000 by the beginning of 1972,[88] combined with a balance of payments surplus, left space for reflation. Reading was not in attendance but subsequently registered his general agreement that 'the degree of spare capacity in the economy should not be under-estimated . . . this is probably a unique opportunity to secure a period of sustained and rapid growth for a period of years, such as we have not seen in this country since the war'.[89] Possible means of triggering it included fiscal measures and cuts in the bank rate.[90] He rejected the idea 'that faster growth is more likely to increase the level of inflationary pay settlements'.[91] There is a notable similarity in the words used by Reading and Heath in justifying the policy. In his memoir, Heath records informing representatives of the TUC at a meeting in March 1972 that 'We now had the best opportunity since 1945 of achieving' the government's objectives, which included 'sustained and steady economic expansion and falling unemployment'. By the time of his first 1972 Budget meeting with Barber on 10 January, Heath was 'already convinced of the case for a generous package'.[92] Perhaps Reading had helped persuade him.

By April 1972, following the Budget, Reading was arguing more enthusiastically than ever in favour of expansionary policy.

If you go faster in the short run you are more likely to be able to go faster in the long. If you go slow in the short run you risk being condemned to slow growth ever after. 'Stop-Go' implies what goes must stop. But it may well be that 'Go-Go' or 'Stop-Stop' are the real alternatives today . . . Rather than attempt to take up capacity carefully and approach full employment on a tangential course, it may be much better to go for explosive growth in the short run.[93]

In May he maintained that 'We must be prepared to push ahead with further reflation at any sign that demand is flagging.' If it should be deemed necessary, he supported 'an early, pre-emptive, exchange rate change'. He also believed that 'we must be prepared to help British industry against foreign competition.'[94] The statement could be taken as implying protection of some kind: certainly no part of a free-market agenda.

Despite Reading's hopes, inflation remained a problem. Given the commitment to growth, the most likely solution was a prices and incomes policy. Initially Reading was opposed to such an approach, which he identified as entailing 'compulsion' and 'a large army of civil servants authorised to enforce' controls on a permanent basis. Furthermore, 'we cannot control incomes and prices unless we are prepared to control the distribution of resources.' Ultimately, he argued, it meant 'the substitution of a state controlled economy for the market place and price mechanism . . . the suspension of the free enterprise system.'[95] On 5 October 1971 Reading sent Heath a paper rejecting the idea of a voluntary incomes policy as a workable solution to economic difficulties. As he put it, trades unions 'are hardly likely to agree with an unpopular Conservative Government except on terms which compromised the Government's policies'. Therefore, in Reading's view, if the course were to be pursued it could only be done by statutory means; but he did not support this either.[96]

Schreiber too, was similarly sceptical regarding the possibility of a deal with the unions. Nevertheless, he held that 'the prospect of a really tough statutory incomes policy – if it is publicly spelt out in detail – may force them to reach an accommodation as the lesser of two evils to their members.'[97] By early 1972 Reading, drawing attention to the perverse combination of large unemployment and a continued balance of payments surplus with high inflation, reluctantly stated that a 'permanent prices and incomes policy may, in the event, prove necessary'. He noted, however, that 'it is tantamount to a change in the nature of our economy' and it was possible that 'the cure would be worse than the disease'.[98]

Over the following months Reading became firmer in his views. In June 1972 he wrote to Rothschild stating that 'inflation is all done by mirrors' and had no

justification whatsoever in the real state of the economy. Unemployment is still staggeringly high by post-war standards; taxation is being reduced; there is still no overseas deficit as yet, and real incomes can rise rapidly . . . What we are suffering today is inflationary psychosis. Wages are rising rapidly because of fears for rapid price increases which themselves are produced by the wage increases.

In such a context, a 'freeze would operate by destroying the expectations of inflation which are the basic cause of our troubles'.[99] It is reasonable to suppose, therefore, that special advisers under Heath, particularly Reading, were influential upon the decision to pursue expansion and, subsequently, to use a statutory incomes policy.

While the supposed free-market agenda was not realised, Heath's major policy accomplishment should not be overlooked. The attainment of British membership of the European Economic Community, which was formally enacted on 1 January 1973, was an event of immense national historical significance with considerable international implications. British membership of the EEC was a source of great domestic controversy. In political terms, Sewill hoped that it 'might break up the class orientation of the two main political parties'.[100] While not elaborating, Sewill seems to have meant that a pro-EEC Conservative Party and anti-EEC Labour Party might emerge. Britain's entry into the Community suggested a tilt away not only from a global role but also from the 'special relationship' with the United States, and towards a regional, continental outlook.[101] At least one special adviser encouraged Heath in such a direction. In October 1971 Schreiber floated a particular interpretation of international affairs to the Prime Minister. 'Russia,' he wrote, 'has not changed her strategic objective of bringing the whole of Western Europe into her bloc.' While Soviet progress had been halted by the formation of NATO, the US was now 'withdrawing from Europe both physically and in heart' and was becoming increasingly less likely to be willing to defend the continent in either a conventional or a nuclear war. The Soviet Union, aware of this, might 'start probing'. A substitute for NATO could be 'an effective integrated EEC nuclear shield, for which Britain would be essential'.[102]

Aside from defence considerations, there was a monetary aspect to European integration. In August 1971 the US President, Richard Nixon, declared the dollar inconvertible into gold. Following a period of enforced floating, exchange rates were fixed again in December. In May 1972 Britain joined the 'German Snake' which had been formed the previous month: a system of currencies centring on the Deutschmark and floating within bands. After six weeks, speculation against sterling drove it out of the snake. The pound then floated, initially as a temporary measure, but continuing for more than a decade.[103]

There is evidence to suggest that Reading was an influence upon the decision to join the Snake. It seems that in May 1971 he warned Rothschild of the likelihood of a dollar crisis in the coming year. Shortly following the declaration of inconvertibility, in September 1971, Reading, returning from leave, 'had a long talk with the Prime Minister' who felt 'the need for a clear strategy at this time'.[104] Within two weeks Reading produced a follow-up paper. It argued that Bretton Woods in its existing form was dead, since the suspension of convertibility, rather than taking place within the 'existing international monetary system . . . undermined the system itself'. In its place, Reading supported 'the creation of a truly international reserve system which winds up the use of sterling and dollars in international trade'. He went on: 'It is sometimes argued that we need a new Keynes. We don't. What we need is acceptance of a solution along the lines of Keynes's original proposals.' In his wartime negotiations with the United States, Keynes had initially pressed for the formation of a world bank which could issue its own currency, thereby guaranteeing sufficient international liquidity. US resistance led to dilution of the proposal. Reading hoped that, within a new system of the type Keynes sought, the value of the pound could be fixed at an appropriate level, presumably lower than the one previously allotted to it.

Reading predicted that EEC member states were likely to establish a currency bloc, with fixed internal rates 'and a managed float . . . against other currencies, notably the dollar and the yen'. Britain should join this group before the trade war that might be looming. An important consideration, of course, would be the level at which the pound was admitted. Prior to membership, therefore, the opportunity for freedom of action afforded by the collapse of Bretton Woods should be exploited in order to pursue sterling depreciation. It would enable Britain to 'establish our own position' before entry into the European bloc.[105] Later on that same month, in a letter to Robert Armstrong, Reading reiterated his belief in the establishment of an international monetary system of the type initially proposed by Keynes, 'in which the principles of domestic banking are extended . . . into the international field'. Membership of a European bloc was a prerequisite for it. As he put it, if 'we can reach agreement with Europe, Europe might be able to do a deal with America. Such a deal would then, of necessity, become generally accepted as the basis of the new system'.[106]

Reading, then, favoured membership of what became the Snake, probably influencing Heath; and yet the Snake was a manifestation of the continental integration project, of which Reading subsequently became an opponent. In 1997 the Referendum Party, which supported a national plebiscite on withdrawal from the EU, contested seats across the country. Heath was 'astonished' to learn that the candidate in his seat, Old Bexley and Sidcup, was Reading. Reading wrote to him personally in December 1996 explaining that since the former Prime Minister was 'bound to be opposed by a Referendum Party candidate' it was better for it to be 'one who holds you in great respect'. Such flattery was lost on Heath.[107]

Heath's administration was criticised by the Conservative right for its failure to control the money supply. A study of special advisers indicates that, while they took an interest in this question, they did not afford it the absolute priority it was given by individuals within the Conservative government formed by Thatcher in 1979. Sewill stated in 1975 that at

> *the Treasury the orthodox view was that while the money supply had an important role, it was not the prime determinant of the rate of inflation . . . I did not dissent from that view . . . even if it is true that a flood of money leads to inflation, the converse does not follow . . . a drastic cut back in . . . money supply would not stop . . . inflation until it had first led to a reduction in economic activity and a rise in unemployment.*[108]

Reading attached an importance to this concern, but, like Sewill, did not regard it as of overriding significance. On 29 October 1970 he wrote to Heath, via Robert Armstrong, drawing attention to the fact that the money supply had increased 'by some £700 million to £800 million in the second quarter of 1970 . . . much larger than would have been consistent with the official policy commitment of the former Labour Government'. He offered two possible explanations: the Bank of

England had been either unable or unwilling to implement the objectives of ministers. Neither interpretation reflected well on it. If the former was the case, then the Bank 'would hardly warrant its respected status, its privileged immunity from interference, criticism and from the need to justify its policies'. Conversely, if 'the Bank could have stopped the growth in the money supply in the second quarter, but would not stop it, it is open to even more severe censure'. On such a basis, Reading argued, there was 'a very strong . . . case for calling the Bank to account for its actions in control of the money supply. The explosion in the second quarter was, after all, a major disaster in the fight against inflation'.[109]

Conscious of the fate of Wilson's administrative experiment, the DEA, in which he was a participant – a fate which he attributed to 'its inability to influence decisions of fiscal and monetary policy' – Reading cautioned that the CPRS 'will equally fail so far as economic policy is concerned unless it can bring monetary and fiscal decisions into the open'. He suggested that 'a useful early task of the Review Staff should be to prepare a report upon the institutional framework within which fiscal and monetary policy issues are decided here and abroad, and to recommend whether or not our system would benefit from a more open approach'.[110] Reading drew attention to the contradictions inherent in the dual government goals of monetary control and growth. The problem was that in 'the longer run . . . monetary policy works by reducing the level of real output, by bankruptcies and by putting up unemployment'. While not suggesting which of the two apparent incompatibles should be favoured, Reading argued that 'we need to make a conscious well-thought-out decision'. In the place of a decision, during the preceding year, he cautioned, 'the Bank and Treasury were allowed to decide monetary policy by default,' leading to an expansion. For the coming twelve months, 'policy . . . should be much more clearly and deliberately decided' following a report by the Bank to the Economic Strategy Committee of the Cabinet.[111]

In April 1972 Rothschild sought and obtained permission from the Prime Minister to draw on the advice of Professor Alan Walters, an LSE economist. A paper Walters had sent to Rothschild suggested that the expansion in the money supply, increased public expenditure (leading to swollen government borrowing) and reduced taxation 'will ensure that the future inflation of British prices will go on apace'. Walters rejected 'the Treasury's standard medicine' for unemployment, namely demand management, which he believed was having the effect internationally of exacerbating not only inflation, but also the joblessness it was designed to reduce.[112] While these strictures were not heeded at the time, Walters was later able to implement some of his ideas as an aide to Thatcher during her premiership.

* * *

Special advisers during 1970–4 did not have the personal status of some of the more prominent appointments of the 1960s. Nor were they as numerous as in later periods. Their potential impact was accordingly less. Moreover, they were part of an administration which, as a whole, was thwarted. All aides were Conservative apparatchiks prior to their appointment and some continued to be paid as such, therefore not quite fitting the category of special advisers. An important motive for their recruitment was the desire for the maintenance of links between party and government – a problematic role for career officials. However, the presence of politically active aides inside Whitehall also resulted in propriety difficulties. The more radical suggestions emanating from special advisers concerning Whitehall reform were not adopted. Although it did have a slightly partisan flavour, the CPRS was not as political or personal to the premier as Schreiber, for one, initially intended it to be. Indeed, the manner of William Armstrong's close association with Heath suggested a need for a committed, prime ministerial source of advice that the CPRS did not provide.

In policy terms, Conservative aides were probably more influential during the opposition period before 1970 than they were inside Whitehall after that date. However, Reading in particular may have influenced the upward revision of growth targets in 1972, prompted in part by the widely held belief that a high level of unemployment inevitably entailed electoral defeat. Adoption of an imposed prices and incomes freeze, although not relished by Schreiber or Reading, followed on from a commitment to expansion combined with the need to combat rising inflation. Encouragement for a European as opposed to US orientation was forthcoming from Schreiber. Reading sought membership of a European currency bloc as a means to a new world exchange rate settlement. While Reading and Sewill took an interest in monetary control as a means of economic management, only Walters regarded it as pre-eminent in importance.

Six

Expertise and politics: Labour in the 1970s

Labour governments under both Wilson, from 1974 to 1976, and Callaghan, from 1976 to 1979, made substantial use of special advisers. This chapter will consider the background to and motivations for Wilson's decision to recruit more aides in 1974, the numbers appointed, the associated costs and the regulations by which they were governed. It is during this period that, some might argue, a marked distinction emerged between those who might be described as political assistants and those who were experts. The representatives of the former group selected here include David Lipsey and Jack Straw, and of the latter Kaldor and Abel-Smith, old hands from the previous Labour term of office, as well as Anthony Lester, appointed by Roy Jenkins at the Home Office. Tony Benn's use of Francis Cripps and Frances Morrell as a team will be considered. Also discussed here is the role of the Policy Unit, a prime ministerial body made up of outsiders and led by a political appointment, set up by Wilson in 1974 and maintained by Callaghan.

'A formidable team of able men and women'

The breakthrough for the special adviser from 1974 onwards took place alongside a more general professionalisation of politics, creating a pool of individuals from which aides might be drawn. Over subsequent decades, increases in MPs' staff allowances, and the appearance of more independent think tanks and public affairs companies, led to a proliferation of career openings. Shortly before

Wilson returned to power, there was an expansion in the funds available to shadow ministers. In June 1971 the Joseph Rowntree Social Service Trust offered support to the three main parties (the Conservatives, in office, declined) which was eventually granted under the title of the Political Fellowship Scheme. Recruited by competitive open selection, the research assistants employed as a result became known as 'Chocolate Soldiers'.[1] In the words of Susan Crosland, most 'of the fortune made from Rowntree chocolate is used beneficially. During 1972, five "chocolate soldiers" were funded as assistants to Shadow Ministers'.[2] Labour chocolate soldiers followed their employers into office. Jenkins describes how, 'thanks to the Rowntree Trust's scheme for helping leading opposition politicians', he 'gained an outstanding assistant in Matthew Oakeshott, then a twenty-five-year-old Oxford graduate student and city councillor, who stayed with me until 1976 and remained a close friend and associate'.[3] After the February 1974 election Wilson began taking steps to transfer responsibility for the Rowntree provision to Parliament. On 20 March 1975 the Leader of the House of Commons, Edward Short, won Commons approval for a scheme of assistance for parliamentary parties, calculated on the basis of the number of seats won in the previous election and the votes cast for them in the one before that.[4]

Short Money, as it became known, was important to the development of the special adviser. It assisted the emergence of a political career structure and the assembly of entourages which politicians might wish, or feel obliged, to take with them into office. For Labour, which had no research group as substantial as the CRD, this funding was particularly valuable. It enabled support to be provided for individual shadow ministers, while stopping short of full state funding for political parties. Lord (Tom) McNally, who served James Callaghan both in opposition and during the Labour governments of 1974–9, suggests that this was the outcome of pragmatism on the part of Wilson. At the time, there was a cleavage between an increasingly radical Labour Party and a more moderate leadership. The state-funding model, if adopted, could be taken as implying that political advisers in both opposition and government would be party employees. Wilson, according to McNally, preferred the idea of aides who were appointed on a basis of ministerial patronage, thereby giving them and their employers greater independence from the party.[5] It seems that, in his premiership from 1974, Wilson was concerned to ensure that links between special advisers and the party were restricted. For example, in November 1975, in one account, he sent 'a minute to all Ministers with political advisers, banning them from attending a meeting' at Transport House.[6]

Wilson's expansion of the use of ministerial special advisers from 1974 and the creation of the Policy Unit were presented as an implementation of Fulton proposals which had not been adopted during 1968–70. This was certainly how Robert Sheldon, a member of the Fulton Committee and the Labour Minister for the Civil Service in 1974, saw them.[7] Wilson's measures were probably also a response to the Conservative use of aides whose roles were tilted towards party liaison, as well as the partisan aspect of the CPRS. Perhaps the retirement of Burke Trend in 1973 was significant in removing an important previous obstacle to such initiatives, especially at Downing Street. Members of Wilson's inner circle, not least Marcia Williams, seem to have urged an increased use of special advisers, as well as the introduction of a prime ministerial body. Writing in 1972, Williams asserted that

> the 1970s require a self-contained top grade personal advisory unit within No. 10. This is more necessary for a progressive government than a Conservative government since the Conservatives can rely on the Civil Service being tuned in to what they want to do. But the Labour government must have a small core of highly qualified, highly expert individuals to initiate policy and ideas which can filter down through the machine. This unit should also assess decisions coming up through the machine via the departments for the Prime Minister's approval. This is what a Labour government for the future must have and it should start planning such a unit now.

Furthermore, Williams argued that 'Labour should . . . start earmarking eager, enthusiastic, able young men and women to be trained in the work they must do when they accompany future Ministers into the departments.'[8] In a 1975 edition of the same book, she described how 'from 1970 to 1974 Labour carefully introduced into each Shadow Minister's office a political administrative assistant.' Some of them were funded by the Rowntree Trust, others were 'personally recruited. All trained for the day when Labour would return to power'. They became, in Williams's words, 'a formidable team of able men and women'.[9]

Wilson's decision to bring in more outsiders in 1974 was also influenced by his experience of Whitehall during his first premiership. When he set up the prime ministerial 'personal advisory unit' to which Williams referred, in the form of the Downing Street Policy Unit, Wilson appointed Bernard Donoughue as its head. In 2002 Donoughue told the Committee on Standards in Public Life that when 'Harold Wilson asked me to do the job and set up the policy unit, he said, "I will not always do what you suggest." He said, "I just want to have the choice of alternative options, particularly alternative options to the Treasury."' According to Donoughue, Wilson's 'experience in the 1960s was having only one option' – and that option, he went on, 'could be painful'.[10] Arguably, an example of Donoughue providing Wilson with a course other than that proposed by the Treasury, which the Prime Minister did take, can be found in the summer of 1975, when the government faced a sterling crisis. In some accounts, at this juncture the Policy Unit fortified Wilson against the Treasury suggestion that a statutory incomes scheme be introduced, arguing instead for a voluntary norm for increases of £6 per week.[11]

Beyond Wilson's immediate entourage, there was what Tony Benn referred to in 1973 as 'growing pressure in the Labour Party for political advisers for ministers'. They would enable government members to maintain contact 'both with their colleagues and the public'.[12] With Labour in office, calls came from within the party for an increase in the use of special advisers, partly on the grounds that career Whitehall was not tuned in to working-class, socialist objectives.[13]

Following his return to office, Wilson oversaw the appointment of special advisers to a number of departments across the government.[14] In the words of Jenkins, ministers 'were positively encouraged to bring in outside advisers'.[15] There were also significant developments at the governmental centre. Contrary to some expectations at the time, Wilson maintained the CPRS;[16] and he established in addition the Downing Street Policy Unit – again supposedly inspired by the Fulton Report – which employed 'seven to ten experts'.[17] Donoughue, a political scientist from the LSE, was the unit's head from 1974 to 1979. Callaghan was, in his own words, 'happy to inherit' the Policy Unit in 1976.[18]

The number of special advisers in employment during 1974–9 ranged from the mid-twenties to the low thirties, far higher than it had been previously. Covering around fifteen offices of government in 1974, the departmental spread was also more extensive than before. The expansion encouraged a higher level of collective and individual media interest in aides.[19] In March 1976, special advisers covered an age range from twenty-five to sixty-seven (for details see appendix). Individual salaries were not revealed, despite opposition demands that they should be. Remuneration was 'determined on a case by case basis and regard is inevitably given in each case to the level of previous salary.'[20] In July 1975 the annual salaries of full-time special advisers ranged from £3,200 to £14,000. In March 1976, there were sixteen aides receiving a higher annual salary than the £5,750 paid to MPs. By 22 March 1976 sixteen special advisers were receiving salaries of over £5,000 per annum, and eight part-time aides were being paid more than £3,000. A total of thirteen were covered by the principal Civil Service pension scheme. Kaldor was the highest paid, receiving £14,000 per annum in 1976.

To set these figures in context, in 1976 the maximum paid to a permanent secretary was £18,675; the Prime Minister earned £20,000 and other Cabinet ministers £13,000; a minister of state received £7,500 and a parliamentary under-secretary £5,500. The additional incomes of government members as MPs ranged from £3,000 to £4,012.

Presumably because of the larger scale of the 1974 innovation, the Prime Minister and the Head of the Home Civil Service, Douglas Allen, agreed a number of ground rules, with, according to Allen, Wilson making most of the suggestions. Appointments were subject to prime ministerial approval and normally no more than two were allowed per minister.[21] A prime ministerial minute to such an effect, it seems, was issued in July 1975.[22] According to Donoughue, 'Wilson introduced a limit of two because one of his Ministers then was threatening to introduce three or four and Wilson had doubts about their mental stability.'[23] When the government changed, special advisers were to leave. Contracts, although varying in length, were all short, meaning ministers, if so inclined, could remove their aides quickly. Crucially, special advisers had no formal power over permanent civil servants.[24] Nevertheless, there is evidence that management roles were assumed, albeit on an occasional, casual, basis. David Owen, Foreign Secretary from 1977 to 1979, informally established 'a separate policy unit working direct to myself'. The staff, composed of career officials, was supervised by Owen's 'special economic adviser' when carrying out 'any work involving economics'.[25]

Wilson initially contemplated continuing the ban on special advisers serving as local councillors. After all, criticism from him had helped prompt Heath to introduce the rule in the first place. However, eventually, in May 1974, a Cabinet decision was taken to the contrary.[26] There seems to have been an understanding, albeit perhaps a vague one, that there were limits to the embroilment in party political activities permissible to aides. In May 1978 Callaghan told Tony Benn, who was Secretary of State for Energy at the time, that 'he had heard rumours' that Benn's aide Frances Morrell 'was doing too much work for the Party'. The following year Callaghan sent Benn a note informing him that Morrell's involvement with *Labour Activist*, an organ of the Labour Coordinating Committee, a left Labour organisation, meant that she was 'in breach of her status as political adviser'.[27]

In December 1974 Wilson 'issued a memorandum of guidance to Ministers in charge of Departments about the terms and conditions of employment of special advisers'. Despite parliamentary pressure that it should be made publicly available, it was not, on the grounds that it had 'not been the practice' to do so. Special advisers, Parliament was informed in 1976, were expected to 'conduct themselves with a proper discretion and to behave with circumspection'.[28] In 1976 guidance on their roles was, for the first time, included in *Questions of Procedure for Ministers*, the then unpublished ministerial guidebook.[29]

The status of special advisers, the Commons was informed in 1977, was that of 'civil servants on limit [*sic*] period appointments'.[30] They were served with dismissal notices which came into effect at the end of an administration, even if they were immediately reappointed. This duly happened following Wilson's resignation in 1976, despite the fact that a general election was not triggered.[31] Donoughue describes how 'I received letters of dismissal in advance of the general elections of October 1974 and May 1979, and on 16 March when Harold Wilson announced his resignation.' After some difficulty, Donoughue managed to negotiate redundancy packages for special advisers. The precarious nature of existence as a temporary civil servant is illustrated by the fact that, following Labour's 1979 election defeat, Donoughue himself 'joined the ranks of the unemployed for five months'.[32]

As Labour approached its fifth year in office since Wilson's return to power in February 1974, a possible technical problem with the employment of special advisers came to light. Under the 1969 Civil Service Order in Council, the Civil Service Commissioners were required to certify the qualifications of all persons proposed for permanent employment. The commissioners worked on the basis that anything over five years constituted a 'permanent' appointment; thus any special advisers who had been present since the beginning of Wilson's first 1974 administration might, in theory, fall due for examination. However, following legal consultations by the commissioners, the decision was taken that 'the appointments of special advisers, limited to the life of the current Administration, are self-evidently not permanent, even if a series of such appointments extended beyond five years, and therefore do not require their certification.'[33]

The complication that had arisen revealed that the scope of the commissioners was probably not as great as some had previously believed it to be. Courts, it had transpired, might regard permanent employment as that which was intended to last until retirement, rather than the five-year definition used by the commissioners. In response, the Civil Service Order in Council 1978 was issued on 28 September 1978.[34] The requirement for approval by the Civil Service Commissioners was extended to take in temporary, in addition to permanent, appointments. While the term did not actually appear in it (or in subsequent ones), it seems that the 1978 Civil Service Order contained the first legal reference to the special adviser. It stated that an exemption from the need for scrutiny by the Commissioners applied in cases 'such that the period for which the situation is to be held thereunder by the person appointed terminates at the end of an Administration'. The Order related purely to the nature of the recruitment and retention of special advisers; not, as Richard Wilson has noted, 'what they could do.'[35] It was minimalist; merely an opt-out from general Civil Service regulations (it did not even state who appointed them or who they worked for).

An alternative had been considered. In 1978, the creation of 'a separate category of Crown servant' for special advisers was apparently countenanced (an idea advocated by Wicks a quarter of a century later). Indeed, under Wilson, in late 1974 a Cabinet committee had examined the same possibility.[36] Possibly, the government ultimately favoured a more ambiguous status for special advisers because that facilitated greater discretion in their deployment. The temptation, in the absence of an immediate and compelling reason to do otherwise, to leave arrangements roughly as they were, was perhaps another factor.

Security status was a subject of opposition interest. In May 1974 Douglas Hurd, by then a Conservative MP, enquired in the House as to whether the government could give 'an assurance covering No. 10 Downing Street, the

Foreign Office and the home Civil Service that in no case do political advisers have access to highly classified . . . information until the appropriate [vetting] procedures are satisfactorily completed'. Sheldon's response was, 'I assure the hon. Gentleman that the procedure which has prevailed in the past is being carried out now.'[37] Sheldon's successor as Minister for the Civil Service, Charles Morris, told the House in February 1976 that 'Special Advisers are subject to the Official Secrets Acts in the same way as are other civil servants.'[38]

At least one special adviser sought to protect her minister from the perceived threat posed by various security agencies. In October 1975 Morrell, who 'had been giving a great deal of attention to the question of agents, MI6 and CIA', came to see Benn and, in his account, told him that he was 'a prime target. There is a real chance you might be Leader of the Labour Party and they'll put their top people on to you.'[39] Increasingly, during his second premiership, Wilson developed the view that various sinister forces were acting to undermine or even topple him. Donoughue was one of a number of Wilson's associates at the time whose houses were burgled. Wilson told him that 'somewhere in South Africa House there must be a room full of grandfather clocks and television sets, including yours'. Aware of Wilson's conspiratorial disposition, Donoughue nevertheless states that he 'was . . . not entirely off the mark, since some South Africans were indeed working to destabilise leading Liberal opponents of apartheid in Britain'. Donoughue goes on:

> *it should never be forgotten that Wilson did have real enemies who were trying to damage him. Right-wing extremists were discussing the need to overthrow the Labour government . . . I never entirely dismissed the suggestion by an old friend of Wilson that my own room was . . . bugged. One day I passed the Head of MI5 in the corridor. I had never met him before, yet he said to me, 'Enjoy your football on Sunday?' I suddenly had a feeling of being watched and have never entirely dismissed Harold as being completely barmy on this subject. Not completely.*[40]

'The "Political Advisers" Experiment'

In May 1975 Wilson delivered a statement entitled 'The "Political Advisers" Experiment' to the Commonwealth Heads of Government Conference in Jamaica.[41] In it he treated the terms 'political adviser' and 'special adviser' as interchangeable. This was to remain the fullest official description of the special adviser in the public domain until 1997 and the publication of the Model Contract for special advisers, which itself drew heavily on Wilson's text. According to Wilson, before the event 'I was urged by other national leaders to make a statement . . . and the host chairman put it on the agenda.'[42] He writes that 'The "Political Advisers" Experiment' was 'prepared by the Cabinet Office at official level, and it warmly expressed on behalf of the Permanent Civil Service approval of the scheme as it was actually working.'[43] However, Donoughue's account suggests that he and McNally wrote the paper.[44]

First, Wilson attempted to explain why such aides were needed. One reason was 'the pressure of work on Ministers'. Increasing emergent difficulties, including 'the immense volume of papers, the exhausting succession of departmental committees, of Party gatherings and meetings with outside interests' meant that, for ministers, achieving detailed oversight of departmental business was difficult, and full engagement in collective Cabinet government even more so. This, then, was the 'overload' theory in all but name. Another motive for the use of special advisers was the nature of the career Civil Service, which 'takes a pride in its political impartiality'. Wilson referred to the existence of a view that 'the social and educational background of senior Civil Servants remains too narrow' and that senior career officials 'can become isolated from changes of mood and structure in our society'.

Heath's innovation, the CPRS, represented an attempt 'to meet these problems' and was of value. However, it was not officially a party political body. Therefore, 'when we came into office in March 1974 I authorised the appointment by Cabinet Ministers of Political Advisers.' Wilson acknowledged the fact that it was 'not . . . a wholly new concept' and that 'previous administrations had brought in advisers from outside, normally chosen from political sympathisers'. However, although even now the numbers were not huge and were spread thinly over a number of offices of government, the proliferation was 'of considerable significance and Political Advisers now play a definite role in our affairs'. Wilson argued, then, that quantitative increase had led to qualitative change, with special advisers constituting a discernible presence inside the administration.

As to the tasks of special advisers, Wilson noted that, owing to the personal nature of their appointments, they varied. He provided a list of possible activities. One was acting as a '"sieve" examining papers as they go to Ministers, drawing attention to problems and difficulties, especially ones having Party political implications'. Next was the 'deviller' function. As well as 'checking facts and research findings outside Whitehall', it could include 'spotting obstacles and ensuring that particularly sensitive political points are dealt with in an appropriately sensitive way' and 'chasing up ministerial wishes'. This suggested that advisers might wield a degree of executive authority. In his 2002 appearance before the Committee on Standards in Public Life, perhaps with this in mind, Richard Wilson referred to the 1975 speech, noting that Harold Wilson 'talked about special advisers chasing up Ministerial wishes, ensuring – note that word – that particularly sensitive political points are dealt with in an appropriately sensitive way. I am not sure that is advice'.[45]

There was also medium- and long-term planning, involving the preparation of 'think pieces', for which the aides had more time than ministers, who were often preoccupied with political, parliamentary and constituency work. Such documents could 'generate long-term policy thinking within the Department'. Again, the job description seemed to extend beyond the mere supply of counsel, as was the case with the fourth activity Harold Wilson suggested: that of participating in 'policy planning within the departments'. Special advisers could take part in departmental committees examining medium- and long-term problems and thereby 'contribute ideas at this early planning stage'. The ideas they brought to such processes might well originate 'from outside the Government machine, and perhaps [run] contrary to long-established departmental views'. By such means, the aide was extending 'the range of options available to a Minister'. There was also liaison with the party, particularly its research department, and outside interest groups, as well as engagement in speech-writing and research work.

Of the functions Wilson listed, he suggested that those which were actually performed partly depended upon the background of the individual concerned. Some were '"ideas men" or academics: others are former Party officials with specialist knowledge of their areas: and others are recent graduates and young Party activists'. Ministers determined which papers their special advisers saw, although they were not normally 'of a high security classification'. Advisers attended departmental, but not interdepartmental, official committees.

In summarising, Wilson described the special adviser as 'an extra pair of hands, ears and eyes and a mind more politically committed and politically aware than would be available to a Minister from the political neutrals in the established Civil Service'. This was particularly important for a 'radical reforming party in government', which was always threatened by Whitehall-induced inertia. There were, Wilson conceded, some problems, although they were not immense. They involved difficulties with relationships, both between special advisers and civil servants, and, more delicately, between aides and 'other ministers'. Wilson also suggested that there had been unauthorised disclosures of information to the press by special advisers, but attributed them to a lack of experience regarding the reticence required when dealing with the media. He noted that the experiment taking place was being carried out in a 'typically British way . . . [working] out the problems as we go along'. While the relatively small number of special advisers did not, and was not intended to, 'overturn our powerful government machine', they could 'make a distinctive contribution'. Senior career officials had welcomed the innovation, and were co-operating to ensure its success.

The speech was probably the most important official pronouncement that has been made concerning the special adviser. Detailed studies of individual aides set out below will demonstrate that while it accurately described many of their activities, it did not tell the whole story. The pursuance of the interests of individual ministers, possibly at the expense of others, was too controversial to be included in the statement, but undoubtedly took place. So too did participation in party factions. Except with his reference to speech-writing, Wilson also failed to mention involvement in presentation, which had been a concern of special advisers from the outset in 1964. Nicholas Jones notes that Roy Hattersley, who was appointed Secretary of State for Prices and Consumer Protection in 1976, recognising the need for assistance in handling the media, employed the services of David Hill, who had joined him as an assistant in the Commons in 1972.[46]

Wilson's audience in Jamaica seems to have been intrigued. He writes that the 'statement I made and circulated caused a great deal of interest, and a number of prime ministers on their way home through London visited the Cabinet Office for talks with the secretariat and with members of the Policy Unit'.[47] Elsewhere in the Commonwealth a similar experiment was taking place. After twenty-three years in opposition, the Australian Labor Party (ALP) took office in 1972. Its leader, Gough Whitlam, was of the view that 'a change from long established positions of administration' was required. He sought to enlarge the limited responsibilities of Australian national government, and felt that in order to achieve the objective, aides recruited on a basis of personal patronage were required. At a press conference in December 1972 Whitlam 'explained the Government's intention to expand the system of ministerial staff'. In his words at the time, there was an intention 'to de-politicise the Public Service so that persons who are responsible for carrying out political decisions will be known to be appointed by a Minister at his whim and disposable at his whim. The Public Service, of course, will be less political if there are such personal advisers known to be appointed'.[48]

It could be argued, then, that there was an international tendency for parties of the left to appoint politically sympathetic outsiders to official posts. A long period out of government could act as a further stimulus to do so when returning to power. Such was certainly the case with Labour in 1964, although not in 1974, and would be again in 1997, as it was for the ALP in 1972. In France the first change in governing party for twenty-three years took place in 1981. The incoming Socialist President, François Mitterrand, appointed an increased number of aides from outside the state service, including personal acquaintances and party loyalists. Ministerial *cabinets* expanded, recruited to a considerable extent from the ranks of assistants who had been made available to members of parliament and senators.[49]

Political and expert advisers

George Bishop, writing in the *New Statesman* in May 1974, described how, alongside academics such as the educational economist Maurice Peston, 'some ministers have gone a step further and brought in purely political assistants . . . young people with no administrative experience or academic expertise.'[50] From 1974 onwards an internal differentiation seems to have been made between political and expert advisers which was to remain in place until May 1997. According to Castle, to avoid controversy, Wilson initially toyed with the idea of having 'the political chaps paid for from outside'.[51] Christopher Foster, who worked at Transport from 1966 to 1969, returned to Whitehall to counsel Crosland and then Shore at Environment. He found that the definition of his role as an 'expert' in the 1970s restricted his activities, compared with the wider brief he had enjoyed in the 1960s. The imposition of the differentiation, he argues, was the result of pressure from officials seeking to confine the activities of special advisers to specific spheres. 'They wanted to know which side of the door you were on,' he says.[52] Specialists were probably in the majority. Of thirty-four special advisers appointed during 1974 whose previous occupations can be identified, probably nineteen were drawn from academia, five of them recently connected to the LSE. Other backgrounds included Transport House, Rowntree-funded research assistance to opposition politicians, and work for bodies such as trades unions and the Race Relations Board.

Clear distinctions were difficult to draw. Individuals such as Abel-Smith were experts, but experts committed to the party of government. As Lord Sheldon puts it, 'you want an expert, but not one who disagrees with you.'[53] Stuart Holland, who reappeared as an aide at Overseas Development in 1974, was an economist who also pursued a political career, serving as an MP from 1979 to 1989. Equally, some political aides had a degree of experience in particular subject fields. Callaghan's special adviser at the Foreign Office from 1974 to 1976, Tom McNally, was previously the secretary of Labour's International Department. As such, he spent a considerable amount of time engaged in policy areas relevant to his work at the Foreign Office.[54] Moreover, a crude division into two groups did not take into account the fact that special advisers each performed distinctive roles, determined by their own qualities, their minister and the office of government in which they were employed. To give an example, David Stephen, whom Owen describes as 'my political adviser . . . involved in all aspects of my activity', at times took on the role of emissary for the Foreign Secretary, embarking on various missions abroad.[55] Nevertheless, the dual classification is useful as a tool of analysis. Although it had precedents, notably John Allen in 1964–5, the political aide was the more novel of the two types of appointment. Detailed studies of political counsellors cast more light on the nature of these positions and how they worked in practice.

David Lipsey provides an example of an assistant to a shadow Cabinet member who accompanied his employer into office as a special adviser. He was born in 1941 and went to Oxford, taking a first in PPE. Funded by Rowntree money, he joined Tony Crosland in 1972 and a strong bond built up between them. As Susan Crosland puts it, '"D. Lip marvellous" Tony said after only a few weeks. "How did I do without him before?"'[56] He is referred to affectionately throughout her book as 'D. Lip'. Lipsey worked for Crosland during the latter's tenure as Secretary of State for the Environment from 1974 to 1976, and then as

Foreign Secretary, a post he held until his early death in 1977. His successor as Foreign Secretary, David Owen, describes how Lipsey 'had been Tony's devoted political adviser and was utterly demoralised by his death'. Owen asked Lipsey to stay on 'as a form of therapy, in the full knowledge that for his own development he needed to move on, which he did, going to work at [the] No. 10 [Policy Unit]'.[57] Lipsey remained at No. 10 until Labour's defeat in 1979, after which he entered journalism. In 2001 Lipsey became the chairman of National Power.

In the context of how he should be categorised, Lipsey has said that, when he arrived in his post, 'I had been doing housing policy in Opposition for two years, which was longer I think than the Deputy Secretary responsible for housing policy, so I was somewhere between being an expert adviser and a pure political adviser.' On the other hand, when he moved to the Foreign Office in 1976, 'I had to get a map put up on the wall pretty sharply, I did not have a deep knowledge of those issues.'[58] At No. 10 he took on a political role, including participating in the drafting of Labour's 1979 manifesto but also monitoring environment policy.[59]

Lipsey has emphasised that 'I think it is important to realise just how *ad hoc* the creation of this whole system was.' Upon Lipsey's arrival at the Department of the Environment in 1974, the 'Permanent Secretary thought he was supposed to stick me in the Departmental Policy Unit which was a civil service thing, and he had not realised that the Minister required a different function of me'. Despite the initial uncertainty, relations built up between Lipsey and Environment officials were harmonious. He 'had the very closest possible working relationship with the civil servants there . . . there was a differentiation between our roles but also, we had ways of rubbing on from day to day'.[60] Indeed, when Lipsey left Environment in 1976, he received a 'panicky call' from the department's permanent secretary, Ian Bancroft. Bancroft was concerned that Peter Shore, Crosland's successor, 'has come here today and he says he does not need a special adviser'. On the grounds that 'we cannot work without a special adviser', the permanent secretary asked Lipsey if he could 'come over and persuade him [Shore] he needs one'.[61]

In addition to the types of work outlined by Wilson in 1975, at which he proved effective, Lipsey assisted Crosland in conflicts between Cabinet ministers. During 1976 Crosland was engaged in what Giles Radice describes as 'a long drawn out struggle' with Denis Healey, the Chancellor, over the spending cuts which Healey sought to impose – and eventually did impose – in the midst of a sterling crisis.[62] This is probably why, in a letter to Crosland that year, Lipsey described himself as not 'wholly inactive!' in advising 'on economic strategy'.[63] Briefing journalists was an element in his work on behalf of Crosland. Around a quarter of a century later Lipsey told the Committee on Standards in Public Life that, on occasion, Crosland

> *wished it to be known . . . that he did not wholly share the views of [Healey] that his top priority of life was to reduce taxation but felt instead that public expenditure should be kept at sustainable but appropriate levels, and he wanted this to appear in newspapers. Well, you could obviously not make a public speech in those terms. So, it might have been given to me to understand that I was to put this in the public domain in the appropriate manner and I would have known how to do that.*[64]

Lipsey took an interest in the furtherance of Crosland's personal ambitions. In a December 1976 submission to his minister Lipsey referred to 'the possibility that you might become Chancellor' – a post Crosland had long coveted.[65] More generally, Crosland was bidding to maximise his importance within the Labour Party. Possibilities had opened up since Jenkins's announcement in mid-1976 of his intended imminent departure to become President of the European Commission from the beginning of 1977, thus vacating the leadership of the Labour right. Lipsey's advice to Crosland was predicated on the assumption that 'your main need is to capture the Jenkinsites'.[66]

To such an end, he helped Crosland cultivate and organise his supporters. In July 1976 Lipsey organised a meeting for Crosland and eleven of his followers within the parliamentary Labour Party (PLP). Lipsey drew up an agenda which included discussion of whether Crosland should stand for the National Executive Committee (NEC) of the Labour Party and the position to be taken in a possible deputy leadership contest. Concerning the latter, Lipsey suggested in his summary of the meeting that Shirley Williams, a rising star on the right, might run and do well, or even win, and implied that Crosland's ambitions might extend even further than the Treasury. Referring to the option of backing a Williams candidacy, he stated that 'Shirley is only 46; therefore if there is another leadership election within 5 years or so it is by no means certain she will feel that she needs to run, and her support could be valuable.'[67] Such activities were not unique to Lipsey and were a clear characteristic of special advisers. For example, McNally was part of the 'small inner team' which Callaghan formed for the purpose of contesting the 1976 Labour leadership contest.[68]

Another political aide was Jack Straw, who served the 1974–6 Secretary of State for Social Services, Barbara Castle. When Callaghan removed Castle from the Cabinet in 1976, Shore, on Lipsey's recommendation, took Straw on at Environment, where he stayed until 1977. Castle records that, in 1974, 'when Harold told us we could appoint a political adviser I was at a loss.' Her husband, Ted, an alderman of Islington Council, recommended Straw, a qualified lawyer and an Islington councillor. Born in 1946, Straw had been a radical student politician.[69] In 2003 much publicity followed the release of Foreign Office files relating to his participation in a student delegation to Chile in 1966. There was a suggestion that he deliberately disrupted the group in order to expose the existing National Union of Students (NUS) executive as poorly organised. Three years later, he became the NUS president. Straw has denied that, while in Chile, he met with Salvador Allende, the Marxist presidential candidate in the 1964 Chilean election, who came to power three years later and died in a CIA-sponsored coup in 1973.[70] In a diary entry for 24 June 1973, Benn, having been at a dinner with him, described Straw as 'a young lawyer on the make who has come up through the National Union of Students'. Castle helped launch Straw on an impressive trajectory:[71] replacing his first ministerial employer as MP for Blackburn in 1979, he eventually became Home Secretary in the 1997–2001 Blair administration, and was appointed Foreign Secretary following the general election of June 2001.

In a private meeting with Castle, William Armstrong, still (just) in post as Head of the Home Civil Service, 'raised no objections at all to my recruiting Jack Straw – even talking in terms of £8,000 a year'. This may have come as something of a surprise. Whitehall was more familiar with temporary academic experts than political aides, tending, in Castle's account, towards suspicion of the latter. Castle notes that

Jack [Straw] did more than any other political adviser to get the civil service to come to terms with this new type of animal. The idea of bringing party activists into the inner citadel of ministerial power was totally alien . . . Civil servants

got used to the fact that Jack, having signed the Official Secrets Act, was entitled to see all the documents which came to me and to give me a political, as against a civil service, briefing on them.[72]

Wilson's decision to permit aides to serve as councillors resulted from Straw's position in Islington, which forced the issue at Cabinet level. Wilson, who had criticised similar practices under Heath, was reluctant to reverse the current ruling, but eventually gave way to Castle. Straw developed a bond with Castle's principal private secretary, Norman Warner, and in 1997 recruited the former career official as his special adviser at the Home Office.[73]

Straw's work for Castle included taking minutes of DHSS ministerial meetings, which, on his suggestion, were sent to the private office. When Wilson proposed raising Ted Castle to the peerage, Straw successfully conducted discreet negotiations with the Privy Council, in order that Barbara could avoid adopting the title of Lady. In July 1974 elements of the press began showing interest in Castle's supposed use of private health-care facilities during the 1960s, and Straw was one of those engaged in the consequent crisis management, helping to draft statements and collect information. In the same year he helped Castle devise a policy proposal for 'maximum incomes', which would entail 100 per cent taxation on pay increases above a certain level. He wrote speeches for Castle to deliver at public occasions; he produced briefs for her for Cabinet meetings. Castle viewed her special adviser as 'an invaluable help to me'.[74]

Castle also obtained assistance from Straw in her opposition to the EEC. Europe was a particularly divisive Cabinet issue. When a referendum was held on continued British membership in 1975, Wilson, who supported a 'yes' vote, partially suspended collective Cabinet responsibility for the duration of the campaign. The leading figures in the so-called 'Dissenting Ministers' group, against the EEC, were John Silkin, Shore, Balogh (by then Minister of Energy), Judith Hart and Benn.[75] Straw, along with Frances Morrell and Tony Banks, who were special advisers to, respectively, Benn and Hart, formed what Castle described as 'The Dissenting Ministers' Secretariat'.[76]

The Dissenting Ministers was not a smoothly running operation, divided as it was by personality clashes and disagreements over approach. At a meeting of the group on 1 May Benn proposed a statement, written by Morrell, to be issued collectively. In her diary Castle described it as 'a rather generalised mish-mash of assertions which were exaggerated'. However, despondent regarding what she saw as the disorganisation of the Dissenting Ministers, she was willing to go along with it. Shore, however, 'entered into a niggling argument about phraseology and we had to leave it to poor Jack, Frances and Tony Banks to sort it out with him'. By 15 May, Straw, Morrell and Banks were, according to Castle, 'furious at the way in which they are being played about with. Decisions are reached on press conferences and statements, on which they work all Friday, only to have some Ministers throw them over'. The following day, Straw informed Castle that Morrell had communicated to him Benn's desire not to issue a particular release on which the Dissenting Ministers had been working. Prompted by this, Castle noted that she was 'sick of Wedgie [Benn] monopolising everything'.[77]

As well as Straw, Castle also employed specialist aides. Referring to her expert counsellors, Castle that 'No one could have described them as party hacks, for they lived in the academic's perfectionist world'. Labour fought the February 1974 election on the basis of the 'Social Contract', which entailed 'practical action by the Government to create a much fairer distribution of the national wealth' in return for voluntary pay restraint by the trades unions. Castle saw herself as 'one of the main custodians of the government's side of the Social Contract'. The fact that she was allowed as many as five special advisers indicates the importance attached to her task. Castle recruited Brian Abel-Smith. As well as providing expertise, he acted as Castle's 'conscience', continually 'reminding me of Labour's first principles'. Castle addressed herself to the modernisation of social security, taking into account trends of the post-Beveridge era, including rising numbers of single-parent families. She was determined to implement the National Superannuation pension policy which Abel-Smith had worked on with Crossman during 1968–70, but in a simplified form, since she felt the complexities of the Crossman proposal had been its undoing. It was introduced in 1978 in the form of the State Earnings Related Pensions Scheme (SERPS).[78]

Other experts with previous experience of the role came back. Kaldor (recently raised to the peerage), in policy terms the most significant special adviser of all during the first experiment, returned to the Treasury, officially from 1 January 1975. His brief extended beyond taxation, to which he had been, theoretically, confined during the 1960s. He insisted on a room in the Treasury building from the outset; and his starting salary of £11,000 was 'nearly double the minimum professorial salary at the time'. While he 'sat on all the Treasury

Committees that he wanted, including the Fiscal Policy Committee consisting of all Heads of Departments', and attended the important meetings at which the Chancellor of the Exchequer was present, Kaldor's actual influence on Healey was, according to Thirlwall, 'minimal'. In Thirlwall's account, Healey proved to be an orthodox Chancellor, favouring the advice of the Bank of England and the more conventional economists within the Treasury.[79] Dell, however, who was Paymaster General at the time, argues that Kaldor became 'a dominating influence within the Treasury'.[80]

Britain's economic problems, relating to inflation, the balance of payments deficit and the public sector borrowing requirement (PSBR), were immense. As during the 1960s, when, with selective employment tax, he had sought to accelerate the relatively slow British growth through the practical application of an economic theory, so Kaldor now sought to develop measures founded in the analysis of the so-called 'new Cambridge school'. This group coalesced around ideas propounded by Kaldor during the 1960s, which attracted a number of converts at the university from 1970.[81] In April 1974 *The Economist*, noting that Kaldor, 'who always does advise British Labour governments', had returned to Whitehall, suggested that 'it is a bit disturbing that the new [Cambridge] school has acquired considerable influence over the Labour Government's policy'.[82] The ideas of the new Cambridge school rested on the view that there was symmetry between the PSBR and the balance of payments deficit. In fact, the equivalency was probably an historical coincidence. Moreover, which side represented cause and which effect was unclear. Kaldor himself later came to doubt the theory.[83] He lobbied for, but did not achieve, 'a strong deflationary package which would cut the PSBR, with an import surcharge/export subsidy scheme'. The latter was intended to mitigate the rise in unemployment entailed by the former.[84]

Kaldor had a close professional and personal relationship with the Permanent Secretary to the Treasury, Douglas Wass. However, some of his interactions were not as happy. Referring to Kaldor's temperament during his second spell as a special adviser, Healey notes that the 'role of the outside expert in Whitehall is a difficult one; if he cannot get on with the civil service he can do more harm than good. Either he will isolate his Minister from what should be his main source of advice, or he will kick his heels with frustration and become a source of continual friction'. In Healey's account, animosity between Kaldor and Kenneth Berrill forced the departure of the latter from his post as Chief Economic Adviser to the Treasury in 1974, to be appointed as head of the CPRS in place of the outgoing Victor Rothschild. As Healey puts it, 'Odium academicum is quite as virulent a disease as odium theologicum; political rivalries pale in comparison.' Berrill disputes this, explaining that he was performing a personal favour for a family friend by relieving Rothschild, who was suffering from poor health. Ultimately, Kaldor's incessant lobbying for his particular objectives alienated him from his own minister, as it had done with Jenkins in the 1960s. Healey acknowledges the economist's intellectual brilliance but doubts his political judgement. He complains of how Kaldor 'would nag me persistently about' the need to introduce import controls to the extent that 'in the end I did not discourage him from going back to academic life'.[85]

Not all experts were economists. During 1965–7 Jenkins was a liberalising Home Secretary, securing parliamentary time for private members' bills decriminalising homosexuality and abortion. His aide, John Harris, helped conduct a complicated lobbying campaign to ensure there was sufficient support for the measures in the free votes that were held. In 1974 Jenkins returned to the Home Office and Harris was raised to the peerage, working in the Lords as a junior minister to Jenkins, who therefore needed a replacement adviser. In May 1974 he appointed Anthony Lester, 'a thirty-seven-year-old junior barrister who was a prominent Fabian and had been a dedicated Gaitskellite'. Lester went on to become an eminent human rights lawyer. A major contribution made by Lester while working for Jenkins was to write, 'almost single-handed', a White Paper on sex discrimination. He required strong backing from Jenkins, who detected 'more departmental opposition at upper-middle level than I had ever previously encountered'.[86] It passed into law in the form of the 1975 Sex Discrimination Act.

Different types of aides could be deployed as teams. Francis Cripps and Frances Morrell, special advisers to Tony Benn, the Secretary of State for Industry from 1974–5 and then Energy from 1975–9, jointly represented the cause of a minister who seems to have been at loggerheads with both certain Cabinet colleagues and career civil servants. Cripps fitted into the category of an expert, while Morrell was a political aide. Benn regarded them as a 'marvellous combination'. In March 1974 he remarked that it 'is a tremendous help to have Frances, who is in touch with the political network through Number 10 and Transport House; as well as Francis Cripps with his access to outside economists'. Cripps and Morrell were both appointed special advisers early in March 1974, with salaries of 'about £4,000 a year', sharing 'a big office on the same floor as' Benn. Together with Benn, who had become the champion of the Labour left, they started as they meant to go on, concerning themselves with means of expanding the economic role of the state. Discussion at their first meeting centred on 'how we would use public ownership in the first instance as an ambulance for failed firms' such as British Leyland. In July 1974 Cripps and Morrell presented their analysis of economic options to a meeting of a number of special advisers from the departments and No. 10, making, in their view at the time, a great impression.[87]

Morrell was born in 1937 and worked as a secondary school teacher from 1960 to 1969 and then as a press officer for the Fabian Society and the NUS. Among other duties, she assisted Benn with the drafting of press releases and speeches, and discussed presentational strategy with him. In February 1977, as part of her 'veto-lifting campaign' against what Benn and some of his entourage perceived as a bar on his expressing his views in public, which entailed 'getting me to talk to people in the media', Benn recorded meeting Alastair Burnet of ITN.[88] She was willing to offer him particularly frank comments, including a warning in March 1974 that the high public profile he was attaining 'had gone to my [Benn's] head and [that] I had damaged my chances of being taken seriously as a political figure'. Benn valued such a quality in his counsellor. In May 1975, having received further critical guidance from her, he noted that Morrell's 'advice is always good'.[89]

It seems there was a degree of tension between her and the permanent machine. In November 1974 she became involved in a dispute with career officials, who were opposed to her attendance at the Labour Party conference. She told Benn that she was 'fed up with the way the civil servants were trying to clamp down on the advisers'. Morrell informed Benn in May 1974 that 'she was convinced that the Department of Industry was sabotaging my [Benn's] industrial proposals'. Benn shared her view; he did not trust the career Civil Service. Returning to his office at the Department of Energy from a Cabinet meeting in March 1976, Benn found that Morrell had left a piece of paper out on her desk listing six topics. They included 'Tony's problem of credibility with the Left of the Party' and 'How to organise the campaign against Treasury strategy'. Benn 'covered the list up', leaving a note reading, 'Is it wise to leave these open on the desk?'[90] Morrell may have been regarded by the Permanent Secretary at Energy,

Sir Jack Rampton, as wont to leak information to journalists. It was an accusation she denied.[91]

Cripps, a Cambridge economist who served under Kaldor in the Treasury in the 1960s, concentrated on detailed policy proposals. After the 1970 election Cripps counselled senior Labour figures including Jenkins, Healey and Dick Taverne. He was brought to Benn's attention by Kaldor in late 1973, as 'a bright chap . . . in Cambridge'. By such advocacy, Kaldor placed a fellow devotee of the new Cambridge school in a position of influence. As well as assisting him with departmental work at Industry and then Energy, Cripps enabled Benn to participate in, and contribute to, broader Cabinet-level deliberation. When, during 1976, Healey sought to introduce public expenditure cuts, Cripps provided Benn with different options, involving proposals such as import controls and freezes on sterling balances. As a result, according to Benn, Healey became 'obsessed with Francis Cripps'.[92]

During the campaign leading to the European referendum of 1975, Morrell was 'thinking seriously about who is going to lead the Party in future'. She recommended that Benn try to ensure that he did not conduct himself in such a way that 'when people look back on this period' he could be seen as having 'rocked the boat'. In March 1976, following Wilson's decision to retire, both Cripps and Morrell were cautious over whether Benn should stand for the Labour leadership. Benn recorded that 'Frances had her doubts. "You might be badly defeated and humiliated," and Francis (who takes his lead from Frances) then added, "Yes, it might damage the policy if you didn't get any support."' When Benn decided to enter the contest anyway, Morrell and Cripps helped draft his initial public statement. Callaghan's victory saw Wilson replaced by an older man, leaving the succession a live question. On 7 April 1976 Benn had 'a long talk to Francis Cripps' on the possibility of his being a future Labour leader and his approach to the premiership. Benn's conclusion was that 'the time for all this is the Eighties. It is not now'.[93] By March 1977 Morrell had apparently decided that 'the only thing worth [Benn] doing was to become Leader of the Party'. In June 1978 Cripps and Morrell were present at a lunch of a small group of allies, of which Benn wrote, 'To be perfectly candid it was a leadership planning meeting'.[94]

The activities of Straw, Morrell, Cripps and Lipsey suggest an involvement of special advisers in Labour factions, coalescing around personalities and ideological approaches, arguably superseding party loyalty. These alignments continued into opposition. In May 1980 Morrell informed Benn of the activities of the Rank and File Mobilising Committee, a body with which she was involved that had been formed to co-ordinate various left-wing Labour groups, officially to campaign on a platform of greater democracy within the party. Benn described its leading figures as 'the people who . . . when the time comes . . . will be the people who organise the Benn election campaign'.[95]

Prompted by the ascendancy of the left within Labour, in 1981 the Social Democratic Party (SDP), a breakaway group composed of exasperated members of the Labour right, was formed by the 'Gang of Four': the former Labour Cabinet ministers, Jenkins, Owen, William Rodgers and Shirley Williams. A number of former Labour special advisers became involved in the new party. At an early, pre-split, Gang of Four meeting in January 1981, Owen records that Jenkins, Rodgers and Williams were all accompanied by their political aides from their periods in office, respectively Matthew Oakeshott, Roger Liddle and John Lyttle. Owen writes, 'My own political adviser was David Stephen, but he was still in the Labour Party, and I was not putting any pressure on him to leave.' Stephen subsequently joined the SDP. In addition, McNally, Callaghan's 'political adviser . . . became a Labour MP and then joined the SDP and became for a time close to' Owen.[96] Derek Scott, aide to Healey, was another defector. In his autobiography, Jenkins lists some of his SDP allies in his support for a merger with the Liberal Party after the 1987 election. Included were three of his former special advisers (John Harris, Anthony Lester, Oakeshott) and Liddle.[97] The SDP drew in special advisers, and although it turned out to be only a temporary home, proved also to be a fertile ground for aides of the future. A number of former members of the party would, in the 1990s, become special advisers to both Conservative and Labour governments.

The Policy Unit

In his 1975 speech to the Commonwealth heads of government Wilson described the purpose of the Policy Unit as, in part, to incorporate expertise into government and extend the range of policy options available, particularly to the Prime Minister. It was also established, 'and its members were selected, to provide a team with strong political commitment to advise on, propose and pursue policies to further the Government's political goals'. The justification, captured in a memorable phrase, was that 'policies without politics are of no more use than politics without policies.' Callaghan saw the Policy Unit's function as being to 'clear away the fog' and help 'me in my efforts to stand back and view developments as a whole'.[98]

According to Wilson, the Policy Unit was a team 'which I have deliberately kept small . . . made up of people with expert knowledge of the fields of economic, industrial and social policy'.[99] Employment within it was arduous. 'As a single adviser covered one departmental policy area, the workload on individuals was enormous,' states Donoughue.[100] In his words, the Policy Unit staff were largely 'policy analysts with a political dimension . . . experts in their field who came in from a situation of prestige and established expertise, and afterwards they went back to that'. As he put it, given 'the fact that I only had three weeks to recruit them, they were not a bad little bunch basically . . . they were people you would take seriously'.[101] One who served inside the Policy Unit as a prelude to a glittering career beyond party politics was Gavyn Davies, a Balliol economist recruited in 1974, who in 1999 became chairman of the Investment Research Department at Goldman Sachs and in 2001 chairman of the BBC Board of Governors. Other members included Andrew Graham, effectively Donoughue's deputy until his departure in 1976. Graham's experience both under and as successor to Balogh was valuable to Donoughue in his dealings with permanent Whitehall. While Donoughue often handled politicians and senior civil servants in No. 10 and the Cabinet Office, Graham maintained contact with top officials in the economics departments and the Bank of England. David Piachaud, from the LSE, was responsible for social policy.[102] Kay Carmichael, from Glasgow University, covered Scottish devolution.[103]

Donoughue was determined not to repeat the experience of earlier aides such as Balogh, who 'had tried fighting the machine on every front and were inevitably defeated. Unless I overcame the innate hostility of the bureaucracy to outsiders, then I would suffer the same fate and the Unit would fail'.[104] At the time of the Unit's launch, therefore, Donoughue engaged in 'prolonged and strenuous talks' with the Cabinet Secretary, Sir John Hunt, regarding its role within Whitehall. Hunt was greatly concerned that the position of the Prime Minister's private office as the formal channel for communication between No. 10 and ministers be maintained. Donoughue sought to ensure 'access to the decision-making process based on the jungle of committees'.[105] As Donoughue told the

Committee on Standards in Public Life in 2002, 'Sir John Hunt and I sat down for at least two weeks to draw up what we called a "concordat" and that effectively defined the boundaries.' While access to papers and committees was important, it did not have to be total. Donoughue thought that it was desirable to avoid 'people just going and sitting in committees for the sake of entertainment, or if they think they might pick up a bit of gossip'.[106]

The agreement eventually struck permitted the Policy Unit to make contact with permanent civil servants in order to ascertain departmental views. Moreover, full support from the Cabinet Office, CPRS and Central Statistical Office was stipulated for Donoughue and his staff. Hunt's 'personal channels of communication to the Prime Minister' were safeguarded. Policy Unit staff, while not being members of official committees, would generally be allowed to attend those they chose to and to be included in the circulation for relevant papers.[107] It was also agreed that 'the individual views of officials expressed in committees should never be conveyed back to the . . . Prime Minister'.[108] Such privileges were more extensive than those afforded to departmental special advisers.[109]

The first Policy Unit offices were located inside No. 10, near the famous dividing door that gives on to the Cabinet Office.[110] During 1974–9 the Unit scrutinised policies emerging from the departments from a political point of view, as well as in the context of overall government co-ordination and strategy.[111] Wilson described its members as advising him directly, both on immediate decisions to be made in Cabinet and elsewhere and on longer-term issues.[112] Individual members of the Policy Unit were given particular areas to cover. This specialisation differed from the approach taken under Balogh in the 1960s, each member of whose small group had to deal with multiple aspects of government business. Nigel Wicks, a Prime Minister's private secretary at the time, has remarked that 'everything [the Policy Unit] put into the Prime Minister was on green notepaper'. This meant that 'You could distinguish it from the official advice and the Prime Minister always used to know where to look, because he just looked for the green notepaper, even if it was tucked right at the end of the sheaf of paper.' The method, according to Donoughue, was the result of Wilson's instruction that 'I want to be able to find it.'[113] Under Wilson, Pimlott argues, the Policy Unit's influence was extensive, particularly on 'health, social administration and economic and financial policy'.[114] While its input into foreign affairs was perhaps more limited, it counselled the Prime Minister on the renegotiation of terms of membership of the EEC during 1974–5.[115]

The Policy Unit played a role in Cabinet disputes during 1974–9. As Secretary of State for Industry from 1974 to 1975, Benn attempted to bring about greater state influence over investment and industry through the creation of a National Enterprise Board and the introduction of planning agreements. Wilson described the draft White Paper on the subject which emerged from the Department of Industry as 'a sloppy and half-baked document, polemical, indeed menacing, in tone'.[116] The Policy Unit was charged with rewriting it, diluting the interventionist content.[117] Wilson was thereby able to assert commitment to the mixed economy, as opposed to the increasing state expansion envisaged by Benn and others on the left.[118] In Benn's account a covert propaganda campaign was mounted against him as well: he referred in a 1975 diary entry to 'all the briefing Bernard Donoughue has done against me and the Department of Industry in the press'.[119] Kenneth Morgan notes that Callaghan used the Policy Unit 'with particular effect during the IMF crisis in November–December 1976 when it supplied much material designed to isolate Tony Benn and explode the credibility of his "alternative economic strategy"'.[120] This episode marked the culmination of the sterling crisis of that year, when £3.5 billion of cuts to the PSBR over two years up to 1979 was eventually agreed to by Cabinet, in return for support from the IMF.[121] Within the Policy Unit, Richard Graham, from British Airways, was employed to keep tabs on Benn while he was at Industry; Jim Corr, from the World Bank, took on the job while Benn was the Secretary of State for Energy.[122]

The creation of the Policy Unit could be regarded as a stage in the development of prime ministerial, as opposed to Cabinet, government. In terms of numbers of aides, the balance favoured the premier. As has been noted, departmental ministers were generally limited to two special advisers each, while the Prime Minister had a staff of up to ten at his disposal (and all appointments across government were subject to approval from Downing Street.)[123] Qualitative change was coupled with quantitative. Callaghan writes that, thanks to the assistance of the Policy Unit, 'I was in a stronger position to challenge Departmental proposals – especially those from the Treasury, which usually fired the heaviest guns.'[124] According to Donoughue, the 'most important contribution of the Policy Unit to central government was that it increased the Prime Minister's capacity for effective intervention in other Ministers' policy areas', especially in respect of matters involving economics.[125] Examples of aides participating in such an exercise of power on the part of the Prime Minister include the establishment of Callaghan's economic 'Seminar' and his public call for the initiation of a national debate on education, both discussed below. The Policy Unit may have, to some extent, facilitated bilateral, as opposed to collective, government. Donoughue briefed Callaghan before the Prime Minister's regular informal 'chats' with individual departmental ministers.[126] In a diary entry from January 1976 Benn noted that the 'PM now has at his disposal his Private Office, the Cabinet Office, the Think Tank and Bernard Donoughue's own policy unit, and in this way power is moving further towards the centre. It is evident that Dick Crossman's theory of prime ministerial government is turning out to be correct.'[127] Benn's remark suggests that significant structural developments, possibly even entailing the establishment of an informal prime ministerial department, were in hand.

However, neither premier during 1974–9 completely dominated his Cabinet colleagues. Especially under Wilson, these were an extremely experienced, powerful collection of ministers from across the leftward half of the political spectrum. Other circumstances rendering command-style leadership unlikely included party divisions and a precarious parliamentary position. Personal style was important. Although determined to control Benn, Wilson was generally more relaxed than during his first premiership. Callaghan was in many (though not all) cases, notably collegiate. He did not feel he needed intermediaries when dealing with ministers. According to Lipsey,

> James Callaghan was . . . a Prime Minister who worked through [secretaries of state] . . . He felt himself to be Chairman of the Committee as head of Government; that was his style of doing things, and the policy unit was very cautious about venturing outside the walls of Number 10 and having direct contact with officials, even the Special Advisers, because that might be seen to prejudice the direct relationship that the Prime Minister liked to have with his [secretaries of state].[128]

In fact, the function of the Policy Unit was often to assist the Prime Minister in working through Cabinet, rather than bypassing it. While special advisers bolstered the premier's position, decision-making nevertheless frequently took place within the context of that collective institution. Indeed, it could be argued that the cumulative effect of the expansion in special advisers during 1974–9 was to enhance Cabinet government. The IMF crisis provides a good example of how this could work. According to Donoughue, the

> *introduction in 1974 of special advisers working to most Cabinet Ministers was another factor which improved the quality of Cabinet debate at that time. It meant that, ideally, Ministers received high-level briefing on fields of policy outside those for which they were departmentally responsible. This was especially important during the IMF crisis, when it was striking how wide a range of Ministers contributed to the discussions ... the minority of Ministers who were often silent ... had in general chosen not to employ special advisers. Indeed, the regular civil servants in the Private Office often mentioned to me that the introduction of a system of special advisers had altered the way in which Cabinet worked by producing much wider debate.*[129]

Owen notes that his special adviser, the economist Michael Stewart, a veteran of Balogh's team in the 1960s, enabled him to feel 'more confident participating in domestic Cabinet economic discussions and in the mysteries of international economics'.[130]

Wilson stated in 1975 that members of the Policy Unit collaborated closely with 'the network of Special Advisers serving other Ministers'.[131] Speaking to the Expenditure Committee after his departure from the premiership, he referred to the Policy Unit as '*doyen* – or perhaps, convenors is a better word – for those [special advisers] in the individual departments'.[132] However, the extent to which special advisers constituted a collective group, with the Policy Unit as their centre of gravity, should not be exaggerated. Donoughue rejected a proposal made in April 1974 that he should be appointed the formal 'head of all the special advisers in Whitehall' on the grounds that 'it would give me responsibility for people over whom I had no control.'[133] Moreover, Lord (David) Lipsey told the Public Administration Select Committee in 2000 that there 'were hopes that ... the special advisers would get together and stop all these departments fighting each other and get them to pull together for a common strategy. Within a few weeks of getting in all the special advisers mimicked their ministers and became the spokesmen for their own departments.'[134]

Bernard Donoughue

Donoughue was born in Northamptonshire in 1934. He went on to become, in the words of Hennessy, 'the first senior policy adviser in No. 10 who could be described as a professional political scientist since Professor W. G. S. Adams headed Lloyd George's Prime Minister's Secretariat'.[135] His father, a factory worker, possessed 'strong left-wing political prejudices'. 'I do not believe,' writes Donoughue, 'that any such hardworking and decent man in such a prosperous country as Britain should have had to endure such a harsh life. My politics, and my determination to improve my lot, were formed by watching him.' Donoughue's surprisingly frank autobiography portrays a family background which might now be termed dysfunctional. Against the odds he obtained a scholarship to Oxford, studying history at Lincoln College. A PhD on the British approach to the American War of Independence followed. In late 1959 he embarked on a career as a journalist, serving an apprenticeship at *The Economist*. In 1963 he secured a lectureship in the LSE Government Department, and, as a member of the Standing Committee of the Court of Governors, he was involved in handling the LSE student riots of 1967–8.[136]

Donoughue's political alignment placed him 'on Labour's radical right wing'. Opposed to the left's 'extreme statist policies', he was associated with the Gaitskellite group, the Campaign for Democratic Socialism, from its inception in 1960. Donoughue first met Wilson in 1971, when interviewing him for a biography of Herbert Morrison, co-authored with George Jones. At the time, Wilson struck Donoughue as 'a very small man with little to say of political interest about his former cabinet colleague'. Two years later Wilson and Donoughue met again, at a City lunch arranged by the businessman Harry Kissin, who had known Wilson for many years. Given his Gaitskellite sympathies, of which Wilson was aware, Donoughue was an unlikely member of the Labour leader's entourage, but in the autumn of 1973 he was asked to join a group supervising opinion polling for the Leader of the Opposition; and he was a member of the inner team during the campaign for the February 1974 election.[137]

Upon meeting Donoughue, Castle noted that he was 'a pleasant – almost ingratiating – chap . . . In himself Bernard is clearly no tiger'.[138] Given his achievement in establishing an effective prime ministerial advisory body, accepted within Whitehall, where similar previous attempts had failed, there was perhaps more to him than Castle saw. Marcia Williams, a rival within the Wilson court, describes Donoughue as both 'complex and contradictory, combining . . . the hard hitting and the charming'.[139] Owen writes that Donoughue 'was a sensitive operator who paced round the Whitehall jungle like a political leopard. He coupled highly manipulative skills with a good academic mind'.[140] Benn's judgements of Donoughue were mixed. In November 1975 he recorded the view that the prime ministerial aide was 'power mad' and intent upon establishing 'a dominant position for himself in Whitehall'.[141] Yet Benn later remarked of Donoughue that he 'is most courteous and respectful'.[142]

The relationship between the Policy Unit head and permanent Whitehall seems to have been uneasy, but not explosive, as Balogh's had been. According to Marcia Williams – not a noted admirer of the career Civil Service herself – initially Donoughue 'had a hawkish approach to the official staff' in Downing Street and 'felt that any who were obviously obstructive should be got rid of with scant ceremony'.[143] He came to an understanding with Hunt, whom he portrays as formidable.[144] However, there was tension between Donoughue and elements within the Treasury, who probably intrigued against him, alleging that he was the source of economic policy leaks.[145]

In 1974 Donoughue was installed in a room inside No. 10 which had previously been occupied by George Wigg.[146] His title was Senior Policy Adviser and his starting salary around £9,000. Donoughue records that he went to Cabinet 'often'; he seems to have been the first special adviser to do so. Sometimes he sent Andrew Graham in his stead.[147] According to Pimlott, Donoughue initially 'asked if he could see every brief coming to the premier. Wilson refused; and defence, foreign affairs and intelligence were largely excluded from the Unit's sphere.'[148] Donoughue was privy to information which many junior Cabinet members were not, for example the formation in 1975 of a ministerial Cabinet committee (MISC 91) on pay policy. The personal proximity to Wilson that Donoughue achieved is suggested by his advance knowledge of the Prime Minister's intention to retire in 1976.[149] Within Wilson's entourage Donoughue formed an alliance with Joe Haines, the Prime Minister's press secretary.

Haines was not formally a special adviser, but fused the roles of political and official spokesman which had existed separately in the previous Wilson administrations. Haines and Donoughue were often at loggerheads with Williams.[150] Harry Kissin, the businessman and associate of Wilson who had first manoeuvred Donoughue into Wilson's entourage, hoped that his protégé would be 'a counter to, and possibly a replacement for, Marcia Williams, whose influence he had often observed and disliked'. For her part, Williams's initial support for Donoughue may have been founded in the hope that he would supplant Haines.[151]

The fact that Donoughue survived the 1976 changeover in prime ministers is indicative of political adeptness on his part. It seems that, during the 1976 Labour leadership contest, some within the Callaghan camp gained the impression that Donoughue favoured their cause.[152] With Callaghan as Prime Minister, Donoughue found life 'more regular, less Byzantine than under Wilson'.[153] From late 1976 Donoughue and the Policy Unit were involved in the formation of Callaghan's inner economic group, a secret mixed committee called 'The Seminar', which Donoughue attended.[154] Callaghan describes his Senior Policy Adviser as possessing a 'keen political insight'.[155] The quality might have gained Labour another term of office. Over the Christmas of 1977, in his account, Donoughue produced a paper recommending that Callaghan opt for a general election the following November. Had Callaghan heeded the advice, he would have gone to the country before the so-called 'Winter of Discontent' of 1978–9, when the government's attempt to impose a 5 per cent limit on pay rises caused large-scale industrial unrest.[156]

From his perspective at the centre of government, Donoughue took an interest in the substantial policy questions of the day. Associated with economic malaise of the 1970s was an erosion of the intellectual credibility of Keynesianism and a growth in support for monetarism, a creed dictating that inflation could be controlled only by restriction of the money supply. Although not fully accepting monetarist doctrine, Donoughue believed that 'a lax monetary stance probably resulted ultimately in higher inflation'. He endeavoured to ensure that Wilson was kept abreast of the theoretical developments, but the Prime Minister, despite his own knowledge of economics, showed little interest. However, with his first speech to the Labour conference as leader in 1976, Callaghan questioned the idea, widely accepted within Labour and elsewhere, that demand management, that is the use of deficit spending and tax cuts, was a means of ensuring high levels of employment in the long term. That part of the text was drafted by Callaghan's son-in-law, Peter Jay, not a special adviser, but was along the same lines as Donoughue's thinking.[157]

As his attitude towards Keynesianism suggests, Donoughue was to some extent thinking beyond many existing Labour attitudes. He notes that, as 'the son of a factory worker from the poorest working class, listening to the aristocratic fantasies of Tony Benn or the middle-class fantasies of Mrs Frances Morrell or Mr Francis Cripps was always entertaining, but it had nothing to do with the realities of industrial life'.[158] Dell draws attention to his advocacy of a scheme which would have 'gone some way to satisfying' the desire of many council tenants to own their own homes.[159] On 16 April 1976 Donoughue produced a memorandum for the incoming Prime Minister entitled 'Themes and Initiatives'. It outlined a number of areas in which he felt new measures were required, including home ownership for council tenants, school curricula and voluntary social service. Morgan suggests that in 'some ways, the Policy Unit under Bernard Donoughue anticipated the keynotes of Tony Blair's "New Labour" philosophy of communal citizenship in the mid-1990s'.[160] Donoughue sought to ensure that increases in expenditure on the NHS would lead to improvements for patients, rather than being absorbed in pay rises. In this, he found himself opposed to labour movement vested interests.[161] Much of the key speech made by Callaghan at Ruskin College, Oxford, on 16 October 1976 was written by Donoughue. Urging the initiation of a 'great debate' on the future of education in Britain, it was of historical importance in placing the issue at the centre of the policy agenda, where it remained.[162] Objectives Donoughue shared with Callaghan in the education field included 'greater monitoring and accountability of teachers ... [and] greater concentration on the basic skills of literacy and numeracy'.[163]

Donoughue had admirers outside the Labour Party. Alfred Sherman, a co-founder of the independent free-market think tank, the Centre for Policy Studies, had worked alongside Donoughue on the newly launched *Sunday Telegraph* in the early 1960s.[164] Sherman subsequently wrote that, during his time at No. 10, Donoughue was 'quick on his feet and possessed all the qualities needed by a successful courtier'. Shortly before she took office in 1979, Sherman urged Thatcher, over whom he had some influence, to maintain the Policy Unit.[165] Donoughue's legacy was preserved, lasting until 2001, when the Policy Unit and private office were merged into the Policy Directorate.

Criticism and verdict

Special advisers were a subject of considerable public controversy during 1974–9. In some quarters it was asserted that they were prone to the improper disclosure of confidential information. In 1975 Donoughue entered into a legal dispute with *Private Eye* over its allegation that he 'had leaked government secrets to the *Sunday Times* and also that I was giving to the City advice on how to evade taxation'. Eventually, in 1976, the publication settled, giving Donoughue 'substantial damages and costs'.[166] In June 1976, in an unrelated case, an item appeared in the *Sunday Times* to the effect that the government wanted to minimise the cost of implementing index-linked pensions for civil servants. In the House, Ian Gow, a Conservative, asked Charles Morris, Minister for the Civil Service, 'whether he is satisfied that none of the leaks . . . came from . . . special advisers'.[167] The implication seemed to be that aides were deliberately briefing the press in order to signal certain viewpoints, or perhaps simply that they were being unintentionally indiscreet.

In Parliament, the opposition made much of the expanded use of temporary civil servants. Ian Sproat MP stated on 29 March 1976 that it was 'totally repugnant that special advisers on political matters should be paid out of taxpayers' money'.[168] Gow in particular conducted a concerted parliamentary campaign. Morris was eventually driven beyond breaking point. In response to yet another question from Gow in June 1976, he pointed out that the

> *hon. Gentleman has tabled over 30 Questions on special advisers in recent months. In addition, he has asked a host of supplementary questions, and on 23rd March we had an adjournment debate initiated by the same hon. Gentleman in respect of special advisers. With the greatest of respect, I appeal to the hon. Gentleman, without infringing any of his parliamentary rights and responsibilities, to bring this squalid campaign against special advisers to an end so that they can get on with the job and make the contribution that the Fulton Committee recognised that they can do.*[169]

There were objections to the use of aides from the government side of the House, too. A number of Labour backbenchers came to resent their party's leadership for what was they saw as an insufficiently radical approach. Moreover, they felt that their own views were being overlooked. Special advisers were perceived not as a means of the administration maintaining contact with the party – one of their supposed functions – but, on the contrary, as part of the problem. During a parliamentary debate on the subject in early 1976, Eric Heffer stated that 'the best advice [ministers] could get would be from Back Benchers on the Government side of the House, and . . . it would be a good idea if we were listened to a little more.'[170] As Marcus Lipton MP put it in late 1977, 'many hon. Members are willing, at no extra expense, to give ample advice to Ministers at any hour of the day or night . . . Why do we have all these extra Special Advisers, who could easily be replaced by Members of this House?'[171]

Political aides in particular were regarded with some suspicion. George Bishop's 1974 *New Statesman* article referred to a 'lack of clarity about what these assistants are supposed to be for'. Their 'fairly hefty salaries' were 'often far above that of' an MP. Most did not 'disguise their ambitions and see their jobs as training for future ministerial careers'. Moreover, some gave 'the impression that they were little more than glorified press officers'. Bishop added that the use of special advisers could 'revive the 18th century spoils system, with the formation of personal coteries', and that certain 'assistants are already mixed up in right and left-wing plotting'. Bishop also regarded the classification of political assistants as civil servants as absurd, since their overtly party political role could not be reconciled with Whitehall traditions of neutrality.[172]

However, as well as criticism, there was encouragement for the use of special advisers. In 1977, in a comprehensive review of the Civil Service, the House of Commons Expenditure Committee remarked that the practice of recruiting special advisers was 'becoming more commonplace and, after some initial resistance to it, is now accepted by the civil service'. It concluded that 'the installation of special advisers should become an accepted feature of administration'. Such a development was necessary since it was the only means by which ministers could 'maintain a level of political control' over a Civil Service which was growing in size. Moreover, the general limit of two per department should be raised. The Expenditure Committee went so far as to suggest that 'Ministers may wish to employ the "Cabinet" system which operates in France.' However, it was stated that special advisers should not be empowered with 'executive authority' and that the permanent secretary should retain control of the department. Nevertheless, there was 'no reason why a Minister's Private Office should not be expanded to include his special advisers, his Press officer and any other persons he considers essential to his day-to-day deliberations'.[173]

The Expenditure Committee took oral evidence from, among others, Hunt, Heath and Wilson. Hunt stated that 'I personally believe in the system of political advisers, and I think that on the whole it has worked well.' Perhaps indirectly suggesting that there were initial tensions which had subsided to some extent, he referred to 'a sea change of attitudes since political advisers first started coming in'. Heath, while valuing the contribution of special advisers, said that 'they ought not to take part in politics outside'. He was probably recalling the fact that, following Labour objections, he forbade aides in his administration from holding local political office. Wilson accurately prophesied that the use of special advisers 'would continue under future Governments' of different political complexions.[174]

Despite the complaints of backbenchers, there was support across the Labour spectrum for the use, even the extended use, of special advisers. Benn's assessment of their value was generally positive. In 1977 he discussed aides with Donoughue. Although expressing concern that 'there was a danger of creating Watergate-type conspirators' and believing that 'we should use MPs more for advice', Benn 'agreed we should certainly build them up'.[175] In a 1981 book, written before the formation of the SDP, Owen described how he had convened the five Foreign Office ministers, two parliamentary private secretaries and two special advisers 'once a week over lunch to discuss issues ... in a party political context'. While believing that the 'introduction of specialist political advisers is a valuable innovation', Owen wanted to go further, advocating 'the more systematic development in Britain of the Continental *cabinet* system'.[176]

Following Labour's 1979 election defeat, the Fabian Society established a study group composed of ministers and special advisers from the 1974–9 administrations, as well as former civil servants, MPs and academics, to discuss the approach a future Labour government should take towards Whitehall. The resulting report, entitled *Making Government Work*, edited by Lipsey, appeared in April 1982. One of its recommendations was for an increased number of political and expert special advisers, to be 'integrated closely into the minister's private office machine where they would be best placed to achieve a strategic position in progress chasing, as heads of *ad hoc* task forces, in generating new policy thinking and generally, in enhancing effective ministerial control'. At No. 10, 'a single institution incorporating a strengthened Policy Unit and Political Office, and undertaking the analytic work at present done for the Prime Minister by the CPRS' was called for. It would provide the Prime Minister with 'strategic political advice' and maintain close contact with 'the party and the public'. It 'would be staffed on the whole by political appointees' who would advise the premier on policy, help 'him write strategic Cabinet papers' and brief 'him' for meetings with the PLP, NEC and TUC.[177] There would be a long wait, however, before Labour had an opportunity to implement such ideas.

* * *

From 1974, for the first time, special advisers constituted a substantial presence across most departments of government. Wilson's role as a constitutional innovator is underlined by the development. The growth in numbers was associated with the increasing professionalisation of politics then under way. Among the motives for the use of aides were the desire to ensure the implementation of party political objectives and the maintenance of contact between the government and the wider party membership. There was also the need, as Wilson's speech suggested, to cope with the problem of ministerial overload. It is likely that, in addition, Wilson wanted to achieve independence from an increasingly radical party, through the use of aides dependent upon ministerial patronage. Regulations, such as they were, were not placed in the public domain. The Policy Unit was larger and more influential, and achieved greater acceptance within Whitehall, than Balogh's staff in the 1960s: a tribute to the achievements of Donoughue and his team. It bolstered the power of the Prime Minister within Cabinet and increased the possibility of prime ministerial interventions and bilateral negotiations with ministers. Neither Wilson nor Callaghan, during this period, sought or were able to maintain a command premiership. Distinctions between experts and political aides existed, but were not absolute. Wilson's 1975 statement referred to functions which appeared to exceed the simple provision of counsel, entailing the exercise of surrogate ministerial authority. Some roles which were being performed, such as press briefing, figured nowhere in his review.

Some of the activities of special advisers reflected and possibly encouraged severe Cabinet divisions. Disagreements were associated with ideological alignment, as the battles between Benn and his aides on the one hand, and the Prime Minister and the Policy Unit on the other, demonstrated. However, personal ambitions were also at stake. Aside from Benn's aspirations, Crosland's interest in the succession, abetted by Lipsey, pitted him against supposed allies on the Labour right. Lipsey was probably not alone in his willingness to brief journalists discreetly in order to signal divergence between ministers. There was some friction between aides and civil servants, and plenty of critical comment in Parliament. However, more sober judgements tended towards the conclusion that the use of special advisers had much to commend it, and should possibly be extended. The authors of *Making Government Work* shared such a view.

Seven

'One of my people':
Thatcher and the heroic mould

This chapter depicts developments during the 1979–90 Conservative administrations of Margaret Thatcher, who used special advisers personally to notable effect. One important area of activity, under Geoffrey Howe, Nigel Lawson and then John Major, was the Treasury. The general role of the Policy Unit in these years is also discussed. In addition, since it was a period in which individual aides in the heroic mould made considerable qualitative impact, there are extended biographical profiles of John Hoskyns, Thatcher's first Senior Policy Adviser, and Alan Walters, her economic counsellor. Both men contributed to the 'Westwell Report' of 1982, a document previously neglected in studies of the Thatcher era. The role played by temporary civil servants in manifesto development is described, and parliamentary criticism of and support for the use of special advisers is examined.

Numbers and regulations

Initially, in quantitative terms, Thatcher and her ministers did not use special advisers as extensively as their Labour predecessors had during 1974–9. The reduction in numbers fitted with the new premier's ideological commitment to smaller, more efficient government.[1] She seems to have been particularly dubious regarding the appointment of aides beyond No. 10. According to Lord (Robert) Armstrong, the Cabinet Secretary from 1979 to 1988, Thatcher 'allowed her departmental colleagues to have their special advisers, if they must; but she took the view that a departmental Minister who had two or three junior Ministers did not really need a special adviser as well to keep him up to date with what politicians were thinking'.[2] By 18 May 1979 six special advisers were officially listed. One of these, Henry James, the No. 10 press secretary, was a career official. Why he was classified otherwise is unclear. The remainder were John Hoskyns, Thatcher's Senior Policy Adviser and head of the Policy Unit; Adam Ridley and Peter Cropper at the Treasury; Robert Shepherd at Employment; and Michael Portillo at Energy.[3]

While Thatcher had doubts about special advisers, she was herself 'in many ways an anti-Establishment "outsider"'.[4] She seems to have been slightly suspicious of career Whitehall, or at least elements within it, and may have doubted whether it was suited to implementing her programme. In her own words, 'as I quickly learnt, some senior civil servants would need more than a conscientious reading of our manifesto and a few speeches truly to grasp the changes we firmly intended to make.'[5] Permanent officials who were deemed ideologically unsound, such as Sir Douglas Wass, the Permanent Secretary to the Treasury and a Keynesian, were to some extent bypassed as a primary source of advice.[6] The use of political appointments fitted well with such a disposition. Forces which had influenced the appointment of special advisers in earlier periods, such as the pressure of work on ministers, perceived national decline and the need for policy ideas, probably also continued to be influential. Nigel Lawson, who held various government posts from 1979 and was the Chancellor of the Exchequer from 1983 to 1989, remarks that while special 'advisers were a Labour innovation to which Margaret Thatcher acceded only slowly . . . eventually every Cabinet Minister ended up with at least one'.[7] By June 1984, the official total (seemingly including prime ministerial aides) was eighteen.[8] On 29 July 1988 there were thirty, spread across fourteen departments, as well as the Cabinet Office and No. 10 (for details see appendix). On 22 March 1989 the total number of special advisers was thirty-two, around the higher end of its usual level during 1974–9.

Of those thirty employed in July 1988, two were unpaid and four were on secondment from the private sector. There was, at the time, a twenty-eight-step pay spine from £13,715 to £40,258, on which twenty-one individuals were placed, fifteen of whom were clustered between £22,927 and £35,952. For purposes of comparison, in 1988 a permanent secretary could earn a maximum of £65,000; an MP earned £22,548, a parliamentary undersecretary in the

Commons £17,897, a minister of state in the Commons £23,887, a Cabinet minister in the Commons £34,157 and the Prime Minister £45,787. The parliamentary salary for ministers in the Commons was £16,911.

The Policy Unit was maintained. Initially it was run at a strength of three, comprising a senior policy adviser, a part-time special adviser and a permanent civil servant. In 1983 the figure rose significantly, and during 1983–90 it 'usually operated with seven to nine staff'.[9] Although representatives of career Whitehall became a constant presence within it, outsiders were in the majority. In November 1986 the Policy Unit had a staff of eight, of which only two were permanent officials. The remainder were three secondments from the private sector and three direct entrants.[10] Thatcher also appointed a small number of aides not located in the Policy Unit, such as the economist Alan Walters, who arrived in 1981; and she recruited certain individuals who, though sometimes officially classified as special advisers, did not quite fit the description. Sir Anthony Parsons, a retired ambassador, counselled Thatcher on foreign affairs in 1982 and 1983. He was succeeded in 1984 by a fellow diplomat, Sir Percy Cradock, who was retained by Major, staying on until 1992. In June 1984 it was announced that eight special advisers were attached to the Prime Minister. A reason cited for the expansion was the abolition of the CPRS following the 1983 election.[11] Technically, the CPRS served the Cabinet as a whole and was non-partisan; so this shift arguably represented both a tipping of the balance towards the centre and greater politicisation. The trend did not go unnoticed. In October 1989 Alan Travis wrote in the *Guardian* that Thatcher 'walked into No. 10 ten years ago determined to employ fewer political advisers. Yet she has been unable to live without them'.[12]

On 27 July 1988 Thatcher provided Parliament with a description of the regulations governing the activities of aides. She stated that their conditions of employment were the same as permanent officials 'except as regards superannuation and severance'. Their conduct was governed by Civil Service rules, except those relating to 'the acceptance of outside appointments after resignation or retirement'. More 'freedom than other civil servants' was allowed in 'two areas of political activity'. Given ministerial approval, they could 'attend party functions' and participate in 'policy reviews organised by the party'. Subject to similar permission, special advisers could 'undertake all forms of local political activity provided they observe the rule of discretion applicable to civil servants'.

However, 'local activities in support of national politics' were not allowed.[13] The regulations permitted them to engage in liaison between government and party. They also enabled continued participation in activities common for those envisaging a future parliamentary career.

The use of special advisers continued to challenge Civil Service traditions. In August 1979 a career official from the Department of Industry, Andrew Duguid, was incorporated into the Policy Unit. Kavanagh and Seldon write that some 'detected the Civil Service establishment's hand, most particularly Armstrong's in persuading Mrs Thatcher to "civilise" the Policy Unit by tempering the enthusiasm of Whitehall outsiders with the experience of some permanent officials'.[14] However, according to Hoskyns, the move was resisted by Sir Ian Bancroft, Head of the Home Civil Service, who 'was opposed to a career official joining a political team', but was eventually persuaded otherwise.[15] If such was the case, it is likely that Bancroft was motivated by a desire to preserve separateness between special advisers and permanent civil servants. The idea of a neutral official answering to a political appointee was presumably considered objectionable. In his memoir Hoskyns records carrying out a work appraisal for Duguid.[16] This was a management function, and its exercise shows that such roles were performed by special advisers long before 1997.

There was a general understanding, which may or may not have been written down somewhere, that political appointees were not permitted to wield executive authority. However, although since 1978 legal provision existed for the appointment of temporary aides without the need for clearance from the Civil Service Commission, in the words of Richard Wilson, 'throughout the 1980s special advisers had no limits on what they could do in law. There may have been rules but in law there were not limits.'[17] In 1989 Thatcher informed the Commons that apart 'from secretarial assistance, permanent civil servants do not work directly for special advisers *except with my express permission*' (emphasis added). The question to which she was responding referred to 'ministerial political and special advisers'.[18] It could be inferred, therefore, that, given clearance, aides in Downing Street and across government were permitted to take on managerial functions. Additionally, special advisers who were perceived as close to their ministers were likely to acquire informal authority. Functions such as the stimulation of policy development, moreover, suggested the performance of more than a mere advisory role.

In a discussion of special advisers, Sir Richard Wilson told the Committee on Standards in Public Life in 2002 that he recalled members of Thatcher's Policy Unit having 'quite a lot of contacts . . . with people in the departments direct, without going through private offices'.[19] Wilson's recollection is important for two reasons. It suggests that the formal Whitehall channels of communication were bypassed, something which John Hunt, at the inception of the Policy Unit, wished to prevent. Furthermore, it is reasonable to assume that such 'contacts' could take the form of the issue of instructions, or at least strong suggestions. Prime ministerial appointments, then, possibly had a degree of authority not only within No. 10 but across the government.

Personnel and roles

A number of important aides during the Thatcher period, including Hoskyns, Norman Strauss, Walters and John Redwood, were associated with the Centre for Policy Studies (CPS).[20] A free-market research body, the CPS was established in March 1974 with Alfred Sherman, a journalist and former communist, playing a leading role. There seems to be some confusion about Sherman's exact position. Correcting an article that appeared in the *Independent* in 1990, he wrote that 'I was not the first director of the Centre for Policy Studies, although I thought it up with Keith Joseph.'[21] A Conservative MP since 1956 and a participant in the Heath administration, Joseph was given a roving policy development brief following the party's return to opposition. A key ally of Thatcher, he introduced her to a wide variety of individuals who were influential upon her political development and activities in office, some of whom went on to serve as special advisers.[22] It has been suggested that Joseph's long-term influence on his party was great. In 1996 one writer, observing a Conservative anti-intellectual tradition, argued that not until 1975 and the 'rise of . . . Sir Keith Joseph, did cleverness become fashionable . . . Four years later, after Mrs Thatcher's election victory, all the little Joseph-clones began infiltrating Whitehall as ministerial special advisers – a process of brains triumphing over common sense'.[23]

A degree of tension developed between the CPS, a newcomer associated with an emergent free-market radicalism, and the long-established CRD, which, in the view of elements on the right of the party, embodied the Conservative establishment's entanglement with social democracy.[24] Lord (David) Young, one of the

CPS's directors in the 1970s, says that the CRD lacked the will to advocate the necessary tough approaches in areas such as state benefits.[25] As Thatcher puts it, much 'bitterness and rivalry . . . built up between the CRD and the CPS'.[26] Arguably, then, Thatcher was working against the grain within her own party. Personal aides, drawn from beyond the usual circles, assisted her in the endeavour.

However, Sir Adam Ridley, who was both a director of the CPS and Deputy Director of the CRD from 1974 to 1979, downplays the extent of the rivalry between the two. There was undoubtedly disagreement between them about both policy and presentation, but it was restricted to certain topics and diminished over time. Unfortunately, he says, 'there is a well-established tendency for some observers to view the relationship between the Research Department and the Centre for Policy Studies as being dominated, in perpetuity, by the pro- and anti-Heath controversies' of 1974–6. In practice, Ridley goes on, 'the thoughtful building of common ground led by Geoffrey Howe, Angus Maude and others lowered the tension markedly by the time of the election, as did Keith Joseph's own diminishing prominence as the Conservative administration found its feet.'[27]

The CPS encouraged Thatcher to take her own aides into government, although she did not make it a priority.[28] According to Hoskyns, from early on in her leadership Sherman encouraged Thatcher to recruit a '"reserve army of advisers" from the outside world'. Sherman argued that they should be 'woven into the Conservative team well before the election' in order to make it possible that an incoming Conservative government could control the Civil Service and master political events. Shortly before the 1979 election Hoskyns tried to persuade Thatcher to attach a group of outsiders to the Prime Minister and to introduce 'a small advisory team of outsiders and insiders for each of the key cabinet colleagues' at the Treasury, Employment, Industry and probably the DHSS. Preoccupied with the campaign, Thatcher showed little interest in the idea.[29] However, Sherman, at least in his own account, managed to secure the future of the Policy Unit and place it in CPS hands. He subsequently wrote that, on 'the eve of the 1979 elections, I succeeded in persuading Margaret Thatcher to retain [the Policy Unit] and to entrust it to John Hoskyns . . . rather than a Conservative Research Department aparatchik [*sic*]'.[30]

Some special advisers were linked to groups more esoteric than the CPS. Peter Shipley was on the Policy Unit staff from 1982 to 1984. In June 1987 he was described in the *Guardian* as a 'keen researcher of groups on the left and on the right since his student days at York University in the late sixties'.[31] Shipley worked for the Conservative Party between 1977 and 1982. According to its convenor, the freelance intelligence operative Brian Crozier, Shipley was a researcher for the 'Shield Committee', an organisation which, during Thatcher's period as leader of the opposition, confidentially briefed her and other senior Conservatives on the supposed extent of communist subversion within British society.[32] Hoskyns confirms that Shipley 'had done research work for Brian Crozier in 1976 on communist subversion of the trade unions' and then became 'a [Conservative] Central Office specialist in union matters and left-wing subversion'.[33]

The Policy Unit maintained contact with a group of business representatives labelled the Argonauts. Hoskyns writes that it was established by Sherman during the steel strike which started late in 1979, involving the smaller companies affected by the action.[34] Special advisers have stressed that, despite the mysterious name, it was not a sinister body. According to Ferdinand Mount, the head of the Policy Unit from 1982 to 1983, 'every couple of months [the anti-socialist pressure group] Aims of Industry arranged a lunch for us to meet spokesmen for the trade associations – the motor manufacturers, the engineering employers and so on. These sober gatherings were somewhat fancifully named the Argonauts, although there was no sign of any golden fleece or even a free woolly jumper on offer.'[35]

Among the Conservative aides of these years were a number of individuals who went on to become MPs. Lawson states that the 'turnover of special advisers was inevitably on the high side, as the pay is not good and the job tends to attract bright youngsters who are contemplating a career in politics'.[36] Two who were particularly successful were John Redwood, head of the Policy Unit from 1984 to 1985, and Michael Portillo, both of whom subsequently became Cabinet members under Major. Portillo was first able to make an impression as a member of the CRD during Thatcher's opposition period. During the 1979 election campaign he was responsible for briefing her for morning press conferences. Thatcher writes that 'he demonstrated not just his grasp of facts, figures and arguments, but also an instinctive shrewdness in suggesting their deployment. One of my impressions of the campaign was that Michael was a young man who would – and deserved to – go far.'[37] Special advisers in the Thatcher period also went on to prominence beyond party politics. Howard Davies, an aide to

Lawson, was subsequently Director-General of the CBI, Director of the Financial Services Authority and Director of the London School of Economics.

While there were some notable appointments, including Walters, experts of the academic variety were not as numerous as they were under Labour in the 1960s and 1970s; nor, indeed, have they been so since. In keeping with the free-market values of Thatcher's administration, individuals recruited for their particular skills or experience had often acquired them in the private sector. The total of thirty-two special advisers employed in March 1989 included individuals on secondment from, previously employed by or still working part-time for Bank of Montreal Capital Markets, British Petroleum, Cazenove (an investment bank), Cluff Investments and Trading, Consolidated Goldfields, Daiwa Europe (an investment bank), Good Relations Group (a public relations company), Hill Samuel (an investment bank), the Institute of Directors, McKinsey (a consul-tancy), the Milk Marketing Board, P&O (the shipping company), Phillips and Drew (an investment bank) and RTZ (formerly the multinational corporation Rio Tinto Zinc). Four more were, respectively, a student, a self-employed person, an MP's secretary and a charity fundraiser; the remainder worked for the Council of the European Communities, City University Business School, the CRD (2), Conservative Central Office (4), the No. 10 Political Office or as career civil servants (2), or were already special advisers (3).[38]

The employment of businessmen in administrative posts, as special advisers and in other capacities, was extensive under Thatcher. Hoskyns sought to convene them as an entity which could impress upon politicians the approach that they brought from the private sector in areas such as expenditure control and management techniques. To this end, a dinner was arranged at the Millbank headquarters of ICI on 25 September 1980. Guests spent much time 'discussing the Westminster–Whitehall culture and why it was so ineffective'. Hoskyns took the opportunity to propose 'an advisers' revolution'. Later on, a smaller gathering considered whether 'we should, as a group, demand an all-day Chequers discus-sion with the members of [the Cabinet Economic Strategy Committee] only and no officials present.' Nothing so dramatic occurred. However, in time, the indi-viduals Hoskyns attempted to galvanise into a businessmen's vanguard at Millbank made a great impact within Whitehall. Included in their number were Derek Rayner, the Prime Minister's Efficiency Adviser, and Robin Ibbs, who, after heading the CPRS, succeeded Rayner. Rayner, although a prime ministerial appointment, was not strictly a special adviser. He was unpaid, non-political and the head of a team carrying out a specific cross-departmental activity. By the time of his departure at the end of 1982 he had begun instilling management efficiency values into Whitehall. In the later 1980s Ibbs was the initiator of the 'Next Steps' reforms, a process of hiving off many state functions to executive agencies. Terry Burns, the Chief Economic Adviser and subsequently Permanent Secretary to the Treasury, also attended the ICI gathering. Special advisers present, other than Hoskyns, included Strauss of the Policy Unit and Peter Cropper, based at the Treasury.[39]

Another businessman aide was David Young. He was unpaid and therefore not actually employed on special adviser terms, although officially listed as one. The only document he signed was the Official Secrets Act. Thatcher is famously said to have remarked once of (Lord) Young that 'other people bring me problems, but David brings me solutions'.[40] Born in 1932, Young was previously a Labour voter. Disillusioned by Britain's economic and social malaise, he briefly emigrated. Young, a property developer, became acquainted with Joseph in the mid-1970s through his business associate Jeffrey Sterling, another adviser during the 1980s.[41] The three men shared a belief in the free-market agenda that came to be known as Thatcherism. Young volunteered his services for the CPS in 1977. In 1979 he was recruited by Joseph, newly installed as Secretary of State for Industry, as a part-time industrial adviser, concentrating 'on the property affairs of the department and their many nationalised industries and agencies'.[42]

In 1980, having obtained the permission of the Prime Minister, Joseph expanded Young's brief to cover wider aspects of the department's work. Matters with which Young then concerned himself included the transfer of British Aerospace and Cable & Wireless into the private sector. (He was the chairman of the latter company from 1990 to 1995.) He attended a committee investigating the feasibility of selling off the Royal Ordnance Factories, and as an advocate of the privatisation of British Telecom was instrumental in driving the policy through government.[43] His functions during an economically depressed period also included exploring ways of saving jobs without resorting to government bail-outs in 1980 he turned his attention to a Philips factory in the constituency of the Secretary of State for Employment, Jim Prior.[44]

When Joseph became Secretary of State for Education in September 1981 he invited Young to accompany him, and the aide's services were eventually shared between Joseph and the new Secretary of State for Industry, Patrick Jenkin. Young was raised to the peerage in 1984 and given a non-departmental Cabinet post with responsibility for unemployment. The following year he was appointed Secretary of State for Employment. In 1987 Young became Secretary of State for Trade and Industry. Such advancement ran against the cultural grain. As Young notes, many 'of my American friends would spend time in academia, then commerce and then government. I assumed that it was natural for us. It is not'.[45]

Michael Heseltine, a Thatcher-era Cabinet minister, distinguished between types of aides thus:

> *Special advisers should be expert in a particular field, concentrate on policy relevant to that expertise and work with civil servants rather than with the minister, but with open access to the minister. The special adviser is quite distinct from the political adviser, who is based near to the minister's private office and works closely with the party as well as the department.*

Heseltine developed a practice of appointing individuals in the former category for six-month periods. The first, recruited in 1979 when Heseltine was Secretary of State for the Environment, was Tom Baron. Baron came into contact with Heseltine when the former was acting in his capacity as a representative of the house-builders Christian Salvesen. He was, Heseltine writes, a

> *wiry terrier of a man, [who] threw out ideas like sparks from a firework. He was voluble, argumentative, amusing and one of those characters who are irrepressible in their enthusiasm. There was only one thing for it. I put it to him that, if he knew so much about what government should be doing, why didn't he come and work for me and show us how.*

One of Baron's contributions was to persuade the Volume Housebuilders, a body comprised of companies such as Barratts and Wimpeys, to build 2,000 new houses a year in London's East End, an important element in the regeneration of the area.[46]

Some special advisers fitted into the mould of general political aide. Norman Fowler, Secretary of State for Social Services from 1982 to 1987, employed the services of Nicholas True, 'an exceptionally able political adviser from outside the civil service . . . who helped me in both policy-making and speech-writing'. Fowler notes that True counselled him on the presentation of reductions in NHS staff numbers in 1983. True was later recruited to Major's Policy Unit.[47] Peter Luff, who worked for Lord (David) Young as Secretary of State for Trade and Industry from 1987, is described by his employer as 'political; he had been around for years and was on the candidates' list, looking for a constituency. He was able to help me with the politics of the job, particularly in maintaining contact with all parts of the party'.[48] Such services were of particular value to Young since, as a peer, he had no constituency party and his interaction with Conservative members in the Commons was restricted.[49] Luff subsequently became a Conservative MP.

Other aides possessed notable public relations skills. Michael Dobbs, later a successful novelist and deputy chairman of the Conservative Party, was a high-flyer at the Saatchi and Saatchi advertising agency, which worked on successive Conservative election campaigns. He was Norman Tebbit's seconded special adviser at various points during 1981–7, serving him at Employment and Trade and Industry, and as Chancellor of the Duchy of Lancaster/Conservative Party chairman.[50] As the Cabinet minister responsible for unemployment from 1984, rather than relying on the services of the Cabinet Office, in which he was located, Lord Young appointed Howell James to perform the role of media liaison. James's background was in independent radio and television. A recent addition to his curriculum vitae was that of press officer to TV-AM, where one of his concerns had been the promotion of the puppet character Roland Rat. 'From the moment he joined my team,' writes Young, 'I could relax about the media, although there were mutterings from the ranks of the Press Officers.'[51] James was brought to Young's attention by Tim Bell, a public relations consultant whose clients included the Conservative Party. According to Bell's biographer James was seconded, with his salary paid by Bell.[52] Young does not think this could have been the case and believes that the money must have been made up from public sources.[53] James arranged press interviews for Young, helped draft his speeches and chaperoned his minister at media events. In 1987 James became Director of Corporate Affairs at the BBC. On first learning that his aide was to leave, Young was 'shattered'.[54] James became Major's political secretary from 1994 to 1997.

The Treasury

The employment of three aides at the Treasury was the norm, both for Geoffrey Howe, Thatcher's Chancellor from 1979 to 1983, and for his successors, Lawson (1983–9) and Major (1989–90). At the outset of the Thatcher premiership there were more special advisers at the Treasury than at No. 10, where there were only two. Howe found temporary Whitehall employment for Peter Cropper, George Cardona and Adam Ridley. They oversaw, respectively, taxation, public expenditure and the general field of economic advice. Ridley, a former member of the CPRS, was the most senior and influential of the three, described by Howe as 'one of my most trusted special advisers at the Treasury'.[55] Technically, Cropper was an aide to John Biffen, Chief Secretary to the Treasury, while Cardona worked for Lawson as Financial Secretary to the Treasury; but in practice all three primarily counselled Howe.[56]

As shadow Chancellor, Howe set up an Economic Reconstruction Group staffed Cardona, Cropper and Ridley of the CRD: Ridley was its secretary, Cardona directed the public expenditure aspects of its work, and Cropper, who came from a City background, covered taxation. In Cropper's area, Howe writes, from 'a ceaseless flow of ideas we were able to distil a formidable array of proposals, which found their way into Nigel Lawson's early Budgets as well as my own'. The goal was 'to switch the tax burden from taxes on income, investment and enterprise to taxes on consumption and expenditure'. Howe's aides were associated with some important policy decisions taken in his early period of office; Ridley was present at Howe's first Budget meeting on 9 May 1979. Howe became convinced of the need to introduce full sterling convertibility following a meeting with Lawson and Ridley on 10 October during the 1979 Conservative Party conference. In the period leading up to the Budget of March 1980, 'our special advisers (George Cardona particularly)' were involved in the development of a downward revision of spending plans up to and including the 1983/4 financial year. Howe records that, in opposition, he, Lawson and Ridley had frequently discussed the idea of a 'medium-term framework for monetary and fiscal discipline'. It appeared in the form of the Medium-Term Financial Strategy, introduced with the 1980 Budget. Precise commitments were made in respect of restrictions on the growth of the money supply, designed to reduce inflationary expectations.[57]

As well as providing policy advice, Ridley, Cropper and Cardona performed political liaison duties. One of their functions was that of taking backbench soundings, 'enabling officials to test the political reaction to proposals below ministerial level'.[58] In 1980 Howe's special advisers held a meeting with the Chelsea Five, an informal group of Conservative backbenchers, in an attempt to allay their concerns regarding the course of economic policy. During this troubled period, the three aides also 'played an equally important . . . role in maintaining smooth relations with and between members of [the Chancellor's] ministerial team'. In March 1980 Howe received a warning from two of his special advisers regarding personality clashes among Treasury ministers. At meetings, they cautioned, Peter Rees, a minister of state, was expressing himself in an irritable, abrupt manner, while Lawson, the Financial Secretary, was talking too much. Howe dealt with these matters personally.[59]

There was some initial suspicion on the part of the permanent Treasury staff regarding special advisers. Referring to the aides recruited to the Treasury in 1979, Lawson suggests that as 'political appointees they were clearly *parti pris*, and were therefore treated initially by the Whitehall machine with the gravest suspicion'. Lawson, however, emphasises the fact that 'it was rapidly realised that they were an extremely useful adjunct to the official machine.'[60] In 2002 Burns told the Committee on Standards in Public Life:

> *I arrived in the Civil Service, in the Treasury, in January of 1980 . . . and I could see then there were some strains and stresses between the roles of Special Advisers and the Civil Servants, because the people who were then Ministers had been used to working with people very closely in opposition . . . over time these issues were resolved . . . People got to know each other, the trust built up.*[61]

Like Howe, Lawson was normally served by three special advisers, to whom he allotted work on an *ad hoc* basis. Sometimes they were given individual tasks; on other occasions they worked jointly on projects. Andrew Tyrie was an aide at the Treasury from 1986 to 1990, serving Lawson and his successor, John Major. Born in 1957, he had joined the CRD in 1983. Tyrie found Lawson extremely demanding, but also rewarding to work for, describing him as 'the cleverest man I have come across in British politics by some way'. Tyrie was responsible for producing the first draft of the Chancellor of the Exchequer's party conference speech (although the Chancellor generally completely rewrote it), had a significant input into the Budget statement and made a lesser contribution to the text for the Mansion House address. A PPE graduate, Tyrie says he learnt his real economics 'on the hoof' at the Treasury, helped by career officials.[62] Major recalls that Tyrie was 'known as "Fang" because he liked to get his teeth into issues' and that he 'had a rigorous intellect and was relentless in pursuit of his preferred policy'.[63]

Although primarily concerned with policy development, Tyrie sometimes spoke to journalists, logging contacts with the Treasury press officer. Lawson describes his three aides, Cropper, Alistair Ross-Goobey and Tyrie, as his 'personal campaign team' during the 1987 election campaign, when their activities included arranging unscheduled press conferences. Lawson had become increasingly frustrated with the way the official Conservative campaign was being handled, especially the failure 'to highlight the implications of Labour's tax and spending plans'. For this reason Lawson and his aides, in particular Tyrie, conducted a freelance operation, priming the media with their projections of the cost of a Labour government. Lawson describes the *Daily Mail* as 'carefully briefed by Andrew Tyrie' for the purposes of one story.[64]

Had his views been heeded in other quarters, Tyrie might have averted a major policy calamity. As a special adviser to Jenkin at Environment, Tyrie was an early opponent of the community charge, or 'poll tax' as it became widely known. In place of the rates system, which was differentiated and levied on properties, it entailed an equal charge for all individuals on a particular local authority electoral register. It was open to criticism for its regressive nature. During 1985 the poll tax was reportedly championed by Oliver Letwin, then a member of the Policy Unit.[65] In the spring of the same year Tyrie was shown an early paper on the proposed measure, under the working title of 'Residence Charge'. 'I saw it,' he says, 'and was shocked.' Appalled by the prospect of a measure which would create millions of new taxpayers, he wrote a note warning that, if implemented, it would destroy the government. Jenkin favoured the measure, however, although Kenneth Baker, the minister of state responsible for local government, took an interest in Tyrie's concerns. Upon his move to the Treasury Tyrie found himself united with a minister, Lawson, who shared his opposition to the community charge. Having shown the Chancellor of the Exchequer his paper from 1985, Tyrie was assigned to the effort to prevent the introduction of the new tax; but he did not prevail.[66] The community charge became a political disaster, the unpopularity of which contributed to the fall of Thatcher.[67]

Remarkably, Tyrie also cautioned against a decision which played a part in the demise of Thatcher's successor. In June 1990, of all those in the Treasury who counselled Major over whether Britain should join the Exchange Rate Mechanism (ERM) of the European Monetary System, 'No one argued for sterling to stay out, though Andrew Tyrie suggested I should consider delaying membership.'[68]

Voices

The Policy Unit (as well as the other aides she employed, particularly Walters) was important to Thatcher's leadership style. She states that 'the value of the Unit . . . lies in its flexibility and involvement in day-to-day policy matters, on the basis of close collaboration with the Prime Minister.'[69] Geoffrey Howe refers to the 'discreet and personalised role for the Prime Minister' performed by the Unit.[70] Thatcher's has been portrayed as a markedly centralised premiership, and it has been argued that she had little regard for collective, Cabinet government.[71] Her emergence as a dominant figure is often traced to around 1982. After a troubled start, her political position was strengthened, partly by success in the Falklands conflict and the removal of dissenting Cabinet members.[72] Significantly, around the same time the number of special advisers at No. 10 began to increase. In 1985 the political journalist Peter Riddell wrote that 'by expanding the unit, Mrs Thatcher has moved slightly further towards Prime Ministerial, as opposed to Cabinet, government.'[73]

The four heads of Thatcher's Policy Unit were Hoskyns (1979–82), Mount (1982–3), Redwood (1984–5) and Brian Griffiths (1985–90). Hoskyns and his small staff deliberately focused only on what he identified as the core policy areas. It has been suggested that, while Hoskyns's approach to the Civil Service was combative, his successors displayed more willingness to work with the grain.[74] Mount, under whom there was an expansion in numbers, 'pioneered the use of seminars to question existing policy and canvas new ideas'.[75] During Redwood's stewardship, each Policy Unit member was allocated a particular zone of responsibility, although questions could still be examined collectively. Griffiths encouraged his staff to spend time outside Whitehall. He himself visited over a hundred schools.[76] Under Thatcher, the practice of the Head of the Policy Unit meeting the Prime Minister on Friday mornings developed.[77] When Walters was not working for Thatcher, the influence of the Senior Policy Adviser over economic decisions increased. It seems that there was little glamour associated with working for the Policy Unit. Mount notes that he was not cultivated by lobbyists. He writes, 'we seldom got asked out. Macaroni cheese and mineral water with the cabinet secretary on Tuesdays was the social highlight of our week.'[78]

Heads of Thatcher's Policy Unit sometimes contributed to her philosophical and moral approach. Mount was a firm advocate of the renewal of discipline and responsibility, particularly for the young, at home and in school, as a means of restoring and renewing the fabric of society. Prompted in part by the urban rioting which took place during 1981, Thatcher came to see Mount's outlook as central to the 'Conservative mission', at the heart of which lay 'something more than economics . . . there is a commitment to strengthen, or at least not undermine, the traditional virtues which enable people to live fulfilling lives without being a threat or a burden to others'. A number of proposals flowed from Mount's philosophy. They included taxation changes for married couples, education vouchers, a more authoritarian approach to policing and increased discounts for council house purchases.[79]

The 'discreet but highly influential' Griffiths also struck up an ideological partnership with the Prime Minister.[80] One commentator stated in 1988 that the two shared 'basic assumptions about family life, religion, and the economy, as well as about personal and social morality'.[81] A Christian monetarist, Griffiths has been described as giving Thatcher 'a moral basis for her ideological convictions'.[82] Referring to Griffiths, in 1989 the Labour MP Frank Field wrote that the 'spirit of [the nineteenth-century Christian scholar] John Henry Newman is not only alive and well but appears to be working in Downing Street'. Field viewed Griffiths as propounding absolute moral values within a free-market context.[83]

Prime ministerial aides were associated with specific policy programmes. The privatisation of a number of state-owned concerns was one of the most significant achievements of the Thatcher premiership: in 1984 the sale of British Telecom shares began; British Gas followed in 1986 and British Airways in 1987. Redwood was recruited to Mount's Policy Unit after the 1983 election, having talked himself, not entirely intentionally, into the job of setting up a government mechanism for implementing the privatisation agenda, which he had been trying to persuade Thatcher to pursue since the early years of her leadership in the mid-1970s. With his initial task complete, and John Moore installed at the Treasury as the responsible minister, Redwood intended to leave; but he was asked to take over from Mount as head of the Unit, an offer he could not refuse. In his new role he continued to observe the progress of the privatisation programme, where necessary accelerating it, or resolving disputes between the Treasury and particular sponsoring departments.[84]

Towards the end of Thatcher's premiership, her interest focused on education. Had she contested another general election it would have been to a large extent on a programme which she and Griffiths were developing. More schools would be encouraged to opt out of local authority control as, in Thatcher's words, 'a way to ease the state . . . out of education'. She wanted to break the monopoly over certification exercised by training colleges. Griffiths was tasked with devising means by which 'at least half' of teachers could qualify through schemes such as apprenticeships. Finally, Thatcher also entrusted Griffiths with the development of proposals to provide leading universities with means by which they could independently raise capital.[85]

Thatcher used her aides to monitor developments on her behalf. It briefed her on papers coming in from the departments and progress-chased on policy decisions. Mount 'was keen to send one of his staff to each Cabinet committee, to find out what was going on'.[86] The practice, Griffiths confirms, continued thereafter.[87] This was significant given that Thatcher came to exercise what Tyrie describes as 'government by Cabinet committee' (by implication, rather than by the full Cabinet).[88] During the spring and summer of 1985 Thatcher endeavoured to bring about a reduction in British Leyland's levels of investment. She states that she was very 'well advised . . . on these matters by my Policy Unit', and that Redwood 'kept a shrewd and sceptical eye on BL's finances, briefing me regularly'.[89] Redwood describes another of his functions as the 'clay pigeon shoot'. It entailed drawing Thatcher's attention to proposals 'for more regulation and more interference in our daily lives, which regularly came forward from the Civil Service' – and which he felt needed to be quashed.[90]

The Policy Unit took part in Thatcher's 'famous "judge and jury" sessions in which ministers would be called to No. 10 and interrogated on their policies and performance and which by the mid 1980s had become a feared and hated part of their lives'.[91] As well as working through Cabinet committees, then, Thatcher monitored her administration bilaterally, assisted by aides. The tendency for these advisers to communicate directly with other parts of Whitehall, bypassing private offices, has already been discussed; increasingly, prime ministerial special advisers seemed to attempt direct intervention in the administration. In March 1988, according to Lawson, Griffiths tried to redraft a section of the forthcoming Budget.[92] The personal power Griffiths acquired was perceived by some as extensive. In the same year the *Guardian* reported that it was 'a grim joke in the Department of Education and Science that Griffiths . . . is more in charge of education policy than the Secretary of State himself'. Griffiths was also believed to have great influence where broadcasting matters, formally the territory of the Home Office, were concerned.[93] However, Griffiths himself emphasises that he had no authority independently of the Prime Minister and was keenly aware that he did not enjoy the mandate of elected politicians. He endeavoured to keep his profile low.[94]

The activities of temporary civil servants based in Downing Street, and the closeness to Thatcher attained by some of them, caused concern among ministers from time to time. Howe has written that the Policy Unit, in combination with special advisers working alongside it in No. 10, 'could have the effect of a loose cannon in destabilising the Downing Street craft. All the more reason . . . for us to keep closely in touch with the Policy Unit and other special advisers at Number 10. At some times this was less easy than at others.' Moreover, he claims that, while he attempted to keep Walters abreast of developments inside the Treasury by including him on circulation lists, 'We were seldom afforded the same insight into the – often assertive rather than analytical – papers which went to Margaret from Walters (or from the rest of the Policy Unit).'[95]

Such grievances related to a negative perception of Thatcher's leadership style which grew among her Cabinet colleagues during her premiership, even those who were formerly her allies. In a discussion of Thatcher's tendency to rely on the advice of special advisers that was not circulated beyond No. 10, Howe writes that 'Margaret would quite often – more frequently as the years went by – cite advice she had received from "one of my people" or "my people". It seemed sometimes as though she was Joan of Arc invoking the authority of her "voices"'.[96] Lawson has also attributed to Thatcher an increasing hubris, with which, he believed, her counsellors were associated. He describes Griffiths as 'inclined to tell her only what she wanted to hear',[97] in contrast to her aides in earlier years. Outside the government, Sherman took a similar view, subsequently stating that the 'policy-unit as it emerged was visibly greying with the years . . . Hoskyns and Mount left fingerprints; their successors did not, but loyally helped compound Thatcher's errors. Unlike comrades of the first hour, appointees cannot be expected to look their patron in the eyes and tell them they are wrong.'[98] Yet Griffiths, for one, had been associated with the same circle of influence upon Thatcher as Sherman in the mid-1970s. Moreover, Griffiths argues that, whatever her popular image, Thatcher was always 'very concerned that every aspect of any proposal should be argued through in extraordinary detail'.[99] Her aides were deployed to such an end.

Personal loyalty and strong commitment to Thatcher's objectives seem to have been characteristics of staff within No. 10 beyond the small band of special advisers. Some career officials were incorporated into her close circle of allies. As Hennessy states, 'it is difficult to exempt her foreign affairs Private Secretary, Charles Powell, and her press secretary, Bernard Ingham . . . from the charge that they were, to some degree, politicised.'[100] The influence of Powell and Ingham was, at times, probably greater than that of the temporaries. Hugo Young credits Powell, 'a man of great ability and great industry . . . [who] developed close personal rapport with' Thatcher, with providing the 'major input' to Thatcher's speech, delivered at Bruges in September 1988, in which she indicated her hostility to the supposed threat of a 'European super-state exercising a new dominance from Brussels'. Ingham, whose public profile was considerable, once famously described John Biffen, who had publicly made an apparently disloyal remark about Thatcher, as a 'semi-detached member of the Cabinet'.[101] Such a comment could be regarded as an excursion into party political territory by a career official.

John Hoskyns

An examination of Hoskyns's career serves to illustrate important aspects of the emergence and enactment of the political programme associated with Thatcher and the role of temporary civil servants in it. He was a significant generator of ideas for Thatcher both in opposition and office, dogged in his efforts to secure their adoption and implementation. Hugo Young describes Hoskyns as 'an archetypal Thatcherite, one of the earliest of the breed'. As such, he believed 'in the business imperative as the sole agent of economic recovery'.[102] His most important contribution was to develop and promote the view that a Conservative government had to tackle trades union power directly. In Howe's words, 'Margaret's gut instincts were never well disposed towards trade unions'; and both he and Joseph were of the view that 'at the right time, reform in this field was essential'. Hoskyns was, according to Howe, the 'key figure' in Joseph's efforts to 'carry the argument forward' while the Conservatives were in opposition.[103]

Born in 1927, Hoskyns attended Winchester College and in 1946 joined the Rifle Brigade, becoming a regular soldier in 1950. In 1957 he took up employment with the computer company, IBM. Seeing business opportunities in a field that had not yet been developed, that of software supply, Hoskyns set up on his own in 1964. By the early 1970s the Hoskyns Group had become one of the largest operations of its kind in the UK. Hoskyns's attempts to apply strategic thinking and systems analysis to politics can arguably be traced respectively to his military and computing backgrounds. Despite his own commercial success, his experiences led him to develop an unfavourable view of the British economy and business culture. Problems he identified and subsequently sought to address included the cost of the welfare state and the nationalised industries, high levels of personal taxation, inflation, union wage pressures and the stop–go cycle. Such an environment placed great pressure on entrepreneurs, of which Hoskyns was one, to sell out to less dynamic, longer-established companies. Successive governments failed to offer solutions and Hoskyns sensed national decline. He writes, 'I had come to feel trapped in a slowly sinking ship.'[104] Importantly, therefore, like other key Thatcher allies including David Young, he sought to represent the interests of first-generation businessmen, whom he regarded as undervalued wealth-creators, penalised by a social democratic political settlement.

By 1973 Hoskyns had decided to leave business and enter politics. A floating voter, he had no prior association with the Conservatives, or indeed any other party. Seeking entry into political circles, Hoskyns encountered an environment he found hostile. He writes that businessmen 'were regarded as intellectual peasants by the intelligentsia of all political persuasions'. Hoskyns was briefly involved, during 1974, with the Campaign for Social Democracy, a group established by Dick Taverne, Financial Secretary to the Treasury from 1969 to 1970. Prompted by the rise of the left within Labour, Taverne left the party in 1972 and held his seat as an independent from 1973 to 1974.[105] Hugo Young refers to Hoskyns as one of a number of associates of Thatcher who had 'the experience of lurching far and wide across the political spectrum'.[106]

Hoskyns developed a novel approach to political diagnosis, constructing diagrammatic representations of British economic malaise in an attempt to move beyond conventional literary depictions. For him, all problems were interlinked and had to be viewed in context as part of the totality. He attracted the interest of Sherman, whom he met for the first time in September 1975. At a CPS lunch the following November, Hoskyns encountered a future member of his Policy Unit, the like-minded Strauss, then working for the chemicals company Unilever. With the help of Sherman, some headway was made in obtaining Joseph's interest in Hoskyns's ideas; and in August 1976 Joseph decided to introduce both Hoskyns and Strauss to Thatcher.[107] Hennessy describes Strauss as

an ebullient, combative businessman who cannot see a conventional wisdom without wishing to puncture it or a vested institutional interest without trying to expose it. He is as abrasive as Hoskyns is smooth . . . Hoskyns and Strauss made an odd but effective pair with Strauss fizzing like a catherine wheel and Hoskyns identifying, isolating and refining the most promising sparks.[108]

In her account, Thatcher was initially 'not very impressed' with Hoskyns's and Strauss's view that 'we could never succeed unless we fitted all our policies into a single strategy in which we worked out in advance the order in which actions had to be taken.'[109] However, on 9 July 1977 the opportunity came. Hoskyns was informed, by Joseph, that Thatcher wanted him and Strauss to turn their ideas into a 'coherent plan to lay ground, campaign and then govern'.[110]

In August 1977 Hoskyns and Strauss began work on a report for the shadow Cabinet. Influenced by the business concept of the 'critical path', which Hoskyns had used in order to develop his proposed series of necessary actions, Joseph suggested the title 'Stepping Stones'.[111] By November 1977 it was completed. Never published, the document warned, in Howe's words, that unless 'a sea change in Britain's political economy' could be achieved, a future Conservative administration was doomed to failure, and Britain to continued decline. The major obstacle to recovery was the 'negative stance of the trade unions'. Specifically, the privileged legal position and immunities they enjoyed had to be eliminated. While this idea was central to 'Stepping Stones', the report made it clear 'that there were plenty of other things that needed to be put right, in management, in education, in government, across the board'.[112] Young wrote that the report 'identified the interlocking nature of the problems to be addressed in the first term: the removal of controls and regulations on the economy, the reduction of inflation, the beginnings of the control of public spending, trade union law reform, public sector pay and the consequent fighting and winning of public sector strikes'.[113]

Thatcher, Joseph and Howe looked favourably on the 'Stepping Stones' programme, but others in the shadow Cabinet were less well disposed towards it. In particular, Jim Prior, who held the Employment brief, did not want to adopt what he saw as a confrontational approach to the trades unions.[114] Young writes that Hoskyns conducted a 'private campaign to get Prior sacked from the Employment portfolio'.[115] The failure of the Labour government's 5 per cent pay norm, resulting in the so-called 'Winter of Discontent' of 1978–9, enabled the proponents of 'Stepping Stones' to make headway. As Howe puts it, suddenly 'the argument that Hoskyns had been urging us to make was being made for us.' As a result, Thatcher publicly committed herself to proposals for the reform of picketing law and the closed shop, and measures designed to ensure that unions bore more of the cost for strikes.[116]

Hoskyns was closely involved in the 1979 general election campaign, speech-writing for Thatcher and attending the twice-daily meetings at Conservative Central Office held by the party chairman, Lord Thorneycroft. Victory seemed likely, and Hoskyns took an interest in where particular advisers would be located within an incoming Thatcher administration. According to Hoskyns, Adam Ridley of the CRD had assumed that he would head the No. 10 Policy Unit. Thatcher, however, had decided to appoint Hoskyns to the post. Personally it was a difficult problem to resolve, Thatcher was loath to disappoint Ridley. Her initial compromise proposal, disliked by Hoskyns (and Ridley), was for the two men to run the Policy Unit jointly. Eventually, probably under the influence of Thatcher's Chief of Staff, David Wolfson, to whom Hoskyns had made his views plain, Ridley was sent to the Treasury while Hoskyns became the sole head of the Policy Unit.[117] Sherman, as shown above, was another advocate of the job being given to Hoskyns.

Ridley, however, says that Thatcher never formed a firm view of whom to put where, and her ideas continued to change right up to the election, indeed beyond it. A few days before the poll, she asked Ridley to put together a team of three or four to work in No. 10, and to that end he had arranged for Cardona, Portillo and Dobbs to go to No. 10 with him, earmarked to work alongside, if not in, the Policy Unit team. However, in the event, Thatcher, 'torn as always between a desire to enforce a tight restriction on staff numbers and to have to hand people on whom she could rely', chose to rely on the official No. 10 machine and asked Ridley to make alternative arrangements for the other members of the CRD. Ridley himself, clear that a divided leadership for the Policy Unit, combined with minimal staff resources, was sure to render the unit ineffective, quickly decided that it would be a better use of his time and resources to take up Howe's standing offer to become a special adviser in the Treasury. In addition he found employment for Cardona at the Treasury and for Portillo at Energy, where, he says, 'both settled in quickly and effectively.' As discussed, Dobbs subsequently worked for Saatchi and Saatchi, and Tebbit.[118]

Hoskyns was appointed, with a rank equivalent to undersecretary, 'Senior Policy Adviser to the Prime Minister', on a salary of £16,524 per annum. He attended the Economic Strategy Committee (E Committee), where he could speak by arrangement or when asked by Thatcher. He secured his presence as an observer at the two major economic Cabinets which took place each year. He went to small prime ministerial meetings in the Downing Street study and ministerial gatherings in the Cabinet room. In addition to numerous memoranda for Thatcher, he prepared papers for bodies such as E Committee and for circulation to senior Cabinet members. Now that the Conservatives were in power, 'colleagues I had come to know . . . were all, it seemed, gathered up in the embrace of Whitehall.' Hoskyns sought to counteract the centrifugal force that threatened to diffuse the close co-operation and energy developed by the team in opposition. He found his reception from permanent officials inside the Prime Minister's office mixed, his office 'shabby'. In his view, civil servants seemed ill-equipped to perform the tasks required for a reversal of national fortunes. They had spent their entire working lives sheltered from the realities of the market; they were associated with policy failures of the past and wedded to social democracy. Moreover, they were intrigue-prone. In September 1979, following what he saw as a duplicitous attempt by senior officials to prevent him from recommending Christopher Foster as the new head of the CPRS, Hoskyns wrote in his diary, 'the Civil Service are the real enemy of hope for the future and they are therefore my enemy.'[119] Once out of government, Hoskyns soon became an outspoken public critic of the structures within which politicians and civil servants operated, which had 'failed us between 1950 and 1980'.[120] Lord Armstrong says of Hoskyns that he was 'better at analysing the problem than proposing workable solutions'.[121]

As to his impact on the course of the Thatcher administrations, in office, according to Howe, Hoskyns 'kept up the pressure of advice on the "Stepping Stones" agenda'.[122] Thatcher records Hoskyns as urging the rapid introduction of trades union legislation.[123] A number of measures were taken over time, including the 1984 Trade Union Act, which made legal immunity dependent upon the conduct of strike ballots and political funds subject to ballots. Even before Thatcher came to power, Hoskyns was urging consideration of how an 'unbeatable' strike, possibly by the miners, might be tackled. The Policy Unit worked with Portillo, the special adviser at Energy, in an effort to ensure that coal stocks were built up for such an eventuality.[124] After Hoskyns's departure, in 1984–5 the government defeated an all-out strike by the National Union of Mineworkers.

Hoskyns probably had a significant influence upon the introduction of public expenditure planning based on cash rather than volume. It was announced with the 1981 Budget, to the general content of which No. 10 aides, Hoskyns included, contributed. He was an advocate of Thatcher carrying out a 'whole-sale recon-struction of the Cabinet', in order to ensure that those who shared her agenda were in key positions.[125] She acted in September 1981, with a reshuffle that included Prior's replacement by Norman Tebbit at Employment. Hoskyns should perhaps be viewed as an advance guard for the Thatcher programme, clearing the path for those who followed him. In 1985 he was described as Thatcher's 'spearhead against the Civil Service machine which she so distrusted in 1979. He was eventually beaten by that machine, but not before Sir Robert Armstrong's army had taken some beatings and remoulded itself better to suit its leader'.[126] A hindrance to Hoskyns, certainly early on, was his lack of government experience – a deficiency that led to errors such as his sending a paper to Geoffrey Howe only a month before the 1980 Budget, believing that he could still interest the Chancellor of the Exchequer in new ideas at such a late stage.[127]

Hoskyns's relationship with the Prime Minister was never personally close, and each had mixed opinions of the other. Thatcher felt that her 'able' aide 'had a refreshingly if sometimes irritatingly undisguised scorn for the *ad hoc* nature of political decision-making'.[128] She refers to his 'strong powers of analysis . . . In government he repeatedly compelled ministers to relate each problem to our overall strategy . . . He kept our eye on the ball'.[129] For his part, Hoskyns writes that in 'personal terms the relationship was, for me, a mixture of affection, loyalty, frequent misunderstandings, exasperation and occasional disappointment. I am sure that the last two feelings were mutual'. He shared political ground with her and felt she was well motivated. However, he found her a poor chairman, prone to inappropriate involvement in microscopic detail and particularly difficult to draft speeches for, owing to the fact that her 'critical faculties were poor'. In August 1981 Hoskyns sent Thatcher a note, co-signed by Wolfson and Ronnie Millar, her speech-writer, warning that her bullying and egotism were demoralising people around her. It seems to have backfired, undermining her confidence in her Senior Policy Adviser.[130]

Hoskyns's departure from office in May 1982 seems to have been prompted in part by what he felt to be a lack of strategic coherence in the government's approach, stemming from Thatcher's inadequacies.[131] According to Sherman, Hoskyns left 'primarily because he found that, contrary to what the media would have us believe, the civil servants soon assimilated Mrs Thatcher'.[132] Hoskyns had stated from the outset that he did not intend his to be a long tenure. The fact that he was drawn into speech-writing activities, a process he found very frustrating, was a more trivial source of discontent. When Thatcher attempted to dissuade him from leaving, he stipulated that he would stay only if he were placed 'formally in charge of a small prime minister's department, with the position of permanent secretary, reporting to' Thatcher. He would be broadly responsible for the CRD and in control of the CPRS. It was the latter requirement that proved to be the stumbling block, making Hoskyns's demand unacceptable to Robert Armstrong, whom Thatcher apparently consulted.[133]

Hoskyns may have influenced an important development in the popular perception of the Civil Service. In January 1980 Anthony Jay, the co-writer of the successful television comedy series *Yes, Minister*, then about to receive its first broadcast, had a meeting with Hoskyns and Strauss. *Yes, Minister* portrayed senior Whitehall officials as able to outwit ministers and pursue their own small-

'c' conservative agenda, an idea which chimed with Hoskyns's views. It became famous for its parody of the tendency for senior civil servants to express themselves in a deliberately understated fashion. Hoskyns suggested phrases such as 'Are you content, Prime Minister?' and 'I am bound to say . . . ' to Jay. As Hoskyns puts it, for 'its creators, and for Paul Eddington [the star], *Yes, Minister* had a more serious purpose than many people realised'.[134] Bernard Donoughue, too, 'acted as a regular chief adviser to the authors Jonathan Lynn and Anthony Jay'. He points out that, in the programme, 'the Prime Minister's personal adviser is named Bernard.'[135] In early episodes a special adviser, named Frank Weisel, is portrayed. The aide attempts to assist his minister, Jim Hacker, appointed to the fictitious Department of Administrative Affairs, in attaining radical policy objectives opposed by the permanent secretary, Sir Humphrey Appleby. Weisel struggles both to obtain an office close to Hacker's and to receive his paperwork. He and Hacker are outmanoeuvred by Appleby.

The Westwell Report

In April 1982 Hoskyns sent Thatcher an eighty-page paper entitled 'Westwell Report – Stepping Stones to 1989'.[136] Intended as the beginning of a follow-up to the original 'Stepping Stones' report,[137] it was based on two discussions held respectively at David Wolfson's house in Westwell in December 1981 and at Hoskyns's Clapham flat in January 1982. In attendance at the first event were three special advisers (Hoskyns, Walters and Strauss) as well as Wolfson himself; the economist and part-time Thatcher aide Douglas Hague; and three junior ministers, David Howell, Cecil Parkinson and Norman Lamont. Lawson submitted a written contribution but did not attend. His subsequent dismissive reference to Westwell was that it 'scarcely mentioned privatisation at all despite the fact that it was drafted by John Hoskyns . . . who continually stressed the need for Ministers to think strategically'.[138] Thatcher was not informed that the Westwell meeting was taking place and was reportedly 'outraged' when she found out, saying that she would have attended herself. Her exclusion was in fact deliberate, in order to foster free expression by the participants. Westwell was subject to what Hoskyns describes as 'the file-and-forget treatment', partly as a result of the departure from office of its main sponsor, Hoskyns.[139] Nevertheless, it merits attention, for it provides insight into the thoughts of some of Thatcher's most important special advisers, and illustrates how radical they were.

The Westwell Report was intended as a 'guide to winning the next election and governing effectively thereafter'. It bears certain Hoskyns hallmarks, such as the use of diagrams. Themes under examination were the economic outlook, means of winning the next election, policies to be pursued after a return to office and the implementation of those policies. Westwell was not optimistic regarding the likelihood that voters knew what was best for them. The electorate was 'still brain-washed into believing that it has rights without obligations'. Tighter regulation of organised labour, already Conservative policy, might not be sufficient; it was possible that it should rather be eradicated, perhaps through deliberate de-industrialisation. The possibility of introducing 'catalytic measures which would accelerate the gradual withering away of unions, together with the sunset industries where they are largely concentrated' was discussed.

Reference was made to '"unthinkable" objectives for . . . the NHS, state education, British Rail'. Greater labour flexibility was favoured, with the abolition of redundancy payments floated. Westwell suggested that there was a need to win public acceptance for the cost of winning the 'Third World War', defined as 'the ideological struggle by subversion and selective military intervention'. Full British membership of the European Monetary System was opposed, a fact which was significant given Thatcher's resistance to participation in continental currency schemes. One means of reducing unemployment might be the reclassification of individuals deemed not to be 'actively seeking work', an approach which 'in the 1930s had a major effect'. Other proposals were for more charges for public services and, perhaps, the introduction of a constitutional limit on state expenditure as a percentage of GDP. Reference was made to the privatisation of nationalised industries, but it was not dwelt on, as Lawson noted. Public-sector strikes had to be fought and won.

The most serious threat to Conservative re-election prospects, Westwell argued, was the possibility of 'riots in the summer of 1983, no doubt orchestrated by Left-wing activists'. The outright abolition of local government, the introduction of education vouchers and the establishment of workers' councils, bypassing trades unions, were raised as options. A desire to move the 'common ground back to the Right' and 'expose, once and for all, the muddied post-War consensus' was expressed, demonstrating that close allies of Thatcher were conscious opponents of the supposed political settlement. More Civil Service jobs should be opened up to outsiders on temporary contracts, at market rates. A purge of holders of various public offices who were opposed to the free market was suggested. Another requirement might be a Prime Minister's department. Extensive discussion was devoted to presentational methods, particularly with a view to developing a public response to the new SDP, which had made initial dramatic headway.

In establishing an election programme, it was argued, the CPRS could be used 'in a more political role'. Having secured a second term, the government should then deal with the Civil Service, which was 'a much more formidable obstacle to national recovery than the trade unions'. Taking as given Whitehall's automatic opposition to any new policy approaches, the Westwell Report called for 'a powerful cadre of market-orientated special advisers' to mount an attempt to 'challenge the Whitehall culture, rather than be meekly assimilated into it'. Attention was drawn to the fact that the 'last Labour Government had about 40 special advisers in Whitehall. We now have less than a dozen'. Economising on them would be 'to risk spoiling the ship for a ha'porth of tar'. This was further evidence of the fact that, often, the most fervent advocates of the use of political aides were the temporaries themselves; it also reflects the repeated pattern whereby instigators of radical programmes from across the political spectrum have envisaged the use of outsiders in Whitehall in order to achieve their objectives.

Alan Walters

From 1981 to 1984 (part-time from 1983) and again during 1989, Thatcher was advised by the economist Alan Walters. He was present at the conception of the Thatcher programme in the mid-1970s, made contributions at critical moments during the course of its existence and was involved in events leading to its demise. Walters was an impressive, intense figure. As Howe puts it, there 'was often a semi-messianic quality about his enthusiasm – about his silences even'.[140] He was an extremely close ally and personal friend of Thatcher, who held him in the highest esteem, and to whom he had direct access. It has been written of Walters that he 'is a man whose belief in simple truths struck a deep chord with Mrs Thatcher'; for his part, in 'her he found a politician who spoke the same language and, moreover, liked the story he had to tell about the limits of government and the need to let markets behave freely'.[141] Thatcher writes that Walters' monetarist ideas helped provide a theoretical framework for her intuition that thrift 'was a virtue and profligacy a vice'.[142] In his own words, he admired Thatcher for her 'strong belief in the morality of individual responsibility, the government's duty to restore and protect freedoms, [and] the need to secure financial stability and a non-inflationary environment'.[143] According to Lawson, Walters' strength was the fact that 'he was prepared to argue with Margaret on issues when he was convinced she was mistaken.'[144] Over the course of the Thatcher premiership, partly as a result of his relationship with her, some colleagues developed increasingly unfavourable opinions of Walters. Howe writes that 'Alan was never happier than when he was making some exclusive input into the Prime Minister's thinking, except when he was taking (or claiming) the credit for having done so.'[145] He has proclaimed his own 'considerable influence on economic policy'.[146] Griffiths, who had an office next door to him at the LSE in the 1970s, insists that Walters was not a difficult personality but that, as an academic, if he did not agree with an idea he said so, which could make him unpopular.[147]

In his own words, Walters was 'born in 1926 of working class parents in a Leicestershire slum'. His father, a communist, was 'revolted' by the excesses of Stalinism, but remained a 'staunch ultra-left-wing socialist until the end'. Walters failed the eleven-plus examination. He studied statistics, sitting a University of London exam externally. In 1960, at Birmingham University, he and some colleagues began researching the money supply in Britain. Walters became a professor at the LSE in 1967. At the time he was associated with the free-market think tank, the Institute of Economic Affairs (IEA), which was under the direction of Ralph Harris.[148]

Walters was, as Howe puts it, one of the 'scattered voices of dissent' to economic policy under Heath, alongside other IEA luminaries and Enoch Powell.[149] Initially Walters believed that the Heath administration was committed to 'a new economic policy based on monetary stability, fiscal rectitude and free and unfettered markets'; but it disappointed him. The concerns he expressed, discussed in Chapter 5 above, led, he writes, to his being 'relieved of my part-time job' in the Cabinet Office.[150] Thatcher describes him as one of the economists 'who had been right when we in Government had gone so badly wrong'.[151] In February 1974 Sherman began having conversations with Joseph, in which the former attacked Heath for his abandonment of the supposed commitment to free-market values and his handling of monetary policy. Walters, who lived near to Sherman in the Kensington High Street area, joined them. So, too, did Thatcher, who was 'as impressed as Joseph by the Sherman–Walters analysis'.[152]

The basis of Walters' approach, as expressed in a 1974 Aims of Industry pamphlet, *Money and Inflation*, was one straightforward proposition. He wrote:

> *the more plentiful a commodity the lower will be its price. Summer strawber-*
> *ries are much cheaper than winter ones. So men have long reasoned that the*
> *same sort of rules must also apply to money. An increase in the supply of money*
> *will cause the 'price' of money to fall . . . This implies that the prices of all other*
> *goods and services rise: hence the simple rule that more money means higher*
> *prices . . . alas, the evidence of recent years shows that distinguished statesmen*
> *have ignored or positively rejected this principle.*[153]

Some time before he became a special adviser, Walters' ideas were an important influence upon Thatcher and, in turn, upon Conservative policy. Partly thanks to his earlier efforts, the party's 1979 manifesto stated that to 'master inflation, proper monetary discipline is essential, with publicly stated targets for the rate of growth of the money supply'.[154]

In 1981, when Walters was recruited as an aide to Thatcher from a lucrative academic post at the Johns Hopkins University in the US, his seniority – equivalent to that of a second permanent secretary – was too great for his inclusion in the Policy Unit; he was therefore given the title of 'Economic Adviser'.[155] His salary of £50,000 was part-funded by the CPS.[156] Walters writes that there was 'much pressure to put me in the cabinet office or in the Treasury, but the Prime Minister and I agreed that I would be most effective at her elbow in No. 10'. He was given a very open-ended brief.[157] Hugo Young suggests that he 'secured more influence in less time at the heart of government than anyone in a comparable position before him'.[158]

Walters arrived at a time of great political and economic strain. With unemployment 'soaring by 100,000 a month',[159] opposition to the prioritisation of control over the money supply extended as far as Thatcher's own Cabinet. Walters, along with others at No. 10, including Hoskyns, although still committed to monetarism, felt that too tight a squeeze was taking place. Matters were complicated further by the fact that the PSBR appeared to be growing out of control. Walters encouraged the adoption of a new approach for the 1981 Budget, entailing the use of tax increases coupled with a reduction in interest rates to ease the pressure on business.[160] The combination represented a very controversial break with much conventional wisdom. As Cairncross puts it, raising 'taxes and tightening fiscal policy in a depression in order to cut the money supply outraged many economists'.[161]

The 1981 Budget was important both as a turning point in policy terms and as an assertion of Thatcher's will over that of the Cabinet.[162] Given its historical importance, competing claims for influence on its content are unsurprising. The extent to which it should be credited to Walters is an area of controversy. Howe records proposing at a No. 10 meeting held on 13 February 1981 that, since the projected PSBR had risen to between £13.5 billion and £13.75 billion, taxes should be increased by £3.5 billion, taking the PSBR down towards £10 billion. Thatcher, Howe writes, baulked at this, but Walters, who subsequently proposed an even larger figure of £7 billion tax increases, provided welcome support for the Chancellor.[163] In Thatcher's recollection of the 13 February discussion, Howe insisted that it would be politically impossible to take the PSBR below £11 billion, with Walters arguing that it should be lower. Thatcher claims that she was gradually won over by the tenacious Walters. At another meeting with Howe, on 24 February, which Walters did not attend, she urged that the PSBR be reduced to approximately £10.5 billion. The following day, she writes, Howe informed her that he was willing to go below £11 billion.[164]

Hoskyns's memoir suggests that, rather than Walters alone, it was the political aides in No. 10 acting collectively who persuaded the politicians of the need for radical action on the PSBR.[165] Howe insists that the Budget decisions were the product of a combined effort by the Treasury and No. 10 and that Walters's role, while significant, has been exaggerated. In accounts of the 1981 Budget, Howe complains, surprisingly 'heroic roles are sometimes attributed to individual performers . . . Some of Walters' champions (not excluding the Professor himself) credit . . . [him] with near-visionary insight.'[166] In his own words, Walters 'worked to bring about immense changes in monetary and fiscal policy' and 'proposed the biggest budgetary squeeze in peacetime history'. His version suggests that after 'much fierce debate, Mrs Thatcher became convinced and, with characteristic courage, adopted this fiscal squeeze'.[167] What is certain is that, whether he was its main or initially its only advocate, Walters wanted the policy that was ultimately adopted, and perhaps something more.

Walters went on to act as a scrutineer of proposed public spending; 'a nonsense-stopper', as Hennessy puts it. One victim was British Rail, which was 'keen on a number of capital projects in the early 1980s'. The Treasury began consulting him prior to making approaches to the Prime Minister.[168] Here was an example of how a special adviser could unofficially obtain authority through obvious proximity to the employing minister. Walters was capable of generating particularly daring schemes of his own, as his response to the Argentinian invasion of the Falkland Islands in 1982 demonstrates. During April and May, with the British task force on its way to the South Atlantic, Walters prepared a paper called 'An Economic Solution for the Falklands'. It proposed that, following the cessation of hostilities and withdrawal of the occupying force, Argentina should be offered the opportunity to purchase sovereignty over the islands. A financial sum would be offered to every inhabitant, followed by a plebiscite on whether to accept it. Walters suspected that a figure of £50,000 would prove to be acceptable to more than two-thirds of the islanders. If the first bid were rejected, however, another could be made after an appropriate period of time had lapsed. Not wishing to appear disloyal at a fraught time, Walters did not send his paper to Thatcher. However, he floated the proposal to Howe late in 1983, who felt that, though intriguing, it was politically unacceptable.[169]

Walters was an opponent of British participation in the ERM, a group of floating currencies pegged to the Deutschmark, within a 6 per cent band. Thatcher's account of his analysis, expressed to her in 1981, was 'that it was wrong to think of the ERM as a force for stability'. Rates were not fixed; rather, they floated within brackets. Moreover, the alignments of currencies within the ERM 'were the subject of political horse-trading rather than the workings of the market – and the market does a better job'.[170] In 1985 Lawson proposed that sterling join the ERM as a means of bringing about monetary discipline. Opinion within Cabinet generally appeared to be moving in his direction. By this time Walters had returned to academia in the United States; nevertheless, his informal advice to Thatcher seems to have been the main basis of her refusal to consent to Lawson's plan.[171]

During his US interlude in the latter half of the 1980s, not only did Walters disagree with Lawson's policies, he engaged in public dissent: behaviour that did not endear him to the Chancellor of the Exchequer. In July 1988, having got wind of the fact that Thatcher was planning to re-employ Walters, Lawson personally pleaded with the Prime Minister not to do so – to no avail.[172] In May 1989 Walters returned. The top-level Cabinet dispute over the ERM, with Thatcher against and Lawson and Howe in favour, was fiercer than ever. Walters became embroiled. Lawson's attempts at surrogate exchange rate management meant rises in interest rates in May and October. Walters counselled Thatcher that the consequent monetary squeeze was excessive.[173] There were soon press references to speculation among politicians and in the City as to 'whether Messrs Lawson and Walters could coexist in Downing Street'.[174] On 8 October 1989 the *Sunday Times* reported that Walters had opposed a recent rise in interest rates from 14 per cent to 15 per cent, on the grounds that 'they were already high enough, and that an increase . . . would be overkill, tipping the economy into a slump'.[175] Warned about the appearance of the story the night before, Lawson 'telephoned Walters at home, who professed complete mystification about the story, swearing he had not spoken to anyone'. However, he 'refused to issue a denial'.[176]

Lawson writes that 'sterling was being put under strain by the habit of financial analysts of treating Alan Walters' views, which . . . continued to be aired to groups of outsiders on both sides of the Atlantic at supposedly private gatherings, as representing the view of Margaret herself'.[177] Lord (Robin) Butler, the Cabinet Secretary from 1988, says that various attempts were made to restrain Walters, all of them unsuccessful. Butler goes on, 'he might also have been of the opinion that he was receiving encouragement from the Prime Minister.' Such a phenomenon was not a historical novelty. As Butler points out, in 1170 Henry II was heard to ask, 'Will no one rid me of this turbulent priest?' Four knights, taking the King at his word, murdered Thomas à Becket, the Archbishop of Canterbury.[178]

Following an article in the *Financial Times* on 18 October 1989, referring to Walters's criticisms of the ERM, Lawson snapped. On the morning of 26 October, in a private meeting, he told Thatcher that public knowledge of Walters' 'disagreement with Government policy . . . over a range of issues, in particular the . . . exchange rate' was making 'my job as Chancellor impossible. The markets heard two voices, and did not know which to believe'. Lawson felt that his authority 'was being almost daily undermined'. Either he, Lawson, or Walters would have to go. In Lawson's account, Thatcher told him that if 'Alan were to go, that would destroy *my* authority'.[179] Thatcher writes that she pointed out that the *Financial Times* quotes were taken from an academic essay written in 1988, before Walters' return to Britain. Moreover, he was an adviser; final decisions on policy resided with ministers. She notes that her relationship with her Chancellor was deteriorating and that his handling of the economy was subject to increasing criticism.[180] Lawson maintains that 'it was well after [Walters] had been re-installed as Margaret's personal economic adviser that he had brought [the essay's] existence to the attention of the *Financial Times* and sent them a copy with explicit permission to quote from it.' Anyway, for Lawson, the problem was the cumulative effect of Walters' views finding their way to a wider audience; the *Financial Times* story was just one particular manifestation of it.[181]

Lawson wrote to Thatcher stating that the 'successful conduct of economic policy is possible only if there is, and is seen to be, full agreement between the Prime Minister and the Chancellor of the Exchequer'. In his view, 'this essential requirement cannot be satisfied so long as Alan Walters remains your personal economic adviser.' For this reason he 'regretfully concluded that it is in the best interest of the Government to resign my office'.[182] With Lawson gone, Kenneth Baker, the Conservative party chairman, prevailed upon Griffiths to encourage Walters, a 'close friend' of Griffiths, to step down.[183] Inevitably, Walters obliged, although it was not Thatcher's wish that he should.[184] This chain of events in turn contributed to Thatcher's downfall.[185] Following Lawson's resignation there was discussion of the 'shadowy role' of special advisers in the press.[186] Walters was not replaced, resulting in speculation that the importance of special advisers at the centre was in decline.[187]

Manifestos

Aides were important to the development of the three Conservative general election manifestos produced during Thatcher's period of leadership. In opposition, Adam Ridley was 'closely involved' with that of 1979.[188] In the summer of 1982 nine policy groups, staffed by the CRD, were established in order to develop proposals for inclusion in the next manifesto. Thatcher records that to 'keep the Government informed, special advisers to the relevant Cabinet ministers would sit in on the meetings', demonstrating their value as 'political appointees . . . free from the constraints of political neutrality which prevent the use of civil servants

in such roles'. Thatcher entrusted primary responsibility for manifesto authorship to Mount, for which as 'head of my Policy Unit at No. 10 . . . [he] was ideally
placed . . . and uniquely gifted'. Along with Howe and Adam Ridley, he worked
on the first draft during February and March 1983.[189] The end result was a classic
statement of Thatcherism. The Conservative Party promised to 'curb the legal
immunity of unions to call strikes without the prior approval of those concerned
through a fair and secret ballot'. Also proposed was the transfer of 'state-owned
businesses to independent ownership', with targets including British Telecom,
British Airways, British Steel, British Shipbuilders, British Leyland and 'as many
as possible of Britain's airports'.[190]

In mid-1986 Thatcher established the Strategy Group (labelled the 'A-Team' by
the press) 'to plan for the next election, discussing policy, presentation and
tactics'. It was composed of the most senior ministers, but Griffiths also 'regularly
attended'. In addition, Griffiths sat on the five-strong Manifesto Committee
subsequently set up by Thatcher under the chairmanship of John MacGregor, the
Chief Secretary to the Treasury. Another member of the Manifesto Committee
was John O'Sullivan, a Policy Unit special adviser who had formerly been an
associate editor at *The Times*. In early 1987 Griffiths, along with Robin Harris,
the director of the CRD, compiled all the proposals produced by ministers and
various policy groups. Thatcher, whose concern was that a party which had been
in office for eight years should continue to present itself in dynamic terms to the
electorate, asserts that the 1987 'manifesto was the best ever produced by the
Conservative Party . . . [it] went to the heart of my convictions'.[191] Howe suggests
that it was imposed on the government and party from the centre.[192] Education
policy was one important aspect. The promotion of 'basic educational skills . . .
moral values: honesty, hard work and responsibility', as well as the facilitation of
parental choice in terms of where to send children, were proposed. Another
important – indeed, as it transpired fateful – commitment was the abolition of
the domestic rating system. It was to be replaced with 'a fairer Community
Charge . . . This will be a fixed rate charge for local services paid by those over
the age of 18.'[193]

The process of manifesto production was often frantic, and it seems that in
1987 one special adviser prevented a major error from occurring, almost
committing another in the process. In his account, shortly before the manifesto's
publication, Jonathan Hill, an aide at Employment, noticed that in the proof that

had supposedly been approved by the Cabinet 'the section dealing with the Conservative's plans for trade union reforms somehow seemed to contain Labour Party proposals'. He rang the CRD and insisted that it be changed. It then fell to him to proofread the corrected version. Taking the document home, Hill accidentally left it in an off-licence. Realising what he had done, he rushed back, to find it there 'in a plastic bag, propped up against the counter'.[194]

Disapproval and encouragement

While the degree of opposition condemnation of the use of special advisers was perhaps not as intense during the Thatcher years as it had been during 1974–9, some Labour MPs did subject the practice to scrutiny. Gordon Brown, who, as Chancellor of the Exchequer from 1997, was to use aides extensively himself, made certain factual enquiries in the House regarding matters such as the numbers in employment.[195] His criticism was implied. Bob Cryer, another Labour MP, was more direct. In February 1989 he called for the initiation of a Commons debate on 'the need for guidelines' governing the employment of special advisers. Cryer described them as 'something of a heterogenous collection since 1979'. Their number, he said, included 'a former member of the National Front, who apparently escaped the scrutiny of special branch', one individual 'who is employed by a company that is being investigated by the Department of Trade and Industry which he is advising' and another, associated with a major shipping company, 'who is apparently meddling in the Department of Transport although ostensibly he is at the Department of Trade and Industry'. The total cost to the taxpayer was 'staggering', Cryer argued, with Thatcher at Downing Street 'paying her Tory chums hundreds of thousands of pounds a year'.[196]

In May 1986 the House of Commons Treasury and Civil Service Select Committee produced a report entitled *Civil Servants and Ministers: Duties and Responsibilities*.[197] It discussed what government members could reasonably ask career officials to do. Disquiet was expressed over a 'recent case where a press officer was instructed by a Minister to disclose to the press the contents of a letter from the Solicitor General to another Minister'. It was stated that the 'act in question would have been no less improper, but the instructions would at least have been fairer to the individual involved, if that person had been a political appointee'. The report went on to propose that 'Ministers who require their press officers to do more than present and describe their policies should make political appointments.' Parliament, then, was actively encouraging the use of special advisers in media briefing roles, as a means of protecting career officials.

The committee noted that none of the witnesses it had interviewed had opposed the practice of ministers appointing their own aides. Generally, 'special advisers and career civil servants have been able to work creatively and harmoniously together,' and 'when used properly special advisers have been able to contribute significantly to the effectiveness of ministers.' The use of special advisers was 'patchy and unsystematic', however. In order to rectify this shortcoming, it was recommended that 'the British system should edge closer to the European model where each Minister appoints a *cabinet* to assist him in running his department.' The 'Minister's Policy Unit', as the committee called it, would be comprised of 'a number of special advisers, together with a number of career civil servants and his Parliamentary Private Secretary'. It would serve to 'strengthen the Minister, increasing his influence and control over the department' as well as enabling participation in 'collective decision-making in cabinet'.

* * *

The reduction in the number of special advisers which followed the changeover in party administration in 1979 was the product of ideology, Thatcher's lack of interest and her reluctance to permit ministers to make their own appointments. Nevertheless, as a political species, they survived. Although quantity was lacking at first, the qualitative impact of individuals such as Walters, Hoskyns and Young was great. Subsequently numbers grew, particularly at Downing Street, with a large private-sector contingent among the recruits. Some went on to political careers, others to success elsewhere. While the CRD supplied staff, the radical newcomer, the CPS, was perhaps more favoured by Thatcher, particularly in the earlier stages of her administration. There were political and presentational aides, but the use of academic experts declined. Special advisers played significant roles at the Treasury.

It would be difficult to conceive of Thatcherism without the contribution of her aides. Both in opposition and office, Walters supplied many economic ideas and Hoskyns bolstered her opposition to trades unionism. Mount and Griffiths added a strong moral dimension during their spells in Downing Street. Privatisation owed much to the efforts of Redwood. Thatcher displayed an openness to influence from beyond the usual Conservative channels. Her personal staff also assisted in the imposition of her control on the government. The increase in the number of special advisers attached to No. 10 took place at the same time as an expansion in her power. However, the resentment engendered by her use of Walters and others ultimately contributed to her downfall. Manifesto development was coordinated from the centre, with participation by departmental aides. Labour criticisms displayed, once again, the opportunism associated with opposition.

Eight

Storm troops, peacemakers and 'bastards': advisers under Major

This chapter describes the use of special advisers during Major's term as premier from 1990 to 1997. This was a period in which the nature and role of special advisers became subject to slightly more legal regulation, and in which hitherto undisclosed guidance on their use was made public. Significant individuals examined include Tessa Keswick, an aide to Kenneth Clarke, a Cabinet member throughout Major's premiership; Tom Burke, who worked at the Department of the Environment from 1991 to 1997; and the two heads of Major's Policy Unit, Sarah Hogg and Norman Blackwell. Cabinet divisions, highlighted by the press, were a feature of the period, and the role of special advisers in them will be considered. Finally, the scrutiny to which aides were subjected, by the Committee on Standards in Public Life, in Parliament and in the press, will be examined.

Regulation

On 1 April 1991 Orders in Council, applying to both the Home and the Diplomatic Service, affirmed in law for the first time the confinement of special advisers, in the course of their duties, to the provision of counsel. The Orders are described by the then Cabinet Secretary, Lord Butler, as a 'general tightening up' of Civil Service regulation, within which provision for the activities of aides formed a part.[1] Previous Diplomatic and Civil Service Orders dating from 1982 specified appointments which terminated 'at the end of an Administration' as being exempt from the need for approval by the Civil Service Commissioners, but did not refer to their exclusively advisory function.[2] They reiterated the first legal definition of the special adviser, contained in the 1978 Order. The 1991 decrees, like their predecessors, listed the exceptions to the rule that career officials should be selected 'on merit on the basis of fair and open competition'. One, which was intended to cover special advisers, was 'where the holder is appointed by a Minister of the Crown for the purpose only of providing advice to any Minister, and under which the period for which the situation is to be held immediately terminates at the end of an Administration'.[3] While the latter part of the definition was not new, the opening, including the phrase 'for the purpose only of providing advice to any Minister', was. The Order in Council now stated who appointed aides and who they worked for (that is, ministers), what their job was (albeit vaguely) and when their employment ceased.

This first attempt to define in law what aides could do occurred some way into their historical development. Richard Wilson told Wicks in July 2002, 'I had not realised until recently that the qualification about advice was only added in 1991.'[4] The Orders were intended to confirm that aides were not integrated into the management structure, and were unable to give orders to career officials. This understanding, which seems to have existed from the outset in 1964, was, however, flawed. The reality of government made its observance problematic, for a number of reasons. The Senior Policy Adviser, who was invariably a political appointment, was effectively responsible for the career civil servants employed within the Policy Unit. Aides at No. 10, certainly since the Thatcher period, communicated with the departments in a manner which presumably sometimes entailed the conveyance of prime ministerial will. Exercise of power was often a more subtle activity than the direct issue of instructions. Special advisers known to be close to ministers could thereby acquire influence, shading into informal authority, over permanent officials, with whom they interacted on a daily basis. For example, the views they expressed in discussions would carry extra weight. As one special adviser during the Major period, Tessa Keswick, subsequently informed the Committee on Standards in Public Life, 'We could not tell civil servants what to do. We asked for things and it was ou job to get on with the civil service.' Since aides, she later went on, 'are alongside the Secretary of State, or a Minister, they have obviously some influence . . . if they are serious people and are taken seriously'.[5] Some activities, including the stimulation of policy development and the chasing of implementation, were arguably more managerial than consultative. Nevertheless, the existence of a convention, and then of Orders in Council, to the effect that such functions were not legitimate must have served to restrain such tendencies.

Major's period of office was characterised by greater openness in and codification of government practice. It was a time in which 'the British Constitution began to move from the back of an envelope to the back of a code.'[6] One manifestation of the trend was the publication of the ministerial guidebook, *Questions of Procedure for Ministers*, for the first time. The edition dated May 1992 referred to special advisers as providing 'a political dimension to the advice available to Ministers' and 'the direct advice of distinguished experts specialising in a particular field of public administration'. This suggested a distinction between types of aide. Appointments, made 'directly by . . . Ministers', were subject to prime ministerial approval, which had to be secured in advance. No reference was made to a numerical limit for each minister.[7]

Possibly as a response to a degree of parliamentary and press criticism, discussed below, a Draft Model Letter of Appointment for Special Advisers was deposited in the House of Commons Library in 1995. For the remainder of the Major period, MPs tabling questions on aides were often referred to it. However, in terms of the functions of special advisers, it merely stated that 'Your duties will be those laid down by the Minister.' Its contents, which probably reflected existing practice rather than introducing anything new, were mainly concerned with practicalities, such as pay reviews, working hours and severance terms. Appointments, the letter stated, were terminated 'at the end of the present Administration . . . when the Minister who appointed you leaves the Government or moves to another appointment . . . in the event of a General Election, on the day after polling day; or . . . on due notice [three months] being given by either side'. One aspect of the regulations contained in the Draft Model Letter lacked credibility. Aides were exempt from the rules which applied to career officials on accepting 'business appointments following resignation or retirement', but 'as a corollary' could not have 'access to the kind of information (e.g. about individual companies), or be involved in the kind of business (e.g. contracts) which necessitate the rules applicable to career civil servants'. Whether or not the regulation was adhered to, public suspicion that it was not observed was always likely to persist. Moreover, other types of knowledge could be equally valuable in the private sector. Accordingly, as will be shown below, amendments were subsequently made to this provision.

The Draft Model Letter further stated that special advisers, like ministers, were not permitted access to papers of previous administrations; and that most of the rules applying to civil servants in the 'politically restricted' group applied also to aides. Any individual in the category publicly identified as a prospective or actual candidate for the European or UK Parliament was obliged to resign his or her post. Similarly, continued employment within Whitehall was not compatible with participation in general, European or by-election campaigns. It was also essential to avoid the use of public funds, in forms such as departmental resources, for party political purposes. However, special advisers were allowed to attend party functions, including conferences and 'policy reviews organised by the party' in order to represent the views of their ministers. At the latter events, however, they were not permitted 'to advocate policies going beyond or departing from those of the Government as a whole'. Public controversy and identification with criticism of the government were to be avoided. Special advisers were permitted to participate in local political activities, except those in support of national ones. If serving on local authorities, however, they had to avoid both involvement in areas which related to the department in which they were employed, and the embarrassment of any government ministers.[8]

There were various concerns regarding adherence to proper practices. In April 1996 the Cabinet Office circulated a memorandum around the departments regarding 'the principles which [civil servants] should observe in relation to the conduct of Government business during the period prior to local and European elections'. (The form it took was standard; a similar caution had been issued in 1994.) It included the provision that special advisers 'should if necessary be reminded of the rules against circulating material on party paper within departments'.[9] Controversy surrounded a 1996 Conservative Party pamphlet entitled *New Labour's Expenditure Plans*, produced through the identification by ministers and special advisers of supposed Labour commitments, which were then costed by career officials. A comparable exercise had been carried out prior to the 1992 election. The senior civil servants' union, the First Division Association (FDA), was reported as stating that a number of its members 'had raised serious concerns about the document, particularly "the stress placed on maximising costings"'.[10] Among a number of enquiries made in the House, it was asked whether 'factual material provided by civil servants . . . was altered by Ministers or special advisers'.[11] However, the existence of political appointments could serve as a protection for permanent officials. In 1996 there were reports that when the government sought to find public service providers willing to act as its 'cheerleaders', Butler insisted that the job of locating individuals be done by special advisers.[12]

A convention seems to have emerged that, given the extremely partisan nature of their role, aides to the Conservative party chairman would be paid from party rather than public sources. When Jeremy Hanley, holder of the chairmanship, recruited Tim Rycroft as his special adviser in September 1994, the party initially announced that he 'would be paid as a civil servant employed by the Cabinet Office'. However, since 'previous special advisers to party chairmen have been automatically paid by the party', the statement was soon retracted. Reportedly, 'Whitehall sources expressed some surprise . . . that the party ever could have thought that Mr Rycroft could have his salary met by public funds.'[13] When Labour created the Cabinet-level post of chairman after the 2001 election it followed suit, arranging for aides to the chair to be paid by the party.

Numbers and personnel

In February 1991 the total number of special advisers in employment was twenty-six. By November 1992 it had risen to thirty-seven and by July 1993 to forty-one; and there were still thirty-eight in post at the end of the period in 1997. The proportion of special advisers located at Downing Street remained steady at six or seven. How can the surge of the early Major years be explained? A tendency towards growth was under way during the Thatcher administration, but there was an acceleration. It may be that the trend was exaggerated by a low figure for February 1991, when special advisers were still being recruited following the changeover in premiers and consequent Cabinet reshuffle the previous November. Major's style as Prime Minister has been portrayed as more relaxed than his predecessor's; perhaps, in the new atmosphere, it was easier for ministers to recruit aides. In his own words, Major 'left ministers with complete freedom to appoint' the special advisers of their choice.[14] However, other accounts suggest that some Cabinet members were strongly encouraged to appoint aides, whether they wanted to or not. John Redwood, formerly

Thatcher's Senior Policy Adviser and the Secretary of State for Wales from 1993 to 1995, suspected that in his case insistence on his having a special adviser was intended as a means of exercising control. According to Redwood, 'I was told originally the aide could be for my junior minister. When the aide was appointed, Number 10 briefed that it was for me.'[15] The special adviser in question, Hywel Williams, states that 'Redwood feared that I was being appointed to spy on him and to report back to the Prime Minister.'[16]

The data available for the Major period also give an indication of the balance between experts and political advisers. In July 1993, of a total of forty-one special advisers eleven were expert and thirty political; by July 1995, of a total of thirty-two, four were expert and twenty-eight political. Remuneration was based on a pay spine, which in 1994 ran from £19,121 to £59,957, although six aides (out of thirty-eight that year) fell outside (presumably above) the scale. At this juncture a permanent secretary could earn a maximum of £87,620; an MP was paid £31,867; a parliamentary undersecretary in the Commons £21,961; a minister of state in the Commons £28,936; a Cabinet minister in the Commons £40,895; and the Prime Minister £54,438. The parliamentary salary for ministers in the Commons was £23,854. (Details of the annual cost of special advisers in the Major years are given in the appendix.)

To some extent, the private-sector flavour of the Thatcher period remained, though party activists and journalists became more prominent. In July 1993, of a total of forty-one special advisers, ten had previously worked in Conservative Central Office; one had been an MP's assistant and one was described as working for Lord Rothschild; one was a barrister and one an academic from the University of California. The connections of the remainder included financial and management consultancies (such as Coopers & Lybrand Deloitte, the Boston Consulting Group and Pieda), investment banks (James Capel), real estate firms (Richard Ellis), pressure groups (the Shopping Hours Reform Council and the National Farmers Union), the *Sunday Telegraph*, *Daily Telegraph* and *European* newspapers, and various other media enterprises (Haymarket Publishing Services and Business Television).

Another group represented among the ranks of Major-era aides was that of former SDP activists.[17] At the end of the 1980s the SDP had split over whether it should merge with the Liberal Party, with which it had formed electoral pacts; the group which remained independent, with three MPs, led by David Owen, was finally dissolved in 1990. Members of the party scattered across the political spectrum. Some, of whom a significant portion were young Owenites, joined the Conservatives, and a number of former SDP apparatchiks became Conservative special advisers. They included Michael McManus, who served at Central Office and then moved to the Welsh Office after the 1992 election;[18] and Chris Hopson, who worked for David Mellor at National Heritage during 1992.[19] By 1 March 1997 Tony Hockley and Tim Rycroft, the final national secretary of the SDP, were at the Department of Health. Nearly two years earlier Andrew Grice had noted in the *Sunday Times* that some 'Tory rightwingers . . . sense a mini-coup at the Department of Health, where Stephen Dorrell, a likely standard-bearer for the left in a future Tory leadership election, has just appointed Tim Rycroft, once SDP national secretary, as his political adviser, and Tony Hockley, Owen's former economic adviser, works for Gerald Malone, Dorrell's deputy.'[20] In addition to Hockley and Rycroft, in March 1997 Tom Burke, although not a partisan convert, was at Environment and Greg Clarke was at Trade and Industry.[21] In 2001 Clarke took over as Director of the CRD from Danny Finkelstein, another former SDP staff member, who was about to contest a parliamentary seat.

Two aides to the Major administrations had served under Labour governments in the 1960s. One, Christopher Foster, was non-political this time around (his case is described in more detail below). The other was Bill Robinson, who counselled Norman Lamont, the 1990–3 Chancellor of the Exchequer. Robinson, 'a taxation expert, from the Institute of Fiscal Studies',[22] had worked inside the prime ministerial team headed by Andrew Graham during 1969. Some were aspiring politicians – such as John Bercow, appointed as a counsellor to the Chief Secretary to the Treasury, Jonathan Aitken, in March 1995. Born in 1963, Bercow studied Government at the University of Essex. During 1986–7 he was National Chairman of the Federation of Conservative Students, and from 1986–90 served as a Conservative councillor in the London Borough of Lambeth. He stood for Parliament, unsuccessfully, in Motherwell South in 1987 and in Bristol South in 1992. After a period working in merchant banking, he joined Rowland Sallingbury Casey, the public affairs branch of Saatchi and Saatchi, and by the time of his appointment as a special adviser had become a director of the company. The involvement prompted questions in the House regarding the possibility of conflicts of interest and the measures that were being taken to avoid them. In response, Kenneth Clarke, the Chancellor of the Exchequer, stated that

'Mr. Bercow has retained no pecuniary interest in any public relations company.'[23] Bercow became an MP, for the safe seat of Buckingham, in 1997.

There were numerous non-expert special advisers. One significant appointment was Tessa Keswick, aide to Kenneth Clarke as Secretary of State for Health from 1989 to 1990, Secretary of State for Education from 1990 to 1992, Home Secretary from 1992 to 1993 and Chancellor of the Exchequer from 1993 to 1995, when she left his service and became director of the CPS. Clarke's biographer, Malcolm Balen, describes Keswick, born in 1942, as 'nothing if not well connected'. Her father was the seventeenth Lord Lovat and she was a founder shareholder in Cluff Oil. Her husband, Henry Keswick, was one of the richest men in Britain.[24] She did not attend university. Formerly a Conservative councillor and parliamentary candidate, she began advising Clarke in January 1989. Their relationship was 'obviously close' to the extent that, eventually, 'she had reached a position where accusing fingers were pointed at her, holding her responsible for what were perceived to be Kenneth Clarke's mistakes.'[25] Commentators have contrasted her 'grandee' image with that of the 'beer-and-skittles' Clarke.[26] Keswick was portrayed in the press as wanting to see Clarke attain the premiership.[27] Upon her departure in February 1995 there was speculation as to whether it might be the result of a 'personal rift' or possibly a 'policy disagreement' between her and Clarke. Keswick was reportedly agnostic over British membership of the European single currency, which Clarke supported.[28]

Keswick's role was wide-ranging. She saw her 'principal duties' as being 'to stick closely to your Minister, to attend all his meetings and share in the policy areas that he was going to pursue'. Keswick went to 'press conferences . . . or occasions that [Clarke] had to appear in front of the press'. She regarded herself as a point of liaison with an outside world which included lobby groups, the press, Conservative Central Office 'and any other bodies or persons who came through us'. She also dealt with external correspondence. Although she was not a specialist, the majority of her work, in her account, was policy-related. It entailed 'looking at the whole role of the public service'. She has said that she spent most of her time 'in meetings discussing policy issues and . . . developing policies'.[29]

According to Keswick, her 'relations with the press department obviously were extremely friendly, but . . . very separate'. Where talking to journalists was concerned, there 'were very strong rules about matters of confidentiality . . . it was extremely unusual for confidential matters to appear in print. If they did so, it was considered to be a leak and the special adviser might get blamed'. She did, however, speak personally to media representatives. Such contact, which Keswick kept to a minimum, had to be conducted with great circumspection, particularly when she was at the Treasury, given the sensitive nature of its business. As she put it, the 'press always wanted to talk to special advisers, for obvious reasons ... You had to be friendly with them because it was important from the point of view of the person you were working for that you should have friendly relations. But, at the same time, obviously you could not give them any information'.[30]

Keswick worked with the Treasury head of information, but only 'if there was an event coming up that related directly to the Secretary of State'. These were

what we call 'good news items', for instance, some initiative was going to be announced in three weeks' time. In consultation with the press office you would decide which day this announcement would go out and you would look at the press release and make sure that the good information was up at the top. It was just rather a minor sort of public relations role that we would play there.

While Keswick downplayed such activities, her reference to them suggests that the news management techniques associated with the Blair administration were not entirely new in 1997, although they may have been less systematic and centralised in the preceding years. Keswick wrote political speeches and press releases issued through party channels for her minister, and 'wrote into some of the departmental speeches as well'. However, she has insisted that 'if we put in even a qualitative adjective which was considered to be exaggerated, we were not allowed to do it.'[31]

Some special advisers were experts not associated with the Conservative Party. One such was Christopher Foster, a veteran aide from Labour governments of the 1960s and 1970s. From June 1992 to November 1993 he worked for John MacGregor, the Secretary of State for Transport. Foster has described himself as a 'non-political' special adviser during this period.[32] He played an important role in the privatisation of British Rail (BR), one of the last of the major sales of its type. Other specialist aides assisted with the policy. Sir Idris Pearce was engaged as a counsellor on 'British Rail privatisation property issues' from June 1992 to July 1994. Roger Salmon and John Swift were also listed as special advisers 'on

British Rail privatisation' from January to November 1993,[33] but the classification was anomalous: they were, respectively, the franchising director and rail regulator, employed as temporary civil servants because the bodies they were to head had yet to be formally established.

The 1992 Conservative manifesto stated that by 'franchising, we will give the private sector the fullest opportunity to operate existing passenger railway services'.[34] The exact approach, however, was not finalised, and the task of doing so fell, in part, to Foster. Foster was a supporter of track separation, which entailed the establishment of an infrastructure controller (created in the form of Railtrack) levying rail access charges on train-operating companies. Foster hoped that this structure would achieve greater efficiency and saw benefits to the introduction of formal contractual relationships into the sector.[35] In 1995 the outgoing chairman of British Rail, Sir Bob Reid, complained that when BR opposed this approach its 'view was subordinated to the view of one consultant, who had never run anything'.[36]

Track separation has been criticised on the grounds that the infrastructure company could increase its income through one or both of only two means. It could exploit its monopoly position by raising access charges, which would harm the profitability of train-operating companies; or expenditure on maintenance could be reduced, thereby possibly compromising safety standards. Division of responsibility for track and trains could be seen as courting harmful confusion.[37] However, greater investment in the network, which Foster had hoped for, was achieved. Before the end of the Major administration all train-operating services, as well as Railtrack itself, were transferred into the private sector. The policy proved to be unpopular. Foster, who had been a member of the working group which produced the proposal for the community charge, was consequently dubbed the 'intellectual father' of both the poll tax and the 'poll tax on wheels'.[38] The label was unfair. Foster himself insisted that 'I was not the intellectual father of rail privatisation in its current form – nor of the poll tax, for that matter.'[39] Indeed, in both instances the decisive political and ideological impetus came from elsewhere.

Tom Burke, another expert not affiliated to the party of government, was a special adviser to Michael Heseltine at the Department of the Environment from 1991, and stayed on to serve his two successors, Michael Howard and John Gummer. He did not expect his appointment. 'I got a phone call from the Deputy

Secretary saying, "What is it you want?" I said, "What do you mean?" and he said "Michael Heseltine wants you to be his special adviser."[40] Born in 1947, Burke had previously run the Green Alliance, an environmental pressure group. He was a Labour and then an SDP activist.[41] By the mid-1980s, having formed the opinion that 'politicians paid more attention to other politicians than to anybody else', he began 'setting out to stimulate . . . a competition between leading political figures to be the most green'. It brought him into contact with Heseltine, who, having resigned as Secretary of State for Defence in 1986, 'had been looking for an issue with which to . . . position himself . . . in relation to the Government he had just left, and I wrote a number of speeches for him . . . chapters in books and so on, and helped get them coverage'.[42]

When Burke was appointed, in March 1991, the *Independent* suggested that it was a sign on Heseltine's part of 'a readiness to listen to "green" economists'.[43] *The Times* referred to Burke's 'detailed knowledge of environmental policy issues and of the green movement' and the fact that 'his influence in government, business and environmental circles is considerable'.[44] In Burke's view, there was 'a certain mischievous quality to the appointment. It was not only that [Heseltine] was entertained by bringing a barbarian inside the gates of the Department of the Environment. I think he was quite entertained by having somebody who was not in his party'.[45] Burke, writes Heseltine, was 'expert in the policy, was politically astute and had a perceptive understanding of the workings of Whitehall'. When recruiting him, Heseltine put it to Burke 'that he had spent his life pointing politicians in the direction he believed environmental policies should go and challenged him to become a special adviser and put his shoulder to the wheel'.[46] It mirrored the manner in which he had approached Tom Baron during his previous spell at Environment a decade earlier. Burke felt that his value to Heseltine was that 'he knew me and I knew a lot about the area and he was confident with the kind of perspective that I took'.[47]

Burke has recalled that, when starting out, he was given no formal induction. In his words, 'I found myself, in effect, given a desk, a telephone, somebody to help me as a private secretary and told to get on with it.' However, he did have a policy area which was already determined by his background, and found the private secretary and deputy secretary helpful in incorporating him into the department. Personalities, in Burke's view, were important to determining the effectiveness of a special adviser. Much depended upon being able 'to work and get on with other people, and the ability of other people to work and get on with you'. He received what he regarded as very valuable advice from one senior departmental official in relation to an issue with which he had been closely associated for a number of years. 'He said, "Don't campaign. You will have more influence and more impact if you don't campaign."'[48] Burke noted that 'I came to my period of service as a temporary [civil servant] with many of the typical public prejudices about civil servants – informed as much by "Yes Minister" as by [any] real knowledge. I found that my actual experience undermined those prejudices. I left with a very high regard for the competence and commitment of the British Civil Service.'[49]

One of his functions, as Burke saw it, was to comment upon policies as they developed through different levels of the formation process. He 'would try to influence policy as it went up'. His licence to dissent was important, and, he felt, distinguished him from career officials. In Burke's view, it was more his different perspective that added value to the government process than any knowledge he possessed which was unavailable to career officials. However, his network of contacts with the outside world was useful, as was his familiarity with the workings of, for example, 'regulatory matters'.[50] Heseltine credits Burke with significant influence on policy. Previously, government had taken a reactive, confrontational approach towards the private sector in protecting the environment. Partly as a result of Burke's contribution, the 'precautionary principle and the concept that the polluter should pay' were developed.[51]

Burke has questioned the idea that special advisers can be cleanly separated into the categories of expert and political. When talking to the Wicks Committee, he drew a distinction 'between partisan and non-partisan advisers' and, while locating himself in the latter category, nonetheless

> *saw myself as advising politically. Part of my job was to take a view on the politics of policy proposals, what would or would not work, not just in Government, not just in the party, but in the wider world as well . . . making the link between a body of technical expertise and the political world is something, I think, that does add value.*

Special advisers met regularly on Wednesdays during the Major period. Burke attended this meeting only once, by invitation, specifically to talk about the environment. As he put it, 'I was there . . . to advise on the politics of the environment, if you like, but I was not there to advise on how the party would take it.' He did not see it as his responsibility to remind his employer of the contents of the manifesto or 'maintain links with the Conservative Party machinery and with the MPs'. He had few dealings with party officials, and then only at their instigation. He had only limited contact with partisan aides within his department, and virtually none with those beyond it.

Burke attended 'a very wide range of Ministerial meetings with Ministers from other Departments or Governments, senior officials and deputations from business and non-governmental organisations'. He wrote speeches and, sometimes, articles. Other duties were 'contributing to Ministerial briefings for meetings of Cabinet or Cabinet Committees and other Ministerial meetings; reviewing and commenting on inter-departmental correspondence on key issues; reviewing and advising on policy submissions to the Secretary of State and attendance at an extensive range of departmental and inter-departmental meetings of officials at an earlier stage of policy making'. He went to a 'large number of international meetings as a member of the UK delegation'.[52]

The maintenance of contact with specialist journalists, briefing them on the background to policy, was, in Burke's words, 'very much part of my job'.[53] Heseltine writes that Burke 'knew his subject backwards [and] rapidly won the confidence of the environmental correspondents'.[54] He did not ask for specific authority before briefing journalists. However, he did keep officials aware of his activities and informed ministers of matters arising from meetings which he thought were of interest. Burke emphasised that it 'certainly was not my job to manage the headlines . . . In any case, all of my experience working in the pressure group world suggested that one's ability to manage the headlines was pretty limited'. He sought to keep his profile low and felt 'that the worst possible thing you could do was become the story'. Burke discussed presentation strategy with the secretary of state and departmental head of information.[55]

Unpaid advice was also used. David Hart was taken on by the Secretary of State for Defence, Malcolm Rifkind, in 1993, and retained in 1995 by Rifkind's successor, Michael Portillo – himself a former aide. Hart's role was officially described as that of a supplier of 'advice on saving money out of the defence budget'.[56] He was a controversial figure. Press articles dwelt on his racial background and portrayed him as a sinister intriguer of the Conservative right. In

November 1993 the *Evening Standard* wondered why 'Defence Secretary Malcolm Rifkind hired the conspiratorial, Thatcherite freebooter David Hart as his special adviser? Millionaire Hart is boilingly Right-wing and isn't thought to be much of a fan of John Major. By contrast, Mr Rifkind worships Mr Major.' One explanation floated, but dismissed, was the fact that both 'men are Jewish'.[57] Previously, Hart had been close to Thatcher, counselling her during the 1984–5 miners strike. In 1994 *Scotland on Sunday* described him as 'a landowner, farmer, novelist, playwright, film-maker and millionaire scourge of anything remotely constituting a left-wing threat to the British way of life'. The same article reported that Hart was 'one of the chief backers of the Committee for a Free Britain, the libertarian right-wing pressure group, and the clandestine British Briefing and World Briefing: briefing papers on subversion which have been edited by ex-CIA and MI5 officials and partly funded by Rupert Murdoch, chairman of News International'.[58]

Hart, 'a keen advocate of US technology', was believed, in 1995, to have encouraged consideration of the possibility of leasing US fighter aircraft rather than updating the Tornado F3.[59] In the following year he was reportedly a supporter of controversial plans to sell off armed forces married quarters.[60] Numerous parliamentary questions were tabled on Hart, including one asking whether he had declared interests in consultancies taken on by the Ministry of Defence.[61] In November 1995, in a Commons debate, Labour MP Peter Mandelson raised the subject of the 'shadowy David Hart'. Hart was

> *that very special of special advisers . . . He is apparently unpaid, yet he inhabits an office near the Secretary of State . . . Mr. Hart is referred to as 'independent', which is more than can be said for the Secretary of State, who apparently jumps every time Mr. Hart opens his mouth . . . that particular individual is viewed within Whitehall as such a dangerous character that . . . even the Prime Minister has tried to have Mr. Hart removed from his job. Of course, the Prime Minister failed.*[62]

Downing Street

Major's elevation to the premiership was so sudden that he had no specific plans for the Policy Unit. In the event it was a discussion with Chris Patten, the newly appointed Conservative party chairman, that led him to the Policy Unit's new head: Sarah Hogg. The daughter of John Boyd-Carpenter, a Macmillan-era Conservative Cabinet member, Hogg was, in the words of Major, 'born to the political purple'. Graduating from Oxford with a first in PPE, she joined *The Economist* in 1967, eventually becoming its economics editor and going on to become a presenter of *Channel Four News*. Hogg was on the staff of the *Independent* at the time of its launch in 1986 and became economics editor of the *Daily Telegraph* and *Sunday Telegraph* in 1989. Following her departure from No. 10 in 1995, she was raised to the peerage. Her husband, Douglas, was a Foreign Office minister at the time of her appointment.[63]

Major refers to Hogg as possessing a 'sharp brain, often hidden behind an engaging giggle'.[64] He had met her 'through her journalistic work when he had been Chief Secretary at the Treasury, and then Chancellor, and they had formed a bond'.[65] An *Evening Standard* article from 1993 suggested that for Major, Hogg 'represents all the breezy intellectual self-confidence that he lacks himself'. She was also described as 'one of the most feared women in Westminster', regarded as being very effective at undermining rival influences within Major's circle.[66] There was, it seems, a personality clash between Hogg and Judith Chaplin, Major's political secretary from 1990 to 1992.[67]

According to Hennessy, Hogg was 'a powerful shaper of Major's detailed thinking'.[68] She was involved in deliberations over official appointments, for example the selection of Rupert Pennant-Rea, then editor of *The Economist*, as the deputy governor of the Bank of England in 1992.[69] Major consulted with Hogg on the timing of the election which was eventually held in April 1992. She also played an important role in devising electoral strategy, planning the campaign and participating in writing the manifesto. Using prime ministerial authority, Hogg made interventions on policy. In the spring of 1991 she grew concerned that the premier, distracted by war in the Gulf, had been unable to devote sufficient attention to the approaching Budget. Having obtained the go-ahead from Major, Hogg, in her account, managed to achieve the agreement of the Treasury to a package consisting of a 2.5 per cent increase in VAT, enabling local authorities to reduce the extremely unpopular community charge by £140 per person to a rate of just over £250 (in England and Wales).[70] However, the version provided by Norman Lamont, the Chancellor of the Exchequer, suggests that he modified the original proposal which emanated from No. 10. He writes that Major's and Hogg's initial intention was to use 'an increase in income tax, of perhaps 2 or 3 pence', but he 'preferred a switch from the Poll Tax to VAT'.[71]

Hogg was present at the key meetings. With Major's backing, she secured the right to sit in on all meetings between the Prime Minister and the Chancellor of the Exchequer.[72] Along with the Prime Minister, ministers and other advisers, she attended policy reviews at Chequers.[73] In 1992 a Cabinet committee called EDX was established under the Chancellor of the Exchequer to conduct the cross-examination, by senior colleagues, of departmental ministers over their spending proposals. Hogg attended EDX, keeping Major abreast of developments.[74] Hogg was a member of the party that accompanied the Prime Minister to the December 1991 EU summit at Maastricht in the Netherlands. It was here that Major, advised by, among others, Hogg, obtained a British opt-out from the EU Social Chapter, a package of measures including a maximum length for the working week.[75]

Hogg tried to help Major avert what turned out to be the greatest disaster of his premiership. Britain's forced exit from the ERM in September 1993 was a setback from which the Conservative government never recovered.[76] Major, as Chancellor, signed sterling up to the ERM, with a central DM rate for the pound of 2.95, in October 1990. By the autumn of 1991 the view that the maintenance of sterling within the ERM was entailing too tight a monetary squeeze, harming the domestic economy, was gaining ground. Major confidentially asked Hogg to prepare a paper discussing how 'the pound might be allowed to settle at a lower rate without leaving the ERM', through a realignment of the currencies within it. One of the possibilities she put forward was a lowering of the Deutschmark rate. Major did not pursue it with Lamont.[77] Lamont says in his own account that during 1992 he advocated the suspension of British membership of the ERM, with the support of Hogg, but that Major did not want to discuss it with them.[78]

Hogg counselled Major through the sterling crisis which culminated in British exit from the ERM. Membership was suspended on 16 September 1992, known as Black Wednesday, when interest rate increases from 10 per cent to 12 per cent and then to 15 per cent were announced in the same day, but failed to halt speculation against the pound. Following this episode, Major considered resignation. He consulted with, among others, Hogg, who told him that it would be an act of 'self indulgence'. The question of whether Major should stand down, for the benefit of the Conservative Party's electoral prospects, was one which he and Hogg revisited subsequently. Following Black Wednesday a new government economic strategy was required. It emerged, with Hogg's participation, in the form of an inflationary target band of 1–4 per cent, combined with greater openness regarding the decisions taken by the Chancellor and the Bank of England.[79]

Major's and Hogg's arrival at No. 10 was accompanied by the departure of all but one of Thatcher's political appointments to the Policy Unit.[80] Major's initial full-strength Policy Unit comprised two career officials and a special adviser who were already in place, and three new political appointments. The latter group included Nicholas True, who was Major's personal choice, the two having worked together as aide and junior minister at the Department of Social Security. Also new to the Policy Unit was Jonathan Hill, formerly a special adviser to Kenneth Clarke at Employment, Trade and Industry, and Health. He became Major's political secretary in 1992. Within the Policy Unit, True 'ranged widely, drafting most of the Prime Minister's key speeches'.[81] As Major puts it, 'he distilled my thoughts into artful speeches.'[82] Other members covered, individually, health, environment, and law and order; industry, finance and Wales; and employment, Scotland and defence. Hill began with housing and transport, 'but pretty soon became the unit's cross-departmental trouble-shooter'.[83] In 1994, of eight staff members, five were outsiders, one of whom was on secondment from the private sector.[84]

Under Major, according to some commentators, collective Cabinet government, as opposed to prime ministerial command government, was restored; similarly, it has been argued that the Policy Unit, in its operations, took on the more conciliatory style that was associated with Thatcher's successor.[85] It was, writes Seldon, 'less a priesthood of true believers' than under Thatcher, with its political appointees spanning 'a range of Conservative views'. Nevertheless, Major's Policy Unit played an important role. At the supposed peak of its influence, during 1990–2, the Policy Unit 'was at the heart of government, involved in all discussions key to the Prime Minister and policy. Secretaries of state would phone up asking if the Policy Unit was happy with what they were proposing, anxious to secure its backing, aware of the influence it carried with the Prime Minister'.[86] However, its status was eroded along with Major's authority, which declined, especially following exit from the ERM.

Hogg co-authored a book with Hill describing the early years of Major's premiership, up to his success in the 1992 election. In it, the Policy Unit's function is described as being 'to keep the Prime Minister in touch with outside thinking, to work on his own ideas and to act as a sounding board for Ministers, advising on the flow of proposals and counter-proposals that pour in continuously from all around Whitehall'. According to Hogg and Hill, the 'Prime Minister can use his unit as storm troops, invading the complacent hinterland of Whitehall; or as peacemakers, building bridges between warring departments and Ministers. In practice, the Unit tries to do a bit of both: to be both grit and oil in the government machine.'[87] Contact between Major and his Policy Unit was regular and informal. He made a habit of 'wandering informally up to [the Policy Unit's] first floor offices whenever I had a spare moment'.[88]

It has been suggested that under Hogg, the Policy Unit was 'applied to contemporary problems, reflecting the fire-fighting policy-making of the Major government, rather than inspiring long-term thinking'.[89] Hywel Williams states that Hogg 'deflected the Policy Unit from its long-term strategic function. Together with other members of the Unit, she briefed the press and intervened in day-to-day administration. She was an incorrigible meddler and sought to manage news when she should have been raising her sights to the policy peaks'.[90] However, the Policy Unit did help to develop, named and participated in the implementation of perhaps Major's most significant policy package: the Citizen's Charter, an 'explicit effort . . . to stimulate public services to use public money better'. Its title was devised by members of the Policy Unit over lunch at the Kundan Indian restaurant in Horseferry Road, Westminster, in March 1991.[91] Central to the 1992 Conservative manifesto, it entailed in part the publication of particular objectives for public services such as hospitals and schools.[92] The Policy Unit, in particular True, played a key role in eliciting Charter commitments from various, often reluctant, Whitehall departments.[93]

Dennis Kavanagh portrays the Citizen's Charter as central to Major's attempt 'to import the best of private sector practice as a means of improving the performance of . . . [public] services'.[94] Hennessy criticises the Citizen's Charter on the grounds that 'it was not justiciable in the courts and there was to be no shot of extra public spending to propel it.' However, he adds, it 'was a useful development in terms of transparency and accountability across the whole Civil Service and public sector . . . The concept of customer care was infiltrated into state services'.[95] With the Citizen's Charter, Major carved out a political identity distinct from that of Thatcher, for whom the quality of public services was not so great a concern. The delivery of tangible enhancements in returns for taxpayers' money was an objective which came to dominate the political agenda for all the main parties as the 1990s progressed. It was taken on enthusiastically by the Labour government which came to power in 1997.

Hogg's successor as head of the Policy Unit was Norman Blackwell. Prior to his appointment Blackwell had been a consultant at McKinsey & Co., and at the time the analogy was drawn that he was mounting a corporate-style rescue of Major's government, 'applying consultancy techniques to his latest job'.[96] As a staff member at the Policy Unit in 1986–7, he had specialised in employment, inner-city regeneration and NHS reforms.[97] Major considered a number of high-profile individuals for the post, but 'Norman appealed to me the moment we met: he had the gift of slow expression but profound analysis that characterises the thorough thinker'.[98] In terms of public portrayal Blackwell was subjected, although to a far lesser extent, to the derision frequently directed at the Prime Minister. In a profile published in November 1995, the *Sunday Times* referred to two of Blackwell's nicknames, 'Mr Nobody' and 'Dr Who'.[99] Alfred Sherman, writing in 1994, suggested that while 'Thatcher enjoyed heterodoxy and paradox, which she wore like a brooch, Major is the same colour all the way through, and feels uncomfortable with too much questioning or heterodoxy. He will die polit-ically as he lived, and Norman Blackwell would seem ideally fitted to accompany him'.[100]

Blackwell's broad policy agenda included the creation of an enterprise economy, helping small firms, education and opportunity, and law and order.[101] In 2000 he told the Public Administration Committee that the value of the Policy Unit was that it could provide the Prime Minister, who lacked a formal depart-ment, with 'a group of people whom he trusts, whom he can talk to, whom he can bounce his ideas round and who can challenge and brief him on the issues independently of departmental advice'. The Policy Unit did not, in Blackwell's view, need to be particularly large and should be of a size that could 'get round a table'. Dealing with the major issues of a particular department did not require great expertise, and with an expansion in the number of aides at the centre came the danger that 'you start to get fragmentation rather than co-ordination'. The meetings around a table to which Blackwell referred sometimes involved the presence of the Prime Minister. They enabled the conduct of 'a single conversa-tion' covering a whole policy area, rather than its breaking up into subgroups.

This was important in Blackwell's view, given the significance he attached to No. 10's role as one of co-ordination.

Blackwell sought to 'engage the special advisers around the ministries as if they were in part of their role an extension of the Number Ten Policy Unit'. He occasionally convened meetings of all aides, or between the members of the Policy Unit and the special advisers who were involved in a particular policy area. All political appointments, in Blackwell's view, 'could and should see themselves as an extension of the Government of the day's need to have a clear idea about where it is going in policy'. It was the responsibility of aides to try to ensure that the activities of their particular departments fitted with the central agenda. However, Blackwell noted, in 'practice it very much depended on the individual and perhaps their Minister to what extent they were part of that or to what extent they would go their own route'. One role for the special adviser, Blackwell felt, was 'to try and create change' since 'the Civil Service machinery is not a generator of radical ideas'. Whitehall outsiders could recommend new courses of action to ministers and 'provide some extra impetus and muscle to require the Civil Service machinery to go through evaluating options that, left to themselves, they would not do'. Blackwell took the view that special advisers were at their most effective when 'dealing in the substance of policy . . . in a way that reflects political objectives or political aspirations'. This differed from 'purely political advice'.

Given his involvement with both the Thatcher and Major premierships, Blackwell was in a good position to compare the two. He was of the view that 'both leaders had a clear sense of where they were going', although he emphasised the fact that, from 1992, Major was operating with a small and dwindling parliamentary majority. Comparing the styles of Major and Thatcher, he has stated that the 'difference in the role of the Policy Unit and the special advisers there was not very great' during their respective tenures at Downing Street. In both cases, he argued, the Policy Unit was engaged in 'trying to think ahead of where the Government policy should be going in three or five years' time, and at the same time giving the Prime Minister advice on the day-to-day policy decisions that were going through'. Another common aspect to the Policy Unit in the Thatcher and Major periods was responsibility for facilitating the conduct and resolution of debates regarding disagreements between the Prime Minister and departmental ministers. It could be argued that through such bilateral methods, Cabinet discussion could be bypassed and prime ministerial will imposed.[102]

Major has said that, had he won a second election victory, he would have bolstered his own staff. In July 2000 he suggested that he would have 'strengthened the Policy Unit' to provide 'a little more direct advice to the Prime Minster'. This could be achieved, Major emphasised, by the secondment of permanent officials as well as the recruitment of temporaries. Additionally, he would have expanded the number employed at the Cabinet Office 'for exactly the same reason, not because I wished to establish a competing barony to the Treasury and the Foreign Office and the other departments but because it is useful to have a source of independent advice on what is happening in government'. Major's extra staff would have been, in his words, charged with 'policy work'. He maintained that he did 'not favour a prime ministerial department as such'. His expansion of the Policy Unit, he said, would not have been as great as Blair's ultimately turned out to be.[103]

Destabilisation?

Famously, in a post-interview conversation with the ITN news editor Michael Brunson in July 1993, Major referred to 'bastards' who were poisoning his government. Unbeknown to the two men, the comment was recorded and its contents leaked. Major has subsequently denied that he meant any members of his Cabinet, although he was interpreted as possibly referring to Peter Lilley along with two former special advisers, Michael Portillo and John Redwood. Compounding the Prime Minister's difficulties associated with plummeting levels of post-ERM public popularity, Major's Cabinet and party were divided, particularly over Europe, a fact which was widely known. During his second term, the press highlighted internal Conservative disputes, showing no mercy to the Major governments.[104] Media deference towards politicians, long in decline, seemed to have almost vanished. Jonathan Haslam, a permanent official, was Major's Deputy Press Secretary from 1991 to 1995 and Chief Press Secretary from 1996 to 1997. As Haslam put it, 'the Government is not treated with the same sort of respect as it had in years past, when interviewers would say, "Is there anything to say to the Nation, Prime Minister?" "No, thank you." We are in an entirely different game.'[105]

Coupled with the tendency for the scrutiny of politics to be constant and unforgiving came technological developments which fostered the increasing emergence of twenty-four-hour, international, electronically driven news media. Deadlines were shorter. The performance of government information officers in the face of such trends was often unimpressive. Haslam suggested to the Committee on Standards in Public Life that 'in some areas the civil service simply was not geared up as effectively as it should have been, and as a member of the senior civil service at the time and a Government Information Officer, I know that I do not think that the Government Information Service was as good as it should have been.'[106] In 2003 Portillo wrote of members of the Government Information Service during the Major period that some 'were woefully inadequate . . . they acted sometimes like mere spectators at the scene of a public relations disaster, occasionally incapable of amassing and conveying even basic information that could have killed a malicious story stone dead'.[107]

The Labour administration which took office in 1997 was influenced by a desire to avoid a repetition of Major's experiences at the hands of the media, with consequences for its deployment of special advisers. However, it is unlikely that Major's problems with the press could have been solved merely by the use of a partisan spokesman at No. 10. Major has argued that he 'would have had the same problems even if I had a party political appointee in terms of press relations. I think the Government were in season'. He 'would not have made a political appointment' on the grounds that 'in these days of a cynical world a dispassionate civil servant, answerable to the head of the Home Civil Service for his honesty and probity, can be seen to be more dispassionate than somebody who is not so answerable.'[108]

Beyond No. 10 and across the government, in Major's view, rather than being a potential remedy, aides were a source of his administration's public relations difficulties. At the time of the 'bastards' comment, he writes, there 'was an open secret that unnamed ministers, their "friends" and their advisers talked to the media in private about their dislike of the Maastricht legislation'.[109] He told the Public Administration Committee that he became 'very disillusioned' with departmental special advisers. 'I think they got out of hand. I think there are too many of them. I think whatever their individual virtues, I think as a collective breed they cause more problems . . . for government than they solve.' They were, he felt, 'too often taken as speaking to their master's voice. I think there are too many occasions when advisers, who have a certain amount of knowledge of their minister, talk to the media or others and it is then reported that happens to be the view of their minister. Whether it is or not, it is not for the adviser to do it'. Whatever their value to ministers, 'they were . . . a significant handicap to the government as a whole'.[110]

With hindsight, Major went on, 'I do wonder how many of the ministerial spats and difficulties that suddenly exploded in the media – unbeknown to me, that I was at terrible loggerheads with someone I was actually having lunch with at that precise moment, for example – came from political advisers.' Coverage of supposed ministerial feuds, he believed, 'often emerge[s] below the salt, as it were, as a result of discussions with people close to the ministers, not always advisers, of course, but in some cases I think it defies logic not to suggest that it was advisers'. He did not name the individuals he felt were responsible.[111]

Aside from Major's testimony, there is other evidence that press briefing by special advisers worsened government divisions. whether or not it was exactly what she had in mind, Keswick may have helped explain a cause of the problem she put it to the Wicks Committee that working as an aide 'is a very difficult job, especially for people who are young, because it is very seductive. If you have a lot of journalists and grand people ringing up and being nice . . . I think that it can go quite wrong and it can go to people's heads'.[112]

In his book *Guilty Men* Hywel Williams provides an account of the Major period which suggests a fascination with political intrigue on the part of its author. Its reliability as a source should be considered in this light. Freely admitting his own use of the media for the purpose of Conservative infighting, he suggests that Redwood was complicit in such activities. Redwood is portrayed as hungry for publicity, becoming 'addicted to the "hit"'. According to Williams, 'the cry, "When am I going to get my next hit?" became familiar.' He writes that 'Leaks at the Welsh Office were often to his [Redwood's] advantage.'[113] Major records 'complaints that reports of private meetings at which John Redwood was present tended to appear in the press. Fairly or unfairly, it was believed that he was either leaking them himself or talking to somebody in his entourage who was doing so. This meant other ministers were unwilling to be frank when he was present'.[114] Williams refers to other methods employed to attain desirable coverage. When Redwood 'wanted to issue a contentious press release or make a controversial speech, both of us became adept at exploiting the ambiguities between the Political Office and the Civil Service side of Number 10 about who was really in charge and who could authorise the final draft'.[115] The attempted centralisation of communications under Alastair Campbell which took place from 1997 seems to have been prompted in part by an observation of such tendencies.

Redwood says that, after his initial lack of enthusiasm for employing a special adviser, he grew to like and trust the individual he appointed, who became a 'sort of travelling companion'. In his account, he later discovered that, during his time in the Cabinet, accounts of disagreements between him and colleagues were supplied to the media by his aide. Some of them were accurate, while others merely represented the views of the temporary civil servant, wrongly attributed to Redwood. None of them did he wish to see publicly aired. Redwood suspects that his special adviser's motive for such activity was simply that 'he liked it'.[116]

Aides were sometimes portrayed in the press as factors in Cabinet rivalry. When Clarke became Chancellor of the Exchequer in May 1993 the *Daily Mail* ran a double profile of Hogg and Keswick, on the grounds that they were now based next door to each other. It was stated that, outwardly, 'these new neighbours will behave impeccably towards each other. Inwardly, however, their struggle for supremacy will certainly be furious,' since Clarke was supposedly the 'heir apparent' to Major.[117] It was reported that Clarke did not allow Portillo, a leading figure on the right, his own special adviser when the latter was Chief Secretary to the Treasury.[118] In March 1995, writing in the *Mail on Sunday*, the Conservative politician Alan Clark decried the fact that 'Cabinet Ministers contradict each other, explain what their colleagues "meant to say" and, either themselves or through their special advisers, brief the Press off the record on the Prime Minister's weaknesses.' He called upon Major to 'get a grip on this'.[119]

In June 1995, to pre-empt a possible challenge, Major resigned the leadership of the Conservative Party in order to seek re-election. In his account, the involvement of aides in intrigue intensified. Major writes that Hart, Portillo's special adviser, 'was telling all who asked that he was doubtful that Michael would enter the contest *on the first ballot*, but did not rule it out [emphasis in original]'. Redwood's aide, Williams, 'sent out . . . hostile signals'. Eventually, Redwood resigned from the Cabinet to run, but was defeated in the first round. Major acquired the assistance of a number of special advisers, including Rachael Whetstone, Gregor MacKay, Michael McManus, Michael Simmonds and Sophie McEwan, 'who effectively took over the internal administration of the media exercise'. Major writes that they 'all resigned their jobs to join the team'.[120] However, in July 1995, in response to a question on the propriety of their participation, Major told the House that 'Special advisers may take part in political activities of the sort described provided they do so during leave or in their own time in addition to fulfilling their normal duties.'[121] It could be inferred from the latter statement that they did not give up their posts.

Major has said that, given another term of office, as 'far as departmental advisers were concerned ... I would have cut back on advisers very dramatically'. As he put it, while it may have been 'very convenient to have someone to pour the drinks, write the speeches and cut out the newspapers and the other useful things ... the downside for government as a whole is greater than the advantage to the individual ministers. It is not good for government'.[122] The view of aides as a liability is corroborated by Williams. He provides a grotesque portrait of the special advisers who met at the Old Cabinet Room in the Cabinet Office at lunchtime on Wednesdays. Williams writes that, like 'dogs, Whitehall special advisers can acquire their masters' characteristics'. He claims that in the Major period there were no individuals of the calibre of Adam Ridley, John Hoskyns or Oliver Letwin, and that the 'intellectual degeneracy' of those who were appointed 'was one of the many factors that led to the electoral collapse of the 1st of May 1997'. The functions of most, according to Williams, were 'to sell their man to the press, to extol his virtues and guard his back ... Few advisers were loyal to the government as a whole'. Moreover, if they 'were meant to be an intellectual officer-class, the nearest military equivalent was Earl Haig and the General Staff of 1915 and 1916'.[123] In a discussion of Cabinet intrigue, Major's biographer writes that some blamed 'less the bosses than their special adviser *éminences grises*', with Williams for Redwood, Hart for Portillo and Clarke's aide, Anthony Teasdale, 'particular subjects, in the highly volatile and charged atmosphere, of suspicion'.[124]

Standards

The mid-1990s saw the emergence of an increasing public concern regarding propriety in official life. A variety of allegations and revelations surfaced, relating to matters such as the external financial interests of MPs. In response to this unease the Committee on Standards in Public Life, initially under the chairmanship of Lord Nolan, was established. The formal terms of reference were to 'examine current concerns about standards of conduct of all holders of public office, including arrangements relating to financial and commercial activities, and make recommendations as to any changes in present arrangements which might be required to ensure the highest standards of propriety in public life'. Over subsequent years the committee took an increasing interest in special advisers. Its first report, however, appearing in May 1995, did not concern itself with them to a great extent. Nevertheless, it pointed out that aides were 'entirely outside the scope of the existing' Civil Service business appointment rules. It was noted that 'in theory they are not permitted to have access to details of individual companies or to become involved in the placing of contracts.' However, Nolan went on, Civil Service regulations went further. When individuals who possessed knowledge of possible future decisions that might be of advantage to a particular firm wished to accept offers of outside employment, they were required to consult with their departments over whether such a move was appropriate. Since special advisers 'probably have a better knowledge of proposed developments in Government policy than most other civil servants in their departments . . . it is not easy to see why they should be exempt from the rules'.[125] On 4 March 1996 the government announced its acceptance of Nolan's argument and that aides would be brought within the business appointments system.[126]

It did not go far enough for some. Speaking in the Commons on the subject of standards in public life in November 1995, the Labour MP Peter Mandelson referred to a 'source of real concern . . . which Nolan touches on but does not delve deeply into – the Government's use of paid, political so-called special advisers'. He acknowledged that previous Labour governments had also used them and expressed the view that 'in appropriate cases, they have a role to play.' However, under Major, there was a 'veritable army of such people at enormous public cost'. Referring to a recent statement by Major that the wage bill since 1988 amounted to £9 million, Mandelson queried 'what all that money is being spent on, how those people fit into the civil service structure and how they can be properly covered by civil service procedures and the civil service code'.

Mandelson was scathing about the fact that a third of the 'current flock' were recruited from Conservative Central Office. Were they, he wondered, 'helping Ministers in pursuit of better government, which would certainly justify the public expenditure involved, or . . . merely assisting politicians in pursuit of their party careers, in which case the payment of their salaries should revert to Conservative central office?' In addition to Nolan's recommendation regarding appointments, 'further transparency is needed in their employment and use.' Mandelson argued that special advisers were 'causing increasing concern and alarm among many in Whitehall'. One of the problems was the knowledge they had of confidential information and the likely future course of policy; their 'value to business is therefore immense', a fact to which 'the traffic of ex-special advisers into well-paid lobbying and consultancy jobs' bore witness. The Committee on Standards in Public Life, Mandelson argued, 'should take a keen interest in such invisible but clearly highly influential individuals at the heart of the Government'.[127]

Disapproval was voiced by the press, too. In December 1993 the *Evening Standard* pointed out that the

> *highest [paid] earn more than £80,000 – more than the Prime Minister! . . . Why do [their salaries] need to be so high? . . . Why on earth do they need to exist at all? Why should the taxpayer pay one penny piece to these proliferating 'special advisers', some of whom are recruited directly from Conservative Central Office? . . . it is . . . a career fast-track for ambitious young Tories . . . it is a fast-track for those who wish to wield political power without submitting to anything so vulgar as a vote by one's fellow citizens. The steadily increasing number of these pampered political bureaucrats sits badly with a Government avowedly committed to tight public spending. And it contributes to a culture in which tomorrow's senior politicians are just party hacks with no experience of earning a living in the real world. 'Special advisers' are expensive passengers on the ship of state. Let's tip them overboard.*[128]

* * *

Under Major, the position of special advisers became subject to greater formal regulation, and certain documents were placed in the public domain; but official definitions remained vague. The growth in numbers was possibly attributable to a post-Thatcher relaxation at the centre. Compared with the Thatcher era, there was a tilt towards the employment of party activists and journalists; there were also some experts who were not Conservative in alignment, such as Burke. It is possible that the long period of one-party government rendered ideologically committed, heroic outsiders redundant; Conservative ministers and the Civil Service were accustomed to working together.

Major did not dominate his government to the same extent as Thatcher. Nevertheless, his Policy Unit was influential, particularly during 1990–2. Its existence meant that there was a structural tendency towards prime ministerial intervention. However, when political circumstances became more difficult, the authority both of Major and of the Policy Unit declined. Communicating with journalists was a common activity for many aides. For some, it seems to have been conducted in order to highlight, or even fabricate, Cabinet-level disagreement. The extent of ministerial sanction for such activities is unclear. Whether a politically appointed press officer at No. 10 would have prevented the presentational chaos of the Major period is doubtful. Concern regarding the conduct of holders of public offices became pronounced in the mid-1990s, and special advisers were not exempt; indeed, such scrutiny would intensify in the future.

Nine

Proliferation and control since 1997

During the Labour governments under Tony Blair that have held office since 1997 special advisers attained the high levels of public attention described in Chapter 1. This chapter will examine the advance preparations for the use of aides made by Labour in opposition, and the expansion in their number that followed rapidly on Blair's election victory. The new regulatory framework that was introduced is assessed. As for the aides themselves, their career paths and the roles they performed are discussed, as is the extent to which individual counsellors could be categorised by type. Their contributions in terms of political liaison and the development of policy will be examined. So, too, will their media-related activities, which became extremely prominent.

At the centre of government, the number of special advisers attached to the Prime Minister grew, and important powers were concentrated at No. 10. The role of the Policy Unit, which was merged with the Private Office to become the Policy Directorate in 2001, is described, along with some of its members. Blair used some unpaid counsellors, most notably Lord Birt; and in 1997, up to three posts were created for political appointments who would be able to issue instructions to career officials; two of them were filled by Alastair Campbell and Jonathan Powell, both of whom are profiled here. Gordon Brown, Chancellor of the Exchequer and the most significant member of the government other than Blair, constructed his own team of special advisers, which included in its number Edward Balls and Charlie Whelan. Their involvement in struggles both with Brown's political rivals and with permanent officialdom is described. Balls's contribution to policy requires examination, as does the establishment of the Council of Economic Advisers, a team of expert aides located at the Treasury.

Planning in opposition

When Labour ministers took office in 1997 they brought with them a large number of aides whose purpose was to ensure the effective implementation and presentation of party policy. The long period of opposition that preceded this moment influenced their approach. In the words of Lord (Robert) Armstrong in 2002, when

> the present Government first took office in 1997, it was understandable that they should wish to keep about them in government some of those with whom they had been working in opposition. The Labour Party had been out of office for eighteen years, and none of those appointed to senior ministerial office had previous experience of working with civil servants in government. This could be said of no previous administration: senior members of the new Governments in 1945, 1951, 1964, 1970 and 1979 had all had previous experience of ministerial office in government.[1]

It is notable that of the participants in Blair's administration who had any sort of administrative experience, Jack Straw, Tony Banks (Minister of Sport) and Lord (Bernard) Donoughue (a minister at the Ministry of Agriculture, Fisheries and Food) had been special advisers in the 1970s.

Labour's use of the British equivalent to a US transition team, imported wholesale by an incoming administration, arguably had implications for the position of regular civil servants. Sir Robin Mountfield, the Permanent Secretary at the Office of Public Service in 1997, subsequently stated that 'this party had been in opposition for 18 years. They had, particularly in the few years before the election, developed very sophisticated internal processes for development of policies, and they came in with a clear agenda, a very clear idea of what they wanted to do, and they did not want anyone to stand in their way.' Consequently, according to Mountfield, a lack of self-confidence was engendered on the part of career officials, some of whom displayed 'almost too much anxiety to please'. As a result, Mountfield concluded, permanent civil servants 'allowed ourselves to be pushed a bit aside'.[2]

Thatcher did not devote much thought to the use of political aides in advance of the Conservative election success of 1979 and was probably not initially convinced of their value. Such was not the case with the Labour leadership in 1997. A view existed at high levels within the party that there would be a substantial role for temporary recruits to the Civil Service in a Blair administration. It was probably prompted in part by uncertainty regarding how Whitehall would react to a change in the party of government – and to a new administration with policy commitments (for example, concerning devolution) that were certainly radical, albeit not entirely in a traditional left-wing sense. Political aides would, it was felt, enable the new regime to bring such measures to fruition swiftly.

By May 1997, many who went on to become special advisers were already in the service of those who became ministers in the first Blair administration. Robin Cook, appointed Foreign Secretary in 1997, had two aides, one paid for prior to the transfer into government through Short Money and the other out of Cook's 'blind trust' (anonymous donations to his office costs). Certain individuals not already employed immediately before the 1997 election had already been earmarked for recruitment as special advisers in the event of victory. In July 1997 the House of Commons was informed that, with three exceptions, all 'paid Special Advisers have at some stage in their careers been employed either by the Labour Party or by individual members of a Labour Shadow Cabinet'.[3]

Considerable thought had been given to planning for deployment. In 1996, anticipating a Labour government, Peter Mandelson and Roger Liddle, who became a special adviser in Blair's Policy Unit, published a book entitled *The Blair Revolution: Can New Labour Deliver?* Containing a series of organisational and policy recommendations for rapid implementation by a Blair administration, it provided an insight into thinking at senior Labour levels regarding the use of special advisers. Liddle and Mandelson argued that Blair 'has to get personal control of the central-government machine and drive it hard, in the knowledge that if the government does not run the machine the machine will run the government'. At No. 10 there was 'a need to make more specialist advice available to the prime minister'. Alongside the requirement for greater expertise was that of commitment to the government of the day. The authors called for 'a stronger political presence in No. 10 . . . to focus on and manage the government's political strategy and programme'. In particular, an expansion of the Policy Unit was required, enabling it to produce 'crisp papers on key policy areas to articulate the prime minister's political agenda'. The Policy Unit would also, along with the Cabinet Secretary, chase progress, reporting back to the Prime Minister. Gordon Brown, at the time the shadow Chancellor of the Exchequer, had to ensure that the Treasury was 'staffed, managed and equipped' satisfactorily.

There would be a need for ministerial 'specialist advisers drawn from outside their departments, but these should work with, not against, the permanent staff'. The Conservative practice, claimed Mandelson and Liddle, was to recruit 'political advisers whose only job, it seems, is to agree with their masters, run political errands, fix the press, and flatter their bosses' egos while they try to get Westminster seats for themselves'. In larger departments, two political aides for each minister, integrated into the private office, might be required; in others, one would suffice. An additional need was for 'people ... who can make a serious contribution to the issues in hand and are able to work closely with departmental officials in developing policy'. The introduction of the full *cabinet* model was rejected by Liddle and Mandelson, on the grounds that the benefits of continuity provided by a career service would be lost. They argued that in certain key departments it might be necessary to appoint some high-ranking special advisers 'to work on the implementation of policies which are central to the New Labour strategy'.[4]

Liddle and Mandelson's book provided in many respects an accurate preview of the use of aides under Blair. Expansion at No. 10 and the Treasury came to pass, as did the focus on driving a single, central political strategy. However, the attention that would be given to media relations, always a major concern for Mandelson, was underplayed. Furthermore, observation of the activities of special advisers in earlier periods suggests that some degree of involvement in furthering the individual causes of ministers was almost inevitable. It will be shown that, as promised, high-powered policy experts were employed from 1997. Nevertheless, however revolutionary it might be, a Blair premiership would not bring about a formal displacement of the private office and permanent secretary by the ministerial *cabinet*.

Proliferation and regulation

Given the preparations, the surge in numbers of special advisers which followed the May 1997 victory was, with hindsight, unsurprising. When Major left office in 1997, his administration employed thirty-eight such aides. By November the same year the figure had nearly doubled to sixty-nine; a year later it was seventy (calculated on the basis of a government description of salary levels).

The determination of exact totals is, however, a complicated process. By late 1999, there were sixty-eight special advisers to ministers. Also listed, at the Cabinet Office, were Keith Hellawell, the UK Anti-Drugs Co-ordinator, and his deputy, Michael Trace. Michael Barber was Standards and Effectiveness Adviser to the Secretary of State for Education and Employment. At the Treasury there were three members of the Council of Economic Advisers (Chris Wales, Paul Gregg and Shriti Vadera). The overall total, then, seems to have been seventy-four. However, it is doubtful whether all of the named individuals should be classified as true special advisers. Hellawell, for example, was recruited by open competition, but deemed to be a political appointment because ministers sat on the committee which selected him.

The increase in numbers continued, reaching seventy-eight by July 2000. In December 2001 there were officially seventy-five special advisers (including Ed Balls, the Chief Economic Adviser). In addition, Pat McFadden was based at the Coalition Information Centre in Islamabad and Keith Hellawell held an advisory role to the Home Secretary on international drug issues. There were five members of the Council of Economic Advisers (Maeve Sherlock and Stewart Wood, as well as Vadera, Wales and Gregg). Lord Birt was referred to as 'the Prime Minister's unpaid strategy adviser'. Sue Nye and David Mathieson were unpaid advisers to, respectively, the Chancellor of the Exchequer and the Leader of the House of Commons/President of the Council. The grand total, then, was eighty-five: probably the peak in the history of the special adviser. They were shared among twenty-three ministers, three of whom were located in the House of Lords and of whom all but two, the Lord Chancellor and the Lord Chief Whip, employed two or more. Details of those departments which employed more than two each are given in the appendix.

By July 2002 the total in employment, taking into account the usual complications, was seventy-five. The Department of Culture, Media and Sport (DCMS) had only one, as did Defence, the Lord Chancellor's Department, Transport, the Wales Office, Work and Pensions, and International Development. The norm of two-per-minister, then, was not quite so prominent as it had been. Perhaps in some cases the high level of unwanted media attention attracted by special advisers had discouraged the immediate replacement of departing aides.

With the increase in numbers came a swollen pay bill, rising from £1.8 million in 1996/7 to £5.1 million in 2001/2 (details of the intervening years are given in the appendix). In November 1998 the average salary of a special adviser was £45,378, as compared with £46,421 under the previous administration (presumably at its end). In the same month the government announced a new band structure, designed to create a clearer framework for remuneration, based on role and responsibility, and comparability to career officials.

In July 2002 there were no special advisers on the bottom rung of the payment scale; most were covered by the middle three bands, with salaries between £34,851 and £89,175 (for details see appendix). The overall maximum for individuals outside the pay bands (at the time, only Jonathan Powell and Alastair Campbell) was £128,125. The £55,118 then received by MPs would have placed them in band 2. For comparison, in 2002 the salary of a permanent secretary fell within the range £115,000–£245,000. A parliamentary undersecretary in the Commons was paid £27,506; a minister of state in the Commons £36,240; a Cabinet minister in the Commons £69,861; the Prime Minister £116,436.

The greatest expansion in numbers, and therefore the greatest cost increase, occurred at the prime ministerial centre. The seven or eight special advisers employed under Major during 1996/7 drew £434,249 in combined salaries. At the beginning of 1998 the Prime Minister's office employed seventeen full-time and two part-time special advisers, costing a total of £849,894. By late 2001 there were twenty-six special advisers attached to the Prime Minister; in July 2002, twenty-seven. Some of them were located in the Strategic Communications Unit (SCU) and the Research and Information Unit (RIU), both established under Blair. To provide a snapshot of deployment, in 2001 there were four in the private office, twelve in the Policy Unit, five in the press office, two in the SCU and three in the RIU.[5]

At the Treasury, by June 1997, there were four paid special advisers: Ed Balls, Charlie Whelan, Edward Miliband and Andrew Maugham. Sue Nye, another aide, was unpaid. In July 2002 five were listed at the Treasury, as well as five members of the Council of Economic Advisers. From 1997 to 2001, the Department for the Environment, Transport and the Regions (DETR) under the Deputy Prime Minister, John Prescott, regularly employed four special advisers.

A conflict was identified with the 1997 Ministerial Code, which stipulated that 'Cabinet Ministers may each appoint up to two Special Advisers.'[6] In 2000 the

Committee on Standards in Public Life drew attention to the fact that 'the Ministerial Code limits each Cabinet Minister . . . to two special advisers, yet . . . several departments exceed that figure . . . For many years . . . the figure in the Prime Minister's Office has exceeded two.' Therefore, the committee recommended, the Ministerial Code should be 'amended to reflect the fact that in certain circumstances more than two special advisers per Cabinet Minister may be appointed'.[7] There was confusion here over whether caps applied to Cabinet members individually or their departments. The 2001 Ministerial Code restated that Cabinet ministers were allowed two special advisers each (adding the stipulation that more could be permitted in special circumstances). Technically, departments such as the Treasury, with two Cabinet ministers, were therefore allowed more than two in total and had been quite legitimately employing four previously (although as has been shown, there was probably a tendency for all Treasury aides to end up working to the Chancellor). The permitted total does not, however, account for the members of the Council of Economic Advisers (discussed below), who came to number five. The 2001 Ministerial Code added that ministers who attended Cabinet regularly but were not formal members might also be permitted one or two aides and that the Prime Minister was subject to no numerical limit.

What was the significance of the expansion? Sir Andrew Turnbull was Permanent Secretary to the Treasury from 1998 to 2002, and thereafter Cabinet Secretary. In his view, despite the proliferation, 'the way they operate is within the long-standing conventions and, although there are more of them, the pattern of their working is recognisable as a pattern that we have seen in earlier administrations.' Turnbull noted that the two per minister rule, which had operated for many years, still held, with a few exceptions.[8] However, one senior Labour politician came to the view that numbers were excessive. In 2002 Charles Clarke, then chairman of the Labour Party, said that 'my very personal view is that there are too many Special Advisors at the moment . . . I think a general sprawling of the number of Special Advisors could . . . lead to a state of affairs where government would be less effective than it is in delivering its policies and what it wants to do.'[9] Blair, reminded of Clarke's comment a week later by the Liaison Committee, said, 'Obviously I think we have the right number otherwise we would have fewer of them.'[10]

Growth in numbers was accompanied by greater formality. May 1997 saw the publication of the first Model Contract for Special Advisers.[11] With the 1997 election approaching, senior officials in Whitehall decided that, given the vague nature of the existing Model Letter of Appointment, a more definitive statement was required. It was discussed with and agreed by both major parties. The section describing the role of the special adviser, Mountfield has said, was 'based to a considerable extent' on Harold Wilson's 1975 paper, with additions taking into account developments in the use of aides in the intervening period.[12] Pay scales and terms and conditions of employment were set out in detail. It was made clear that aides 'do not work directly under a permanent civil servant or have permanent civil servants working directly for them apart from providing assistance through the Minister's private office'. Their role was described as being 'to advise the Minister in the development of Government policy and its effective presentation'. It was in these 'two areas of activity that the Government and the Party overlap'. Special advisers were two-way conduits. They could both ensure that the 'Party's policy analysis and advice' were taken into account by ministers, and 'liaise with the Party to make sure that Party publicity is factually accurate with Government policy'.

The most significant additions to Harold Wilson's list of possible functions were those of 'encouraging presentational activities by the Party', 'helping to brief Party MPs and officials on issues of Government policy' and adding 'party political content to material prepared by permanent civil servants' for inclusion in speeches. Limitations on party-related pursuits were similar to those of earlier administrations. Local but not national political activities were permitted. There was no specific reference to contact with journalists; however, it was noted that participation in public controversy was forbidden, and special advisers were required to 'observe discretion and express comment with moderation, and avoid personal attacks; and they would not normally speak in public for their Minister or the Department'. It could be inferred, therefore, that anonymous briefing of reporters was allowed, provided it was not malicious or hyperbolic. The fact that 'the Government needs to present its policies and achievements positively' was iterated. Reinforcement of the status of the Model Contract was provided by the 1997 Ministerial Code, which stated that all such 'appointments should be made, and all Special Advisers should operate, in accordance with the terms and conditions of the Model Contract'.[13] Unlike its 2001 successor, the 1997 Model Contract did not contain a 'Code of Conduct'. However, much of the content of the Code was present in the 1997 Model Contract, but not grouped under such a heading. The main addition in 2001 was in the form of guidance offered on contacts with the media.

Personnel and functions

The legal challenge to the Lord Chancellor's appointment of an aide on grounds of discrimination, discussed in Chapter 1, was politically undesirable for a government committed to providing opportunities for groups previously excluded or disadvantaged. How far was the intention reflected in the make-up of the special advisers it recruited? In February 1999 Parliament was informed that, of sixty-nine special advisers, sixteen were women. A survey identified fifty-eight as being white; the remaining eleven had not responded.[14] Two months later it was revealed that there were fewer than five special advisers from ethnic minority backgrounds across government as a whole.[15] For comparative purposes, in 2001 there were six women in a twenty-three-member Cabinet, and twenty among the sixty-nine junior ministers: an overall proportion of 31 per cent across the government. Of 3,200 senior civil servants in 2001, all but 750 were male. In October 2002, 2.8 per cent of the Senior Civil Service was known to be non-white (27.1 per cent unknown). None of the nine members of the Prime Minister's Private Office in April 1999 were from ethnic minorities.[16]

Service as a special adviser continued for many to be a stage in a career within or related to politics. Wendy Alexander was appointed as an aide to Donald Dewar, the Scottish Secretary, in 1997. She came from a background in 'Scottish Labour Action, a home-rule pressure group within the Labour party which fought for devolution in the wake of a second crushing Labour defeat at the polls in 1983'. She was 'closely involved in drafting the white paper that [led] to the creation of the Scottish parliament'. Alexander went on to become a member of the new parliament and of the Scottish Executive, from which she resigned in 2002.[17] Hilary Benn, the son of Tony, was an aide to the Secretary of State for Education, David Blunkett, from 1997. He had served for more than a decade as a west London councillor and was elected as the MP for Leeds Central in 1999. In 2001 he became a government minister. In 2002 Andrew Hood, previously a special adviser at the Ministry of Defence and before that at the Foreign Office, took up employment with the public relations firm Brunswick – a move which generated a degree of controversy, since Brunswick had defence companies among its clients.[18]

Some special advisers moved around within the government. Robert Hill was a member of the Policy Unit from 1997. He became the Prime Minister's political secretary in 2001 and then, in 2002, joined the newly appointed Secretary of State for Education, Charles Clarke. Between 1997 and 2002 Kieran Simpson served ministers in the Chief Whip's Office, the Ministry of Agriculture, Fisheries and Food, and the Department for Work and Pensions. Equally, there were those who stayed put even when ministers departed. Dan Corry served Margaret Beckett, Peter Mandelson and Stephen Byers at the Department of Trade and Industry.

A number of aides had previously been associated with think tanks. Indeed, it was even suggested in the *Sunday Times* in May 1997 that the research bodies Demos, the Institute for Public Policy Research (IPPR) and the Fabian Society faced a difficult future, many of their associates and staff members having been elected as MPs or appointed as ministers or special advisers. Geoff Mulgan, the director of Demos, was recruited to Blair's Policy Unit. Dan Corry was previously a 'staff economist' at the IPPR. Other aides with IPPR links were Liz Kendall (working for Harriet Harman, the Secretary of State for Social Security), Wendy Alexander, and David Miliband and James Purnell (both in the Policy Unit).[19]

In 1997 the internal differentiation between expert and political special advisers seems to have been dropped. The decision reflected the difficulties in maintaining an absolute distinction between the two types, with many aides performing mixed roles. According to Pat McFadden, who spent time at No. 10 as a member of the Policy Unit and the Deputy Chief of Staff, later becoming Political Secretary,

> the term 'Special Adviser' covers several different kinds of job. Sometimes it is policy expertise . . . general speech writing . . . contact with the media. It is quite difficult in government and in politics to put people into separate boxes and say that the person who deals with the media does not have policy expertise because they might have both. The person who has a lot of policy expertise might have no expertise at all with dealing with the media or they may.

During Labour's long period of opposition, the relatively small number of professional staff that could be afforded applied themselves to a variety of duties;

and they took this approach with them into government.[20] In Charles Clarke's view, 'Special Advisors have a range of different responsibilities ... The ones that occur to me are policy, press and media, diary organisation ... and representation generally. This is a range of different functions and different Special Advisors have different combinations of those.'[21]

Andy Burnham, who was a special adviser to Chris Smith, Secretary of State at the DCMS between 1998 and 2001, provides evidence for Clarke's argument. Previously, Burnham, born in 1970, was a researcher to Tessa Jowell MP and administrator to the Football Task Force; later he became a Labour MP and the chairman of Supporters Direct, a publicly funded body set up to promote supporters' ownership of football clubs. Primarily, he regarded himself as a political aide. However, while he was not, for example, a distinguished academic, he had personal experience of an aspect of the work of the department to which he was attached. As he subsequently put it, 'I suppose, crudely, I would be the ... "spotty upstart from Millbank [the Labour Party headquarters until 2002]" kind of special adviser and the others would fit into "distinguished expert". But the truth of it is too blurred.'[22]

Burnham enjoyed what he saw as a 'good working relationship with departmental officials'. Lacking a detailed knowledge of the workings of the Civil Service, he was given a considerate induction by the permanent secretary, followed by introductions to all the key officials. On the basis of his experiences, he came to the view that special advisers were able to contribute to the work of a department in a number of ways. They could 'help make the policy-making process more efficient. By working with civil servants at the early stages of policy development, political priorities can be reflected. This can help focus policy work and ensure time is spent productively'. They were also important to 'improving cross-departmental working'. For example, DCMS sport policy decisions often required agreement from Education, and special advisers were well placed to 'oil those wheels'. Finally, aides were in a good position to 'help renew and refresh thinking, challenge assumptions on how things are done and generally act as a source of creativity'.[23]

Burnham welcomed the Wicks inquiry on the grounds that 'it might demystify the job in some sense and just perhaps shed light on what, in many ways, can be a fairly mundane and fairly functional role'. He saw his job as 'to provide policy and political support and advice to the Secretary of State ... to add political shading to the general work of the department'. Although it was not his principal function, he engaged in 'regular contact with the media . . . there was very close liaison with the Press Office'. Burnham also maintained contact with the parliamentary Labour Party. By such means, he believed ministerial account-ability to Parliament could be enhanced. He divided work with his fellow DCMS special adviser, John Newbigin, roughly along policy lines: Burnham tended to concentrate upon sport and the National Lottery, Newbigin more on the arts.[24]

Most comment on special advisers under Blair emphasised their media roles. This tended to give a skewed picture of the balance of their work overall; as many inside government were at pains to argue, much of the work done by aides related to the development and implementation of policy. Figures produced by the Public Administration Select Committee in 2001 suggested that, of a total of seventy-six advisers, eight (of those whose departments were willing to reveal their primary function) were primarily political or presentational while for ten policy work was the foremost concern.[25]

Special advisers were closely involved in many of the defining policy approaches taken under Blair from 1997. David Clark, who was born in 1966, joined Robin Cook, Foreign Secretary from 1997 to 2001, in opposition in 1994. While he did not consider himself an expert and came from a political background, Clark worked closely with his employer on the development of an agenda for Labour. Important aspects to it were a much more positive, although not uncritical, approach towards European integration and efforts to promote the international cause of human rights. One manifestation of the former commitment was Britain's acceptance of the Social Chapter, from which Major had famously obtained an opt-out. The latter became what was termed the 'ethical dimension to foreign policy'. Controls on the export of armaments from Britain were tightened. Military interventions were also pursued. In 1999 Britain was a leading advocate of NATO's use of air strikes against Serbia, intended to end atrocities against Albanians in Kosovo. Clark helped Cook develop the concept of the use of international law to prosecute war criminals, which was applied to the case of the former Serb leader Slobodan Milosevic. Eventually, the International Criminal Court was established, its jurisdiction coming into force in July 2002. While Britain could not, of course, claim sole credit for this achievement, it did play a part.[26]

While he was able to see many of the policies he supported implemented, Clark grew weary of serving in the Blair administration. He resigned as a special adviser in advance of the 2001 election, ostensibly to enable him to participate in the campaign. However, he had no intention of returning. He had, he says, become 'frustrated with the government in terms of policy and style'. In his view, loyalty to the United States had become the dominant motif of foreign policy, and this approach, imposed by the 'elected monarchy', as he describes it, at No. 10, was a source of increasing concern for him, particularly in the light of the changeover to a right-wing Republican administration under George W. Bush following the 2000 US election. Enhancements to Britain's European status achieved since 1997 were being reversed. Clark, an advocate of British membership of the European single currency, felt that it was being blocked by Gordon Brown. Cook was moved from the Foreign Office to become Leader of the House of Commons following Labour's poll victory in June 2001. His subsequent resignation from the Cabinet in March 2003, over his objections to British participation in a US-led invasion of Iraq, without clear UN backing, suggests that he shared much of Clark's outlook.[27]

Aides played an important role in the implementation of Blair's central domestic agenda, which was focused on the delivery of measurable improvements in public services. In return for the resources they were allocated, departments were expected to achieve specific agreed objectives, set out in Public Service Agreements (PSAs). For example, the Department of Health had a range of detailed targets, including ones to reduce the lengths of waiting times for NHS treatment. Special advisers participated in the monitoring process. Turnbull told Wicks that when the 'Prime Minister has one of his stock-takes there are a number of special advisers in the room. There are special advisers from the [No. 10] policy directorate and any special advisers that the Secretary of State brings along. So the scrutiny of a department's progress against its PSA targets is something that special advisers take an interest in'.[28]

One aide who made the delivery concept his own was Michael Barber, a special adviser to David Blunkett at the Department for Education and Employment (DfEE) from 1997 to 2001. In 2003 he described the government's objective as being 'to achieve high quality public services which means rising average standards of performance . . . particularly . . . in the most disadvantaged communities so as to ensure equity'.[29] There was, then a dual objective: efficiency and social justice. Barber was born in 1955 and became a history teacher. Working for the National Union of Teachers from 1985 to 1993, Barber contested Henley-on-

Thames for Labour in 1987. Immediately before his appointment, he was Professor of Education at the Institute of Education, London, and a counsellor to the Labour leadership. Blunkett writes that Barber proved himself to have 'a refreshingly open approach to school reform, which was too often absent amongst his academic colleagues'.[30]

In his 1996 book *The Learning Game* Barber called for 'a government which puts education at the heart of its work' and was committed to the concept of a 'learning society', that extended beyond schools. He sought to combine goals of economic efficiency with the preservation of diversity and 'liberal traditions'. *The Learning Game* made plain Barber's support for Blunkett, stating that he 'has already proved himself the most formidable Opposition Spokesperson on Education for a generation'. Barber advocated that Blunkett should be placed at the head of a Department of Lifelong Learning (DOLLY), which would be given the status of 'a great office of state on a par with the Foreign Office or the Home Office'.[31] His views were reflected in Labour's 1997 manifesto, which, as well as proclaiming education as the party's top priority, stated that under 'Labour the Department for Education and Employment will become a leading office of state'.[32]

Once appointed, according to the Education permanent secretary, Michael Bichard, Barber 'ran the School Improvement Division and ran the Literacy and Numeracy Strategy'. He did not, however, have executive responsibilities. It was, Bichard said, a 'slightly odd relationship in that he was driving what that unit was doing, but actually we had a civil servant managing the unit'. Bichard described Barber as the 'best expert adviser I have ever worked with'. Although recruited on a patronage basis, Barber's credentials as an expert in his field were not in doubt. As Bichard put it, 'we might as well have just advertised for the person to run that unit and Barber would have got it.'[33] Not all who worked with Barber were as impressed. In 2001, having recently resigned as the Chief Inspector of Schools, Chris Woodhead described how, when he raised concerns over policy, he found Barber dismissive. Moreover, in his own account, Woodhead's 'experience was not unique. Others have commented on the professor's messianic conviction that all was well, and that no right-minded person could possibly question the Government's "world class" programme of educational reform'.[34]

A particular objective towards which Barber worked was the implementation of a literacy target for eleven-year-olds. He has recounted that the argument against it was that there would be 'perverse effects' on other parts of the national curriculum, which would be neglected. According to Barber, this did not happen; and, as well as progress being made towards the central target, improvements were made elsewhere.[35] In 2001 Ian Kendall and David Holloway wrote that there 'is evidence that some of the new initiatives are having an impact, with dramatic improvements in English and Maths'.[36] Following Blair's second election victory, Barber moved on from his role as a special adviser to take an even more high-powered post as head of the newly established Delivery Unit, reporting to the Prime Minister, under the supervision of the Minister for the Cabinet Office.

Ever since 1964 special advisers had taken an interest in public relations, which could entail, as well as functions such as planning presentational strategy and speech-writing, the maintenance of contact with journalists. In the words of Burns, 'Special Advisers talking to the press . . . has gone on . . . since the beginning of time. The idea that this started in 1997 is far from the truth.'[37] However, it is arguable that there was a change in emphasis from 1997. In certain accounts, most notably that of Nicholas Jones, the advent of the Blair administration signified a breakthrough for the special adviser as 'spin doctor', both inside No. 10 and beyond. It has been shown that a number of special advisers dealt with enquiries from the press, even if it was not their main function. Many came from media backgrounds. There was a contingent of former BBC employees.[38] For some, handling journalists was the principal duty. As Jones puts it, in 1997 many 'of the Labour Party press officers who had worked for members of the shadow cabinet in opposition were smartly found jobs inside government departments where they were appointed as special advisers to ministers'.[39] The most prominent such individual was Alastair Campbell, who was appointed as the Prime Minister's Chief Press Secretary in 1997. Another was Conor Ryan. He was recruited as an aide to Blunkett in 1997, having served as his 'workaholic mouthpiece for nearly four years' in opposition. Ryan was previously a journalist and press officer.[40] Charlie Whelan worked for Brown at the Treasury, and Ed Owen for Jack Straw both as Home Secretary and at the Foreign Office. Joe McRea pursued an 'eager, hands-on approach to the task of gaining favourable publicity' for the Secretary of State for Health, Frank Dobson, and other health ministers.[41]

What proportion of aides were engaged in dealing with journalists? In 1998 Campbell said that the 'vast majority do not have any contact with the press whatever'.[42] Less than four years later, in February 2002, Mike Granatt, Head of

Profession of the Government Information and Communication Service (GICS), was asked at his appearance before the Public Administration Committee how many special advisers dealt with the media. His response was that it was 'difficult to tell because some advisers operate on policy matters; some advise on presentation and talk to the media – some do both.' However, Granatt guessed that 'taking into account No. 10 and the adviser departments, about half of them. We are talking about 40 people but as I say, that is an imprecise figure.' It included individuals for whom it was not the sole or primary task.[43] As noted in Chapter 1, in mid-2002 the number who were predominantly presentational assistants was probably eleven.

According to Granatt, much of the media relations activity undertaken by special advisers was similar to that of career officials, that is, 'answering factual questions' when journalists telephoned the press office. The difference between special advisers and permanent civil servants was that the former could 'explain the party political background to a decision, to a policy, to a range of discussions. That is something that Civil Service press officers cannot and should not do'. In talking to the press, special advisers could 'add that extra dimension – to an extent be the Minister's voice'. Baroness Jay, Leader of the House of Lords from 1998 to 2001, described how the press office would forward enquiries to her aide 'when they were being asked things which required political interpretation or something beyond their information giving responsibilities'.[44]

Granatt emphasised that special advisers did not have *carte blanche* to partake in partisan point-scoring. As he put it, they 'can explain the party politics, [but] they cannot indulge in party politics'. They were certainly not allowed to 'attack individuals' or 'enter into the party political fray in some aggressive, personalised fashion'. Aides, Granatt has noted, contributed to the wording of press releases, a practice to which he had no objections. There were occasions, however, on which 'the Special Adviser, for some reason, generally and inadvertently in my experience, suggests something which it would not be right to be distributed with public funds, in which case one would seek to distribute that information through the party machine'.[45]

It could be argued that politically committed civil servants, in carrying out presentational duties, might – while not fabricating information – be more selective in their use of facts than career officials. Granatt's view was that 'telling the truth . . . does not, and cannot, mean in every circumstance every single fact is revealed, but the test for me has always been that if somebody came into possession of every single fact, they would see that . . . whatever is being said, was consistent with the truth and was indeed itself truthful.'[46] Turnbull has insisted that it 'is possible to present information neutrally'. In the area of data, this was achieved through the 'designation of certain statistics as national statistics that are released by the ONS [Office of National Statistics], or by departments, and that is to a particular timetable . . . and to a particular framework presentation'.[47] There was, it seems, a difference of philosophical approach between permanent Whitehall and at least one member of Blair's Cabinet. Charles Clarke, in a general discussion of the concept of impartiality, told Wicks that 'I do not fit the description "totally objective" to anything. I do not believe such a thing exists. I think it is a nonsensical concept. I did mathematics at University and I maybe would accept that totally and objectively two plus two equals four most of the time, but I do not think it is a helpful description from this point of view.'[48]

There is evidence that the presence of proactive, politically committed public relations advisers within a traditionally neutral Civil Service created problems. Whelan, said to be a 'volatile, publicity-seeking' individual, apparently trod on Whitehall toes. The Jo Moore affair was the most heavily publicised example of such tension. Difficulties were not inevitable, however. Ed Owen, for example, was able to fit in with the permanent machine very easily.[49] Presentational contradictions within and between departments were a danger. Granatt has said that 'confusion has arisen, where the Special Adviser and, for instance, the Director of Information or Head of News are not effectively communicating, they are saying different things. Sometimes to the same people.'[50] In many cases, according to Mountfield, journalists discovered that special advisers could reflect the views of their ministers more accurately than official press officers. It could lead to correspondents 'squirreling away to find discrepancies between one Minister's views and another by virtue of discussing it with special advisers'.[51] In October 1997 much confusion was created when Whelan was overheard in a bar stating on his mobile phone that Brown had ruled out membership of the single European currency in the present parliament, in contradiction of previously stated official government policy.[52]

The belief was widely held that certain special advisers supplied journalists with off-the-record briefings designed to further the causes of their employers, often at the expense of other ministers. According to the BBC's Political Editor,

Andrew Marr, 'there are examples of Ministers who . . . have almost sub-contracted parts of their personality to special advisers. They go off and will say things and do things on behalf of the Minister that the Minister would not dream of saying and doing as Minister in front of a journalist or a colleague.'[53] Campbell was adamant that No. 10 staff did not behave in such a way, writing in 2000 that 'the vast bulk of spin comes from what I call journalist spin doctors . . . If you read about a senior insider, the place the insider is from is likely to be the journalist's head.'[54] Jones argues that the extent of such hostile activity from 1997 undermined the value of special advisers.[55] As a junior minister at the Department of Social Security during 1997–8, Frank Field felt he was briefed against by aides because his ideas for welfare reform conflicted with Brown's. Field says that 'they are a destabilising force. The sum of human happiness would not be reduced if they all received their cards tomorrow.'[56]

Blair has conceded that, in his first term, public relations were overvalued. As he told the Liaison Committee in 2002, 'When you are in Opposition for 18 years, as we were, there was a tendency (because this is the way that Opposition works) that you believe the announcement is the reality. In many ways . . . it is, because what matters is the policy you are announcing; you are not actually in a position to deliver anything on the ground.' Consequently, 'for the first period of time in Government there was a tendency to believe . . . that the same situation still applied. It does not, in fact. For Government the announcement is merely the intention; the reality is what you have to go on and deliver on the ground.'[57]

That excessive focus on public relations can be explained in part by the fact that, historically, Labour's experience of the press was not a happy one. From the outset of Blair's leadership of Labour in 1994 his closest allies, including Mandelson and Campbell, had placed great emphasis upon the importance of communication techniques. Thanks partly to their efforts, in the years immediately prior to the 1997 election success traditionally pro-Conservative newspapers had become more sympathetic to Labour. However, within the Blair camp, it was suspected that such 'conversions' were not wholehearted. During the 1980s and 1990s, according to Campbell, 'the bias against Labour in the press was so strong it amounted in my view to a democratic injustice.' While, subsequently, the 'press may well have changed . . . parts of it are deeply hostile'.[58] There was, therefore, a determination to devote full attention to presentation in office, an effort in which special advisers played an important part. It has been argued that certain newspapers, in particular *The Times* and the *Sun*, which had previously espoused the Conservative cause, but became sympathetic to Blair, achieved numerous exclusive political stories.[59]

In addition to its use of special advisers in presentational roles, the Labour government overhauled the GICS. Following a request from Sir Robin Butler, the Cabinet Secretary, the Working Group on the Government Information Service was established under Mountfield in September 1997, its members including Campbell, Granatt and Ryan. It reported the following November. Jones portrays Mountfield's group as delivering suggestions very much in keeping with what Campbell wanted.[60] Mountfield, however, has insisted that he fought the career Civil Service corner. As he put it, there 'was an attempt to politicise appointments of press officers after the 1997 election. Our 1997 report went into a lot of detail to explain why that was not possible'.[61] Much of its content related to proposals for improvements in the efficiency and professionalism of the GICS. As far as aides were concerned, it was stated that 'the Special Adviser and the permanent Civil Service Press Officer will each have a role which is at once distinctive, legitimate and important.' The value of 'close co-ordination' and good relationships between 'Departmental Press Offices and Special Advisers advising on communications' was stressed. Following legal advice, it was determined that ministers could not appoint special advisers as heads of information, since aides were precluded by Order in Council from 'acting in an executive role'.[62]

'A strong centre'

Partially in reaction to the perception of Major as a weak leader, government was deliberately and openly centralised under Blair. As he put it to the Liaison Committee in 2002, 'I make no apology for having a strong centre. I think you need a strong centre.' Such had been his style in opposition. In office, the emphasis on public service delivery encouraged the tendency, as did the increased uncertainty over international security after September 2001. Even before the Al-Qaeda attacks in America, Blair had authorised military action in Iraq and Kosovo, events requiring a streamlined approach to decision-making.[63] Successive large parliamentary majorities afforded him political strength, particularly since they followed a long run of electoral failure for Labour. Blair's No. 10 was constructed with the intention of, as Hennessy puts it, 'driving policy and presentation from the centre'.[64] Political appointments were central to the development; and their authority was arguably greater than under any previous administration. As well as being more numerous than ever before, their distribution extended considerably beyond the Policy Unit, previously the most usual location for aides at No. 10: appointments were made to the private office and press office and, later, the newly established SCU and RIU.

The US spoils system was an influence on the organisation of Downing Street. Ties between Blair's circle and that of the Democratic President, Bill Clinton, were close. In the *Sunday Times* of 4 May 1997 Andrew Grice wrote that just 'as Labour strategists deployed slick campaign techniques learnt from Bill Clinton's presidential election in 1992, so they have looked to America in recent months for guidance on how to drive the machinery of government'.[65] In keeping with the US model, Blair's personal team, including Campbell, Powell and Miliband, made a seamless transition from opposition to administration in May 1997.[66] Among the others introduced was Anji Hunter, who had known Blair since his youth and had been his Commons assistant for most of the previous decade. With the title Special Assistant, she established herself as Blair's 'gatekeeper'.[67]

In Mountfield's view, the 'very large number of special advisers' at the centre constituted 'a critical mass'. In conjunction with certain regular officials, 'a sort of inner clique' was created, which had become 'very often the primary source of advice, with the civil service advice being seen as secondary'.[68] However, as Mountfield indicated, while the collective significance of permanent Whitehall may have lessened, individual career officials were still able to become influential. Clare Short's 'in group' (referred to in the Prologue) included Sir David Manning, who led the Downing Street Foreign Policy Adviser's office from 2001. Discontinuity with the past was not complete. In 2002 Richard Wilson said that 'the role [of special advisers] in Number 10 is changing, partly because of the numbers, partly because there is a real wish to have a stronger centre . . . But if I may just describe . . . what Harold Wilson said about Number 10 [in his 1975 speech], he said "The policy unit was set up to provide a team with strong political commitment to advise on, propose and pursue policies to further the government's political goals." That is not a bad description of the role of Number 10 now'.[69]

What was the relationship between aides at the centre and those spread across the government? John Newbigin, a former DCMS aide, has referred to 'a government-wide network of special advisers, which has its centre of gravity on

Number 10 and therefore has quite a lot of special advisers attached to Number 10'.[70] Weekly meetings were held for all political appointments. Initially they were chaired by David Miliband of the Policy Unit, but the responsibility was later handed over to the political office. According to some who were expected to attend, the gatherings were generally considered to be of little value. The most animated discussions which took place reportedly related to terms and conditions of employment for special advisers. Nevertheless, there were strong bilateral relations between individual aides at Downing Street and their counterparts elsewhere.

Particular efforts were made to control government announcements from Downing Street.[71] According to Campbell, the centralised approach to public relations was influenced by 'a desire to learn the lessons of past governments of both parties about the need for a strong centre and a strong sense of strategic direction'. The Major administrations in particular, Campbell argued, provided evidence for such a requirement.[72] In 1997 the Ministerial Code stated that 'all major interviews and media appearances . . . should be agreed with the No. 10 Press Office.' In addition, the 'policy content of all major speeches, press releases and new policy initiatives should be cleared . . . with the No. 10 Private Office: the timing and form of announcements should be cleared with the No. 10 Press Office'.[73] In 2001 the latter instruction was amended to refer to the Strategic Communications Unit (SCU), which was located at No. 10.[74] By such means, considerable authority was concentrated in the hands of, generally, the premier's office, and, particularly, Campbell.

The *Report of the Working Group on the Government Information Service* reinforced the tendency. It proposed the formation of the SCU, to be 'based in No. 10, answerable to the Prime Minister, working through the Chief Press Secretary'. The purpose of the SCU was to facilitate the cross-departmental co-ordination of the presentation of 'initiatives and events'. Its staff of perhaps six would be composed of 'a mix of civil servants and Special Advisers'. Its formation was announced in January 1998. The first head, Philip Bassett, a journalist, was a special adviser. The SCU introduced the 'Agenda' computer system, which created an all-encompassing grid for government announcements, replicating methods used by the Labour Party at Millbank.[75] Through the SCU and the grid, it could be ensured, for example, that major policy packages from different departments were not unveiled on the same day as each other, thereby reducing their impact. Equally, it might be argued, politically inconvenient information could be made public at times when it was likely to receive minimal attention. In 1999 the RIU was established at No. 10 under Bill Bush, formerly the head of BBC Research. A small body, it was charged with creating a database for use by No. 10 staff to assist in the rapid rebuttal of hostile press items.

A need 'to ensure that authentic Government statements, especially from the Centre, carry due authority' was identified by the working group report. Partly in order to combat the problem of 'anonymous stories which increasingly dominate political journalism', it was recommended that, in future, the non-attributable twice-daily lobby briefings conducted by the Prime Minister's Chief Press Secretary be made on the record. Campbell would not, however, be named, since 'this could tend to build up an official . . . too much into a figure in his own right'. Rather, the source would be the 'Prime Minister's official spokesman'. However, some journalists began referring to Campbell.

Other members of the Downing Street press office would speak on the record when dealing with enquiries, unless agreed otherwise. Referring to routine stories, they would be known as 'an official Downing Street spokesman', and for major ones, 'the Prime Minister's official spokesman'. Aside from the Chief Press Secretary, other special advisers in No. 10 could be designated as official, except 'on those occasions where there was a significant political dimension'. In such instances they would either agree a form of words with the Chief Press Secretary, which would then be attributed to the 'Prime Minister's official spokesman', or speak as 'a political adviser to Mr Blair'. In other departments, special advisers would always be referred to as 'a political adviser to' the minister and not 'an official spokesman'.[76] These changes in attribution etiquette were obviously intended to ensure that the government spoke with a single voice. As well as the public relations difficulties experienced by Major, the desire to avoid a re-emergence of Labour's tendency to play out its internal divisions in public, particularly evident during the 1980s, was probably an influence.

As was the case throughout government, presentation was far from being the only concern of special advisers in Downing Street. The Policy Unit/Directorate was central to Blair's style of leadership. It was larger than in earlier periods and composed predominantly of special advisers. In 2000, of a total of fourteen senior staff in the Policy Unit, twelve were outsiders. As had been the case since Redwood was its head, and when Donoughue first established the body, individual staff monitored particular policy areas. The Policy Unit held collective, themed meetings and maintained contact with various outside groups. Its members, with Ed Richards foremost, played important roles in the development of the 2001 manifesto. From 1997 onwards they worked very closely with career officials at No. 10. When Labour secured a second term, the distinction between the private office and the Policy Unit was abolished, both being subsumed in a 'Policy Directorate'. The change in the status of this body took place as part of a more general reorganisation, which divided No. 10 into three sections: 'Communications and Strategy', 'Policy and Government' and 'Government and Political Relations'.[77] Commentators noted signs of a trend towards a presidential approach. Writing in the *Financial Times* in July 2001, Brian Groom detected 'a strong White House flavour about changes affecting Downing Street'.[78] The new No. 10, in which more of the formal barriers between seconded civil servants and outsiders were now removed, was also comparable to a continental *cabinet*.

David Miliband, who was already performing the role in an acting capacity, was confirmed as head of the Policy Unit in 1998. Described as an 'enthuser with a fluid mind',[79] Miliband was born in 1965, the son of the distinguished socialist academic Ralph, and the brother of Gordon Brown's special adviser, Edward. David took a first in PPE and was a research fellow at the IPPR from 1989 to 1994. In 1994 he became the head of Blair's policy office. Elected to Parliament in 2001, Miliband was appointed school standards minister in 2002.

Miliband helped develop Blair's ideological approach. The political consultant Philip Gould, a close Blair ally, refers to a 'constant dialogue' between himself and Miliband during 1995–6 leading to the emergence of the agenda Blair would present to the electorate.[80] Miliband was an advocate of what came to be labelled the 'Third Way', a political approach endorsed by Blair and other leaders of progressive governments. In Britain it was an alternative to the statism particularly prevalent in the Labour movement during the 1970s and 1980s – a form of socialism abandoned by Labour for reasons including its electoral unpopularity and the fact that it was rendered less relevant by the successful implementation of the Thatcher programme. The name 'Third Way' implied that a new path, one of neither unfettered capitalism nor traditional interventionism, would be followed.

In 1994 Miliband edited a collection of essays entitled *Reinventing the Left*. Contributors included Gordon Brown and the academic Anthony Giddens, a leading Third Way theorist. In his introduction Miliband stated that, in the face of social trends such as the reduction in the size of the working class and the lowered credibility of social democracy, 'the Left needs a radical and new identity if it is to do more than rail against the (many) injustices of the present, and provide realistic hope of change in the future.' He argued for the 'constant reapplication of a set of values to changing circumstance' as opposed to utopianism.[81] In practical terms, it meant acceptance of market economics as a framework within which governments seeking to enhance social justice had to operate. Labour had begun moving towards such a position under Neil Kinnock, who became leader in 1983. When Blair took the helm in 1994 the transformation became more overt. Symbolically, the commitment to 'common ownership of the means of production' contained in Clause Four of the Labour Party constitution, often interpreted as meaning nationalisation of large sections of the economy, was dropped in 1995. The new text (part of which was written by Peter Hyman, a future Policy Unit special adviser) was a less specific articulation of collectivism. Miliband had senior responsibility for authorship of the 1997 Labour manifesto. Its foreword, credited to Blair, stated that government 'and industry must work together to achieve key objectives aimed at enhancing the dynamism of the market, not undermining it'.[82] Once Labour was in office, the Third Way manifested itself, Dell writes, in the form of 'welfare-to-work programmes ... public–private partnerships ... [and] incentives for excellence'.[83]

Blair's Policy Unit/Directorate included former associates of the SDP; a presence which, beginning in opposition, inevitably provoked resentment within Labour. It could be argued that the SDP, the formation of which was a reaction against Labour extremism in the early 1980s, provided a precedent for Blair's Labour Party. In 2001 Robert Shrimsley noted in the *Financial Times* that

> *Mr Blair welcomed the hated social democrats who had defected back into his party when he took up the party leadership, seeing them as spiritual fathers to his new Labour vision. He has two leading lights of that party in his Downing Street policy unit. Derek Scott is the prime minister's economic adviser while Roger Liddle helps to shape his European policy. A third policy unit member, Andrew Adonis, was a member of both the Liberals and SDP, before the two merged.[84]*

Not only were Scott and Liddle former SDP members, both had been Labour special advisers in the 1970s. Derek Scott counselled Denis Healey as Chancellor of the Exchequer, while Liddle was an aide to William Rodgers, the Secretary of State for Transport and one of the original 'Gang of Four'. Liddle's and Scott's disagreement over whether Britain should join the single European currency has been portrayed in terms of their previous attachment to the respective rival SDP factions of Roy Jenkins and David Owen. Rawnsley writes that Blair's 'adviser on Europe, Roger Liddle, a former Social Democrat of the Jenkinsite persuasion, was as passionately for the single currency as his adviser on economics, Derek Scott, another refugee from the SDP but of an Owenite inclination, was against the euro'.[85] Adonis became the senior member of the newly formed Policy Directorate in 2001. An Oxford graduate in modern history, he was the co-author of a book on the poll tax. In 2002 a group of commentators wrote that 'his school boffin appearance belies an underlying steeliness that has seen him rise to senior positions in three professions: academia, journalism and politics.' It was suggested that 'Although Adonis is personable and rarely confrontational, his influence is renowned, as is his habit of bombarding Ministers with "10 ideas a day, of which about one sticks," says one colleague.'[86]

As noted above, many individuals associated with think tanks were employed. Geoff Mulgan, a member of the Policy Unit, was 'the driving force behind . . . Demos'.[87] In May 1997 the *Financial Times* described Mulgan, a 'former adviser to Mr Gordon Brown', as 'one of the most fashionable proponents of post-modern thinking on big subjects such as work, the family and democracy'.[88] The employment of Mulgan could be read as reflecting Blair's desire to transcend rigid ideological frameworks and absorb influences from across the political spectrum. Like Barber, Mulgan moved on to a permanent Civil Service post, being appointed the head of the Performance and Innovation Unit (PIU) in 2000. He was recruited through open competition. Nevertheless, opposition allegations of politicisation followed.[89]

What was the impact of the Policy Unit/Directorate? In 2002 Blair told the Liaison Committee that departments 'are charged with policy, but the reality is for any modern Prime Minister you also want to know what is happening in your own Government, to be trying to drive forward the agenda of change on which you were elected'. He emphasised bilateralism: dealing with departments individually to achieve agreement on issues before they reached Cabinet. In his words, 'if there were particularly very contentious issues and the first I ever heard of it was at Cabinet then I would think some process of communication between

Departments and the centre had broken down.'[90] To such an end, the Policy Unit/Directorate was systematically involved in the development of departmental proposals from a very early stage, representing the Prime Minister's preferences in particular areas.

Often such interactions were harmonious, but not always. Blair's idea of good management could be perceived elsewhere as interference. In 1998 there were reports that Geoffrey Norris, a special adviser in the Policy Unit, blocked proposals by Prescott to introduce measures designed to decrease car usage, and that Prescott's displeasure was thereby incurred. Prescott was said to refer to staff members at Downing Street as 'teeny-boppers' (although Norris, who was in his forties, was rather an old teeny-bopper).[91] The following year, in an interview with *The Times*, the Deputy Prime Minister referred to the 'faceless wonders' in Downing Street who were opposing his plans for congestion charges for motorists.[92] It was understood that Estelle Morris, who resigned as Secretary of State for Education in October 2002, was uncomfortable with the introduction of variable tuition fees for universities, a policy advocated by Adonis.[93] However, Blair was insistent that the 'idea that [special advisers] determine the policy of the Government, I really believe is something that would not be recognised by any Cabinet Minister, even if you were talking to them off the record in private'.[94] In 2003, Dan Corry, no longer employed within government, was quoted in the *Financial Times* as saying that a 'secretary of state who knows what he wants and is prepared to argue it can say No to Number 10'.[95]

Some suspected that No. 10 aides, rather than representing the views of the Prime Minister, often pursued their own agenda. Mountfield told the Wicks Committee that

> *if one tries to dissect the activities, for example, of the Number 10 policy unit or whatever it is now called, their people are conveying the views of the Prime Minister to civil servants, sometimes I suspect claiming prime-ministrative authority for views that they made up themselves, but acting in effect as surrogate Ministers to some extent. That seems to me to be going beyond the proper role.*[96]

Policy aides, nevertheless, insisted that they were no more than emissaries for the premier and did not act on their own initiative. Their value was that they knew Blair's mind and did not always need to consult him in advance of expressing what his view would be on a particular issue. Were they wrong, the fact would have emerged, eroding their credibility.

One former No. 10 special adviser provided a detailed account of his activities to Wicks. For much of his first spell in Downing Street, Pat McFadden was a member of the Policy Unit working on constitutional reform. His career began as an opposition research assistant to Donald Dewar MP. He then transferred to the office of John Smith, Blair's predecessor as Labour leader, who died in 1994. McFadden was described in the Glasgow *Herald* in July 1997 as 'one of the few aides in Mr Smith's office who effortlessly made the transition to Tony Blair's New Labour while maintaining loyalty to his former boss'. He was 'closely identified with the reforming wing of the party and was a key player in the ... reform of Clause 4'.[97] For three years prior to the 1997 election, his work for Blair included contributing to speeches, particularly on devolution, a project Blair inherited from Smith.

While McFadden was loath to refer to himself as an expert, he did have, in his words, 'a long and deep familiarity with the issues that I was working with'. Nevertheless, he also took pains to point out that he was 'a political person'. He 'was a Labour party person for many years. I was a party member. I was close to the politicians I worked with. One of the reasons they employed me was the party affiliation as well as what I could bring to the job'. On the subject of presentational activities, he has said, 'Of course you talk to the press. I did not do much on a day-to-day, news of the day, kind of stories but ... quite often the press will ring special advisers and say, "Can you just give me a feel for it? How does the Minister think about this?"'[98]

McFadden's introduction to Whitehall was abrupt and preceded by nothing in the way of formal training. Immediately after Labour's 1997 poll victory, he was appointed to the Policy Unit and began attending, 'as an observer, the various Cabinet Committees during the devolution and other constitutional reform issues'. He also read as many as he could of the relevant papers. They were plentiful during the first two years of Blair's premiership, a period of 'very speedy enactment of quite a big agenda'. In particular, he worked with the constitutional secretariat, staffed by seconded permanent officials, who had less knowledge of the areas they were dealing with than he did. McFadden has said that he found them 'talented' and quick to learn.[99]

His functions included keeping the Prime Minister 'involved' and maintaining contact with the various ministers concerned. He also ensured that members of the No. 10 private office, who were not available to attend the meetings at which he was present, were informed of developments. In turn, career officials 'would advise me on many things to do with Whitehall procedure, how things got done in government and so on'. He has emphasised the team spirit which existed, saying that the government 'had a manifesto commitment to legislate within the first parliamentary year and we were determined to meet it. So we moved fast. That was probably a bigger thing in our minds than worrying about whether somebody was a special adviser or whether somebody was a civil servant'.[100]

In 1999 McFadden moved from the Policy Unit to become Deputy Chief of Staff under Powell. He maintained his existing policy interest, acting as a point of contact for the devolved Scottish Executive. He regularly spoke to its representatives, in particular his former employer Dewar, who became the Scottish First Minister, 'on the phone about various things that were coming up, things that might be problems between the devolved administrations and the UK Government. I managed to deal with an awful lot of things that never became problems'. McFadden also handled numerous assorted issues which his senior, Powell, 'did not have the time to deal with'. Some of them were 'parliamentary' matters. He did not share Powell's power to exercise authority over civil servants.[101]

McFadden left No. 10 in June 2000, 'to work for the Labour Party in the run-up to the 2001 General Election'. His career then took another turn. He 'agreed, at No 10's request, to work on two short-term contracts for the Coalition Information Centre [CIC] in Islamabad and then in Kabul'. The work entailed communicating 'the [anti-terrorism] Coalition's case and to respond to reports emanating from the ongoing conflict in Afghanistan'. In addition to McFadden, the CIC team consisted of 'civil servants from No. 10, the MoD, the Treasury and Lord Chancellor's Dept, personnel from the UK and US Military forces, [US] State Department officials, Republican political appointees from the White House, and retired US Ambassador Kenton Keith, who was the Coalition's spokesman in Islamabad'.[102] He was listed as a special adviser during his CIC spell.

Blair also took on in policy roles some unwaged counsellors, who were not located inside the Policy Unit/Directorate. The most famous of them was Lord (John) Birt, Director General of the BBC from 1992 to 2000. On 24 July 2000 the Prime Minister informed Parliament that

I have asked Lord Birt to take a long-term, strategic look at criminality and long-run social trends . . . He will be reporting to me and to . . . the Home Secretary as well as working closely with . . . the Lord Chancellor and the Attorney-General . . . he will be entitled to claim out-of-pocket expenses, to have appropriate use of Government office accommodation and to have access to relevant Government papers.

There were numerous Parliamentary queries regarding Birt's role and qualifications.[103] In October 2001 Birt was appointed as the Prime Minister's 'unpaid strategy adviser for a period of up to three years'. He supplied 'private internal advice to [the Prime Minister] and other Cabinet Ministers', which was exempt from public disclosure.[104] Birt worked in conjunction with the newly established Forward Strategy Unit, with an 'overarching role' on a number of projects supported by it.[105] In the press, attention was drawn to the controversy that surrounded his tenure at the BBC. 'Birtism', David Walker remarked in the *Guardian* in August 2001, 'especially cuts in production staff and the importation of US management techniques and language – led to widespread anger against him. The playwright Dennis Potter famously called him a Dalek.'[106] Birt became particularly involved in transport strategy. In January 2002 the *Daily Telegraph* posed the question, 'Who is in charge of the transport system? Is it Stephen Byers, the Transport Secretary, or Lord Birt, the former BBC Director-General appointed as Tony Blair's trains supremo?'[107]

While the Policy Unit/Directorate was very important to Blair's method of government, his two most senior special advisers were located elsewhere. Ever since 1974, except perhaps when Walters was counselling Thatcher, the head of the Policy Unit had been the leading temporary in No. 10. Such was no longer the case. Before his election success, it became apparent that, as Prime Minister, Blair intended to employ, in the words of Mountfield, 'a chief of staff and a chief press secretary who would be special adviser appointments'.[108] Sir Robin Butler, the Cabinet Secretary, took legal advice.[109] The conclusion was that it would be necessary to amend the 1995 Order in Council in order 'to include the power to instruct civil servants', as Mountfield put it, within the remit of Blair's senior aides. It applied to three positions, in No. 10 only, two of which were taken up,[110] by Campbell, Blair's Chief Press Secretary, and Powell, his Chief of Staff.

Why was the third post not filled? In 2000 Sir Richard Wilson, the Cabinet Secretary and Head of the Home Civil Service, protested ignorance.[111] It is said that a high-profile appointment as Senior Policy Adviser, who perhaps would have been empowered by Order in Council, was sought but not found. Reportedly, Adair Turner, Director General of the Confederation of British Industry, was sounded out. Others who supposedly declined were Bob Ayling, chief executive at British Airways, and, on the career official side, Rachel Lomax, Permanent Secretary to the Welsh Office.[112] Although, as head of the Policy Unit, Miliband was not given executive authority, he was able to perform his duties effectively without it. In 2001 it was suggested in the press that Anji Hunter sought, unsuccessfully, to be given 'the same powers as Mr Campbell and Mr Powell to manage civil servants'.[113] Appointed to the new role of Head of Government and Political Relations after the 2001 election, she left to take on the senior communications role at British Petroleum in November of that year. Her replacement was Baroness (Sally) Morgan, who had been a minister in the Cabinet Office and before that Blair's political secretary from 1997 to 2001.[114]

It has been shown in earlier chapters of this book that special advisers in No. 10 had assumed effective line responsibilities for career officials under previous administrations. In November 2000 Richard Wilson said that the 1997 Order in Council was 'in reality a technical change' since 'there has been a certain amount of management by Special Advisers going on in Number 10 under previous governments'.[115] Since the time of Hoskyns's stewardship in the Thatcher era, the Policy Unit had included a significant permanent Civil Service presence. In the words of Turnbull, 'in the old policy unit, it was almost the case that in some sense special advisers directed the work of civil servants. I mean, heads of the policy units chose those civil servants, decided what their portfolios were.'[116]

Campbell's and Powell's powers extended beyond No. 10. Appearing before the Committee on Standards in Public Life in July 2002, Granatt stated that Campbell (and, by implication, Powell too) could issue instructions to 'any Civil Servant'. Pressed on the comment, he said, 'I am not trying to wriggle out of the question, but I mean Number 10 has a general authority over the Civil Service, if it did not it could not do its job.' Richard Wilson confirmed that 'Those powers, for the two or three individuals you ask about, do not apply just in Number 10. They apply through the Civil Service.' It was probably proximity to the Prime Minister, rather than the Order in itself, which was the true source of authority. As Granatt put it, 'whether or not the Director had powers under the Order in Council, the fact that he issued some advice, some instruction, on behalf of the Prime Minister, would mean that people would comply with it.'[117]

What form did the use of the power take? Wilson was insistent that it was the communication of instructions from ministers, not the making of decisions, that was carried out. He added,

in practice I think the exercise of the managerial side of the role is actually rela-tively light. I think what it does is give them authority without people worrying about whether they are crossing over a boundary or not. It gives them the right to become engaged in management issues, or the right to discuss things with civil servants and to ask civil servants to take things on, without people debating whether or not a boundary has been crossed.[118]

Campbell's memorandum of June 2003 to the Foreign Affairs Select Committee seemed to provide an example of activities of the type referred to by Wilson. During the run-up to the war in Iraq, Campbell chaired the cross-departmental Iraq Communications Group, which included, among others, senior officials from No. 10, the Foreign Office, the Ministry of Defence, the Department for International Development, the Cabinet Office and the Secret Intelligence Service (or MI6). It met weekly 'to discuss and review forward communications strategy'. He 'also chaired the regular morning media meeting of key departments to help take the strategy forward on a day-to-day basis'.[119]

The 1997 Order in Council tested the traditional career Civil Service model. Lord (Robert) Armstrong's judgement was that career officials 'should not be responsible or accountable to Special Advisers, and Special Advisers should not be given responsibility for managing or giving instructions to civil servants. Though the decision to confer such responsibility on Jonathan Powell and [Alastair] Campbell was effected by due process of Order in Council, I believe that that was unwise'. The suspicion, whether well founded or not, was that the exercise of such authority was likely to be influenced by 'party political consid-erations'.[120] From 1999 the First Division Association, which was initially open-minded on the subject, favoured the removal of executive powers from the Downing Street special advisers.[121]

Other aides, in addition to Campbell and Powell, possessed de facto executive authority, although not as extensive as theirs. Granatt has said that, inside No. 10, non-executive special advisers 'may convey guidance from the Prime Minister, from the private office, which Civil Servants will take on board and work with in the work that they do'.[122] Indeed, it was commonplace across government for aides to communicate instructions from ministers to career officials. McFadden suggested that the 'authority of a special adviser in the eyes of the civil services would probably come from how much weight they think the Minister or Prime Minister attaches to that person's views', rather than from his or her formal authority.[123]

Jonathan Powell

Powell, Blair's Chief of Staff, was born in 1956, the son of an air vice marshal and the younger brother of Charles, Thatcher's Foreign Affairs Private Secretary. Rawnsley writes that for 'twenty years in British politics, there has been a Powell behind the throne'.[124] An Oxford history graduate, Jonathan Powell worked at the BBC and Granada television during 1978–9, joining the Foreign Office in 1979, and became a member of Blair's opposition team in January 1995. Gould writes that he 'added new skills to the operation: he understood government and how it worked and was vital in making Labour's transition to power so smooth'.[125] In 1995, the *Daily Mail* said that 'Powell has a reputation as an energetic "fixer" who combines managerial discipline with diplomacy'.[126]

Serving at the British Embassy in Washington in 1992, Powell observed 'the Clinton campaign at first hand'. The success of the Democrats, channelled partly through Powell, had a great influence upon Labour under Blair. Gould notes that the results included the establishment of Labour's opposition 'war room' in Millbank Tower, the rapid rebuttal mechanism using the 'Excalibur' computer, 'an obsession with message; and a tough, unremitting focus on hard-working people and their concerns'.[127] In office, the influence of the US spoils system could be detected in both Powell's title and his role.

Powell was committed to the extension of prime ministerial influence over government. Shortly before the 1997 election he was quoted as stating that, under Blair, there would be 'a change from a feudal system of barons to a more Napoleonic system'.[128] Inside Downing Street, Powell was located in an office very close to the Prime Minister's base.[129] Until July 2000 he chaired weekly presentational strategy meetings. Another function was to assist Blair in dealing with Cabinet members and the Labour Party.[130] In May 1997 it was reported that one of Powell's roles was 'to liaise with Robin Cook, the foreign secretary, and John Prescott, the deputy prime minister, both of whom have a prickly relationship with Brown'.[131] Aside from his general tasks, he has been described as the 'most influential voice on foreign affairs at the Blair court'. His realist approach probably clashed with that of the more idealistic Foreign Secretary, Cook. Powell played an important role in the brokering of the 'Good Friday Agreement' between Republican and Loyalist parties in Northern Ireland in April 1998.[132] Alongside Campbell, Powell frequently accompanied Blair on overseas visits.

Blair's initial intention was to appoint Powell as the principal private secretary. The plan raised questions of propriety. Certain sensitive tasks, such as liaison with the Palace and the opposition at election time, could be appropriately performed only by a neutral official. Butler says that, shortly before the 1997 poll, he met Blair and asked him to leave the post in the hands of the career Civil Service. Blair agreed to do so, initially for a trial period, which became permanent.[133] Powell's position had less recent precedent than Campbell's. Under Wilson from 1974 to 1976 Joe Haines, who was a political appointment, although not classified as a special adviser, ran the No. 10 press office. However, Downing Street private secretaries have always been permanent civil servants since the 1920s. Tim Bligh, principal private secretary under Macmillan and Home from 1959 to 1964, may have developed a problematically close association with the Conservative Party. Similarly, Charles Powell acquired a strong personal attachment to Thatcher during his 1984–90 spell as her overseas affairs private secretary. Nevertheless, an overtly political appointment as the senior civil servant at No. 10, if this was what Powell was, certainly represented a break with seven decades of tradition.

Which of the two, the Chief of Staff and the principal private secretary, was in charge? In February 2000 Richard Wilson supplied the Public Administration Committee with an organisation chart for No. 10, in which all lines of responsibility, including the one running from the principal private secretary, Jeremy Heywood, led to Powell.[134] In his appearance before the committee Wilson grappled with this, saying that there were 'a number of issues which the Principal Private Secretary deals with, without answering to Jonathan Powell. He answers to me on them'. Wilson's contention was that, whatever the diagram might suggest, in practice Powell was ultimately responsible for the Policy Unit and communications side of No. 10 (although Miliband and Campbell ran these), while Heywood oversaw the private office, Garden Rooms, honours and appointments, and operations.[135] The following year, a novel approach was taken to explaining the hierarchy within No. 10. In a diagram which Wilson presented to the committee there were no lines. Instead, staff were categorised by boxes and colour codes.[136]

Parliamentary scrutiny of the Chief of Staff was resisted. While Campbell made an appearance before the Public Administration Committee in 1998, Powell, despite requests that he do so, did not; Richard Wilson, appearing in his stead in November 2000, explained Powell's non-attendance on the grounds that there was no precedent for the cross-examination of a civil servant 'about himself and what he did', which appeared to be the committee's intention.[137]

Alastair Campbell

Campbell was born in 1957 and went to Cambridge University. His skill at mass communication was such that it left an imprint on the English language. To give two examples, Campbell was credited as the creator of the slogan 'New Labour, New Britain',[138] and 'supplied the phrase "People's Princess"' for Blair's statement on 31 August 1997 following the death of Diana, Princess of Wales.[139] His biographer, Peter Oborne, portrays a colourful character who, 'as a young man . . . worked as a busker, as a writer of soft pornography and as a croupier', and then went on to a successful career in tabloid journalism, eventually becoming Political Editor of the *Daily Mirror*.[140] Peter Stothard refers to a 'focused survivor of alcoholism and mental breakdown'.[141] The relationship between the Prime Minister and his press secretary was extremely close. In 2000 Campbell said of Blair that 'he was, and is, a friend of mine.'[142] Campbell attended Cabinet. Hennessy describes him as 'arguably the closest and most influential individual within [Blair's] innermost circle'.[143] Fiona Millar, Campbell's partner, was also a special adviser at No. 10 from 1997, counselling Blair's wife, Cherie.

Campbell was an informal adviser to Neil Kinnock during the latter's tenure of the Labour leadership.[144] Joining the leader of the opposition's team in 1994, he was an important figure in Blair's overhaul of the Labour Party, for example participating in the successful attempt to alter Clause Four of its constitution.[145]

This was not likely to win him approval from the left. Neither was an association with an emphasis on presentation, an approach mistrusted by many within the Labour movement. In 1996 Michael Barratt Brown and Ken Coates disparagingly portrayed Blair's leadership as treating the party as a 'product to be prepared, packaged and marketed'. They identified Campbell as a member of the 'inner group around the party leader' which was pursuing such a course.[146]

Much has been written about Campbell, not all of it reliable. In June 1998 he took the opportunity provided by his appearance before the Public Administration Committee to provide his own account of his role. He described the Prime Minister's need for an aide 'whom he can trust, who knows his mind, who knows what he thinks about the big issues of the day, and indeed about the small issues of the day, and who can brief at the drop of a hat'. As Chief Press Secretary, his function was to 'provide effective support for the elected politicians in the communication of policy'. He divided his tasks into two categories. First, he was the Prime Minister's official spokesman, giving on-the-record briefings. This, he said, was the only capacity in which he spoke to the press. Second, there was 'a co-ordinating role' which, at the time, he carried out in conjunction with Mandelson as minister without portfolio. Campbell was additionally responsible for the Strategic Communications Unit, which was charged with 'taking . . . a strategic overview of how the Government should communicate the policies and its activities'.[147]

As well as expressing Blair's views publicly, Campbell was able to speak for the Prime Minister within government. In January and February 1998 Campbell sent faxes, subsequently leaked to the press, to Harriet Harman, the Secretary of State for Social Security, and Frank Field, a junior minister in the same department. The two politicians were locked in a well-publicised dispute over welfare policy. Campbell instructed them to remain silent on the issue. Jones describes it as 'proof that Campbell had been caught red-handed ordering ministers to do what they were told'.[148] Campbell insisted that it did not mean that he was more important than ministers, stating that 'I do not have any power independently of the Prime Minister.'[149]

The media, from Campbell's viewpoint, were inconvenient and hostile but, unfortunately, had to be used in communicating with the public. Writing in the *Mirror* in July 2000, he indicated that he saw the Labour administration as under siege from 'a media herd always ready to give a lot of space to attack the

Government'.[150] Discussing how journalism had changed since his time in the profession, Campbell said that there 'is more of it. I think it is more competitive. I think there has been a bringing together of the market'. His philosophy was founded in the belief that there were 'two worlds'. The first was 'a media village that tries to envelop the political process' while the second was 'what is happening out there'; and it was 'out there', that is to say in the real world, that the government had to show that it was delivering on its commitments, Campbell felt. Hence the value of Blair's appearance on, for example, the lowbrow Des O'Connor Show.[151]

A charismatic person, though he could be charming, Campbell was capable of abrasiveness. In 1998 he was asked whether Blair had telephoned the Italian prime minister, Romano Prodi, in order to intervene on behalf of the media tycoon Rupert Murdoch. It was reported that Campbell responded by saying, 'I can certainly say that it's balls that the Prime Minister intervened over some deal with Murdoch. That's C-R-A-P.' When pressed by the Public Administration Committee, Campbell conceded, 'I may well have said that.' Asked whether he thought journalists were intimidated by him, Campbell maintained that he liked 'to think that I am fair with people'. However, he did 'not mind engaging in robust argument with people who I think are writing stories that happen to be wrong'.[152] Such an approach became particularly evident during his dispute with the BBC in the summer of 2003. In January 1998 Andrew Rawnsley reported that someone close to Blair had described Brown as characterised by 'psychological flaws'.[153] When asked about the episode in June of that year, Campbell insisted that 'I have not briefed against any member of the Cabinet.'[154] Two years later he reiterated the point, referring in the *Mirror* to his 'golden rule in speaking to journalists: I never say anything bad about anyone in this Government'.[155]

Campbell's appointment meant that the Prime Minister's official spokesman was a special adviser, not formally bound by Civil Service rules regarding objectivity and impartiality. According to Richard Wilson, Campbell was

freer than permanent civil servants to present the policies of the Government in the political context. He is overtly political. He is able to point out how the Government and the policy may differ from that of his predecessors in a way that a civil servant would feel inhibited from doing. But I do not think his job

is to go over the top and attack the Opposition with bricks and bottles . . . [or]
to focus on an out-and-out attack on the Opposition.[156]

Wilson conceded that 'there is a grey area here which is a matter of judgement.'
He could

imagine a situation where it would be proper for him [Campbell] to say . . .
that something the Opposition had said was absurd; the Government was not
doing what the Opposition had said, it was doing X, Y or Z; and that it was
very different from what the Opposition had done when it was in power . . . I
can imagine that kind of thing could be described as attacking the Opposition
but not attacking with bricks and bottles.[157]

Campbell described himself to the Public Administration Committee as 'freer
than my predecessors' in that 'if the Prime Minister is the subject of a political
attack I am in a position to rebut it.' However, he would only be 'reactive in
terms of any party political activity, not proactive'.[158] Such restraint was difficult
for a former partisan tabloid journalist. As he put it in 2000, 'sometimes I just
have to stop myself because I want to start whacking the Tories. So I don't go to
briefings and say, right, here are ten reasons why Michael Portillo is a complete
prat.'[159]

Nicholas Jones's criticisms of Campbell's behaviour centre on the view that
the Prime Minister's spokesman failed to fulfil the commitments made to the
Public Administration Committee. For example, Jones argues that in lobby
briefings during 1999 and 2000 Campbell engaged energetically in opposing Ken
Livingstone, the Labour MP who sought selection as Labour's candidate for
London Mayor but was not favoured by the party leadership. Jones also draws
attention to an event in relation to the 'bricks and bottles' rule. In January 2001,
in a lobby briefing, Campbell described Conservative spending commitments as
'an insult to Mickey Mouse' – a comment which led to Conservative demands for
his resignation. Another matter raised by Jones is that of Campbell's involvement
in arranging the defection of the Conservative MP Shaun Woodward to Labour
in late 1999. Had it been conducted in working hours, it would have tested the
terms of the Model Contract. The official line was that, once he knew what
Woodward intended, Campbell acted out of office time.[160]

Oborne writes that 'at the beginning of 1999 . . . well-informed people started calling Campbell "Deputy Prime Minister".'[161] The frequent public portrayal of Campbell as a manipulative operator and the power behind the throne served to glamorise a role which was, in reality, often arduous and not necessarily rewarding. Richard Wilson has suggested that Campbell's job was 'extremely hard work and quite often has a lot of grind in it. I see every day the note of his briefings in the Lobby. A lot of that is extremely dull.'[162] Campbell himself has said that 'I actually think that my role . . . is hugely overstated. I could not move policy even if I wanted to. If I suddenly started saying, "I want to do this on policy. I do not believe in this policy, let's move it", then I would very quickly be sitting back with these guys [the press lobby].'[163] The inflation of his influence, he suggested, was a result of 'the media being obsessed with its own little world. Most political journalists probably see me more than anybody else and I think they elevate my significance because of that. It makes them feel important.'[164]

While not the most retiring individual, Campbell nevertheless seemed to grow weary of the critical scrutiny to which he was constantly subjected. He complained that the Conservative Party was 'mildly obsessed about me'.[165] He began withdrawing from the business of day-to-day briefings, concentrating more on strategy. By late 2000 he was talking to the lobby only on Monday morning, on Wednesday after Prime Minister's Questions and on Thursday after Cabinet.[166] Eventually he handed over the task altogether to his two deputies, and in 2001 his job title became 'Director of Communications and Strategy'. But he remained a strong presence in the public arena. In 2002 he engaged in a public dispute with the *Evening Standard*, *Mail on Sunday* and *Spectator* over supposed attempts by the Prime Minister's office to expand Blair's role in the funeral of the Queen Mother;[167] and the following year his profile grew yet further following his appearance before the Foreign Affairs Select Committee.

Campbell's influence over the government publicity machine was extensive. However, while Bernard Ingham, Thatcher's press secretary, eventually took direct control of the Government Information Service, as it was then called, Campbell did not. Aside from the GICS, another official organisation which had an important role in the conduct of public relations was the Central Office of Information (COI), established in 1946 following the abolition of the Ministry of Information. By the time Blair took office, the COI's main responsibility was to advise departments and agencies on marketing communication, that is, paid-for publicity. In the early twenty-first century government was the largest purchaser in this market, and the expansion in expenditure in this area became the subject of criticism. While most official advertising campaigns were, on the surface, innocuous, relating to, for example, health and safety, there were suggestions in some quarters that a sinister pursuance of partisan interest was taking place.

Was Campbell in a position to supervise such an operation? The head of the COI reported to the Cabinet Office minister, not Campbell. However, Campbell and the head of the COI, did have, in the words of Granatt, 'a relationship'. The establishment of this arrangement followed a proposal by the quinquennial review of the COI, conducted between March and September 2001 and reporting in February 2002. The intention, according to Granatt, was 'to provide the Director of Communications Strategy . . . with an overview of the totality of the government's marketing effort'. Nevertheless, Granatt emphasised that there was 'not a reporting line to Number 10, it is not a line management line to Number 10, it is a line for information and advice'.[168]

Special advisers at the Treasury

While Blair has been a powerful Prime Minister, with an apparent preference for bilateral over collective Cabinet decision-making, No. 10 has been to some extent counterbalanced by the Treasury under Brown. Indeed, Treasury influence 'across a wide range of economic and domestic policy' has arguably reached its highest point to date. In 1997 Brown installed his 'very personal *coterie*' in office as special advisers. He was, Hennessy suggests, 'close to running a *cabinet* system'.[169] Reviewing Brown's group of aides, Geoffrey Robinson, the Paymaster General from 1997 to 1998, describes Ed Balls as Brown's 'deputy in all his roles, and in charge of policy and tactics in his own right'. Charlie Whelan was able to 'take out an opponent – press or political – as soon as look at them'. Sue Nye and Ed Miliband, brother of David, were also 'crucial players' within the set-up.[170]

Balls and Whelan were both recruited around late 1993 to serve the then shadow Chancellor. Balls, previously a *Financial Times* leader writer, was an economic adviser, while Whelan handled the press. Following the death of John Smith in 1994 the question arose whether Brown should bid against Blair, the first declared runner for the succession. According to Brown's biographer, Paul

Routledge, Balls was present (although he left early on) at the meeting between the two held on 31 May at Granita, a restaurant in Islington, where Brown conceded the leadership. Brown's 1997 appointment of both Balls and Whelan as special advisers, along with Miliband and Nye, was apparently a source of discomfort to Blair.[171]

Between them, Balls and Whelan have been described as comprising 'an operation that had as much interest in preserving and enhancing Brown's political power in the government and the party as worrying about the next spending round or the preparations for entering the euro. They weren't Treasury men, they were "Gordon's men".[172] Lord (Terry) Burns was Permanent Secretary to the Treasury when Labour assumed power in 1997. He left his post the following year. Rawnsley refers to the conduct of 'low intensity warfare between Brown's aides and Sir Terry Burns'. Shortly after the 1997 election Burns, according to Rawnsley, challenged Whelan over his former membership of the Communist Party, which the special adviser had not mentioned on his clearance form. Whelan pointed out that Denis Healey was also an ex-communist. Balls was an open critic of monetarist policies pursued by the Treasury under the Conservatives, on which Burns had advised.[173] The permanent secretary 'found it difficult to be treated as less than an equal to Ed Balls', while Balls 'struggled to mask his disdain for' Burns.[174] In May 1997 it was reported in the *Financial Times* that officials were complaining that 'they are not being kept in touch by the "Brownies", the fiercely loyal aides [Brown] has brought to the Treasury with him'.[175] Burns reportedly complained about leaks of Brown's first Budget in July 1997.[176]

During Burns's appearance before Wicks, Chris Smith, a committee member and formerly a minister in Blair's government, put it to him that when

the new government came in and you were Permanent Secretary of the Treasury, you will have had experience of one particular Special Adviser who was extremely overtly political and who saw his role entirely as dealing with the press and doing so in a very robust way and who has cheerfully and openly admitted never knowingly to have told an unvarnished version of events! Did that sort of proactive, highly political, Special Adviser role cause any problems?

Burns responded in the affirmative, stating that

it caused a great deal of problems . . . there is a tendency for some of these problems to emerge in the early days of new governments . . . the particular person that you refer to did pose more challenges than most of the people that I had to deal with, indeed probably I should say any of the people that I had to deal with. But, all I could say is, the system has a tendency to be able to deal with these problems. It may take a little longer than you might have hoped for but the problem was, in the end, resolved.[177]

Whelan has been described by Oborne as 'one of the most improbable and, in his way, appealing figures ever to have strutted his stuff on the Westminster stage'. He was, Oborne goes on, a 'hard-drinking, foul-mouthed, ex-Communist bruiser'.[178] Portrayed as adept at inspiring pro-Brown articles in the press,[179] he is often referred to in accounts of the tension between the Brown and Blair camps. Campbell supposedly maintained a 'capacious file of Whelan-related cuttings in his office'.[180] Whelan's fame spread widely and rapidly. On 3 May 1997 there was a reference in the *Mirror* to how, during the recent election campaign, 'Gordon Brown's aide Charlie Whelan ensured Chancellor Kenneth Clarke looked as trustworthy as Arfur Daley'.[181] In January 1999 Whelan decided to resign following intense speculation over the source of revelations regarding the personal finances of the Secretary of State for Trade and Industry, Peter Mandelson.[182] By then Whelan had outlived his usefulness since, in the words of Frank Dobson in a radio interview at the time, 'you can be a successful poisoner or a famous poisoner but you can't be both.'[183] Out of office, Whelan became an open critic of the methods he alleged were being used by No. 10 to undermine out-of-favour Cabinet members. In July 2000 he wrote that 'most Labour MPs I know are thoroughly fed up with the unattributable briefings emanating from No.10 against people they don't like.'[184]

In May 1997 the *Observer* described the partnership between Brown and Balls as 'curious', contrasting Balls's sophisticated, outgoing personality with Brown's.[185] Curious or not, their relationship was extremely close. As David Clark puts it, 'it is difficult to know where Gordon Brown ends and Ed Balls begins.'[186] Balls's father was the chair of a ward Labour Party, which Balls joined at sixteen. Unconventionally, at university he was, according to Routledge, a member not only of the Labour club, but also of its Conservative and Liberal equivalents.[187] Continuing his education after Oxford at Harvard, Balls was only thirty in 1997.

His partner, Yvette Cooper, was elected as a Labour MP in the same year. From Brown's point of view, it was argued, Balls's most attractive feature was that he had 'a brain the size of a planet'. Yet he had 'something more than intellect. He has demonstrated an ability to learn the black arts of news management. He has acquired political nous'.[188] In October 1999 Balls was appointed Chief Economic Adviser. In order to make his position within the Treasury workable, an arrangement was adopted similar to that which had applied to Robert Neild and Alec Cairncross after 1964, whereby Gus O'Donnell, a career official and head of the Government Economic Service, and not Balls, was responsible for staff management.[189]

Balls was an intellectual force behind New Labour economic policy. In his first week at Harvard he attended a lecture by Professor Greg Mankiw, a leading 'new Keynesian' (Mankiw's dog was called Keynes), in which he 'eulogised Milton Friedman', the promulgator of monetarism. For the first time, Balls, in his own words, 'realised that the world was more complicated than the sterile and over-ideological "Keynesian v Monetarists" essays that I wrote as an undergraduate'. It was Balls's intention to bring about 'macroeconomic stability – low and stable inflation and sound public finances'. However, this objective was not an end in itself. Rather, he aimed 'to deliver high and stable levels of growth and employment by ensuring economic and employment opportunities for all'. It was a familiar long-term Labour intent, that of efficiency combined with social justice. For example, Balls's predecessor at the Treasury, Kaldor, sought to attain such objectives through the use of taxation.

Balls was not a monetarist, denying 'the stability of the link between the money supply and inflation'. Equally, while he saw the role of government as extending 'well beyond macroeconomic policy-making', he was not an interventionist in the traditional sense. He did not believe in 'picking winners [i.e. selective intervention] or responding to market failures by trying to replace the market in its entirety'.[190] In 1992 he wrote that 'Old-style Keynesianism, pursued for too long, simply leads to high and rising inflation, unwieldy fiscal deficits and finally damaging recessions. This is the stuff of which boom-bust cycles are made.'[191] In Balls's model, the role of the state was to tackle 'short-termism and market failures by making markets work more dynamically and encouraging investment in the broadest sense – not just in machines, but in technology and innovation, skills and infrastructure – the fuel for growth in the modern economy'.[192]

The extent of Balls's influence on economic policy from 1997 would be difficult to exaggerate. In 1998 Routledge wrote that he was 'reckoned by Whitehall insiders to be the most influential outsider in the Treasury since John Maynard Keynes'.[193] Although Kaldor was probably in the same league, the judgement was defensible. In the words of Robinson, 'I can think of no policy or decision in which he was not centrally involved.' For example, Robinson attributes to Balls the establishment of five criteria against which an assessment could be made regarding whether Britain should join the European single currency.[194] One of the most dramatic and momentous initiatives which Balls inspired took place five days after Labour's 1997 election victory, when Brown announced that responsibility for monetary policy would be transferred from the Treasury to the Bank of England. In addition, two weeks later it was stated that banking supervision would no longer be conducted by the Bank of England, but henceforth by a new Financial Services Authority. Reform and formalisation of the way in which the Bank was financed was also intended. The arrangements found legislative expression in the 1998 Bank of England Act.[195]

Balls's advocacy of the 1997 measures dated back at least as far as 1992, when, in a Fabian Society pamphlet, he called for an independent central bank, adding that the Bank of England 'would perform its macroeconomic task better if it were not also responsible for City supervision'.[196] According to Robinson, Balls first floated the idea to Brown in mid-1995. Brown, having cleared it with an enthusiastic Blair, gave Balls the go-ahead to produce a detailed proposal.[197] The Bank of England was primarily charged with conducting monetary policy in order to attain an average inflation target of 2.5 per cent. There was a secondary objective of meeting the government's growth and employment intentions. It was intended, according to Balls, that there would be 'no doubt about the Government and the Bank's sound long-term objectives'. At the same time, there was a degree of flexibility, allowing the Bank to 'respond intelligently to . . . shocks'. Balls labelled the approach 'constrained discretion'.[198] Linked to monetary policy changes was the introduction of a new fiscal framework. Again the intention was to introduce long-term clarity and certainty. There was a 'golden rule' that, over the economic cycle, the government would borrow not to finance current expenditure but only to fund investment. In addition, the principle was established that public debt, as a proportion of GDP, would be maintained at a stable and prudent level over the economic cycle.[199]

A body which was in some respects a Treasury equivalent to the Policy Unit emerged in the form of the Council of Economic Advisers. It was, according to Turnbull, 'not a council in the sense that they meet as a collectivity in a group', but rather 'a heading under which they are employed'. Each member had a particular speciality, variously 'poverty and the labour markets, corporate finance, local government, the voluntary world, taxation'. They were experts, personally selected by Brown, and were, in Turnbull's words 'definitely special advisers'. The Council was established in August 1997, following the disbanding of the Panel of Independent Forecasters which had served the previous administration. Its terms of reference were 'to advise the Chancellor of the Exchequer on the design and implementation of policies for the achievement of the Government's economic objectives'.

The initial members were Chris Wales and Paul Gregg who covered, respectively, taxation and employment. Wales moved from a position as a tax partner at Arthur Andersen; Gregg was a senior research associate at the Centre for Economic Performance at the LSE, a role he continued on a part-time basis. His speciality was the dynamics of the UK labour market. Subsequent recruits included Maeve Sherlock, who joined in May 2000. Director of the National Council for One Parent Families, she provided Treasury ministers with counsel, in particular, on 'welfare-to-work' measures and child poverty. By 2001 the Council had reached a strength of five. Did it pose a threat to the position of the permanent Civil Service? Turnbull thought not. Since they worked in clearly defined areas, the members of the Council did not engender the feeling that 'there is a great mass of them up there sitting on top of the department . . . it does not feel like a kind of managing group.'[200] Nevertheless, taken together, the Council and Brown's other aides constituted a group of special advisers larger not only than any present at the Treasury before, but also than at No. 10 in virtually any period before 1997. Their collective impact, as well as Balls's personal influence on policy, was pronounced.

* * *

In opposition, particularly under Blair, Labour built up a contingent of aides who proved to be very effective at developing and presenting proposals. Given the long period of Conservative government, the career Civil Service was something of an unknown quantity to the Labour administration that took office in 1997. Partly in order to ensure the implementation of a considerable number of radical policies, the largest number of political appointments to have served any government to date was made. Many had worked for their employers in opposition. A number were associated with think tanks. Here was further evidence for the professionalisation of politics, feeding into the use of special advisers. They achieved great influence in office, thereby reducing that of the career Civil Service. However, a complete overthrow of the Whitehall machine and installation of the *cabinet* system was not attempted. Individual career officials were able to achieve prominence. Centralised communications methods employed by Labour before May 1997 were also transferred into government. These developments were encouraged by a desire to avoid the repetition of public relations difficulties which had characterised the Major administration, as well as by Labour's past experience of the press. The proliferation in numbers of special advisers after May 1997 was to a large extent attributable to the expansion at Downing Street, with the Treasury also a significant area of growth. It could be taken as a reflection of and factor in the importance of Blair and Brown within the administration. Various measures, including the introduction of the Model Contract, were adopted with the intention of bringing greater certainty and clarity to the use of special advisers. Perversely, the existence of a clearer framework provided a means by which their activities could be more easily judged and possibly condemned.

The division of aides into different types, no longer applied within government, was difficult, since many performed a variety of functions. Political liaison continued to be important. There were major contributions to policy from, among others, Barber and Balls, and from the Policy Unit/Directorate. Media-related activities were significant, but received disproportionate levels of attention. The GICS received an overhaul for which it was in all probability due. Attempts to establish a single voice for the government represented as much a desire to control departmental special advisers and ministers as to alter the values of the official machine. Almost certainly, the Policy Unit/Directorate played a more systematic, proactive role in the development of measures across government than ever before. Furthermore, it contributed to Blair's ideological approach. Taking all of this into account, it could be argued that special advisers at Downing Street were facilitating prime ministerial, as opposed to Cabinet, government. The obvious US influence on the Blair camp gave some validity to the presidential analogy. In structural terms the *cabinet* model was another important comparison. Yet however powerful Blair was, at the Treasury Brown had his own effective team. Special advisers were a factor in the competition between these two power bases. Hostility was probably worsened by media briefing. Journalists, for their part, were often eager to seize upon supposed differences between the Prime Minister and the Chancellor of the Exchequer.

Ten

Trends and achievements

In this concluding chapter the significance of the special adviser is discussed in the context of the themes outlined in Chapter 1, taking into account all the periods that have been examined. The government response to the Public Administration Committee's report on the Jo Moore affair will be described, along with the findings of the Wicks Committee's investigation into the boundaries within the executive. An assessment is made of whether the numerous publicly voiced concerns regarding the use of political appointments under Blair were justified. The extent to which aides have changed in nature since their initial introduction in 1964 is considered.

Throughout the four decades examined, individual connections between special advisers and the ministers they worked for were crucial. Relationships were frequently long-standing. Personal bonds could be close, as demonstrated by that between Thatcher and Walters. Inner circles around Cabinet members often included political appointments. Aides depended for influence upon their employers' confidence: if that were lost, so too was the chance of effectiveness, as Kaldor found through his relentless pressure on Healey. Conversely, Cabinet members could come to feel extremely dependent upon their counsellors, who might not only provide support but also perform the role of critical, candid friend, as Frances Morrell did for Benn. The linkage between the fates of temporary civil servants and those of their ministers fostered a tendency for the former to seek to advance the particular interests of the latter, sometimes fighting factional battles or endeavouring to undermine others in the government. Rivalries between senior members of the 1974–9 Labour administrations, for example, in which special advisers played a role, were intense. It was common for ministers and their personal appointments to share ideological alignment and develop policy approaches together. However, not all matches were perfect. Donoughue was from a Gaitskellite background, yet served as Senior Policy Adviser to Wilson. He then managed to survive the transition to the new Prime Minister.

Partisanship was an important characteristic. Special advisers were recruited to help implement manifesto programmes, which they had often helped to construct, and many were active in party circles prior to their appointment. Their interests in securing political success and re-election were clear; and employment as a temporary civil servant could be a stage in a political career. However, not all aides were partisan. Tom Burke at Environment from 1991 was not a Conservative and Hoskyns's association was with the party was fairly recent in 1979. Commitments could be flexible. A number of Labour special advisers joined the SDP, two of whom returned to serve under Blair from 1997. Certain younger SDP activists went on to serve ministers under Major. During 1974–9, special advisers appeared to be a means by which the leadership could reduce dependency upon the Labour machine. Both Thatcher and Blair introduced changes of policy direction, to which there was some resistance within their parties, with the assistance of personal aides who subsequently served in office.

From the first appointments, special advisers have been concerned with the presentation of party and government activity. This facet of their work was prompted in part by the pressure of an increasingly critical media, associated with declining social deference from the late 1950s. Aides' association with the government of the day encouraged a more proactive approach to public relations than might be expected from career officials. Their tasks in this field included the development of strategy, speech-writing and the cultivation of relations with journalists – whether the end in view was the benefit of the government as a whole, or the profile of individual ministers. A high degree of suspicion surrounded such functions, particularly that of dealing with the press. During 1974–9, for example, aides were believed to be associated with leaks of official information.

Special advisers were often the subject of media interest themselves, either as individuals (for example, Balogh) or as a group (particularly the case from 1997). Frequently notable in various ways, special advisers provided good copy, particularly in comparison to civil servants, who were often perceived as grey and anonymous. It should be noted that attempts at government news management certainly predated 1964. The Ministry of Information, although founded in extreme circumstances, was a fully fledged propaganda department. Moreover, selective leaking in order to pursue particular agendas was practised by Charles Trevelyan in the nineteenth century and, in the twentieth, William Beveridge.

For much of the period under examination, national economic and political decline was a prominent concern in Britain. Wilson's initial decision to recruit special advisers was motivated by a desire to reverse it. Many aides, including Hoskyns, had their own prescriptions for the cure of the 'British malaise'. Some historians regard the political and economic difficulties experienced from the late 1950s as undermining the supposed cross-party political consensus established after 1945. It is notable that in the mid-1970s, around the point at which a final collapse in the postwar settlement is believed to have occurred, the number of special advisers expanded considerably. It could be argued that the appearance of partisan aides was a reflection of the increased polarisation which consequently emerged. Certainly, whether the consensus was a reality or not, Mark Schreiber believed it existed, as did Hoskyns and probably other special advisers to Thatcher; and they wished to see it overturned. Another tendency associated with decline was that of overload. As problems mounted up, so did the pressure on Cabinet members. Wilson's 1975 speech indicated that special advisers were intended to ease the burden, presumably by taking on functions which career officials could not perform or were not suited to carrying out.

Wilson's 1964 introduction of aides was a genuine innovation. There were, admittedly, numerous instances of the recruitment of outsiders into Whitehall prior to 1964, and the new entrants shared various characteristics with their post-1964 counterparts. In the early twentieth century the Liberals had made temporary appointments in order to implement a party programme. The two most significant experiments prior to 1964, involving both personal aides and bodies of experts, took place under the extraordinary circumstances of world war, in which coalition government reduced the significance of political alignment. In the post-1945 period, at No. 10, Attlee employed Jay, while Macmillan had John Wyndham.

However, Wilson's creation of special advisers was innovatory because it led to the simultaneous combination of a number of pronounced features. The new aides were the product of a deliberate, stated, strategy, which sprang in part from

Labour/Fabian ideology, and they were introduced simultaneously across different offices of government in 1964. Their partisanship was important and they were associated with individual ministers. A particular job title, not previously widely used and only in a different context in Britain, was attached to them. They were placed inside, although not absorbed by, the Civil Service, receiving papers and attending committees. As Pimlott puts it, previous 'prime ministers had sometimes employed non-civil service staff . . . But Wilson was the first to do so . . . on a substantial scale, and as a matter of principle. The innovation stuck: what was pioneering and risqué in 1964 became an established practice, copied and institutionalised by later administrations.'[1]

Wilson is responsible both for the first use of special advisers and for the expansion in their number in 1974. Without him, while there might well have been an increasing use of political appointments, it might have taken place in an even more *ad hoc* fashion than it did. Whatever other judgements might be made of his qualities and performance, Wilson must take the credit for at least this one significant, lasting development. Special advisers should also be seen as Labour's constitutional contribution. In government it has tended to make more use of them than the Conservatives, although the latter have tacitly acknowledged their value.

The perceived need for more expertise within government was an extremely important motivation for the introduction of aides. Most of the initial appointees during 1964–70 were economists with university connections. Such a recruitment practice not only reflected cross-party views since the late 1950s, but was particularly in keeping with the Fabian outlook. Indeed, technocratic considerations, which were arguably elitist in flavour, seem to have been generally more important to Labour's use of outsiders in Whitehall than the class-based analysis of the senior Civil Service which might have been expected to loom large (although that approach did have some currency within the party, for example in the 1970s). Over the history of the special adviser a number of prominent academics have been employed as aides, Kaldor and Walters among them. Not all were economists: Donoughue was a political scientist and Michael Barber's expertise was in education. The definition of a specialist could be extended beyond university professors and lecturers. Others might, for example, come from the private sector, as during the 1980s. Indeed, in a sense, journalists such as John Harris and Alastair Campbell were also specialists, applying their own particular skills and experience. Over time the use of academics, as a proportion of the total number of aides in employment, declined, though it did not die out. However, the assertion that the role of special adviser was introduced purely as a means of employing experts, but was subverted at some point for the pursuance of partisan gain, is not supported by the evidence. Other considerations, described in this work, were influential from the outset in 1964.

It is possible to identify different types of aide, but overlapping roles were common. Balogh, for example, was an economist and Labour partisan who also took an interest in public relations. Non-expert aides often developed considerable knowledge of their policy areas. The emergence of independent think tanks and increased funding for shadow ministers led to the development of a pool of individuals who were both politically partisan and well acquainted with particular issues. It is perhaps more useful to distinguish between the functions that were performed than the individuals who carried them out. Presentation was important, as was political liaison, for example with the parliamentary party. The supply of expert advice was also a significant activity. Under Thatcher, the application of business experience was particularly valued. The types of work required of aides could reflect the approach of the administration they served.

Special advisers often sought to influence events on their own accounts and pursued their own agendas. Hoskyns was an example of this, as was Kaldor. In order to achieve their ends, aides might conduct lobbying campaigns. However, with such activities came the danger of isolating themselves from their ministers or the Civil Service. Personalities could be important, and some individuals' overbearing traits served to reduce their impact. The extent to which the more controversial activities of special advisers were sanctioned by those they served was not always clear. A perceptive politician, however, would surely become aware if his or her aide was persistently campaigning against others within the administration without approval, and call a halt to it.

In discussing special advisers as individual actors core executive theory provides a useful model. This is founded in a view of government as an arena in which multiple actors trade resources such as information and authority in order to achieve particular objectives; it is positioned in opposition to the command model, in which ministers instruct others.[2] Perhaps special advisers could be viewed as participants in such a process, rather than mere tools of their ministers.

Employment as an aide became an element in many successful individual career paths, both within and beyond party politics. At the time of writing, the

Foreign Secretary, the chairman of the BBC, the Master of Balliol College, Oxford, and the incoming director of the LSE, along with numerous front- and backbench government and opposition politicians are all former special advisers. However, for others, such as Hoskyns, far from being a career move, entry into public affairs entailed a considerable sacrifice in terms of earning potential.

Prime ministers have almost always employed more aides than other government members. While the premier has no formal department, it is arguable that, particularly following the establishment of the Policy Unit, an unofficial one began to emerge. At least from the 1980s, it began to communicate directly with other parts of the machine. Interventions from the centre were made easier by a larger number of staff. Certain prime ministers, most notably Thatcher and Blair, used outsiders to great effect in determining the course of their governments, for instance as a means of conducting bilateral as opposed to Cabinet government. There was also a structural tendency towards centralisation, as demonstrated by the fact that less interventionist premiers such as Callaghan nevertheless used their special advisers to obtain desired results. However, numbers of staff were not the only factor determining prime ministerial influence; political circumstances were also very important. Major appeared to lose control of his administration and it is doubtful whether a greater number of political appointments at No. 10 would have restored his authority. In certain instances, such as that of Roy Jenkins and John Harris, aides elsewhere in the government appeared to undermine the premier. While the recruitment of all special advisers was, in theory, subject to approval from No. 10, the right of veto, as with other prime ministerial powers, could surely not be exercised with impunity. For example, even if Blair was troubled by the presence of Balls and Whelan at the Treasury, he did not prevent Brown from taking them there in 1997. Special advisers facilitated the participation of secretaries of state in Cabinet debates, for example during the 1976 sterling crisis. Moreover, perceived overuse of aides could provoke a backlash, as was the case with Thatcher and Walters.

Particularly under Blair, the use of special advisers at No. 10 has encouraged presidential analogies. There are of course structural distinctions between the British and US systems, notably the lack of separation of powers in Britain; nevertheless, it is possible to argue that, assisted by aides, British prime ministers have developed a separateness from their cabinets and parties. Michael Foley argues that the cult of the personality prevalent in US politics has come to the fore in Britain in recent decades, leading to the emergence of a British presidency.[3] The continental *cabinet* was a clear influence upon the development of special advisers from the outset. The full adoption of the model, although encouraged by parliamentary reports in the 1970s and 1980s, never occurred, although the staff of No. 10, consisting of seconded officials and outsiders, began to take on the features of a *cabinet*, as, to a lesser extent, did those of other offices of government, including the Treasury. The British constitutional tradition, however, is a very strong one – arguably the most influential of all across the world – and should be examined in its own right, not merely as a receptacle for outside ideas.

The contribution of special advisers to policy was immense. They introduced ideas and skills not necessarily present within Whitehall. Many of the important packages developed from 1964 onwards were influenced by outsiders. Brian Reading, for example, encouraged the Heath administration's decision to stimulate economic expansion. Particularly from 1979, political appointments saw their initiatives successfully adopted. Key programmes of the Thatcher period which altered the role of the state, such as privatisation, were developed in part by aides. Major's Policy Unit contributed to the Citizen's Charter. Under Blair, special advisers were associated with a considerable range of measures including devolved government and the establishment of an independent central bank. Taking into account all the periods studied, the influence upon policy was the most significant result of their introduction to government.

As elements inserted temporarily, and perhaps rather awkwardly, into the career Civil Service, special advisers inevitably gave rise to some friction. Certain outsiders were hostile in their attitude towards Whitehall; and there is evidence that elements within the permanent machine worked to undermine some of the incomers, with a degree of initial success. However, over time, particularly after 1974, the balance of power shifted. The trend was probably partly a product of the expansion in numbers. In addition, ministers increasingly valued outside counsel as the prestige of Whitehall, along with that of numerous other traditional institutions, declined, overload increased and the media became more hostile. Propriety difficulties associated with the introduction of political appointments into a traditionally neutral Whitehall were inevitable. The possibility that information and contacts obtained inside Whitehall might be exploited to commercial advantage by outsiders was a perennial and understandable concern. While aides were supposed to provide advice only, they informally took on management functions over permanent civil servants (in addition to their secretarial assistants). This came about in part because, though special advisers were attached to individual ministers and therefore supposedly separate from the hierarchy, the nature of their roles meant that they worked alongside and interacted with career staff. In 1997 two appointments were officially granted such authority. Many special advisers, including Schreiber, had particular prescriptions for Civil Service reform. While they were sometimes intended to break the dominance of the Treasury as the senior office of government, this was never fully achieved; indeed, under Gordon Brown the Treasury became more powerful than ever, albeit subject to significant political control. Tensions existed between regulars and outsiders, but were not inevitable or insurmountable. The implementation of policies required a degree of co-operation; and permanent Whitehall was not itself an entirely homogeneous entity, with all staff acting as one.

At various times, special advisers have referred to the need for 'revolution' or the removal of established governing elites through the incorporation of outsiders into Whitehall. For Balogh, this meant *dirigiste* Labour economists replacing generalists. Hoskyns sought to displace permanent civil servants, cushioned against economic realities, with market-hardened businessmen. While neither succeeded in fully realising his objectives, both saw individuals of the types they favoured introduced in greater numbers than previously. However, political appointments have generally reflected their neutral counterparts in terms of educational background. Many special advisers were graduates with Oxbridge connections. Although there has been a considerable LSE presence, it hardly constituted a major upheaval. Women, as in the senior levels of many other walks of life, were underrepresented, although not completely absent. For a time under Major, Sarah Hogg and Tessa Keswick were two of the most important aides in Whitehall. Ethnic minorities, similarly, were broadly neglected. Various dynasties have been represented in the forms of, for example, Hilary Benn, the Miliband brothers, Jonathan Powell, Hogg and Keswick. Dan Corry was the son of Bernard, a Labour special adviser in the 1970s.

Did the introduction of the special adviser lead to the advancement of previously alienated groups? It is difficult to make generalisations. However, in examining specific cases it is clear that individuals with contributions to make who, owing to certain characteristics, might otherwise not have held public office, have been recruited to Whitehall by this route. For example, Abel-Smith's sexual orientation meant that he considered himself ineligible for election to Parliament. Balogh and Kaldor, as Jews and Hungarians, had already met with barriers to their progress. It is doubtful whether Hoskyns would have made an impact upon government other than by the route that he did. And Ed Balls was able to attain substantial influence much earlier in life than is likely had he opted to work his way up the Civil Service hierarchy or in Parliament as a Labour MP.

In Chapter 1 it was shown that, although it existed previously, interest in the special adviser reached a new peak after 1997, often taking the form of anxious or even hostile concern. During 2003 certain consequences of this attention manifested themselves. In February the government produced a response to the Public Administration Committee's report on the Jo Moore affair.[4] Lines of accountability, which were unclear at the DTLR during 2001–2, were clarified. It was stated that 'ultimate responsibility for disciplining an individual special adviser should fall to the Minister who made the appointment.' If a permanent secretary was unhappy with a decision taken by a minister in this respect, it could be raised with the Cabinet Secretary, who in turn would bring the matter to the attention of the Prime Minister. The premier possessed the ultimate right 'to terminate employment by withdrawing his consent to the appointment concerned'. For the benefit of career officials who might wish to voice concerns about the activities of special advisers, the government promised that, following discussions with the Civil Service trades unions, specific guidance would be included in the Civil Service Management Code. It was announced that a group, under the chairmanship of Robert Phillis, chief executive of the *Guardian* Media Group, would be established to conduct an external review of government communications.

The government drew attention to the fact that the first ever special adviser induction training session was held on 21 November 2002. Moreover, it added, 'special advisers have been invited to think about their development needs – individually and collectively', as well as to participate, on a pilot basis, in the Engaging with Government programme, designed to give new entrants to the Civil Service at senior level a broad understanding of the administration. However, the government was insistent that the appointment of aides would continue to be conducted on a basis of personal patronage and that posts would not be publicly advertised, since 'Ministers seek a combination of political and personal commitment, relevant expertise and personal trust and confidence.' The core principles underpinning the nature of the special adviser, therefore, were defended.

On 8 April 2003 Sir Nigel Wicks's Committee on Standards in Public Life published what was, in part, the most detailed official assessment of the special adviser to have been conducted to date. Wicks's central proposal was for a 'short Act to cover the Civil Service and special advisers'. It would enshrine the Whitehall values of impartiality and open recruitment, and provide for their thorough enforcement. The report, entitled *Defining the Boundaries within the Executive: Ministers, Special Advisers and the Permanent Civil Service*, noted on the basis of the evidence it had received that, in most cases, relations between civil servants, ministers and special advisers were harmonious and that the latter group were widely regarded, by insiders and outsiders, as having a valuable role to play in government.[5] However, it made a number of proposals in relation to aides with the aim of ensuring the maintenance of high standards.

First, Wicks recommended that 'Special advisers should be defined as a category of government servant distinct from the Civil Service.' This proposal was prompted by concerns that their status as personal appointments, not subject to impartiality and objectivity obligations and able, to some extent, to represent their ministers' views to the media in a partisan manner, was not compatible with categorisation as permanent officials. Nevertheless, they should, it was argued, continue to be employed as government servants, rather than being paid out of party funds. Terms similar to those contained in the Civil Service Code, Civil Service Management Code and Code of Conduct for Special Advisers should still apply to them.

Wicks – like this author – argued that special advisers could not necessarily be separated cleanly into distinct categories and therefore stated that there should be 'a single category of special adviser'. Following a view advanced by Richard Wilson, the report proposed that appropriate behaviour for civil servants should be defined negatively. Under such a system, political appointments would not be allowed to ask career officials 'to do anything improper or illegal', to undermine their impartiality, or to play a part in their 'appraisal, reward, discipline or promotion'. With the exception of staff in the Prime Minister's office exempted by the 1997 Order in Council, they would be prevented from authorising expenditure, participating in the line management of permanent civil servants, directing members of the GICS or possessing 'any other executive powers'. All of this should be defined in primary legislation. In terms of positive definition of roles, the Code of Conduct for Special Advisers would continue to list the sorts of work aides might perform. Upon making appointments, ministers would set out in a contract the functions to be carried out. Where this entailed any significant departure from the descriptions contained in the Code of Conduct, prior written prime ministerial approval and a public explanation would be required.

There were clear difficulties for permanent secretaries who were forced to make judgements regarding the conduct of temporary civil servants, since the latter were personal selections of secretaries of state. Wicks suggested, therefore, that the Ministerial Code should stipulate clearly that ministers were 'personally accountable to the Prime Minister and to Parliament for the management and discipline' of their aides. Investigation of alleged infringements of the Code of Conduct would be mandatory. Every year a report would be made to Parliament, providing, for example, the names, roles, cost (by department) and total number of special advisers. Following a parliamentary debate, an absolute cap on the latter figure should be introduced. There were also proposals to bring unpaid advisers within the fold of accountability and discipline. Wicks was concerned that the public might find it difficult, when reading reports in the media, to distinguish between off-the-record comments made by members of the GICS and those emanating from special advisers. The report therefore suggested that 'Wherever possible, GICS press officers should speak on the record as "the department's spokesman/spokeswoman"' – a stipulation presumably intended to isolate and thereby identify the briefing activities of aides. The relationship between special advisers and career officials, it went on, should be explained in the Guidance on the Work of the Government Information Service.

Wicks argued that, within a global cap on the number of aides, the distribution across the various departments and No. 10 was a matter for the government. There would, therefore, be no sublimit applied to prime ministerial appointments. As was to be the case for other ministers, the Prime Minister would be responsible for the special advisers employed at No. 10. The premier's senior aide would be entrusted with ensuring day-to-day compliance with the Code of Conduct for Special Advisers. Wicks noted that, although up to three of the premier's aides were exempted from the 'only ... advice' stipulation, there was no positive guide as to what form their activities should take. It was suggested that the special advisers in question should not be permitted to 'have any role in the appraisal, reward, discipline or promotion of permanent civil servants', but that they could 'authorise . . . spending . . . have a role in the line management of civil servants . . . [and] have charge of and direction over the work of GICS members'. Importantly, they should not be allowed to direct civil servants working outside No. 10. The existence of the two executive positions then held should be subject to parliamentary debate and affirmation. There was no need, it was argued, for the third one, which had not been taken up, to be preserved. The Prime Minister's principal private secretary would be entrusted with the new responsibility of raising with the Prime Minister any concerns regarding threats to the impartiality of career officials within Downing Street.

The press response to Wicks, predictably, not only emphasised the aspects of the report related to No. 10, but seemingly overlooked the fact that Powell shared Campbell's empowerment under the Order in Council. The *Independent* ran the headline 'Powers of Blair aides "should be reduced"', stating that 'Alastair Campbell should be stripped of his power to give orders to all civil servants, the Prime Minister was told.'[6] Similarly, the *Daily Telegraph* proclaimed 'Whitehall watchdog calls for curbs on Campbell.'[7] Peter Riddell, writing in *The Times*, stated that many of the charges against the Blair government were 'overblown', but suggested that, in order to protect itself, the administration should adopt the Wicks proposals.[8] It was now for the government to decide whether it would bring forward a Civil Service Act, to which it was officially committed on taking office in 1997, as advocated by Wicks.

In May 2003 Clare Short, nearly seven years after her 'people who live in the dark' comment, resigned as Secretary of State for International Development. In explaining her decision to the House she cited, in addition to policy disagreements over the war in Iraq, 'the style and organisation of our Government, which is undermining trust and straining party loyalty in a way that is completely unnecessary'. The primary shortcoming in the first term, she said, 'was spin: endless announcements, exaggerations and manipulation of the media that undermined people's respect for the Government and trust in what we said'. From 2001 the problem was 'the centralisation of power into the hands of the Prime Minister and an increasingly small number of advisers who make decisions in private without proper discussion'. Cabinet was no longer a viable entity; there was 'no real collective responsibility because there is no collective;

just diktats in favour of increasingly badly thought through policy initiatives that come from on high'. There were implications for parliamentary democracy since 'those who are wielding power are not accountable and not scrutinised. Thus we have the powers of a presidential-type system with the automatic majority of a parliamentary system.'[9]

Short's comments raised, once again, many of the criticisms described in Chapter 1. During the agitation which built up against them from 1997, special advisers were likened to rent boys, Al-Qaeda suicide pilots, Hitler Youth and even Adolf Hitler himself. By the early twenty-first century, the conspiracy theorist David Icke had named Jonathan Powell, Alastair Campbell and Anji Hunter as elements in a plot by reptilian aliens to enslave the human race.[10] Aside from such far-fetched claims, a litany of more credible charges emerged. That numbers had grown in relation to previous administrations was indisputable. Whether this was in itself a problem was harder to establish. Relative to other democracies, Britain had only a small number of political appointments. Furthermore, a number of official reports from the 1960s onwards had endorsed expansion. The costs were inevitably greater as a result; but, in the context of government expenditure, they could not seriously be portrayed as a major drain on resources.

Did the occupying army of partisan recruits threaten the neutrality of Whitehall? On the one hand, it could be argued that special advisers protected the impartiality of career officials by performing party political functions for ministers. However, there was evidence that departmental aides were in informal positions of authority over permanent civil servants. The government submission to Wicks was revealing. While it stated that, other than the two exceptions at No. 10, outsiders did not perform 'line management' roles, it also noted that 'special advisers work very closely on a day-to-day basis with civil servants, including conveying Ministers' views'. The distinction, though probably not technically correct, was a fine one. Performance of such a role could be seen as the assumption of informal management responsibilities. Moreover, if this function were not handled very carefully, there was a likelihood that resentment would be engendered among career civil servants on the receiving end of the conveyance of views. It was a matter of office politics. In this sense the neutrality of Whitehall was compromised. However, although it probably became more widespread and systematic thereafter, the tendency towards de facto executive authority of various sorts existed before 1997. It was, after all, not until 1991 that the 'only . . . advice' stipulation was included in an Order in Council; prior to that, provision to this effect did not exist in legal form.

Nevertheless, the particular quasi-management role of conduit for ministerial communications seemed to be more pronounced under Blair, and certain observers believed that a worrying qualitative change had taken place. Lord Armstrong noted in his memorandum to Wicks that

> *I have always seen considerable value in the institution of Special Advisers. A Special Adviser can be a useful source of advice to a Minister on the political aspects of policies and decisions which he is called upon to consider. His advice can then be read or heard by the Minister alongside the advice which he receives from other sources (including his departmental civil servants), so that he can weigh the various strands of advice and make up his mind what policy he wishes to follow or to recommend to his ministerial colleagues.*

However, Armstrong suspected that since 1997 some

> *Ministers . . . have tended to rely heavily on their Special Advisers, and have found it difficult to develop the sort of relationship with their civil servants that is needed if the British system of government is to work effectively. That has led to over-reliance on Special Advisers, and a tendency to look to Special Advisers to do things which they should not be asked to do, and had better be done by civil servants.*

There was a danger that, if special advisers were 'used as a channel for the communication of Ministerial instructions or requirements . . . civil servants may fear that their ability to give their own professional advice to the Minister is impaired'.[11]

As to the authority of aides at the centre, the 1997 Order in Council gave its beneficiaries the freedom to act with greater impunity, but its importance should not be overplayed. An exchange between Richard Wilson and Wicks effectively conveyed the ambiguous nature of the exercise of authority within Whitehall. Asked whether the two executive special advisers could issue instructions to career officials beyond No. 10 directly, rather than through the private office of the relevant department, the supposed traditional means of contact, Wilson said,

'I think communications still take place primarily between private offices, though I accept it may be different from what it was.' He then recalled, 'warming to my theme, that members of the policy unit had quite a lot of contacts in the 1980s with people in departments direct, without going through private offices.'

Wicks, who was Thatcher's principal private secretary from 1985 to 1988, probed further. 'Contacts, yes. But instructions?' Wilson replied,

> *I think instructions are actually not what happens . . . people discuss what should be done in the particular situation, and agree what should be done. If you think back to situations you have been in, I think there is a lot more done in a way that is more shaded that [sic] the word 'instruction' would imply. Instruction is a direct order, I think direct orders are relatively rare. I think much more often what happens is either someone says 'Look, the Prime Minister wants X to happen' or, 'I think the Prime Minister would think X is the right thing to do' or 'What are we going to do about this? What do you think?' You have a discussion about it and then both parties . . . go back to their Ministers and discuss that and the dialogue goes on. I think that is a much more common situation than someone banging the table, as the word 'instruction' implies, and giving an order'.[12]*

The possibility that the Northcote–Trevelyan settlement was under threat was also raised. Growth in patronage-based recruitment was by definition an erosion of an important aspect of the Victorian reforms. On the other hand, many who were appointed were extremely able. However, if government was receiving advice from a narrower, partisan perspective, then, arguably, bad decision-making would eventually result. It should be noted that, in many respects, the Victorian reforms were inspired by objectives that were soon to be obsolete: for example, the aim to preserve mid-nineteenth-century social structures and administer a *laissez-faire* state. Tension between special advisers and career officials was a characteristic which could be traced back to the outset of their cohabitation in 1964. The clash between Balogh and Burke Trend, for example, was in many ways a more serious difficulty than that involving Jo Moore at the DTLR; but it was not publicly aired. Complaints that aides were attaining excessive influence under Blair mirrored similar concerns of earlier periods, relating to, for example, Donoughue and Walters. Similarly, allegations that special advisers were not generally in possession of valuable skills dated back at least as far as 1974.

Accusations of moral unsoundness were prompted in part by the belief that aides were often the conscious initiators of malicious gossip targeted at individuals. Such activities, however distasteful, were and are a part of what politicians sometimes do, and have probably always done, in order to achieve personal advancement. Aides, given their attachments to individual ministers, were likely to become embroiled in such intrigue. Indeed, they made it easier, sometimes encouraged it, or possibly even engaged in it without being asked to. It could be argued that more special advisers inevitably meant more hostile briefing. Opposition parties felt that, in recruiting unprecedented numbers of partisan counsellors, the Labour government was unfairly exploiting control over public funds for political gain. Suspicions that links with outside business concerns might lead to corruption were understandable, but again such anxieties predated 1997. The extent of aides' genuine commitment to the Labour movement has been questioned. In many cases this scepticism was unfair. Moore, for example, had a long record of serving Labour. Campbell's partisanship verged on the obsessive. There were those who had been members of other parties: for example, Whelan was a former communist, and Blair's Policy Unit/Directorate had a contingent of former SDP members. However, in earlier periods, for example during Thatcher's premiership, aides including Hoskyns also came from 'impure' backgrounds.

In the Blair administrations presentation was valued highly. However, from the outset of the special adviser experiment there were aides whose main occupation was dealing with journalists. Others took an interest, if not a primary one, in the media. It seems unreasonable to blame special advisers for any supposed decline in the quality of political reporting. The advance leaking of announcements, it is fair to say, was a problem for career officials and raised legitimate concerns about the bypassing of Parliament. Moreover, the non-appearance of Powell before the Public Administration Committee was unsatisfactory from the perspective of accountability. On the other hand, the use of aides who enter and leave office with an elected administration could be seen as an enhancement of democracy; career officials, after all, never have to submit themselves to the popular vote. There is no doubt that Blair's own special advisers assisted a centralisation of government. He has been criticised for the tendency. However,

Major was condemned for the opposite reason. Special advisers and the characteristics often associated with them became a focus for censure of the Blair administration from across the political spectrum. In this sense, their usefulness was undermined, although not negated. It could be argued that they acted as lightning conductors, attracting the denigration that might otherwise have been targeted at ministers. Aides were undoubtedly involved in power struggles. Moreover, at times their mere presence inside the administration was enough to create suspicion.

In conclusion, many of the main characteristics associated with aides today existed from the outset. Rather than startling new functions emerging, most changes took place in the form of a combination of tendencies already established. It is arguable, however, that there was an increasing assumption of management functions, especially latterly. 'Unfortunate events', related to personality, clashes between ministers and the tension which resulted from the incorporation of outsiders into an established organisation, were a perennial phenomenon. There have been different emphases at different times. During 1964–70, to some extent, a revival of the wartime use of experts occurred. Under Heath, a full-time party staff was incorporated into Whitehall, although the Conservatives continued to pick up part of the tab. From 1974 to 1979, there was a large presence, with a full range of experts and political aides, some of whom were embroiled in infighting. The Thatcher years had a centralised, private-sector flavour, with individuals making a great impact. In Major's premiership, temporary civil servants were less remarkable, subject to more formal regulation and perhaps more intrigue-prone. Finally, the Blair period saw expansion in terms of significance and numbers, and the exercise of pronounced managerial and media roles, leading to high levels of publicity. If there was a change over time, it was in aides becoming more firmly established and accepted, and, to a limited extent, officially defined.

A study of the special adviser over the last four decades reveals a typical British tendency, namely for the gradual, informal emergence of an administrative fixture. Only late in the twentieth century were any attempts made at proper codification. The controversy regularly and increasingly generated by aides has been in part a product of the challenge they posed to the traditional constitutional model. To take a mid-twentieth-century view of British arrangements, provided by S. B. Chrimes in *English Constitutional History*, 'The essence of the

Constitution to-day is the temporary entrusting of great powers to a small Cabinet . . . who are politically responsible to the electorate . . . and who are served by a corps of permanent civil servants.' 'England,' Chrimes wrote, 'has happily avoided the "spoils system", and the personnel of the Civil Service does not change with every change of government.' Without permanency among officials, 'we might have to endure a Civil Service as amateurish and transient as many Ministers are, not to mention the evils and corruption inseparable from a political Civil Service.'[13]

Views such as Chrimes's, although eloquently expressed, neglected experiments that had already taken place and probably served to exaggerate the dangers that might be associated with the limited use of outsiders. Moreover, they now belong to the past. National malaise, social trends, ideological approaches and certain individual efforts, all leading to the emergence of political appointments, mean that Britain's constitution must be partially redefined. A significant component within the Civil Service is now temporary. Government cannot be fully explained without reference to special advisers. While their role and presence may alter under different administrations, for the foreseeable future their continued existence is assured.

Appendix

Special advisers: names and figures

Numbers of special advisers, 1974–1977

Date	No. of special advisers (of which part-time)	
2 May 1974	31	(9)
22 March 1976	28	(11)
21 February 1977	25	(6)

Total cost of special advisers, 1974–1976

Date	Approximate annual cost
January 1974 (Heath admin.)	£15,000
1974/5	£169,000
1975/6	£196,000

Special advisers in employment, 2 May 1974

Department	Names
Cabinet Office	Lord Crowther-Hunt
	Mr G. R. J. Richardson
No. 10 Downing Street	Dr B. Donoughue
	*Mrs C. Carmichael
	*Mr A. Graham
	*Mr R. Graham
	*Mr R. H. Kirwan
	*Mr D. F. J. Piachaud

cont'd

Department	Names
Department of Education and Science	Professor M. Preston [sic]
Department of Energy	Mr S. Bundred
Department of the Environment	Mr D. Lipsey
	Mr P. Barry
Foreign and Commonwealth Office	Mr T. McNally
Department of Health and Social Security	*Professor Abel-Smith
	Mr J. Straw
	Mr A. Lynes
	Mr Chapman
Home Office	Mr M. A. Oakeshott
Department of Industry	Mr F. Cripps
	Mrs F Morrell
	Mr K. J. Griffin
Northern Ireland Office	Mr R. Darlington
Ministry of Overseas Development	Miss M. Jackson
	Dr S. Holland
Department of Prices and Consumer Protection	Mr J. Lyttle
	*Dr J. Mitchell
Privy Council Office	Mr T. J. Pitt
	Miss V. Kidd
Department of Trade	*Mr M. Stewart
Her Majesty's Treasury	Mr A. Ham
Welsh Office	*M. G. Prys-Davies

* Working part-time.

Special advisers by age group, 1976

Age range	25–34	35–44	45–54	55+	Total
No.	13	8	5	2	28

Special advisers appointed during 1983

Department	Appointee	Full/ part-time	Previous/concurrent outside occupation	Date appointed
Treasury	R. Lord	Full	*Daily Telegraph* leader writer	27 June
Treasury	Mr A. Ridley	Full	Asst Director CRD	10 June
Treasury	Dr L. Rouse	Full	Head of Economic Dept CRD	27 June
Treasury	Mr M. Portillo	Full	Consultant to the Oil Industry	14 November
Transport	Mrs K. Ramsay	Full	Conservative Central Office, Research Department	1 September
DHSS	Mr N. True	Full	Research Officer	21 June
FCO	Mr J. Houston	Full	Political Adviser to the Vice-President, European Commission	19 September
Energy	Dr L. Rouse	Full	See above	1 January
Energy	Prof S. Edwards	Part	Prof. of Physics, Cambridge University	17 October
Trade and Industry	Mr M. Portillo	Full	See above	1 July
Trade and Industry	Mr J. Sterling	Part	Chairman, Town and City Properties Ltd	1 July
Trade and Industry	Mr M. Dobbs	Part	Saatchi & Saatchi Garland Crompton Ltd	28 October
Home Office	Mr R. D. R. Harris	Full	Research Assistant, CRD	20 June
Employment	Mr M. Dobbs	Part	Saatchi & Saatchi, Director	22 June
Northern Ireland	Mr E. Bickham	Full	Conservative Central Office, Research Department	26 September
Wales	Mr C. Butler	Part (later full)	Market Research Desk Officer, Conservative Central Office Wales area; part-time with British Consortium for Innovation while special adviser	17 October

cont'd

Department	Appointee	Full/ part-time	Previous/concurrent outside occupation	Date appointed
Education and Science	Mr S. Sexton	Full	Stood in 1983 general election. Conservative Central Office	16 June
Environment	Sir R. Cooke	Part	MP	10 January
Environment	Sir R. Cooke	Part	See above	13 June
Environment	Mr C. G. Mockler	Full	Conservative Central Office, Research Department	18 July
No. 10	Sir A. Parsons	Part	Retired Ambassador	1 January
No. 10	Hon. C. Monckton	Full	Researcher, Centre for Policy Studies	10 June
No. 10	Mr F. Mount	Full	Freelance columnist	10 June
No. 10	Sir A. Parsons	Part	See above	11 June
No. 10	Mr P. Shipley	Full	Not known	10 June
No. 10	Mr O. Letwin	Full	Conservative Central Office	1 August
No. 10	Mr J. Redwood	Full	Secondment from Rothschilds & Sons Ltd	1 October
No. 10	Mrs C Ryder	Part	Secretary	14 November
Chief Whip	Dame F. Yonge	Full	Private Secretary to Opposition Chief Whip	10 June
Chief Whip	Miss A. Ward	Full	Secretary	28 November

Note: Some of these were already in employment, re-appointed following the general election of this year, or transferred to different departments during the year.

Departments employing more than one special adviser, July 1988

Department	No. of special advisers
Cabinet Office/No. 10	9
Foreign Office	2
Treasury	3

cont'd

Department	No. of special advisers
Health and Social Security	2[a]
Trade and Industry	2
Home Office	2
Environment	2

[a] Department in process of being split.

Annual cost of special advisers, 1993/4–1995/6

Year	Cost
1993/4	£1,133,590
1994/5	£1,460,733
1995/6	£1,512,622

Special advisers to ministers, 18 April 1994

Name	Department
K. Adams	Environment
A. Allen	Trade and Industry
P. Barnes	Social Security
C. Blunt	Defence
T. Burke	Environment
J. Caine	Northern Ireland Office
D. Cameron	Home Office
Dr. E. Cotterell	Agriculture, Fisheries and Food
Dr. W. Eltis	Trade and Industry
M. Fraser	Foreign and Commonwealth Office
J. Gray	Environment
C. Grantham	Education
D. Green	Prime Minister's Office
Mrs S. Hogg	Prime Minister's Office
Ms S. Hole	Chief Whip's Office
A. Kemp	Trade and Industry
Mrs T. Keswick	Treasury
Mrs E. Laing	Transport
D. Loehnis	National Heritage
G. MacKay	Scottish Office
M. MacLay	Foreign and Commonwealth Office
R. Marsh	Health
Mrs S. McEwen	House of Lords
M. McManus	Employment

cont'd

Name	Department
P. Moman	Privy Council Office
Dr. J. Nicholson	Office of Public Service and Science
L. O'Connor	Environment
Sir I. Pearce	Transport
Lord Poole	Prime Minister's Office
Ms K. Ramsay	Prime Minister's Office
P. Rock	Home Office
D. Ruffley	Treasury
D. Rutley	Office of Public Service and Science
Lady Strathnaver	Trade and Industry
N. True	Prime Minister's Office
Miss A. Warburton	Prime Minister's Office
H. William	Welsh Office
A. Young	Scottish Office

Total salary cost of special advisers, 1996/7–2001/2

Year	Cost
1996/7	£1.8 million
1997/8	£2.6 million
1998/9	£3.6 million
2001/2	£5.1 million

No. 10 staff and responsibilities, 30 October 1997

Name	Responsibility
Jonathan Powell	Chief of Staff
Kate Garvey	Diary
Anji Hunter	Planning and visits
Fiona Millar (part-time)	Assistant to Mrs Blair
Roz Preston (part-time)	Assistant to Mrs Blair

No. 10 Policy Unit

Name	Responsibility
David Miliband	Director of Policy, Education
Derek Scott	Economy
James Purnell	Culture, Media and Sport and Office of Public Service
Robert Hill	Health and Local Government
Liz Lloyd	Agriculture, Environment and Home Affairs
Pat McFadden	Constitutional Reform
Geoffrey Norris	Trade and Industry, Transport and Regional Policy
Roger Liddle	Europe, Defence

cont'd

Name	Responsibility
Peter Hyman	Communications
Geoff Mulgan	Social Exclusion
No. 10 Press Office	
Alastair Campbell	Press Secretary
Tim Allan	No. 10 Press Office
Hilary Coffman	No. 10 Press Office

Departments employing more than two special advisers, July 2000

Department	No. of advisers
Prime Minister	27
Treasury	5 (3 Chancellor, 2 Chief Secretary) +5 Council of Economic Advisers
Deputy Prime Minister	4 (2 part-time)
Home Office	4 (1 part-time)
Trade and Industry	3 (1 part-time)

Paid and unpaid special advisers, 24 July 2000

Minister	Special Adviser
The Prime Minister	Jonathan Powell
	Alastair Campbell
	Kate Garvey
	Anji Hunter
	David Miliband
	Hilary Coffman
	Roger Liddle
	James Purnell
	Derek Scott
	Robert Hill
	Geoff Mulgan
	Geoffrey Norris
	Peter Hyman
	Liz Lloyd
	Phil Bassett
	David Bradshaw

cont'd

Minister	Special Adviser
	Andrew Adonis
	Ed Richards
	Bill Bush
	Phil Murphy
	Catherine Rimmer
	Bob Bartram
	Carey Oppenheim
	Carl Sobhan
	Chris McShane
	Fiona Millar
Chief Whip (Commons)	Ian McKenzie
	Sue Jackson
Chief Whip (Lords)	Margaret Ounsley
Minister of Agriculture, Fisheries and Food	Kieran Simpson
	Jack Thurston
Secretary of State for Defence	Alasdair McGowan
	Andrew Hood
Secretary of State for Education and Employment	Conor Ryan
	Leala Padmanabhan
	Tom Engel
	Nick Pearce
	Michael Barber (Standards and Effectiveness Adviser)
Deputy Prime Minister	Joe Irvin
	Paul Hackett
	Joan Hammell
	Adrian Long
	David Wilson
Secretary of State for Foreign and Commonwealth Affairs	David Clark
	Michael Williams
Secretary of State for Health	Simon Stevens
	Darren Murphy
Secretary of State for the Home Department	Ed Owen
	Justin Russell
Lord Chancellor	Garry Hart
Secretary of State for International Development	David Mepham
	Dee Sullivan

Minister	Special Adviser
Leader of the House of Lords and Minister for Women	Clare Cozens Jo Gibbons
Minister for the Cabinet Office	Nigel Warner Andrew Lappin Keith Hellawell (UK Anti-Drugs Co-ordinator) Michael Trace (Deputy)
President of the Council and Leader of the House of Commons	Sheila Watson Nicci Collins
Secretary of State for Scotland	Richard Olszewski Michael Elrick Professor Mike Donnelly
Secretary of State for Social Security	Andrew Maugham Elsbeth Johnson
Secretary of State for Trade and Industry	Dan Corry Jo Moore
Chancellor of the Exchequer	Ed Balls (Chief Economic Adviser) Ian Austin
Council of Economic Advisers	Chris Wales Paul Gregg Shriti Vadera Maeve Sherlock
Chief Secretary	Paul Andrew Ed Miliband
Secretary of State for Wales	Andrew Bold Adrian Mcmenaman

Pay bands for special advisers and numbers within each, July 2002

Payband	Salary range	No. of advisers
0	<£34,850	0
1	£34,851–£45,760	13
2	£45,101–£58,240	26
3	£57,401–£89,175	21
4	£76,876–£92,250	4

A note on historiography and sources

There is no comprehensive history of the special adviser. However, during certain periods, observers have written on the subject. In his chapter from Richard Rose's 1969 collection, *Policy Making in Britain*, called 'The Irregulars', Samuel Brittan provided an overview of the extensive use of outside economists made by Harold Wilson's first two administrations. Brittan emphasised the fact that, while it was presented as a means of bringing about a reversal in economic fortunes, none was forthcoming. The practical difficulties experienced by outsiders within Whitehall were also discussed.

Following his return to office in 1974, Wilson brought about the first considerable expansion in special advisers. Some journalistic and academic interest was prompted. In 1975 George Jones, a pioneering dissector of the Prime Minister's Office, wrote an article in the *Spectator*, 'Harold Wilson's Policy-Makers' dealing in part with the Downing Street Policy Unit, formed the previous year.[1] It seemingly inadvertently provoked an argument within the entourage of the Prime Minister: Marcia Williams felt that it neglected her and implied that Donoughue had influence on policy.[2] Jones has returned to the subject, more than once, since.[3] Two essays appeared in academic journals on the subject of special advisers during the 1974–9 Labour term of office. The first, by Rudolf Klein and Janet Lewis, entitled 'Advice and Dissent in British Government: The Case of the Special Advisers' was published in 1977. Klein and Lewis argued that special advisers signified a response to 'overload', that is the growth of demands upon the government machine to an unmanageable level (a concept espoused in the mid-1970s by Anthony King); the breakdown of the political consensus; and the declining reputation of the permanent Civil Service. They also emphasised the importance of personal link between aide and minister.[4] Joan E. Mitchell served as an aide to the Labour minister Shirley Williams. Her 1978 article,

'Special Advisers: A Personal View', stated that in 'practice there are two kinds of advisers . . . those who act as an extra political arm, and those having technical or departmental expertise'. It also suggested that a 'few more ground-rules and short induction sessions might be useful'.[5]

In 1987 David Willetts provided an insider's view of the operation of Margaret Thatcher's Policy Unit.[6] Two of John Major's most senior prime ministerial aides, Sarah Hogg and Jonathan Hill, co-authored a memoir of the period 1990–2. Biographies of two aides, *Nicholas Kaldor* by Anthony Thirlwall and *Alastair Campbell* by Peter Oborne, have been published. The former portrays the career of a great economist, while the latter is a contemporary view of a journalist turned special adviser, by one of his former kind. Thomas Balogh, Wilson's senior aide during his first premiership, has two essays devoted to him. Andrew Graham was a member of Balogh's team from 1966 and took over as Wilson's senior economic adviser in 1968, serving until 1969. His article, entitled 'Thomas Balogh (1905–1985)', portrays its subject as an intuitive, if flawed, genius, as well as emphasising the closeness of his relationship with Wilson. It argues that, during his time as a special adviser, Balogh reduced his own effectiveness through a tendency to try to achieve too much. June Morris, whose biography of Balogh will appear soon, follows a similar line to Graham in 'Thomas Balogh and the Fight for North Sea Revenue'.

General studies drawn on for all chapters include Peter Hennessy's *Whitehall*, the only full history of the Civil Service. Hennessy emphasises the importance of the declinist school which emerged in the late 1950s in influencing subsequent Civil Service reforms, including the use of special advisers. *The Powers behind the Prime Minister*, by Dennis Kavanagh and Anthony Seldon, analyses organisation and staff at No. 10, including special advisers. The argument the authors present is that, while the number of aides attached to prime ministers has grown, there has been no absolute increase in the power of the premier. Hennessy's *The Prime Minister*, and *The Chancellors*, written by the former Labour politician and academic Edmund Dell, have both been used as reference works. So, too, have biographies of prime ministers and other senior politicians.

Kevin Theakston's *Leadership in Whitehall* consists of a series of profiles of senior civil servants, covering a period from the nineteenth through to the late twentieth century. Its group-biographical approach is followed in parts of this book. Also by Theakston, *The Labour Party and Whitehall* offers a clear thesis regarding Labour's approach to the Civil Service. He identifies a Fabian/techno-cratic tradition within Labour, as well as a tendency to doubt whether the existing official machine was willing or able to implement socialism. Theakston casts doubt on the notion that Labour failures in office have resulted from subterfuge on the part of permanent civil servants. James Walter's *The Ministers' Minders*, a study of personal aides in Australian government, has helped provide a model for a study of their British counterparts.

Theoretical texts used include *Advising the Rulers*, a collection edited by William Plowden. This provides accounts of various international forms of counsel. Of particular use are its descriptions of the continental cabinet and the US 'spoils system'. Michael Foley's *The Rise of the British Presidency* argues that the cult of personal leadership prevalent in US politics has come to the fore in Britain in recent decades. Special advisers, who are attached to individual ministers rather than departments, particularly those at No. 10, could be regarded as symptomatic of the trend. Martin J. Smith's *The Core Executive in Britain* summarises a fairly recent development in political science, core executive theory. It is founded on a view of government as an arena in which multiple actors trade resources such as information and authority in order to achieve particular objectives. Special advisers could be viewed as participants in such a process.

Bernard Donoughue, the first head of the Policy Unit from 1974–9, has produced a chapter in a collection,[7] a memoir of the period and an autobiog-raphy. His successor, John Hoskyns, who was Senior Policy Adviser to Thatcher from 1979 to 1982, has also published an account of his time in government. Lord (David) Young, another aide in the Thatcher era, wrote a book which partly deals with his work as an unpaid special adviser. Hywel Williams, a counsellor at the Welsh Office from 1993 to 1995, describes his activities in *Guilty Men*. Numerous political memoirs refer to the use of temporary civil servants. Private papers and diaries provide a vivid image of the subject under examination. While not always supplying reliable technical detail, such sources offer insight into the impressions and perceptions of practitioners. A number of collections of personal papers have been studied, including those of three special advisers, Brian Abel-Smith, Nicholas Kaldor and Stuart Holland, as well as the journals of the Labour politicians Richard Crossman, Tony Benn and Barbara Castle and the diary kept by Alec Cairncross, Head of the Government Economic Service from 1964 to 1968.

Archives of organisations including the Fabian Society and the Centre for Policy Studies have been consulted. There are a large number of relevant and revealing Public Record Office files for the period up to 1972. They contain plentiful evidence of internal views of the appointment of special advisers, as well as evidence of the latters' own experiences. Participation by various aides in policy formation is apparent, too, and sensitive information relating to security issues is recorded.

More than forty interviews, both on and off the record, have been conducted. Over a hundred transcripts of oral evidence from parliamentary select committee inquiries and investigations conducted by the Committee on Standards in Public Life were studied. Finally, the internet has proved to be a valuable tool, both for viewing government and other websites containing electronic versions of documents, and for pursuing various leads.

Notes

Prologue

1 Foreign Affairs Select Committee, Oral Evidence, 25 June 2003.
2 Ibid.
3 *The Decision to Go to War in Iraq*, Foreign Affairs Select Committee.
4 Foreign Affairs Select Committee, Oral Evidence, 17 June 2003.
5 Foreign Affairs Select Committee, Oral Evidence, 25 June 2003.
6 Nicholas Watt, 'War claims row', *Guardian*, 28 June 2003.
7 Interview with Robert Jackson.
8 This section draws on a PhD thesis by the author, 'The Origins and History of the Special Adviser, with Particular Reference to the 1964–70 Wilson Administrations', Queen Mary, University of London, 2002.

Chapter 1

1 See e.g. N. Jones, *The Control Freaks*.
2 For further analysis, see Walter, *The Ministers' Minders*, p. 8.
3 Addison, *British Historians and the Debate over the 'Post-War Consensus'*, pp. 5–8.
4 Committee on Standards in Public Life, Public Hearings, 9 July 2002.
5 Tony Wright, 'Warfare in Whitehall', *Guardian*, 22 Feb. 2002.
6 Steve Richards, 'The people who are trying to turn Tony Blair into a macho man are making a wrong judgment and they endanger our victory', *New Statesman*, 9 Aug. 1996; Philip Webster, 'Short attacks Blair's "dark forces"', *The Times*, 8 Aug. 1996.
7 David Wighton, 'Troubleshooting team reveals a youthful face', *Financial Times*, 5 May 1997.
8 John Deans, 'Blair to rule with a rod of iron', *Daily Mail*, 6 May 1997.
9 Kamal Ahmed, 'The in-crowd', *Guardian*, 21 May 1997.

10 See e.g. Patrick Hennessy and Alex Renton, 'New Labour, new old boy network', *Evening Standard*, 4 June 1997.
11 See Ferdinand Mount, 'Whatever became of the policies?', *Sunday Times*, 12 July 1998.
12 N. Jones, *The Control Freaks*, p. 190.
13 Antony Barnett and Gregory Palast, 'New Labour insiders offer secrets for cash', *Observer*, 5 July 1998.
14 Anthony Bevins, 'Woman goes to war on Lord Chancellor's "old boys' network"', *Independent*, 7 Feb. 1998.
15 Jean Eaglesham, 'Ruling "would end headhunting"', *Financial Times*, 29 Nov. 2000.
16 N. Jones, *Sultans of Spin*; N. Jones, *The Control Freaks*.
17 Oborne, *Alastair Campbell*.
18 Naughtie, *The Rivals*, p. 234.
19 Allen, *The Last Prime Minister*, p. 29.
20 Major, *The Autobiography*, pp. 743–8.
21 Public Administration Committee, Minutes of Evidence, 24 Jan. 2001.
22 *Time for Common Sense* (Conservative Party, London, 2001).
23 Ken Follett, 'Blair's blackest art', *Observer*, 2 July 2000.
24 *Reinforcing Standards: Review of the First Report of the Committee on Standards in Public Life*.
25 *The Government's Response to the Sixth Report from the Committee on Standards in Public Life*.
26 *The Government Information and Communication Service*, Public Administration Committee.
27 *Special Advisers: Boon or Bane?*, Public Administration Committee.
28 'Daily Star says', *Daily Star*, 13 Oct. 2001.
29 'If Mr Byers will not sack his spin doctor, he is unfit to remain a minister', *Independent*, 13 Oct. 2001.
30 'Tell Jo to go', *Mirror*, 13 Oct. 2001.
31 Martin Samuel, 'This twisted spin is just as hideous as terrorism', *Express*, 12 Oct. 2001.
32 Simon Walters and Jonathan Oliver, 'Shamed spin doctor drove colleagues out of their jobs', *Mail on Sunday*, 14 Oct. 2001.
33 Graeme Wilson, 'Archbishop joins attack on Byers in storm over his spin doctor', *Daily Mail*, 13 Oct. 2001.

34 Lorraine Kelly, 'Go Jo', *Sun*, 13 Oct. 2001.

35 *"These Unfortunate Events": Lessons of Recent Events at the Former DTLR*, Public Administration Committee.

36 T. Wright, 'Warfare in Whitehall'.

37 Peter Oborne, 'Uncivil to the servants', *Scotsman*, 26 Feb. 2002.

38 Peter Oborne, 'You've reached the top, now stop this rot', *Evening Standard*, 23 April 2002.

39 Hugo Young, 'The Blairites have wrecked the best of the civil service', *Guardian*, 28 Feb. 2002.

40 Iain Duncan Smith, 'This is how I will clean up Number Ten', *Sunday Telegraph*, 3 March 2002.

41 *Hansard, House of Lords Debates*, 1 May 2002, cols 703, 704, 714–15.

42 http://news.bbc.co.uk/1/hi/uk_politics/2030737.stm.

43 Joe Haines, 'Blair, the Pontius Pilate of politics', *Mail on Sunday*, 9 June 2002.

44 Marie Woolf, 'Why Tony Blair is the worst Labour Prime Minister I've known', *Independent*, 10 June 2002.

45 'In a spin', *The Economist*, 8 June 2002.

46 David Clark, 'In defence of special advisers', *Guardian*, 1 March 2002.

47 T. Wright, 'Warfare in Whitehall'.

48 'Portrait of a Profession Revisited', speech by Sir Richard Wilson to the Centre for Management and Policy Studies, 26 March 2002.

49 Liaison Committee, Minutes of Evidence, 17 July 2002.

50 Civil Service Order in Council 1995.

51 Civil Service (Amendment) Order in Council 1997.

52 *The Ministerial Code: A Code of Conduct and Guidance on Procedures for Ministers* (Cabinet Office, London, 2001).

53 *Model Contract for Special Advisers* (Cabinet Office, London, 2001).

54 *Guidance on the Work of the Government Information Service* (Cabinet Office, London, 1997).

55 'Code of Conduct for Special Advisers', July 2001, attached to the 2001 *Model Contract for Special Advisers*.

56 Committee on Standards in Public Life, Public Hearings, 27 June 2002.

Chapter 2

1 Hennessy, *Whitehall*, pp. 20–1.

2 Elton, *England under the Tudors* p. 76.

3 Roseveare, *The Treasury*, pp. 13–14.

4 Bridges, *Portrait of a Profession*, p. 6.

5 Parris, *Constitutional Bureaucracy*, pp. 42–4.

6 Peter Barberis, *The Elite of the Elite*, p. 5.

7 Hennessy, *Whitehall*, p. 27.

8 Chapman and Greenaway, *The Dynamics of Administrative Reform*, p. 23.

9 Theakston, *Leadership in Whitehall*, pp. 20–1.

10 Roseveare, *The Treasury*, pp. 136–7.

11 Theakston, *Leadership in Whitehall*, pp. 23–4.

12 Reproduced in *The Civil Service*, vol. 1: *Report of the Committee 1966–68*, appendix B.

13 Donajgrodzki, 'New Roles for Old', p. 83.

14 M. Wright, *Treasury Control of the Civil Service*, p. xv.

15 Fry, *Statesmen in Disguise*, p. 36.

16 Chapman and Greenaway, *The Dynamics of Administrative Reform*, pp. 38–41.

17 See e.g. Annan, *Leslie Stephen*, p. 3.

18 Roseveare, *The Treasury*, pp. 143–4.

19 Balogh, 'The Apotheosis of the Dilettante', p. 83.

20 Hennessy, *Whitehall*, p. 51.

21 See e.g. Balogh, 'The Apotheosis of the Dilettante', pp. 83–5, 109.

22 Chapman and Greenaway, *The Dynamics of Administrative Reform*, pp. 42–4.

23 Ibid., pp. 42–4, 45; Hennessy, *Whitehall*, p. 371.

24 Chapman and Greenaway, *The Dynamics of Administrative Reform*, pp. 48–9.

25 M. Wright, *Treasury Control of the Civil Service*, pp. 329–40.

26 Fry, *Statesmen in Disguise*, pp. 33–6.

27 Roseveare, *The Treasury*, p. 214.

28 Bridges, *Portrait of a Profession*, p. 13.

29 S. Webb, *Twentieth Century Politics: A Policy of National Efficiency*, p. 7.

30 Scally, *The Origins of the Lloyd George Coalition*, pp. 3–28.

31 Searle, *Country before Party: Coalition and the Idea of 'National Government' in Modern Britain, 1885–1987*, p. 53.

32 See e.g. Earl of Rosebery, 'Foreword' to Alfred Stead, *Great Japan: a Study of National Efficiency*.

33 Co-efficients Collection, 'Subjects of Discussion, 1902'.

34 Hennessy, *Whitehall*, pp. 57–8, 55.

35 Peter Rowland, *Lloyd George* (Barrie and Jenkins, London, 1975), p. 377.

36 Balogh, 'The Apotheosis of the Dilettante', p. 87.

37 Hennessy, *Whitehall*, pp. 57–8.

38 Skidelsky, *John Maynard Keynes*, vol. 1, pp. 293, 297–9.

39 Hennessy, *Whitehall*, pp. 61–2.

40 Turner, *Lloyd George's Secretariat*, pp. 1–26; F. Lloyd George, *The Years that are Past*, pp. 100–1.

41 Kavanagh and Seldon, *The Powers behind the Prime Minister*, p. 46.

42 Turner, *Lloyd George's Secretariat*, pp. 191–2.

43 Theakston, *Leadership in Whitehall*, pp. 57–8; Hennessy, *Whitehall*, pp. 70–1.

44 Chapman and Greenaway, *The Dynamics of Administrative Reform*, p. 106.

45 Theakston, *Leadership in Whitehall*, pp. 51–4.

46 Hennessy, *Whitehall*, p. 75.

47 Theakston, *Leadership in Whitehall*, p. 50.

48 Balogh, 'The Apotheosis of the Dilettante', p. 86.

49 Fry, *Statesmen in Disguise*, pp. 60–1.

50 Kavanagh and Seldon, *The Powers behind the Prime Minister*, p. 49.

51 Ramsden, *The Age of Balfour and Baldwin, 1902–1940*, p. 291.

52 Howson and Winch, *The Economic Advisory Council, 1930–1939*, pp. 17–29.

53 Skidelsky, *Politicians and the Slump*, pp. 134–6.

54 Attlee, *As It Happened*, p. 84.

55 Milward, *War, Economy and Society, 1939–1945*, p. 102.

56 Hennessy, *Whitehall*, pp. 88–104. For an example of how one economist, Evan Durbin, found his way into the Ministry of Supply, see Durbin Collection, 3/11, 'Correspondence about Durbin's wartime employment'.

57 Barberis, *The Elite of the Elite*, p. 13.

58 Chester (ed.), *Lessons of the British War Economy*, p. 9.

59 Cairncross and Watts, *The Economic Section 1939–1961*, p. 32.

60 Wilson, *Memoirs*, pp. 57–8.

61 Cairncross and Watts, *The Economic Section*, p. 55.

62 MacDougall, *Don and Mandarin*, pp. 22–3.

63 Ibid., pp. 29–30.

64 MacDougall, 'The Prime Minister's Statistical Section', p. 68.

65 Harrod, *The Prof*, pp. 186–7.

66 Churchill, *The Second World War*, vol. 1, p. 369.

67 Harrod, *The Prof*, p. 188.

68 Addison, *The Road to 1945*, pp. 170–1.

69 Roseveare, *The Treasury*, pp. 274–6.

70 Harrod, *The Life of John Maynard Keynes*, pp. 501–2.

71 Ibid.; Stone, 'The Use and Development of National Income and Expenditure Estimates', pp. 83–5.

72 See e.g. Harrod, *The Life of John Maynard Keynes*, pp. 506–14.

73 *Keynes, the Treasury and British Economic Policy*, p. 53.

74 PRO T 230/283, 1943–53, Keynes to Robbins, 1 Feb. 1943.

75 Addison, *The Road to 1945*, pp. 118–9, 188.

76 Cairncross and Watts, *The Economic Section*, p. 65; MacDougall, *Don and Mandarin*, pp. 33–4.

77 F. Lloyd George, *The Years that are Past*, pp. 228–9.

78 Harris, *William Beveridge: A Biography*, pp. 362–6.

79 Harrod, *The Life of John Maynard Keynes*, p. 489.

80 Wilson, *Memoirs*, p. 65.

81 Hennessy, *Whitehall*, p. 103.

82 *Social Insurance and Allied Services: Report*, Cmnd 6404 (HMSO, London, 1942).

83 Wilson, *Memoirs*, p. 64.

84 Addison, *The Road to 1945*, pp. 211–28, 242–3.

85 McLaine, *Ministry of Morale*, pp. 12–13, 13–14.

86 Hennessy, *Whitehall*, p. 97.

87 Crick, introduction to George Orwell, *1984* p. 22.

88 Crick, *George Orwell: A Life*, p. 455.

89 Evidence of this is contained in Durbin Collection, 3/12, 'Appointment Mr Durbin: personal doper [*sic*]: remnants from war files'.

90 Cairncross and Watts, *The Economic Section*, p. 80.

91 Chester, 'The Central Machinery for Economic Policy', pp. 25–6.

92 See e.g. MacDougall, *Don and Mandarin*, p. 21.

93 Cairncross and Watts, *The Economic Section*, p. 79.

94 Ibid., p. 42.

95 PRO CAB 87/72, 'The role of the economist in the machinery of government', 'Report by the committee', 15 Nov. 1943.

96 Brittan, *The Treasury under the Tories, 1951–1964*, p. 70.

97 For evidence of this, see Edwin Plowden, *An Industrialist in the Treasury, The Post-War Years* (Andre Deutsch, London, 1989), p. 8.

98 MacDougall, *Don and Mandarin*, p. 40.

99 PRO CAB 87/72, 'The Roll [*sic*] of the economist in the future machinery of government', Notes by Lord Keynes, 9 April 1943.

100 Cairncross, *Years of Recovery*, p. 50.

101 Dalton, *The Fateful Years*, p. 479.

102 Cairncross, *Years of Recovery*, p. 55.

103 Ibid., p. 53.

104 Ibid., p. 44.

105 Addison, *The Road to 1945*, p. 263.

106 Addison, 'The Road from 1945', in Hennessy and Seldon (eds), *Ruling Performance*, p. 7.

107 Morgan, *Labour in Power*, p. 88.

108 Ibid., pp. 48–9.

109 For Jay's description of his time at No. 10, see Douglas Jay, *Change and Fortune*, pp. 128–56.

110 Dalton, *The Fateful Years*, p. 419.

111 Jay, *Change and Fortune*, pp. 128–9.

112 Cairncross, *Years of Recovery*, p. 52.

113 Plowden, *An Industrialist in the Treasury*, pp. 7–10, 19–22.

114 Theakston, *The Labour Party and Whitehall*, p. 99.

115 Ibid., p. 85.

116 For Laski's critique of the Civil Service, see Laski, *Parliamentary Government in England*, pp. 309–59.

117 Balogh, 'The Apotheosis of the Dilettante', pp. 117–18.

118 Hennessy, *Whitehall*, p. 137.

119 Theakston, *The Labour Party and Whitehall*, p. 26–7.

120 Miliband, *Parliamentary Socialism*, pp. 275–6.

121 Theakston, *The Labour Party and Whitehall*, pp. 3–4.

122 Barberis, *The Elite of the Elite*, p. 14.

123 Hennessy, *Whitehall*, p. 138.

124 Balogh, 'The Apotheosis of the Dilettante', p. 121.

125 Interview with Sir Derek Mitchell.

126 Hennessy, *Whitehall*, p. 15.

127 'Portrait of a Profession Revisited', speech by Sir Richard Wilson to the Centre for Management and Policy Studies, 26 March 2002.

128 Bridges, *Treasury Control*, p. 6.

129 Bridges, *Portrait of a Profession*, p. 22–3.

130 Bridges, *Treasury Control*.

131 Bridges, *The Treasury*, pp. 95, 107.

132 Bridges, *Portrait of a Profession*, pp. 15, 17, 13.

133 *The Reform of the Higher Civil Service* (Fabian Society, London, 1947), p. 5.

134 Peter Hennessy, *Whitehall*, pp. 170–1.

135 Morgan, *The People's Peace, British History since 1945*, p. 145.

136 *The Administrators*, p. 2.

137 Hennessy, *Whitehall*, p. 171.

138 Morgan, *The People's Peace*, p. 145.

139 See e.g. Chapman, *British Government Observed*, p. 7.

140 See e.g. Thomas, 'The Establishment and Society', p. 15.

141 Hennessy, *The Great and the Good, An Inquiry into the British Establishment*, p. 4.

142 Thomas, 'The Establishment and Society', pp. 14–15.

143 Sampson, *The New Europeans*, p. 347.

144 Hennessy, *The Great and the Good*, p. 6.

145 Thomas (ed.), *The Establishment*.

146 Barberis, *The Elite of the Elite*, fig. 6.2, p. 103.

147 Interview with Robert Neild.

148 Balogh, 'The Apotheosis of the Dilettante', pp. 110–12.

149 Sampson, *The New Europeans*, p. 332.

150 *The Administrators*, p. 23.

151 Brittan, *The Treasury under the Tories*, p. 309.

152 *The Administrators*, p. 42.

153 Ibid., p. 40; *Whitehall and Beyond* (BBC, London, 1964), p. 19. For a description of presidential appointments in the US, see Stephen Wayne, 'The United States', in Plowden (ed.), *Advising the Rulers*, pp. 71–91.

154 Hennessy, *Whitehall*, p. 175; interview with Sir Samuel Brittan.

155 Fabian Society Collection, K 65/1, 'Civil Service', 1963; 'Civil Service Group, notices, lists of members, minutes', Minutes of First Meeting, 31 July 1962.

156 James, *British Cabinet Government*, p. 242.

157 Pierre Gaborit and Jean-Pierre Mounier, 'France', in Plowden (ed.), *Advising the Rulers*, p. 108.

158 Balogh, 'The Apotheosis of the Dilettante', p. 124.

159 Brittan, *The Treasury under the Tories*, p. 309.

160 Balogh, 'The Apotheosis of the Dilettante', p. 126.

161 Balogh, *Planning for Progress*, p. 7 and fn.

162 Fabian Society Collection, K 66/1, 'Civil Service', 1963; 'Civil Service Group, draft sections of memoranda', 'Advising the Ministers', Balogh, undated, probably from 1963.

163 Tiratsoo and Tomlinson, *The Conservatives and Industrial Efficiency*, pp. 31–3.

164 Balogh, *Planning for Progress*, p. 3.

165 Tiratsoo and Tomlinson, *The Conservatives and Industrial Efficiency*, p. 20.

166 See Callaghan, 'The Left and the "Unfinished Revolution"', esp. pp. 77–8.

167 Zaleski, *Stalinist Planning for Economic Growth*, pp. 43–6.

168 Balogh, 'The Apotheosis of the Dilettante', p. 126.

169 Ibid., p. 111.

170 Harrod, *The Prof*, p. 258.

171 MacDougall, *Don and Mandarin*, pp. 82–3.

172 Macmillan, *Riding the Storm*, pp. 192–3.

173 Interview with Sir Derek Mitchell.

174 PRO PREM 11/3742, Macmillan to Selwyn Lloyd, Chancellor of the Exchequer, 9 Dec. 1962.

175 MacDougall, *Don and Mandarin*, p. 137.

176 Roseveare, *The Treasury*, p. 331.

177 MacDougall, *Don and Mandarin*, p. 136.

178 *Whitehall and Beyond*, p. 14.

179 Theakston, *The Labour Party and Whitehall*, p. 7.

180 Webb and Webb, *A Constitution for the Socialist Commonwealth of Great Britain*, pp. 175–6.

181 Laski, *A Grammar of Politics*, p. 405.

182 Fabian Society Collection, J 38/2, 'New Fabian Research Bureau', 'Memoranda on Parliament, the Government and electoral reform 1932–35', 'Reorganisation of government departments and ministerial functions', Ernest Bevin and Colin G. Clark, 21 Jan. 1932.

183 Ibid., J 38/3, 'Civil Service', 'Memorandum on the Civil Service', Kingsley Smellie, 5 Nov. 1932.

184 Laski, *The Limitations of the Expert*, p. 4.

185 See e.g. Pimlott, *Harold Wilson*, p. 347.

186 Laski, *A Grammar of Politics*, p. 405.

187 Wells, *The Shape of Things to Come*, p. 257.

188 Reproduced in *Purpose in Politics*, p. 27.

189 *Whitehall and Beyond*, p. 14.

190 Hennessy, *The Prime Minister*, p. 287.

191 *Whitehall and Beyond*, p. 20.

192 Crossman, 'Scientists in Whitehall', in *Planning for Freedom*, pp. 144–5.

193 Thirlwall (ed.), *Keynes as a Policy Adviser*, p. 175.

194 *Whitehall and Beyond*, p. 19.

195 Cairncross, *The Wilson Years*, p. 7, diary entry for 19 Oct. 1964 and fn.

196 Interview with Lord Shore.

197 Thirlwall (ed.), *Keynes as a Policy Adviser*, p. 175.

198 Interview with Robert Neild.

199 Theakston, *The Labour Party and Whitehall*, pp. 45–7.

200 Lansbury, *My England*, pp. 145, 147.

201 Fabian Society Collection, J 62/4, 'International and Commonwealth Bureau', 'Buscot Park Conference on "The British Government's Public Relations Information Services"', 13–15 Feb. 1948.

202 Parris, *Constitutional Bureaucracy*, pp. 59, 67–8.

203 Interview with Lord Shore.

204 Theakston, *The Labour Party and Whitehall*, p. 115.

205 Balogh, *Planning for Progress*, pp. 47–8.

206 Benn, *Out of the Wilderness*, p. 25, diary entry for 25 May 1963.

207 Interview with Sir Samuel Brittan.

208 Interview with Lord Shore.

209 Brown, *In My Way*, pp. 87–8, 91.

210 See Kaldor Papers, NK 11/1, '"Labour Party working party on taxation": Minutes, reports and memoranda', 1959–67; NK 11/4, '"Labour Party Finance and Economic Policy Sub-Committee": correspondence, minutes and policy documents', 1959–82.

211 *Let's Go with Labour for the New Britain* (Labour Party, London, 1964). For Kaldor's pre-election activities, see e.g. Jay, *Change and Fortune*, p. 313.

212 Interview with Lord Shore.

213 Benn, *Out of the Wilderness*, p. 13, diary entry for 2 May 1963; p. 25, diary entry for 25 May 1963; p. 33, diary entry for 19 June 1963.

214 Ibid., pp. 65–6, diary entry for 30 Sept. 1963.

215 *Whitehall and Beyond*, pp. 17–8.

216 *The Administrators*, p. 40.

217 Samuel Brittan Collection, p. 6, diary entry for 9 Nov. 1964.

218 *Whitehall and Beyond*, p. 19.

219 Cairncross, *The Wilson Years*, p. 12, diary entry for 25 Oct. 1964.

220 Crossman, *The Diaries of a Cabinet Minister*, vol. 1, p. 246, diary entry for 13 June 1965; Ziegler, *Wilson*, p. 181.

221 George and Bewlay, *Advice – and Dissent*, pp. 8, 6–7.

222 *Whitehall and Beyond*, p. 63, p. 70.

Chapter 3

1 See *Federal Reclamation by Irrigation. Message from the President of the United States Transmitting a Report Submitted to the Secretary of the Interior by the Committee of Special Advisers on Reclamation* (Washington: Department of the Interior, 1924).

2 See e.g. *Letter to the President on Foreign Trade from George N. Peek, Special Adviser to the President on Foreign Trade* (Washington: US Government Printing Office, 1934).

3 See e.g. discussion within the Colonial Office of the special advisers who were to accompany delegates attending a Kenya Constitutional Conference at Lancaster House in 1960: PRO CO 822/2355, 'Special advisers', 1960.

4 For details of this appointment, see PRO T 199/706, 'Appointment of Special Adviser on Middle East Oil Supplies (Admiral Sir Matthew Slattery)', 1957–60.

5 Interview with Sir Derek Mitchell.

6 PRO T 199/1164, 'Mr Kaldor', 23 Oct. 1964.

7 Cairncross, *The Wilson Years*, p. 7, diary entry for 19 Oct. 1964.

8 Interview with Robert Neild; Callaghan, *Time and Chance*, p. 153.

9 Cairncross, *The Wilson Years*, p. 2.

10 Thirlwall (ed.), *Keynes as a Policy Adviser*, p. 175.

11 Samuel Brittan Collection, p. 6, diary entry for 9 Nov. 1964.

12 PRO T 199/874, 'Organisation and Staffing of the Economic Section', 1963–5, William Armstrong to Callaghan, 23 Oct. 1964.

13 Interview with Robert Neild; Cairncross, *The Wilson Years*, p. 2.

14 T 199/999, 'Management Committee for the *Economist* and Statistician Classes. Circulated Papers and Minutes of Meetings 1966'.

15 PRO T 199/875, 'Government Economic Service', Cairncross to Sir Philip Allen, Second Secretary, Treasury, 8 Jan. 1965.

16 PRO CAB 160/1, Heaton to Elsie Abbot, Establishment Officer, Third Secretary, Treasury, 23 Oct. 1964.

17 *Hansard, House of Commons Debates*, 10 Nov. 1964, col. 812.

18 PRO CAB 160/1, David Heaton, Principal Establishment Officer, Cabinet Office, to Sir Burke Trend, Secretary of the Cabinet, 19 Oct. 1965.

19 Ibid.

20 PRO T 199/1063, Andrew Collier, Assistant Secretary, Treasury, to Heaton, 29 Oct. 1964.

21 PRO CAB 160/1, Trend to The Master, Balliol College and the Vice Chancellor, Oxford University, 27 Oct. 1964.

22 PRO CAB 160/1, 'Action Sheet – On Joining', 17 Oct. 1964.

23 Ibid., Heaton to Trend, 19 Oct. 1965.

24 Ibid.

25 Ibid.

26 PRO CAB 160/1, Balogh to Heaton, 25 April 1966.

27 PRO T 199/1164, Abbot to Armstrong, 24 June 1966.

28 PRO T 199/1063, Balogh to Louis Petch, Treasury Second Secretary, 13 Feb. 1967.

29 PRO CAB 160/2, Balogh to Heaton, 18 July 1966.

30 Ibid., Balogh to Heaton, 28 Sept. 1966.

31 *Imperial Calendar 1965*, p. 23.

32 PRO T 199/1164, 'Note for the Record', Abbot, 23 Oct. 1964.

33 Ibid., 'Professor Kaldor', Abbot to Collier, 22 June 1966. In fact, Neild did reach this level.

34 PRO CAB 160/1, Heaton to Balogh, 9 Nov. 1964.

35 Ibid., Balogh to Heaton, 21 March 1966.

36 Interview with Lord Croham.

37 PRO T 199/891, Ken Couzens, Chairman, First Division Association, Treasury Branch, to Collier, 18 Nov. 1964; Collier to Abbot, 2 March 1965.

38 CAB 160/1, Heaton to Trend, 19 Oct. 1964.

39 Interview with Lord Croham.

40 PRO PREM 13/518, Mitchell to Wilson, 17 June 1965.

41 See Kaldor Papers, NK 10/5, 'Treasury Political Papers', 1966–8.

42 PRO CAB 160/1, Note, 3 March 1966.

43 PRO T 199/1063, Collier to Abbot, 4 April 1966; Collier to Petch, 14 Feb. 1967; Collier to Abbot, 4 April 1966.

44 PRO PREM 13/15, 'Note', 4 Nov. 1964.

45 PRO T 199/1164, 'Note for the Record', Abbot, 23 Oct. 1964.

46 See PRO PREM 13/168, Balogh to Trend, 14 April 1965; Trend to Mitchell, 3 May 1965.

47 *Hansard, House of Commons Debates*, 10 Nov. 1964, cols 811–2.

48 PRO PREM 13/15, 'Nationality Rules: Dr. Balogh and Mr. Kaldor', 3 Nov. 1964.

49 PRO CAB 160/1, 'Action Sheet – On Joining', 17 Oct. 1964; Heaton to Trend, 3 Nov. 1964.

50 Private information.

51 PRO PREM 13/15, 'Nationality Rules: Dr. Balogh and Mr. Kaldor', 3 Nov.1964.

52 PRO CAB 160/1, Heaton to Trend, 19 Oct. 1964.

53 Ibid., Heaton to Balogh, 9 Nov. 1964.

54 PRO CAB 160/2, Heaton to Balogh, 14 April 1967.

55 PRO CAB 160/1, Trend to Mitchell, 18 March 1966.

56 Interview with Sir Derek Mitchell.

57 PRO CAB 160/1, Balogh to Theobald, 8 March 1966.

58 Interview with Sir Christopher Foster.

59 Cairncross, *The Wilson Years*, p. 142, diary entry for 19 June 1966.

60 Interview with Robert Neild.

61 PRO T 199/1164, 'Note for the Record', Abbot, 23 Oct. 1964; 'Note for the Record', Armstrong, 4 Nov. 1964.

62 Thirlwall, *Nicholas Kaldor*, pp. 231–2.

63 PRO CAB 160/1 Heaton to Abbot, 23 Oct. 1964.

64 Ibid., Note by William McIndoe, Private Secretary, Cabinet Office, 23 Oct. 1964.

65 Interview with Lord Shore.

66 PRO PREM 13/3094, Balogh to Wilson, 2 March 1967.

67 PRO CAB 160/1, Note made by McIndoe, 23 Oct. 1964.

68 See e.g. M. Williams, *Inside Number 10*, pp. 357–8.

69 Interview with Sir Derek Mitchell.

70 PRO CAB 21/5248, Armstrong to Trend, 6 Nov. 1964.

71 PRO PREM 13/1955, Balogh to Wilson, 1 Feb. 1966; 'Treasury Committees', Mitchell to Wilson, 2 Feb. 1966.

72 Cairncross, *The Wilson Years*, p. 201, diary entry for 10 March 1967.

73 PRO CAB 147/75, Balogh to Sir Richard Clarke, Second Secretary, Treasury, 21 Oct. 1965; Armstrong to Balogh, 19 May 1966; Balogh to Armstrong, 31 March 1966; Stewart to Balogh, 6 March 1967.

74 PRO PREM 13/1955, 'Note for the Record', 7 March 1967.

75 PRO PREM 13/839, 'Implementation of the Radcliffe Report', April 1966, Balogh to Wilson, 25 April 1966.

76 MacDougall, *Don and Mandarin*, p. 151.

77 Cairncross, *The Wilson Years*, p. 46, diary entry for 5 April 1965; p. 54, diary entry for 22 May 1965; p. 80, diary entry for 14 Sept. 1965.

78 See e.g. 'Callaghan calls in tax expert', *Daily Express*, 30 Oct. 1964.

79 Cairncross, *The Wilson Years*, p. 23, diary entry for 10 Dec. 1964.

80 Details of this press campaign are contained in PRO PREM 13/15.

81 Graham, 'Thomas Balogh (1905–1985)', pp. 194, 197.

82 Interview with Wilfred Beckerman.

83 'Mr Wilson's S.C.R.', *Financial Times*, 30 Oct. 1964.

84 Interview with Wilfred Beckerman.

85 Keynes was certainly referring to Balogh here and probably Kaldor as well. See Robert Skidelsky, *John Maynard Keynes*, vol. 3, p. 445.

86 *The Diary of Hugh Gaitskell*, p. 432, diary entry for 1 Feb. 1956.

87 PRO PREM 11/4190, 'Sterling', Harold Macmillan, Prime Minister, to Reginald Maudling, Chancellor of the Exchequer, 13 March 1963; Maudling to Macmillan, 14 March 1963.

88 *Hansard, House of Commons Debates*, 10 Nov. 1964, col. 812.

89 PRO CAB 160/1, Heaton to McIndoe, 13 Nov. 1964.

90 *The Civil Service*, vol. 1: *Report of the Committee 1966–68*.

91 Hennessy, *Whitehall*, p. 204.

92 Theakston, *The Labour Party and Whitehall*, p. 132.

93 Ibid., pp. 64–5.

94 Crossman, *The Diaries of a Cabinet Minister*, vol. 1, p. 616, diary entry for 11 Aug. 1966.

95 PRO T 199/1164, 'Note for the Record', Abbot, 23 Oct. 1964.

96 *The Robert Hall Diaries*, p. 147, diary entry for 10 Feb. 1958.

97 Brown, *In My Way*, p. 93.

98 PRO CAB 147/14, 1965, Balogh to Roll, 9 May 1966.

99 Wigg Collection, 4/56, Balogh to Wilson, 3 Feb. 1965.

100 PRO PREM 13/360, 'Note on the Experiences with the Government Machine', Balogh to Wilson, 25 Feb. 1965.

101 PRO CAB 147/12, 'Economic Strategy and Tactics', Balogh to Wilson, 12 May 1966.

102 PRO CAB 147/155, Balogh to Wilson, 9 Aug. 1966.

103 Pimlott, *Harold Wilson*, p. 350.

104 Interview with Wilfred Beckerman.

105 Hennessy, *The Prime Minister*, p. 289.

106 MacDougall, *Don and Mandarin*, p. 152.

107 See Brittan, 'The Irregulars', pp. 334–5. Brittan writes that Pryke was employed from 1965, but other sources suggest May 1966. For Pryke's subsequent critique of economic policy during the first Wilson administration, see Pryke, *Though Cowards Flinch*.

108 MacDougall, *Don and Mandarin*, p. 173.

109 Balogh, *Planning for Progress*, pp. 24–5.

110 MacDougall, *Don and Mandarin*, p. 153.

111 Callaghan, *Time and Chance*, p. 159.

112 S. Crosland, *Tony Crosland*, p. 135.

113 Samuel Brittan Collection, p. 23, diary entry for 9 Dec. 1964.

114 PRO PREM 13/852, 'Economic-Strategy', Balogh to Wilson, 6 April 1966.

115 Thirlwall, *Nicholas Kaldor*, pp. 283–4. Advocated in an unpublished Fabian paper from 1952, Nicholas Kaldor, 'Foreign Trade and the Balance of Payments', reproduced in Kaldor, *Essays on Economic Policy*, vol. 2, p. 50.

116 Cairncross, *The Wilson Years*, p. 72, diary entry for 25 July 1965.

117 Kaldor Papers, NK 10/2, 'Fixed or Flexible Rates', Kaldor to Armstrong, 22 July 1965.

118 PRO CAB 147/14, 'Economic Strategy.' It is not clear to whom, if anyone, this was sent.

119 Interview with Robert Neild.

120 Wilson, *The Labour Government 1964–70*, p. 571.

121 Cairncross, *The Wilson Years*, pp. 17–18, diary entry for 25 Nov. 1964.

122 Interview with Sir Derek Mitchell. So far, investigations in the PRO suggest Mitchell was successful.

123 PRO PREM 13/250, 'Brief for Washington', Balogh to Wilson, 4 Dec. 1964.

124 Interview with Robert Neild.

125 Cairncross, *The Wilson Years*, p. 230, diary entry for 22 Sept. 1967.

126 PRO T 312/1401, 'Note of a Meeting Held in Sir William Armstrong's Room', 5 April 1965.

127 PRO T 312/1398, 'Guarantees and Compensations'.

128 This paper is referred to in PRO T 312/1636, 'Devaluation Dossier', 21 Feb. 1966.

129 PRO T 312/1401, 'Note of a Meeting Held in Sir William Armstrong's Room', 16 June 1965; 'Note of a Meeting Held in Sir William Armstrong's Room', 13 Sept. 1965.

130 Ibid., 'Note of a Meeting Held in Sir William Armstrong's Room', 29 July 1965.

131 Interview with Sir Donald MacDougall.

132 Interview with Sir Derek Mitchell.

133 Cairncross, *The Wilson Years*, p. 73, diary entry for 26 July 1965.

134 This is referred to in PRO T 312/1636, 'Devaluation Dossier', 21 Feb. 1966. It may be the one he sent to Armstrong, referred to above.

135 Interview with Robert Neild.

136 Interview with Sir Derek Mitchell.

137 Cairncross, *The Wilson Years*, p. 73, diary entry for 26 July 1965 and fn; p. 75, diary entry for 29 July 1965.

138 Interview with Michael Posner.

139 See PRO CAB 147/75, Balogh to Armstrong, 28 Nov. 1967.

140 PRO PREM 13/1447, 'Exchange Rate: Measures to Devalue Pound Sterling; "Operation Patriarch"', Balogh to Wilson, 16 Nov. 1967.

141 Cairncross, 'Economic Advisers in the United Kingdom', p. 237.

142 Castle, *Fighting All the Way*, 397.

143 See e.g. Cairncross, *The Wilson Years*, p. 285, diary entry for 15 March 1968.

144 Tony Benn, *Out of the Wilderness*, p. 319, diary entry for 13 Sept. 1965.

145 Crossman, *The Diaries of a Cabinet Minister*, vol. 2, p. 160, diary entry for 11 Dec. 1966.

146 Benn, *Out of the Wilderness*, p. 41, diary entry for 15 July 1963.

147 Crossman, *The Diaries of a Cabinet Minister*, vol. 2, p. 160, diary entry for 11 Dec. 1966.

148 Benn, *Out of the Wilderness*, p. 319, diary entry for 13 Sept. 1965.

149 Crossman, *The Diaries of a Cabinet Minister*, vol. 2, p. 296, diary entry for 27 March 1967; p. 304, diary entry for 6 April 1967.

150 Pimlott, *Harold Wilson*, pp. 338–9.

151 For example, Crossman, *The Diaries of a Cabinet Minister*, vol. 1, p. 363, diary entry for 26 Oct. 1965; Crossman, *The Diaries of a Cabinet Minister*, vol. 2, p. 718, diary entry for 17 March 1968.

152 Crossman, *The Diaries of a Cabinet Minister*, vol. 1, p. 12.

153 Crossman, *The Diaries of a Cabinet Minister*, vol. 2, p. 43, diary entry for 19 Sept. 1966.

154 Booker, *The Neophiliacs*, pp. 18, 252, 254.

155 See PRO PREM 13/284, 'Investment in Real Estate in Non-Sterling Area by UK Residents. Moves to Frustrate Train Robbers: Cost of Re-issuing Bank Notes', 1965.

156 See Reynolds, Reynolds and Parker, *The Great Train Robbery*.

157 PRO PREM 13/284, Ian Bancroft, Principal Private Secretary to the Chancellor of the Exchequer, to Derek Mitchell, Principal Private Secretary to the Prime Minister, 22 July 1965; Mitchell to Stewart, 26 July 1965; 'Bank Notes and Train Robbers', Mitchell to Wilson, 26 Nov. 1965; 'Train Robbers and Bank Notes', Mitchell to Bancroft, 3 Dec. 1965.

158 Benn, *Out of the Wilderness*, p. 146, diary entry for 23 Sept. 1964.

159 See Hennessy, *The Prime Minister*, pp. 55–7.

160 Crossman, 'Introduction' to Bagehot, *The English Constitution*, pp. 51–6.

161 PRO PREM 13/360, 'Note on the Experiences with the Government Machine', Balogh to Wilson, 25 Feb. 1965.

162 Crossman, *The Diaries of a Cabinet Minister*, vol. 2, pp. 569, diary entry for 12 Nov. 1967.

163 *Whitehall and Beyond*, pp. 18–20.

164 Crossman, *The Diaries of a Cabinet Minister*, vol. 1, p. 249, diary entry for 13 June 1965.

165 See e.g. Crossman, *The Diaries of a Cabinet Minister*, vol. 2, p. 219, diary entry for 1 Feb. 1967.

166 Wigg Collection, 4/56, 'Progress Chasing', Balogh to Trend, 29 May 1965.

Chapter 4

1   'John Allen', *The Times*, 2 July 1998.

2   PRO CAB 160/1, Heaton to Abbot, 23 Oct. 1964.

3   Ian Aitken, 'Obituary', *Guardian*, 1 July 1998.

4   Tony Benn, *Out of the Wilderness*, p. 149, diary entry for 4 Oct. 1964.

5   Ibid., p. 172, diary entry for 25 Oct. 1964.

6   Interview with Sir Derek Mitchell.

7   Benn, *Out of the Wilderness*, p. 172, diary entry for 25 Oct. 1964; p. 207, diary entry for 21 Jan. 1965; p. 198, diary entry for 29 Dec. 1964; p. 198, diary entry for 30 Dec. 1964; p. 198, diary entry for 29 Dec. 1964; p. 173, diary entry for 25 Oct. 1964.

8   Pimlott, *Harold Wilson*, p. 347. This has been corroborated by others (private information).

9   M. Williams, *Inside Number 10*, pp. 325, 332.

10 'John Allen'.

11 Aitken, 'Obituary'.

12 'John Allen'.

13 T 171/803, 'Teenage Compulsory Saving Scheme', Neild to Callaghan, 23 Oct. 1964; 'Teenage Compulsory Saving Scheme', Ian Bancroft, Principal Private Secretary to the Chancellor of the Exchequer, to Neild, 26 Oct. 1964.

14 Thirlwall, *Nicholas Kaldor*, p. 228.

15 Cairncross, *The Wilson Years*, p. 1, fn.

16 See Kaldor Papers, NK 10/5.

17 Thirlwall, 'Kaldor as a Policy Adviser', p. 122.

18 See e.g. Cairncross, *The Wilson Years*, p. 196, diary entry for 20 Feb. 1967.

19 Interview with Sir Samuel Brittan.

20 Interview with Sir Douglas Wass.

21 Interview with Robert Neild.

22 Thirlwall, *Nicholas Kaldor*, p. 239.

23 Interview with Lord Shore.

24 Richard Whiting, *The Labour Party and Taxation*, p. 199.

25 Kaldor, 'Causes of the Slow Rate of Growth in the UK', pp. 282, 285, 288.

26 Thirlwall, *Nicholas Kaldor*, pp. 241–3.

27 Callaghan, *Time and Chance*, pp. 192–3.

28 Stewart, *Politics and Economic Policy since 1964*, pp. 64–5, 67–8.

29 Interview with Lord Shore.

30 Wigg, *George Wigg*, p. 321.

31 *Action not Words: The New Conservative Programme* (Conservative Party, London, 1966).

32 The only participant in the Wilson administrations named in the George Harrison song 'Taxman', from the *Revolver* album, however, is 'Mr Wilson', alongside 'Mr Heath'. See MacDonald, *Revolution in the Head*, pp. 177–8.

33 Castle, *The Castle Diaries, 1964–70*, p. 121, diary entry for 2 May 1966.

34 Cairncross, *The Wilson Years*, p. 46, diary entry for 5 April 1965.

35 Dell, *The Chancellors*, p. 357.

36 Interview with Michael Posner.

37 Jenkins, *A Life at the Centre*, p. 232.

38 Cairncross, *The Wilson Years*, p. 274, diary entry for 14 Feb. 1968.

39 Ibid., p. 276, diary entry for 21 Feb. 1968.

40 Jenkins, *A Life at the Centre*, p. 232.

41 Interview with Lord Croham.

42 Kaldor Papers, NK 10/35, Crossman to Jenkins, March 1969. See also Richard Crossman, *The Diaries of a Cabinet Minister*, vol. 3, p. 568, diary entry for 14 July 1969.

43 Crossman, *The Diaries of a Cabinet Minister*, vol. 3, p. 568, diary entry for 14 July 1969.

44 PRO T 199/1164, 'Research Assistance for Professor Kaldor', Richard Sharp, Establishment Officer, Under-Secretary, Treasury, to Allen, 17 Nov. 1969.

45 PRO T 199/1164, Sir Alec Johnston, Chairman of the Board of Inland Revenue, to Sir William Armstrong, Joint Permanent Secretary to the Treasury, 20 Oct. 1964; Abbot to Collier, 17 Jan. 1967.

46 Kaldor Papers, NK 10/24, "'Structural Factors in Economic Growth: A Cross Section Study of the

International Statistics," written by C. Allsopp under NK's direction', 1967.

47   See Kaldor Papers, NK 10/23. Details of Kaldor's recruitment of assistants can be found in Kaldor Papers, NK 10/32, 'Correspondence Concerning the Conditions of Employment and Accommodation of NK's staff, F. Cripps and C. Allsopp', 1966–8.

48   Conradi, *Iris Murdoch: A Life* , pp. 177–9.

49   Anne Chisholm, 'Iris's Sexual Roundabout', *Sunday Telegraph*, 23 Sept. 2001.

50   PRO CAB 147/169, 'Budget, 1965–66', 1965, 'Short Term Policy', Balogh, 18 Feb. 1965.

51   Balogh, *Unequal Partners*, vol. 2, pp. 1–3.

52   Ibid., p. 4.

53   Healey, *The Time of My Life*, p. 30.

54   Balogh, *Unequal Partners*, vol. 2, p. 2.

55   Balogh, *Fact and Fancy in International Economic Relations*, p. 28.

56   Skidelsky, *John Maynard Keynes*, vol. 3, p. 190.

57   Balogh, *Unequal Partners*, vol. 2, pp. 4, 7.

58   Cairncross, *The Wilson Years*, p. 93, diary entry for 18 Nov. 1965.

59   Marquand, *Ramsay MacDonald*, p. 524.

60   PRO CAB 87/72, Sir Hubert Henderson to Thomas Padmore, 4 Feb. 1943.

61   See Principal Memoranda of Evidence Submitted to the Committee on the Working of the Monetary System (HMSO, London, 1960), 'Memorandum of Evidence Submitted by Mr. Thomas Balogh'.

62   Balogh, *Planning for Progress*, p. 48.

63   Balogh, *Unequal Partners*, vol. 2, pp. 4, 47.

64   Graham, 'Thomas Balogh (1905–1985)', p. 201.

65   See e.g. PRO PREM 13/31, 'Radical International Monetary Reform: Dr Balogh Reported Conversation with Arthur Schlesinger', 1964, 'Brief for Washington', Balogh to Wilson, 4 Dec. 1964.

66   PRO PREM 13/250, 'Foreign Investment Policy', Balogh, 22 Dec. 1964.

67   Graham, 'Thomas Balogh (1905–1985)', p. 196.

68   Howard and West, *The Making of the Prime Minister*, pp. 15–16.

69   Wigg Collection, 4/56, Balogh to Wilson, 28 July 1965.

70   Cairncross, *The Wilson Years*, p. 1, fn.

71   Castle, *The Castle Diaries, 1964–70*, p. 7, diary entry for 2 Feb. 1965.

72   PRO CAB 21/5248, Balogh to Armstrong, 24 Nov. 1964.

73   Wigg Collection, 4/14, Balogh to Wilson, 1 Feb. 1965.

74   PRO CAB 147/2, 'Costing of the Tory Manifesto', Balogh to Wilson, 7 March 1966.

75   Wigg Collection, 4/14, Balogh to Wigg, undated; ibid., Balogh to Wigg, undated.

76   Crossman, *The Diaries of a Cabinet Minister*, vol. 2, p. 125, diary entry for 14 Nov. 1966.

77   PRO PREM 13/360, 'Note on the Experiences with the Government Machine', Balogh to Wilson, 25 Feb. 1965.

78   *The Robert Hall Diaries, 1947–53*, ed. Cairncross, p. 64, diary entry for 11 July 1949.

79   'Mr Wilson's S.C.R.', *Financial Times*, 30 Oct. 1964.

80   *Observer*, 22 Nov. 1964.

81   Crossman, *The Diaries of a Cabinet Minister*, vol. 2, p. 87, diary entry for 22 Oct. 1966.

82   PRO CAB 160/1, Balogh to Heaton, 9 Feb. 1966.

83   Cairncross, *The Wilson Years*, p. 73, diary entry for 26 July 1965.

84   See e.g. Castle, *The Castle Diaries, 1964–70*, p. xvi.

85   Crossman, *The Diaries of a Cabinet Minister*, vol. 1, p. 92, diary entry for 9 Dec. 1964.

86   See e.g. ibid., p. 566, diary entry for 10 July 1966.

87   Graham, 'Thomas Balogh (1905–1985)', p. 203.

88   See e.g. Castle, *The Castle Diaries, 1964–70*, p. 51, diary entry for 26 July 1965; Cairncross, *The Wilson Years*, p. 217, diary entry for 19 June 1967; Jay, *Change and Fortune*, p. 67.

89   Crossman, *The Diaries of a Cabinet Minister*, vol. 2, p. 304, diary entry for 6 April 1967.

90   Interview with Robert Neild.

91   Interview with Sir Michael Palliser.

92   Crossman, *The Diaries of a Cabinet Minister*, vol. 2, p. 304, diary entry for 6 April 1967.

93   Benn, *Office without Power*, p. 90, diary entry for 12 July 1968.

94   Crossman, *The Diaries of a Cabinet Minister*, vol. 3, p. 96, diary entry for 17 June 1968.

95   See *Hansard, House of Commons Debates*, 6 April 1965, cols 269–73.

96   See Morris, 'Thomas Balogh and the Fight for North Sea Revenue'.

97   Graham, 'Thomas Balogh (1905–1985)', p. 204.

98   Cairncross, *The Wilson Years*, p. 124, diary entry for 23 March 1966.

99   Details of appointments to Balogh's team have been obtained from PRO T 199/1063, cross-referenced against Graham, 'Thomas Balogh (1905–1985)', p. 207 fn. Generally, these two sources agree, although Graham does not refer to John Allen, who had gone before he arrived.

100   PRO PREM 13/1955, 'Staff and Papers', Balogh to Wilson, 22 April 1966.

101   Crossman, *The Diaries of a Cabinet Minister*, vol. 2, p. 348, diary entry for 9 May 1967.

102   PRO PREM 13/1955, Halls to Allen, 8 Nov. 1968.

103   See PRO CAB 147/30, 'Prices and Income Policy', 1968–9.

104   PRO PREM 13/1955, 'Papers', Graham to Halls, 29 Oct. 1968.

105   PRO T 199/1063, Neild to Petch, 7 March 1967.

106 Ibid., 'Mr. M. J. Stewart – Outline of Duties and Responsibilities', Heaton to Collier, 22 Nov. 1966.

107 Interview with Stuart Holland.

108 Interview with Sir Michael Palliser.

109 Interview with Stuart Holland; and M. Williams, *Inside Number 10*, p. 246.

110 Crossman, *The Diaries of a Cabinet Minister*, vol, 2, p. 37, diary entry for 13 Sept. 1966.

111 M. Williams, *Inside Number 10*, p. 180.

112 PRO PREM 13/182, 'Commonwealth Trade and Aid', Memorandum by Dr. Balogh, 11 March 1965.

113 For Chamberlain's campaign for imperial preference, see Jay, *Joseph Chamberlain, A Political Study*, pp. 248–303.

114 Stuart Holland private papers, 'EEC Entry', Holland to Balogh, 10 Oct. 1966.

115 Stuart Holland, 'Britain and Europe since 1945', text of paper presented to Institute of Contemporary British History; the East Germany associate status idea can be found in Stuart Holland private papers, 'Observations on EEC Entry after Visits of the Prime Minister and Foreign Secretary to the Capitals of the Six', 31 March 1967.

116 Holland, 'Britain and Europe since 1945'.

117 Stuart Holland private papers, 'Visit to Paris, Thursday and Friday June 15th –16th 1967', 16 June 1967.

118 Stuart Holland private papers, 'Meeting with Louis Joxe, Friday 19 May 1967', 24 May 1967.

119 Stuart Holland private papers, 'Visit to Paris, Thursday and Friday June 15th –16th 1967', 16 June 1967.

120 Interview with Stuart Holland.

121 Stuart Holland, 'Special Advisers and Security', written statement to author, 16 July 2002.

122 PRO T 199/1164, 'Note for the Record', 30 Nov. 1967.

123 Inteview with Stuart Holland.

124 PRO T 199/1164, 'Note for the Record', 30 Nov. 1967.

125 Holland, 'Special Advisers and Security'.

126 Interview with Stuart Holland.

127 Holland, 'Special Advisers and Security'.

128 Interview with Stuart Holland. This is also suggested by Marcia Williams: see *Inside Number 10*, pp. 246, 248.

129 'Passion, principle and economics', *Guardian*, 11 Jan. 1999.

130 For a full discussion of the suspicions held by some regarding Wilson, see Pimlott, *Harold Wilson*, pp. 697–723.

131 Hennessy, *Muddling Through*, p. 265.

132 Andrew and Mitrokhin, *The Mitrokhin Archive*, pp. 527–9.

133 Ziegler, *Wilson*, p. 476.

134 Ramsay, 'Wilson and the Security Services', p. 154.

135 Interview with Stuart Holland.

136 Interview with Sir Christopher Foster.

137 Private information.

138 Interview with Stuart Holland.

139 Crossman, *The Diaries of a Cabinet Minister*, vol. 3, p. 583, diary entry for 20 July 1969.

140 Tony Benn, *Years of Hope*, p. 313, diary entry for 22 Sept. 1959.

141 Interview with Lord Harris.

142 Benn, *Years of Hope*, p. 343, diary entry for 30 Sept. 1960.

143 *The Backbench Diaries of Richard Crossman*, ed. Janet Morgan, p. 873, diary entry for 20 Sept. 1960; Ibid., p. 864, diary entry for 4 Aug. 1960.

144 See e.g. ibid., p. 931, diary entry for 23 Feb. 1961 and p. 936, diary entry for 3 March 1961.

145 *The Political Diary of Hugh Dalton, 1918–40, 1945–60*, ed. Pimlott, p. 694, diary entry for 11 Oct. 1959.

146 Castle, *The Castle Diaries, 1964–70*, p. 487, diary entry for 15 July 1968.

147 Interview with Lord Harris.

148 This is suggested by the Library of Congress Online Catalogue. See e.g. Lee Meriwether, special assistant to the American ambassador to France, *The War Diary of a Diplomat* (New York: Dodd, Mead & Co., *c.*1919).

149 Jenkins, *A Life at the Centre*, p. 182.

150 M. Williams, *Inside Number 10*, p. 223.

151 Interview with Lord Harris.

152 PRO PREM 13/508, 'John Harris', Derek Mitchell, Prime Minister's Principal Private Secretary, to Wilson, 31 May 1965; Sir Laurence Helsby, Joint Permanent Secretary to the Treasury, to Mitchell, 17 June 1965.

153 Interview with Lord Harris.

154 Crossman, *The Diaries of a Cabinet Minister*, vol. 2, p. 636, diary entry for 5 Jan. 1968.

155 Jenkins, *A Life at the Centre*, pp. 181–2.

156 Cairncross, *The Wilson Years*, pp. 336–7, diary entry for 3 Nov. 1968.

157 Jenkins, *A Life at the Centre*, pp. 285, 219, 270.

158 Interview with Lord Croham.

159 Castle, *The Castle Diaries, 1964–70*, p. 414, diary entry for 28 March 1968.

160 Interview with Lord Shore.

161 See e.g. Benn, *Office without Power*, p. 63, diary entry for 30 April 1968; Crossman, *The Diaries of a Cabinet Minister*, vol. 3, pp. 43–4, diary entry for 3 May 1968.

162 Crossman, *The Diaries of a Cabinet Minister*, vol. 2, p. 368, diary entry for 7 June 1967.

163 Ibid., p. 373, diary entry for 8 June 1967.

164 Benn, *Out of the Wilderness*, pp. 467–8, diary entry for 9 Aug. 1966.

165 S. Crosland, *Tony Crosland*, p. 171.

166 Castle, *The Castle Diaries, 1964–70*, p. 414, diary entry for 28 March 1968.

167 Crossman, *The Diaries of a Cabinet Minister*, vol. 3, p. 269, diary entry for Friday 22 Nov. 1968.

168 See e.g. 'Will he be Britain's man of the year?', *Daily Mirror*, 1 Jan. 1968.

169 Crossman, *The Diaries of a Cabinet Minister*, vol. 2, p. 636, diary entry for 5 Jan. 1968.

170 Benn, *Office without Power*, pp. 49–50, diary entry for 25 March 1968.

171 Castle, *The Castle Diaries, 1964–70*, p. 487, diary entry for 15 July 1968.

172 Crossman, *The Diaries of a Cabinet Minister*, vol. 3, p. 269, diary entry for Friday 22 Nov. 1968.

173 Ibid., p. 690, diary entry for 21 Oct. 1969.

174 For a description of the way in which such information was supplied to journalists by Harris and others, see ibid., pp. 582–3, diary entry for 20 July 1969.

175 S. Crosland, *Tony Crosland*, pp. 170–1.

176 Interview with Lord Shore.

177 Interview with Lord Harris.

178 Interview with Lord Marsh.

179 Crossman, *The Diaries of a Cabinet Minister*, vol. 3, pp. 582–3, diary entry for 20 July 1969; Castle, *The Castle Diaries, 1964–70*, p. 414, diary entry for 28 March 1968.

180 Interview with Lord Croham.

181 Castle, *The Castle Diaries, 1964–70*, p. 455, diary entry for 6 June 1968.

182 Interview with Lord Harris.

183 Gordon Walker, *Political Diaries*, p. 316, diary entry for 24 June 1967.

184 Ibid., pp. 321–2, diary entry for 27 May 1968.

185 Ibid., p. 323, diary entry for 4 July 1968.

186 Ibid., pp. 324–5, diary entry for 7 May 1969.

187 Ibid., p. 325, diary entry for 13 May 1969.

188 Ibid., p. 325, diary entry for 13 May 1969.

189 For possible explanations as to why this was so, see Pimlott, *Harold Wilson*, pp. 504–5.

190 Castle, *The Castle Diaries, 1964–70*, p. 487, diary entry for 15 July 1968.

191 See Butler and Pinto-Duschinsky, *The British General Election of 1970*, p. 181.

192 Jenkins, *A Life at the Centre*, p. 297.

193 Crossman, *The Diaries of a Cabinet Minister*, vol. 3, p. 921, diary entry for 14 May 1970.

194 Castle, *The Castle Diaries, 1964–70*, p. 517 fn.

195 *The Backbench Diaries of Richard Crossman*, ed. Morgan, p. 583, diary entry for 1 May 1957.

196 *The Political Diary of Hugh Dalton*, ed. Pimlott pp. 508–9 and fn, diary entry for 2–4 March 1951.

197 Ibid.

198 Peter Townsend, 'Obituary: Professor Brian Abel-Smith', *Independent*, 9 April 1996.

199 Crossman, *The Diaries of a Cabinet Minister*, vol. 3, p. 35, diary entry for 29 April 1968; pp. 183–4, diary entry for 10 Sept. 1968; p. 186, diary entry for 11 Sept. 1968.

200 Crossman, *The Diaries of a Cabinet Minister*, vol. 3, p. 362, diary entry for 10 Feb. 1969; p. 456, diary entry for 25 April 1969; p. 833, diary entry for 24 Feb. 1970.

201 See PRO MH 166/13, 'N.H.S. Green Paper', 1969–70.

202 See PRO CAB 152/10, 'Proposed White Paper on the Mentally Handicapped', 1970–1.

203 Brian Abel-Smith and Peter Townsend, *New Pensions for the Old* (Fabian Society, London, 1955), pp. 2–3.

204 For a summary of the principles involved see Glennerster, *British Social Policy since 1945*, pp. 103–4.

205 Labour Party, *National Superannuation*, pp. 70–3.

206 Interview with Sir Christopher Foster.

207 Peter Jenkins, 'Mrs Castle brings in the economists', *Guardian*, 6 Jan. 1966.

208 *Let's Go with Labour for the New Britain*; *Time for Decision* (Labour Party, London, 1966), p. 301.

209 Interview with Sir Christopher Foster.

210 Castle, *Fighting All the Way*, pp. 368–72.

211 Wilson, *The Labour Government 1964–1970*, p. 320.

212 See PRO MT 160/8, 'Plan for a National Freight Authority', 1966.

213 Interview with Sir Christopher Foster.

214 Jenkins, 'Mrs Castle brings in the economists'.

215 Interview with Sir Christopher Foster.

216 See e.g. Castle, *The Castle Diaries, 1964–70*, p. 276, diary entry for 11 July 1967.

217 Ibid., pp. 334–5, diary entry for 7 Dec. 1967.

218 Interview with Sir Christopher Foster.

219 Interview with Lord Marsh.

220 Castle, *The Castle Diaries, 1964–70*, p. 559, diary entry for 27 Nov. 1968.

221 Interview with Sir Christopher Foster.

222 Crossman, *The Diaries of a Cabinet Minister*, vol. 2, p. 151, diary entry for 5 Dec. 1967 and fn.

223 Ibid., p. 581, diary entry for 19 Nov. 1967.

224 Interview with Michael Posner.

225 T 199/1029, 'Mr. Posner and Mr. Berrill', Cairncross to Armstrong, 7 Aug. 1967.

226 Interview with Sir Kenneth Berrill.

227 Wilfred Beckerman, *Growth, the Environment and the Distribution of Incomes* (Aldershot: Edward Elgar, 1995), p. xxxi.

Chapter 5

1 Kavanagh and Seldon, *The Powers behind the Prime Minister*, p. 80.

2 Ramsden, *The Winds of Change*, p. 326.

3 Hurd, *An End to Promises*, pp. 37–8.

4 Kavanagh and Seldon, *The Powers behind the Prime Minister*, p. 80.

5 John Campbell, *Edward Heath, A Biography* (Pimlico, London, 1994), p. 325.

6 Hurd, *An End to Promises*, p. 38.

7 Interview with Robert Jackson.

8 Wilson, *The Governance of Britain*, p. 91.

9 David Jones, 'Whitehall gets more advisers', *The Times*, 18 July 1970; 'Tory Party research chief moves to Treasury', *The Times*, 18 Sept. 1970.

10 Miles Hudson, 'Special advisers', *The Times*, 6 March 2002.

11 Interview with Lord Marlesford.

12 'Widening Whitehall's corridors', *The Economist*, 4 July 1970.

13 PRO PREM 15/022.

14 Hurd, *An End to Promises*, p. 37.

15 *Civil Servants and Ministers: Duties and Responsibilities*, Treasury and Civil Service Select Committee, vol. II.

16 PRO PREM 15/407, Reading to Robert Armstrong, 5 Oct. 1971, 'Government Strategy, A Review of the Review', marked for the Prime Minister and to be included in folder for 8 Oct. 1971 CPRS Chequers meeting.

17 Interview with Lord Howell.

18 PRO CAB 184/39, 'Presentation of Policy', Reading to Robert Armstrong, 18 Jan. 1972.

19 Ibid., 'Lopsided Economic Management', Reading to Robert Armstrong, 19 Nov. 1971.

20 Ibid., 'Next Week's News', Reading to Robert Armstrong, 2 Dec. 1971.

21 Heath, *The Course of My Life*, pp. 311, 512.

22 See *Hansard, House of Commons Debates*, 11 Feb. 1971, cols 784–6.

23 PRO PREM 15/264, 'Party Political Activities of Civil Servants', Robert Armstrong, Prime Minister's Principal Private Secretary, to Sir William Armstrong, Permanent Secretary to the Civil Service Department and Head of the Home Civil Service, 12 Feb. 1971.

24 Ibid., 'Party Political Activities of Senior Civil Servants', William Armstrong to Robert Armstrong, 25 March 1971.

25 Ibid., Robert Armstrong to Heath, 26 March 1971.

26 Ibid., 'Party Political Activities of Senior Civil Servants', Robert Armstrong to William Armstrong, 29 March 1971.

27 PRO PREM 15/084 'The Formulation of Economic Policy', Reading to Robert Armstrong, 3 Dec. 1970.

28 PRO CAB 184/39, Reading to Rothschild, 1 Sept. 1971.

29 Sewill, 'A View from the Inside: In Place of Strikes', p. 44.

30 Interview with Lord Marlesford.

31 'Widening Whitehall's corridors'.

32 Heath, *The Course of My Life*, p. 332.

33 PRO PREM 15/084 'The Formulation of Economic Policy', Reading to Robert Armstrong, 3 Dec. 1970.

34 Ibid., 'The Formulation of Economic Policy', Robert Armstrong to Reading, 15 Dec. 1970.

35 Howell, *The Edge of Now*, p. 319.

36 PRO PREM 15/407, 'Government Strategy', Schreiber to Robert Armstrong, 7 Oct. 1971.

37 Dell, *The Chancellors*, p. 375.

38 Hennessy, *Whitehall*, pp. 210–12.

39 Ibid., p. 221.

40 *The Reorganisation of Central Government*.

41 Blackstone and Plowden, *Inside the Think Tank*, pp. 6, 10.

42 Interview with Lord Howell.

43 Howell, *The Edge of Now*, p. 350.

44 PREM 15/406, Schreiber to Lord Privy Seal, Lord Jellicoe, 14 Aug. 1970.

45 Blackstone and Plowden, *Inside the Think Tank*, p. 10.

46 Interview with Lord Marlesford.

47 Hurd, *An End to Promises*, pp. 36–7.

48 See Theakston, *Leadership in Whitehall*, pp. 192–6.

49 *Hansard, House of Commons Debates*, 6 May 1974, col. 21.

50 Interview with Lord Sheldon.

51 Theakston, *Leadership in Whitehall*, pp. 195–6.

52 Heath, *The Course of My Life*, p. 315.

53 Hennessy, *Whitehall*, p. 223.

54 Lord Rothschild, *Meditations of a Broomstick* (Collins, London, 1977), p. 112.

55 Heath, *The Course of My Life*, p. 315.

56 Blackstone and Plowden, *Inside the Think Tank*, pp. 27–8.

57 See e.g. PRO PREM 15/927.

58 See Blackstone and Plowden, *Inside the Think Tank*, p. 30.

59 Interview with Sir Adam Ridley.

60 Ibid., pp. 30, 67; interview with Lord Marlesford.

61 PRO PREM 15/407, 'CPRS Presentation, 8 Oct.', Hurd to Robert Armstrong, 17 Sept. 1971.

62 Ibid., Robert Armstrong to Heath, 22 Sept. 1971.

63 Ibid., 'Strategy Meeting at Chequers', Robert Armstrong to Trend, 1 Oct. 1971.

64 See PRO PREM 15/927.

65 *A Better Tomorrow* (Conservative Party, London, 1970).

66 Dell, *The Chancellors*, p. 377.

67 For a discussion of this, see Peter Hennessy, *The Prime Minister*, pp. 333–6.

68 Interview with Lord Marlesford.

69 Ibid.

70 Sewill, 'A View from the Inside: In Place of Strikes', p. 31.

71 Interview with Lord Howell.

72 Sewill, 'A View from the Inside: In Place of Strikes', p. 31.

73 Brian Reading, 'Tripping up in a dash for growth', *The Times*, 9 Oct. 1988.

74 Brian Reading, 'The speech that swung an election', *Financial Times*, 14 April 1997.

75 Heath, *The Course of My Life*, p. 304.

76 Reading, 'The speech that swung an election'.

77 Heath, *The Course of My Life*, p. 304.

78 Dell, *The Chancellors*, p. 387.

79 Reading, 'Tripping up in a dash for growth'.

80 Interviews with Lord Marlesford, Lord Armstrong.

81 Interview with Lord Howell.

82 PRO PREM 15/809, 'The Summer Short Term Forecasts', Reading to Robert Armstrong, marked for the Prime Minister, 8 July 1971.

83 PRO PREM 15/407, 'Government Strategy, A Review of the Review', Reading to Robert Armstrong, 5 Oct. 1971, marked for the Prime Minister and to be included in folder for 8 Oct. 1971 CPRS Chequers meeting.

84 Ibid., Reading to Robert Armstrong, 5 Oct. 1971, 'Government Strategy, A Review of the Review', marked for the Prime Minister and to be included in folder for 8 Oct. 1971 CPRS Chequers meeting.

85 Heath, *The Course of My Life*, p. 398.

86 Sewill, 'A View from the Inside: In Place of Strikes', p. 45.

87 PRO PREM 15/407, 'Government Strategy', Schreiber to Robert Armstrong, 7 Oct. 1971.

88 Cairncross, *The British Economy since 1945*, p. 182.

89 PRO CAB 184/39, 'Spare Capacity', Reading to Robert Armstrong, 13 Oct. 1971.

90 Ibid., 'Roundabouts and Ratchets – or The Consequences of Dirty Floating in a Clean Sink', Reading to Robert Armstrong, 13 Oct. 1971.

91 Ibid., Reading to MacDougall, 7 Dec. 1971.

92 Heath, *The Course of My Life*, pp. 397–8.

93 PRO CAB 184/39, 'Meditations upon Multipliers, Accelerators, Go–Go and Stop–Stop', Reading to Rothschild, 24 April 1972.

94 Ibid., 'Policy Decisions in 1972', Reading, 16 May 1972.

95 PRO PREM 15/055, 'The Money Supply in the Second Quarter', Reading to Robert Armstrong, 7 Dec. 1970.

96 PRO PREM 15/407, Reading to Robert Armstrong, 5 Oct. 1971, 'Government Strategy, A Review of the Review', marked for the Prime Minister and to be included in folder for 8 Oct. 1971 CPRS Chequers meeting.

97 Ibid., 'Government Strategy', Schreiber to Robert Armstrong, 7 Oct. 1971.

98 PRO CAB 184/39, 'Economic Management in 1972', Reading, Jan. 1972.

99 PRO CAB 184/39, 'How to Maintain Control over the Economy', Reading to Rothschild, 28 June 1972.

100 Sewill, 'A View from the Inside: In Place of Strikes', p. 33.

101 For a discussion of Heath's international orientation, see John W. Young, *Britain and European Unity 1945–1999* (Macmillan, Basingstoke, 2000), pp. 109–10.

102 PRO PREM 15/407, 'Government Strategy', Schreiber to Robert Armstrong, 7 Oct. 1971.

103 Dell, *The Chancellors*, pp. 385–91.

104 PRO CAB 184/39, Reading to Rothschild, 1 Sept. 1971.

105 Ibid., 'The Passing of the Parities', Brian Reading, 13 Sept. 1971.

106 PRO CAB 184/39, 'International Monetary Reform', Reading to Robert Armstrong, 23 Sept. 1971. For a description of Keynes's initial proposal, see Robert Skidelsky, *John Maynard Keynes*, vol. 3, pp. 179–230.

107 Heath, *The Course of My life*, pp. 719–20.

108 Sewill, 'A View from the Inside: In Place of Strikes', pp. 36–8.

109 PRO PREM 15/055, 'The Money Supply Incomes Policy and the Bank o England', Reading to Robert Armstrong, 29 October. 1970.

110 Ibid.

111 PRO PREM 15/084, 'Monetary Policy', Reading to Robert Armstrong, passed to Prime Minister, 31 Dec. 1970.

112 PREM 15/808, 'Problems in the Management of the Economy: A Comment', Alan Walters, April 1972.

Chapter 6

1 Roger Darlington, 'The public must pay for effective MPs', *The Times*, 17 June 1974;.

2 S. Crosland, *Tony Crosland*, p. 246.

3 Jenkins, *A Life at the Centre*, p. 355.

4 *Hansard, House of Commons Debates*, 25 March 1975, cols 1869–70.

5 Interview with Lord McNally.

6 Benn, *Against the Tide*, p. 454, diary entry for 4 Nov. 1975.

7 Interview with Lord Sheldon.

8 Williams, *Inside Number 10*, pp. 358, 359.

9 Ibid., p. 284.

10 Committee on Standards in Public Life, Public Hearings, 9 Sept. 2002.

11 Haines, *The Politics of Power*, pp. 43–63.

12 Anthony Wedgwood Benn, 'A little light in dark corners', *The Times*, 11 July 1973.

13 See e.g. Peter Hennessy, 'A more political Whitehall urged', *The Times*, 23 May 1977.

14 Wilson, *Final Term*, p. 19.

15 Jenkins, *A Life at the Centre*, p. 375.

16 Hennessy, *Whitehall*, p. 244.

17 Donoughue, *Prime Minister*, p. ix.

18 Callaghan, *Time and Chance*, p. 404.

19 See e.g. 'More party supporters given Whitehall jobs', *The Times*, 10 June 1974.

20 HC Written Answers, 1 March 1977, col. 124.

21 Interview with Lord Croham.

22 Roger Darlington, 'Why there should be more special advisers in Whitehall', *The Times*, 18 July 1978.

23 Committee on Standards in Public Life, Public Hearings, 9 Sept. 2002.

24 Interview with Lord Croham.

25 Owen, *Face the Future*, p. 301; Owen, *Time to Declare*, p. 263.

26 Castle, *The Castle Diaries, 1974–76*, pp. 66–7, diary entry for 4 April 1974; p. 105, diary entry for 23 May 1974.

27 Benn, *Conflicts of Interest*, p. 303, diary entry for 23 May 1978; p. 470, 11 March 1979.

28 *Hansard, House of Commons Debates*, 10 May 1976, col. 23.

29 Baker, *Prime Ministers and the Rule Book*, p. 95.

30 HC Written Answers, 21 Feb. 1977, col. 472.

31 Castle, *The Castle Diaries, 1974–76*, p. 707, diary entry for 29 March 1976.

32 Donoughue, *Prime Minister*, pp. 20, 25.

33 HC Written Answers, 1 Aug. 1978, cols 226–7.

34 Civil Service Order in Council 1978. The fact that it came into force late in the year (1 December) may be the reason for apparently mistaken references made by some to a 1979 Order in Council defining the appointments of special advisers.

35 Committee on Standards in Public Life, Public Hearings, 9 July 2002.

36 Darlington, 'Why there should be more special advisers in Whitehall'.

37 HC Written Answers, 6 May 1974, col. 22.

38 HC Written Answers, 27 Feb. 1976, cols 360–1.

39 Benn, *Against the Tide*, p. 446, diary entry for 10 Oct. 1975.

40 Donoughue, *The Heat of the Kitchen*, pp. 185–6.

41 Reproduced in Wilson, *The Governance of Britain*, pp. 202–5.

42 Wilson, *The Governance of Britain*, p. 99.

43 Wilson, *Final Term*, p. 19.

44 Donoughue, *The Heat of the Kitchen*, p. 222.

45 Committee on Standards in Public Life, Public Hearings, 9 July 2002.

46 N. Jones, *The Control Freaks*, pp. 76–7.

47 Wilson, *The Governance of Britain*, p. 99.

48 Whitlam, *The Whitlam Government*, p. 695.

49 Pierre Gaborit and Jean-Pierre Mounier, 'France', in Plowden (ed.), *Advising the Rulers*, pp. 109–15.

50 George Bishop, 'Labour's private army in Whitehall', *New Statesman*, 10 May 1974.

51 Castle, *The Castle Diaries, 1974–1976*, p. 67, diary entry for 4 April 1974.

52 Interview with Sir Christopher Foster.

53 Interview with Lord Sheldon.

54 Interview with Lord McNally.

55 Owen, *Time to Declare*, p. 263; Owen, *Face the Future*, pp. 299–300.

56 S. Crosland, *Tony Crosland*, p. 246.

57 Owen, *Time to Declare*, pp. 281–2.

58 Public Administration Committee, Minutes of Evidence, 12 July 2000.

59 Benn, *Conflicts of Interest*, p. 481, diary entry for 2 April 1979.

60 Committee on Standards in Public Life, Public Hearings, 27 June 2002.

61 Public Administration Committee, Minutes of Evidence, 12 July 2000.

62 Radice, *Friends and Rivals*, p. 243.

63 Crosland Collection, CAR 5/13, David Lipsey to Tony Crosland, 22 Dec. 1976.

64 Committee on Standards in Public Life, Public Hearings, 27 June 2002.

65 Crosland Collection, CAR 5/13, David Lipsey to Tony Crosland, 22 Dec. 1976.

66 Ibid., CAR 5/12, 'Meeting with Supporting MPs', Lipsey to Crosland, 20 July 1976.

67 Ibid.

68 Callaghan, *Time and Chance*, p. 392.

69 Castle, *Fighting All the Way*, p. 460.

70 Alan Hamilton and Sam Coates, 'Troublemaker in chief', *The Times*, 7 March 2003.

71 Benn, *Against the Tide*, p. 50, diary entry for 24 June 1973; Castle, *The Castle Diaries, 1974–1976*, p. 34, diary entry for 5 March 1974 and fn.

72 Castle, *The Castle Diaries, 1974–1976*, p. 40, diary entry for 11 March 1974; Castle, *Fighting All the Way*, pp. 460–1.

73 Nichola Timmins and Simon Targett, 'Straw and Blunkett pick policy specialists', *Financial Times*, 6 May 1997.

74 Castle, *The Castle Diaries, 1974–1976*, p. 125, diary entry for 1 July 1974; p. 78, diary entry for 9 April 1974; pp. 99–100, diary entry for 5 May 1974; pp. 130–1, diary entry for 5 July 1974; p. 177, diary entry for 11 Sept. 1974; p. 247, diary entry for 11 Dec. 1974; p. 635, diary entry for 29 Jan. 1976.

75 See e.g. Tony Benn, *Against the Tide*, p. 363, diary entry for 17 April 1975.

76 Castle, *The Castle Diaries, 1974–1976*, p. 367, diary entry for 17 April 1975.

77 Ibid., p. 383, diary entry for 1 May 1975; p. 391, diary entry for 15 May 1975; p. 391, diary entry for 16 May 1975.

78 Castle, *Fighting All the Way*, pp. 461, 462, 463–4;

Wilson, *Final Term*, p. 5; *Let Us Work Together: Labour's Way Out of the Crisis* (Labour Party, London, 1974); Castle, *The Castle Diaries, 1974–1976*, p. 38, diary entry for 6 March 1974.

79 Thirlwall, *Nicholas Kaldor*, pp. 250–1.

80 Dell, *The Chancellors*, p. 412.

81 Thirlwall, *Nicholas Kaldor*, p. 251.

82 'The Cambridge debate', *The Economist*, 27 April 1974.

83 Thirlwall, *Nicholas Kaldor*, p. 251.

84 Dell, *The Chancellors*, pp. 412–13.

85 Thirlwall, *Nicholas Kaldor*, p. 250; Healey, *The Time of My Life*, pp. 390–1; Hennessy, *Whitehall*, p. 249; Interview with Sir Kenneth Berrill.

86 Jenkins, *A Life at the Centre*, pp. 375–6.

87 Benn, *Against the Tide*, p. 210, diary entry for 31 July 1974; p. 120, diary entry for 11 March 1974; p. 115, diary entry for 6 March 1974; p. 210, diary entry for 31 July 1974.

88 Benn, *Conflicts of Interest*, p. 41, diary entry for 17 Feb. 1977.

89 Benn, *Against the Tide*, p. 122, diary entry for 17 March 1974; p. 218, diary entry for 15 Aug. 1974; p. 216, diary entry for 7 Aug. 1974; p. 124, diary entry for 20 March 1974; p. 376, diary entry for 12 May 1975.

90 Ibid; p. 267, diary entry for 19 Nov. 1974; p. 152, diary entry for 12 May 1974; p. 531, diary entry for 11 March 1976.

91 Benn, *Conflicts of Interest*, pp. 269–70, diary entry for 11 Jan. 1978.

92 Benn, *Against the Tide*, p. 103, diary entry for 3 Feb. 1974; p. 82, diary entry for 31 Dec. 1973; p. 580, diary entry for 15 June 1976.

93 Ibid., p. 360, diary entry for 7 April 1975; pp. 536–7, diary entry for 16 March 1976; p. 537, diary entry for 17 March 1976; p. 555, diary entry for 7 April 1976.

94 Benn, *Conflicts of Interest*, p. 55, diary entry for 2 March 1977; p. 313, diary entry for 21 June 1978.

95 Ibid., p. 599, diary entry for 30 May 1978.

96 Owen, *Time to Declare*, pp. 477, 522, 282–3.

97 Jenkins, *A Life at the Centre*, p. 598.

98 'The "Political Advisers" Experiment' (reproduced in Wilson, *The Governance of Britain*, pp. 202–5); Callaghan, *Time and Chance*, pp. 404–5.

99 'The "Political Advisers" Experiment'.

100 Donoughue, *Prime Minister*, p. 24.

101 Committee on Standards in Public Life, Public Hearings, 9 Sept. 2002.

102 Kavanagh and Seldon, *The Powers behind the Prime Minister*, pp. 121–2.

103 Donoughue, *The Heat of the Kitchen*, p. 131.

104 Ibid.

105 Donoughue, *Prime Minister*, p. 22.

106 Committee on Standards in Public Life, Public Hearings, 9 Sept. 2002.

107 Donoughue, *Prime Minister*, pp. 22–4.

108 Committee on Standards in Public Life, Public Hearings, 9 Sept. 2002.

109 Donoughue, *Prime Minister*, pp. 23–4.

110 Ibid., pp. 20–1.

111 Kavanagh and Seldon, *The Powers behind the Prime Minister*, pp. 119–20.

112 'The "Political Advisers" Experiment'.

113 Committee on Standards in Public Life, Public Hearings, 9 Sept. 2002.

114 Pimlott, *Harold Wilson*, pp. 620–1.

115 Donoughue, *The Heat of the Kitchen*, pp. 150–7.

116 See Wilson, *Final Term*, p. 33.

117 Donoughue, *Prime Minister*, p. 52.

118 Wilson, *Final Term*, p. 35.

119 Benn, *Against the Tide*, p. 454, diary entry for 4 Nov. 1975.

120 Morgan, *Callaghan*, p. 495.

121 Radice, *Friends and Rivals*, pp. 256–63; Dell, *The Chancellors*, p. 436.

122 Donoughue, *The Heat of the Kitchen*, pp. 130–1.

123 Hennessy, *The Prime Minister*, p. 359.

124 Callaghan, *Time and Chance*, p. 404.

125 Donoughue, *Prime Minister*, p. 24.

126 Callaghan, *Time and Chance*, p. 408.

127 Benn, *Against the Tide*, p. 488, diary entry for 5 Jan. 1976.

128 Committee on Standards in Public Life, Public Hearings, 27 June 2002.

129 Donoughue, *Prime Minister*, pp. 36–7.

130 Owen, *Time to Declare*, p. 263.

131 'The "Political Advisers" Experiment'.

132 *The Civil Service*, Expenditure Committee, vol. 2, part 2.

133 Donoughue, *Prime Minister*, p. 24.

134 Public Administration Committee, Minutes of Evidence, 12 July 2000.

135 Hennessy, *The Prime Minister*, p. 380.

136 Donoughue, *The Heat of the Kitchen*, pp. 3, 5, 6, pp. 3–87.

137 Ibid., pp. 91, 91–2, 101, 101–2, 105–6.

138 Castle, *The Castle Diaries, 1974–1976*, pp. 59–60, diary entry for 1 April 1974.

139 Falkender, *Downing Street in Perspective*, p. 99.

140 Owen, *Time to Declare*, p. 282.

141 Benn, *Against the Tide*, p. 454, diary entry for 4 Nov. 1975.

142 Benn, *Conflicts of Interest*, p. 171, diary entry for 21 June 1977.

143 Falkender, *Downing Street in Perspective*, p. 99.

144 Donoughue, *The Heat of the Kitchen*, pp. 131–2.

145 Haines, *The Politics of Power*, pp. 62–3.

146 Falkender, *Downing Street in Perspective*, p. 85.

147   Donoughue, *The Heat of the Kitchen*, p. 162.

148   Pimlott, *Harold Wilson*, p. 620.

149   Donoughue, *Prime Minister*, pp. 65, 86–7.

150   See e.g. Haines, *The Politics of Power*, p. 165.

151   Donoughue, *The Heat of the Kitchen*, p. 101.

152   Morgan, *Callaghan*, p. 472.

153   Donoughue, *The Heat of the Kitchen*, p. 237.

154   Donoughue, *Prime Minister*, p. 101.

155   Callaghan, *Time and Chance*, p. 404.

156   Donoughue, *Prime Minister*, pp. 157, 163–4.

157   Ibid., pp. 79–82; Callaghan, *Time and Chance*, pp. 425–7.

158   Donoughue, *Prime Minister*, pp. 54–5.

159   Dell, *A Strange Eventful History*, p. 501.

160   Morgan, *Callaghan*, p. 493.

161   Donoughue, *Prime Minister*, pp. 114–15.

162   Morgan, *Callaghan*, p. 503.

163   Donoughue, *Prime Minister*, p. 111.

164   Donoughue, *The Heat of the Kitchen*, p. 80.

165   Alfred Sherman, 'A little grey matter in Downing St', *Guardian*, 23 Dec. 1994.

166   Donoughue, *The Heat of the Kitchen*, pp. 210–11.

167   *Hansard, House of Commons Debates*, 21 June 1976, col. 1091.

168   Ibid., 29 March 1976, cols 887–8.

169   Ibid., 21 June 1976, col. 1091.

170   Ibid., 23 Feb. 1976, cols 20–1.

171   Ibid., 21 Nov. 1977, col. 1089.

172   Bishop, 'Labour's private army in Whitehall'.

173   *The Civil Service*, Expenditure Committee, vol. 1.

174   *The Civil Service*, Expenditure Committee, vol. 2, part 2.

175   Benn, *Conflicts of Interest*, p. 172, diary entry for 21 June 1977.

176   Owen, *Face the Future*, pp. 300–1.

177   Lipsey (ed.), *Making Government Work*, pp. 9, 15.

Chapter 7

1   Lee et al., *At the Centre of Whitehall*, p. 100.

2   Lord Armstrong, 'Malaise in Whitehall', *Spectator*, 26 Feb. 2002.

3   HC Written Answers, 18 May 1979, cols 7–8.

4   Theakston, *Leadership in Whitehall*, p. 227.

5   Thatcher, *The Downing Street Years*, p. 18.

6   Hennessy, *Whitehall*, pp. 658–9.

7   Lawson, *The View from No. 11*, p. 25.

8   HC Written Answers, 19 June 1984, cols 99–100.

9   Kavanagh and Seldon, *The Powers behind the Prime Minister*, p. 192.

10   Lee et al., *At the Centre of Whitehall*, p. 103.

11   HC Written Answers, 19 June 1984, cols 99–100.

12   Alan Travis, 'Hidden persuaders: The role of ministers' special advisers', *Guardian*, 25 Oct. 1989.

13   HC Written Answers, 27 July 1988, col. 253.

14   Kavanagh and Seldon, *The Powers behind the Prime Minister*, p. 155.

15   Hoskyns, *Just in Time*, p. 119.

16   Ibid., p. 265.

17   Committee on Standards in Public Life, Public Hearings, 9 July 2002.

18   HC Written Answers, 20 March 1989, col. 419.

19   Committee on Standards in Public Life, Public Hearings, 9 July 2002.

20   Cockett, *Thinking the Unthinkable*, p. 265.

21   Alfred Sherman, 'Facts about the men who made Thatcher', *Independent*, 26 Nov. 1990.

22   Howe, *Conflict of Loyalty*, pp. 86, 98.

23   Robert Harris, 'Kick in the teeth for the clever classes', *Sunday Times*, 17 Nov. 1996.

24   Hoskyns, *Just in Time*, p. 56.

25   Interview with Lord Young.

26   Thatcher, *The Path to Power*, p. 292.

27   Interview with Sir Adam Ridley.

28   Cockett, *Thinking the Unthinkable*, pp. 275–6.

29   Hoskyns, *Just in Time*, pp. 78, 89–90.

30   Alfred Sherman, 'A little grey matter in Downing St', *Guardian*, 23 Dec. 1994.

31   David Pallister, 'Election 87: Labour seeks assurance on "dirty tricks"', *Guardian*, 6 June 1987.

32   Crozier, *Free Agent*, p. 129.

33   Hoskyns, *Just in Time*, p. 129 fn.

34   Ibid., p. 159.

35   Ferdinand Mount, 'Whatever became of the policies?', *Sunday Times*, 12 July 1998.

36   Lawson, *The View from No. 11*, p. 263.

37   Thatcher, *The Path to Power*, p. 443.

38   HC Written Answers, 22 March 1989, cols 418–19.

39   Hoskyns, *Just in Time*, p. 227. For the Rayner reforms, see Theakston, *Leadership in Whitehall*, pp. 227–46. For the report leading to the Next Steps reforms, see *Improving Management in Government: The Next Steps*, Efficiency Unit.

40   H. Young, *One of Us*, p. 516.

41   Interview with Lord Young.

42   Lord Young, *The Enterprise Years*, pp. 17, 31–2, 37–8.

43   Ibid., pp. 48–9, 60; Baker, *The Turbulent Years*, p. 78.

44   Young, *The Enterprise Years*, p. 50.

45   Ibid., pp. 60–3, 123, 159, 251–3, 359.

46   Heseltine, *Life in the Jungle*, pp. 199–200.

47   Fowler, *Ministers Decide*, pp. 273–4, 192–3.

48   Young, *The Enterprise Years*, p. 266.

49   Interview with Lord Young.

50   Tebbit, *Upwardly Mobile*, pp. 252, 270, 312.

51   Young, *The Enterprise Years*, pp. 151–2.

52   Hollingsworth, *The Ultimate Spin Doctor*, p. 167.

53   Interview with Lord Young.

54   Young, *The Enterprise Years*, p. 266.

55   Howe, *Conflict of Loyalty*, pp. 125, 73.

56   Lawson, *The View from No. 11*, p. 25.

57   Howe, *Conflict of Loyalty*, pp. 98–9, 126, 142, 160, 155. For the 1980 Budget, see *Hansard, House of Commons Debates*, 26 March 1980, cols 1439–90.

58   Lawson, *The View from No. 11*, p. 25.

59   Howe, *Conflict of Loyalty*, pp. 167–8.

60   Lawson, *The View from No. 11*, p. 25.

61   Committee on Standards in Public Life, Public Hearings, 9 July 2002.

62   Interview with Andrew Tyrie.

63   Major, *The Autobiography*, p. 135.

64   Lawson, *The View from No. 11*, pp. 697–8, 702–3.

65   Lee et al., *At the Centre of Whitehall*, p. 123; David Butler et al., *Failure in British Government* (Oxford University Press, Oxford, 1994), p. 95.

66   Interview with Andrew Tyrie.

67   See Jones, 'The Downfall of Margaret Thatcher', p. 90.

68   Major, *The Autobiography*, p. 158.

69   Thatcher, *The Downing Street Years*, p. 30 fn.

70   Howe, *Conflict of Loyalty*, p. 260.

71   Hennessy, *The Prime Minister*, pp. 400–4.

72   Kavanagh and Seldon, *The Powers behind the Prime Minister*, p. 173.

73   Peter Riddell, 'In the Thatcher mould', *Financial Times*, 1 Oct. 1985.

74   Ibid.

75   Kavanagh and Seldon, *The Powers behind the Prime Minister*, p. 160.

76   Interview with Lord Griffiths.

77   Lee et al., *At the Centre of Whitehall*, p. 116.

78   Mount, 'Whatever became of the policies?'

79   Thatcher, *The Downing Street Years*, pp. 278–9.

80   Nicholas Wood, 'Members of the kitchen cabinet reap rich rewards', *The Times*, 21 Dec. 1990.

81   David Gow, 'Round Brian quiz', *Guardian*, 19 July 1988.

82   Colin Brown, 'Thatcher rewards the defenders of her political faith', *Independent*, 21 Dec. 1990.

83   Frank Field, review of *Privatised Parables: Morality and the Market-place* by Brian Griffiths, *Independent*, 25 May 1989.

84   Interview with John Redwood.

85   Thatcher, *The Downing Street Years*, pp. 597–9.

86   Kavanagh and Seldon, *The Powers behind the Prime Minister*, p. 192.

87   Interview with Lord Griffiths.

88   Interview with Andrew Tyrie.

89   Thatcher, *The Downing Street Years*, p. 438 and fn.

90   Interview with John Redwood.

91   Hennessy, *The Prime Minister*, p. 424.

92   Lawson, *The View from No. 11*, p. 798.

93   Gow, 'Round Brian quiz'.

94   Interview with Lord Griffiths.

95   Howe, *Conflict of Loyalty*, pp. 260, 201.

96   Ibid., p. 201.

97   Lawson, *The View from No. 11*, p. 116.

98   Sherman, 'A little grey matter in Downing St'.

99   Interview with Lord Griffiths.

100 Hennessy, *The Prime Minister*, p. 405.

101 H. Young, *One of Us*, pp. 445, 551–2, 496.

102 Ibid., p. 113.

103 Howe, *Conflict of Loyalty*, pp. 104–5.

104 Hoskyns, *Just in Time*, pp. 3–8, 7.

105 Ibid., pp. 15, 12.

106 H. Young, *One of Us*, p. 113.

107 Hoskyns, *Just in Time*, pp. 10–12, 18–23.

108 Hennessy, *Whitehall*, p. 638.

109 Thatcher, *The Path to Power*, p. 420.

110 Hoskyns, *Just in Time*, p. 28.

111 Ibid., p. 39.

112 Howe, *Conflict of Loyalty*, pp. 104–5.

113 H. Young, *One of Us*, pp. 117–18.

114 Howe, *Conflict of Loyalty*, pp. 104–5.

115 H. Young, *One of Us*, p. 117.

116 Howe, *Conflict of Loyalty*, pp. 107–8.

117 Hoskyns, *Just in Time*, pp. 91–4, 102–3.

118 Interview with Sir Adam Ridley.

119 Ibid., p. 106; Hennessy, *Whitehall*, p. 640; Hoskyns, *Just in Time*, pp. 100, 98–102, 128.

120 Robin Pauley, 'Civil Service accused of incompetence', *Financial Times*, 29 Sept. 1983.

121 Interview with Lord Armstrong.

122 Howe, *Conflict of Loyalty*, p. 260.

123 Thatcher, *The Downing Street Years*, p. 104.

124 Hoskyns, *Just in Time*, pp. 73, 178.

125 Ibid., pp. 213–20, 163.

126 Peter Stothard, 'Too good for Downing Street', *The Times*, 27 Aug. 1985.

127 Hoskyns, *Just in Time*, p. 164.

128 Thatcher, *The Path to Power*, p. 420.

129 Thatcher, *The Downing Street Years*, p. 30.

130 Hoskyns, *Just in Time*, pp. xiv, 74, 131, 326–8, 364.

131 Ibid., pp. 351–2.

132 Sherman, 'A little grey matter in Downing St'.

133 Hoskyns, *Just in Time*, pp. 355–6, 362–3.

134 Ibid., p. 150.

135 Donoughue, *The Heat of the Kitchen*, p. 131.

136 Centre for Policy Studies Collection, CPS 7, 'The Westwell Report'.

137 Hoskyns, *Just in Time*, p. 358.

138 Lawson, *The View from No. 11*, pp. 204–5.

139 Hoskyns, *Just in Time*, pp. 358, 376.

140 Howe, *Conflict of Loyalty*, p. 201.

141 Simon Holbertson, 'The rise of a journeyman economist', *Financial Times*, 27 Oct. 1989.

142 Thatcher, *The Path to Power*, p. 567.

143 Alan Walters, 'My deviationist economics', *Independent*, 26 Oct. 1989.

144 Lawson, *The View from No. 11*, p. 116.

145 Howe, *Conflict of Loyalty*, p. 187.

146 Walters, 'My deviationist economics'.

147 Interview with Lord Griffiths.

148 Walters 'My deviationist economics'.

149 Howe, *Conflict of Loyalty*, p. 75.

150 Walters, 'My deviationist economics'.

151 Thatcher, *The Path to Power*, p. 254.

152 Cockett, *Thinking the Unthinkable*, p. 233.

153 A. A. Walters, *Money and Inflation* (Aims of Industry, London, 1974), p. 1.

154 *The 1979 Conservative Manifesto* (Conservative Party, London, 1979).

155 Lee et al., *At the Centre of Whitehall*, pp. 124–5.

156 Hennessy, *Whitehall*, p. 642.

157 Walters, 'My deviationist economics'.

158 H. Young, *One of Us*, p. 212.

159 Cairncross, *The British Economy since 1945*, p. 244.

160 Lawson, *The View from No. 11*, p. 63.

161 Cairncross, *The British Economy since 1945*, p. 245.

162 Hennessy, *The Prime Minister*, pp. 410–11.

163 Howe, *Conflict of Loyalty*, p. 202.

164 Thatcher, *The Downing Street Years*, pp. 133–6.

165 See e.g. Hoskyns, *Just in Time*, p. 273.

166 Howe, *Conflict of Loyalty*, pp. 200–1.

167 Walters, 'My deviationist economics'.

168 Hennessy, *Whitehall*, p. 642.

169 Howe, *Conflict of Loyalty*, pp. 452–3.

170 Thatcher, *The Downing Street Years*, p. 693.

171 Ibid., pp. 694–5l; Howe, *Conflict of Loyalty*, pp. 449–50.

172 Lawson, *The View from No. 11*, p. 842.

173 Thatcher, *The Downing Street Years*, p. 707.

174 'Outsider at the heart of Thatcherism', *Independent*, 17 June 1989.

175 David Smith and David Hughes, 'Interest rise "puts Britain on brink of recession"', *Sunday Times*, 8 Oct. 1989.

176 Lawson, *The View from No. 11*, p. 951.

177 Ibid., p. 926.

178 Interview with Lord Butler.

179 Lawson, *The View from No. 11*, pp. 960–1.

180 Thatcher, *The Downing Street Years*, pp. 714–15.

181 Lawson, *The View from No. 11*, pp. 955–6.

182 The letter was reproduced in *Guardian*, 27 Oct. 1989.

183 Baker, *The Turbulent Years*, p. 308.

184 Thatcher, *The Downing Street Years*, pp. 715–18.

185 Jones, 'The Downfall of Margaret Thatcher', pp. 94–5.

186 Hazel Duffy, 'The Chancellor's resignation', *Financial Times*, 28 Oct. 1989.

187 Ralph Atkins, 'Role of advisers "may not be so great"', *Financial Times*, 3 Nov. 1989.

188 Howe, *Conflict of Loyalty*, p. 279; *The 1979 Conservative Manifesto* (Conservative Party, London, 1979).

189 Thatcher, *The Downing Street Years*, pp. 282–3.

190 *The 1983 Conservative Manifesto* (Conservative Party, London, 1983).

191 Thatcher, *The Downing Street Years*, pp. 565, 570–2.

192 Howe, *Conflict of Loyalty*, p. 519.

193 *The Next Moves Forward* (Conservative Party, London, 1987).

194 Hogg and Hill, *Too Close to Call*, p. 182.

195 See e.g. HC Written Answers, 19 June 1984, cols 99–100.

196 *Hansard, House of Commons Debates*, 2 Feb. 1989, col. 436.

197 *Civil Servants and Ministers: Duties and Responsibilities*, Treasury and Civil Service Committee, vol. 1.

Chapter 8

1 Interview with Lord Butler.

2 Civil Service Order in Council 1982; Diplomatic Service (Amendment) Order 1982.

3 Civil Service Order in Council 1991; Diplomatic Service Order 1991.

4 Committee on Standards in Public Life, Public Hearings, 9 July 2002.

5 Ibid.

6 Hennessy, *The Prime Minister*, p. 452.

7 *Questions of Procedure for Ministers*.

8 *Draft Model Letter of Appointment for Special Advisers*.

9 HC Written Answers, 3 April 1996, col. 250.

10 Stuart Trotter, 'New row over use of civil servants', *Herald*, 21 Nov. 1996.

11 HC Written Answers, 17 Dec. 1996, col. 502.

12 Clare Garner, 'Memo shows Heseltine wanted civil servants to find supporters', *Independent*, 11 Nov. 1996.

13 Donald MacIntyre, 'Hanley slips up again over funding of adviser', *Independent*, 19 Sept. 1994.

14 Public Administration Committee, Minutes of Evidence, 18 July 2000.

15 Interview with John Redwood.

16 Williams, *Guilty Men*, p. 46.

17 See Michael White 'Children of the Gang of Four', *Guardian*, 14 April 1997.

18 HC Written Answers, 18 Nov. 1992, col. 215.

19 HC Written Answers, 29 March 1995, col. 638.

20 Andrew Grice, 'The discreet rise of the SDP', *Sunday Times*, 30 July 1995.

21 HC Written Answers, 1 May 2001, cols 607–8.

22 Lamont, *In Office*, p. 32.

23 HC Written Answers, 30 March 1995, col. 723.

24 Balen, *Kenneth Clarke*, p. 262.

25 McSmith, *Kenneth Clarke*, p. 228.

26 Balen, *Kenneth Clarke*, p. 262.

27 'Pass notes no. 297: Tessa Keswick', *Guardian*, 2 Dec. 1993.

28 Paul Eastham, 'Mystery as Clarke sees his Girl Friday sail away', *Daily Mail*, 25 Feb. 1995.

29 Committee on Standards in Public Life, Public Hearings, 5 July 2002.

30 Ibid.

31 Ibid.

32 Public Administration Committee, Minutes of Evidence, 28 Feb. 2001.

33 HC Written Answers, 1 Dec. 1994, col. 801.

34 *The Best Future for Britain* (Conservative Party, London, 1992).

35 Jon Shaw, 'Designing a Method of Rail Privatisation' in Roger Freeman and Jon Shaw (eds), *All Change, British Railway Privatisation* (McGraw-Hill, Maidenhead, 2000), p. 22.

36 Rebecca Smithers, 'Just read between the lines', *Guardian*, 25 Feb. 1995.

37 See Christian Wolmar, *Broken Rails* (Aurum, London, 2001).

38 Nicholas Faith, 'Breaking up is hard to do', *Independent*, 27 March 1994.

39 Sir Christopher Foster, 'Rationale for railways policy', *Independent*, 3 April 1994.

40 Committee on Standards in Public Life, Public Hearings, 5 July 2002.

41 M. Crick, *Michael Heseltine: A Biography*, p. 309.

42 Committee on Standards in Public Life, Public Hearings, 5 July 2002.

43 Stephen Goodwin, 'Heseltine seeks out "green" advice', *Independent*, 13 March 1991.

44 Michael McCarthy, 'Heseltine to appoint environment adviser', *The Times*, 18 Feb. 1991.

45 Committee on Standards in Public Life, Public Hearings, 5 July 2002.

46 Heseltine, *Life in the Jungle*, pp. 345, 379.

47 Committee on Standards in Public Life, Public Hearings, 5 July 2002.

48 Ibid.

49 'Statement by Mr Tom Burke' to Committee on Standards in Public Life, 5 July 2002.

50 Committee on Standards in Public Life, Public Hearings, 5 July 2002.

51 Heseltine, *Life in the Jungle*, p. 401.

52 'Statement by Mr Tom Burke' to Committee on Standards in Public Life, 5 July 2002.

53 Committee on Standards in Public Life, Public Hearings, 5 July 2002.

54 Heseltine, *Life in the Jungle*, p. 379.

55 Committee on Standards in Public Life, Public Hearings, 5 July 2002.

56 *Hansard*, 2 Nov. 1995, col. 486.

57 'By George there's life after your sell-by date', *Evening Standard*, 19 Nov. 1993.

58 'Ultra-blue Hart keeps life in campaign for Portillo', *Scotland on Sunday*, 11 Sept. 1994.

59 Bernard Gray, 'UK may lease US aircraft instead of updating Tornado', *Financial Times*, 25 Sept. 1995.

60 Colin Brown, 'Revolt on MoD homes sell-off', *Independent*, 26 June 1996.

61 *Hansard, House of Commons Debates*, 23 Jan. 1996, col. 137.

62 Ibid., 2 Nov. 1995, cols 483–4.

63 Major, *The Autobiography*, p. 211.

64 Ibid.

65 Seldon with Baston, *Major: A Political Life*, p. 139.

66 Henry Porter, 'Sarah and the lost horizons', *Evening Standard*, 13 July 1993.

67 Hennessy, *Prime Minister*, p. 447.

68 Ibid.

69 Lamont, *In Office*, p. 322.

70 Hogg and Hill, *Too Close to Call*, pp. 122, 163–82, 64–5. See also *Hansard, House of Commons Debates*, 19 March 1991, cols 180–1.

71 Lamont, *In Office*, p. 44.

72 Seldon with Baston, *Major: A Political Life*, p. 140.

73 Hogg and Hill, *Too Close to Call*, pp. 87–9.

74 Major, *The Autobiography*, p. 666.

75 Hogg and Hill, *Too Close to Call*, pp. 138–62.

76 See Seldon with Baston, *Major: a Political Life*, pp. 309–23.

77 Hogg and Hill, *Too Close to Call*, pp. 187–8.

78 Lamont, *In Office*, pp. 225–6.

79 Major, *The Autobiography*, pp. 329–34, 336, 691, 667–8.

80 Seldon with Baston, *Major: A Political Life*, p. 139.

81 Hogg and Hill, *Too Close to Call*, pp. 27–8, 88 fn.

82 Major, *The Autobiography*, p. 211.

83 Hogg and Hill, *Too Close to Call*, p. 88 fn.

84 Lee et al., *At the Centre of Whitehall*, p. 104.

85 Ibid., pp. 122–4.

86 Seldon with Baston, *Major: A Political Life*, p. 141.

87 Hogg and Hill, *Too Close to Call*, p. 24.

88 Major, *The Autobiography*, p. 212.

89 Porter, 'Sarah and the lost horizons'.

90 H. Williams, *Guilty Men*, p. 37.

91 Hogg and Hill, *Too Close to Call*, pp. 93–4.

92 *The Best Future for Britain* (Conservative Party, London, 1992).

93 Hogg and Hill, *Too Close to Call*, pp. 94–105.

94 Kavanagh, 'A Major Agenda?', p. 10.

95 Hennessy, *The Prime Minister*, pp. 449–50.

96 Andrew Grice and David Smith, 'Tories believe they can rely on Nobody', *Sunday Times*, 12 Nov. 1995.

97 Seldon with Baston, *Major: A Political Life*, p. 542.

98 Major, *The Autobiography*, p. 701.

99 Grice and Smith, 'Tories believe they can rely on Nobody'.

100 Sherman, 'A little grey matter in Downing St.'.

101 Seldon with Baston, *Major: A Political Life*, p. 542.

102 Public Administration Committee, Minutes of Evidence, 22 Nov. 2000.

103 Ibid., 18 July 2000.

104 Hennessy, *The Prime Minister*, pp. 470–2.

105 Committee on Standards in Public Life, Public Hearings, 27 June 2002.

106 Ibid.

107 Michael Portillo, 'When politics spin out of control', *The Times*, 19 March 2003.

108 Public Administration Committee, Minutes of Evidence, 18 July 2000.

109 Major, *The Autobiography*, p. 343.

110 Public Administration Committee, Minutes of Evidence, 18 July 2000.

111 Ibid.

112 Committee on Standards in Public Life, Public Hearings, 5 July 2002.

113 H. Williams, *Guilty Men*, pp. 97–8.

114 Major, *The Autobiography*, p. 621.

115 H. Williams, *Guilty Men*, pp. 97–8.

116 Interview with John Redwood.

117 Sandra Parsons, 'Are these the most powerful women in Britain?', *Daily Mail*, 29 May 1993.

118 Michael White, 'New Treasury political job points to poll preparations', *Guardian*, 11 March 1995.

119 Alan Clark, 'The "feel proud" factor is what Tory voters really need', *Mail on Sunday*, 19 March 1995.

120 Major, *The Autobiography*, pp. 628, 630.

121 HC Written Answers, col. 392, 10 July 1995.

122 Public Administration Committee, Minutes of Evidence, 18 July 2000.

123 H. Williams, *Guilty Men*, pp. 58–60.

124 Seldon with Baston, *Major: A Political Life*, p. 684.

125 *First Report of the Committee on Standards in Public Life*.

126 HC Written Answers, 4 March 1996, col. 5.

127 *Hansard, House of Commons Debates*, 2 Nov 1995, col. 482.

128 'Expensive advice', *Evening Standard*, 7 Dec. 1993.

Chapter 9

1 'Ministers, Special Advisers and the Permanent Civil Service', Memorandum by Lord Armstrong of Ilminster to the Committee on Standards in Public Life, 11 July 2002.

2 Committee on Standards in Public Life, Public Hearings, 27 June 2002.

3 HC Written Answers, 18 July 1997, col. 341.

4 Mandelson and Liddle, *The Blair Revolution*, pp. 235–49.

5 *Special Advisers: Boon or Bane?*, Public Administration Committee.

6 *Ministerial Code* (1997).

7 *Reinforcing Standards: Review of the First Report of the Committee on Standards in Public* Life.

8 Committee on Standards in Public Life, Public Hearings, 5 July 2002.

9 Ibid., 9 July 2002.

10 Liaison Committee, Minutes of Evidence, 16 July 2002.

11 *Model Contract for Special Advisers* (1997).

12 Public Administration Committee, Minutes of Evidence, 23 June 1998.

13 *Ministerial Code* (1997).

14 HC Written Answers, 15 Feb. 1999, col. 39.

15 HC Written Answers, 14 April 1999, col. 239.

16 Ibid.

17 Torcuil Crichton, 'Wendy and Jack', *Sunday Herald*, 5 May 2002.

18 Jean Eaglesham, 'Political adviser's career switch adds to rumpus', *Financial Times*, 13 June 2002.

19 Kirsty Milne and Richard Cockett, 'Who'll do Blair's thinking?', *Sunday Times*, 18 May 1997.

20 Committee on Standards in Public Life, Public Hearings, 1 July 2002.

21 Ibid., 9 July 2002.

22 Committee on Standards in Public Life, Public Hearings, 9 Sept. 2002.

23 Ibid.

24 Ibid.

25 *Special Advisers: Boon or Bane?*, Public Administration Committee.

26 Interview with David Clark; Carr, 'Foreign and Defence Policy', pp. 228–9, 232–5.

27 Interview with David Clark.

28 Committee on Standards in Public Life, Public Hearings, 5 July 2002.

29 Public Administration Committee, Minutes of Evidence, 27 Feb. 2003.

30 Blunkett, *On a Clear Day*, p. 222.

31 Barber, *The Learning Game*, pp. 291, 9, 296.

32 *New Labour: Because Britain Deserves Better* (Labour Party, London, 1997).

33 Committee on Standards in Public Life, Public Hearings, 28 June 2002.

34 Chris Woodhead, 'Blair and Blunkett have not delivered. The children have been betrayed', *Daily Telegraph*, 1 March 2001.

35 Public Administration Committee, Minutes of Evidence, 11 July 2002.

36 Kendall and Holloway, 'Education Policy', p. 172.

37 Committee on Standards in Public Life, Public Hearings, 9 July 2002.

38 N. Jones, *The Control Freaks*, pp. 72–4.

39 N. Jones, *Sultans of Spin*, p. 17.

40 John Carvel, 'New set of brains', *Guardian*, 6 May 1997.

41 N. Jones, *Sultans of Spin*, pp. 74, 78.

42 Public Administration Committee, Minutes of Evidence, 23 June 1998.

43 Ibid., 28 Feb. 2002.

44 Committee on Standards in Public Life, Public Hearings, 9 July 2002.

45 Ibid.

46 Ibid., 9 July 2002.

47 Ibid., 5 July 2002.

48 Ibid., 9 July 2002.

49 N. Jones, *Sultans of Spin*, p. 74.

50 Committee on Standards in Public Life, Public Hearings, 9 July 2002.

51 Ibid., 27 June 2002.

52 N. Jones, *Sultans of Spin*, pp. 83–9.

53 Committee on Standards in Public Life, Public Hearings, 27 June 2002.

54 Alastair Campbell, 'Why it is foolish to forget about loyalty', *Mirror*, 3 July 2000.

55 N. Jones, *Sultans of Spin*, pp. 279–80.

56 Interview with Frank Field.

57 Liaison Committee, Minutes of Evidence, 16 July 2002.

58 Campbell, 'Why it is foolish to forget about loyalty'.

59 Oborne, *Alastair Campbell*, pp. 174–7.

60 N. Jones, *Sultans of Spin*, pp. 126–7.

61 Committee on Standards in Public Life, Public Hearings, 27 June 2002.

62 *Report of the Working Group on the Government Information Service*.

63 Liaison Committee, Minutes of Evidence, 16 July 2002.

64 Hennessy, *The Prime Minister*, p. 477.

65 Andrew Grice, 'All power to the kitchen cabinet', *Sunday Times*, 4 May 1997.

66 Hennessy, *The Prime Minister*, p. 479.

67 Rawnsley, *Servants of the People*, p. 26.

68 Committee on Standards in Public Life, Public Hearings, 27 June 2002.

69 Ibid., 9 July 2002.

70 Ibid., 5 July 2002.

71 Hennessy, *Prime Minister*, pp. 483–4.

72 Public Administration Committee, Minutes of Evidence, 23 June 1998.

73 *Ministerial Code* (1997).

74 *Ministerial Code* (2001).

75 Kavanagh and Seldon, *The Powers behind the Prime Minister*, p. 255.

76 *Report of the Working Group on the Government Information Service*.

77 Public Administration Committee, Minutes of Evidence, 1 Nov. 2001, 'Organisation Chart for No. 10'.

78 Brian Groom, 'President Blair beefs up Downing Street', *Financial Times*, 9 July 2001.

79 Rawnsley, *Servants of the People*, p. 26.

80 Gould, *The Unfinished Revolution*, pp. 243–4.

81 David Miliband, introduction to David Miliband (ed.) *Reinventing the Left* (Polity, Cambridge, 1994), pp. 2, 6.

82 *New Labour: Because Britain Deserves Better*.

83 Dell, *A Strange Eventful History*, p. 568.

84 Robert Shrimsley, 'The Party may be over for the Social Democrats but the spirits linger on', *Financial Times*, 24 Jan. 2001.

85 Rawnsley, *Servants of the People*, p. 74.

86 Kamal Ahmed, Gaby Hinsliff and Martin Bright, 'The Morris resignation', *Observer*, 27 Oct. 2002.

87 Michael White, 'Blair shuns MPs and party chiefs in policy group', *Guardian*, 15 July 1995.

88 James Blitz and David Wighton, 'Policy think-tank set for overhaul', *Financial Times*, 9 May 1997.

89 Jill Sherman, 'Blair adviser switches to Civil Service', *The Times*, 2 Sept. 2000.

90 Liaison Committee, Minutes of Evidence, 16 July 2002.

91 'The faceless wonders', *The Times*, 8 July 1999.

92 'Prescott berates Blair's "faceless wonders"', *The Times*, 8 July 1999.

93 Ahmed et al., 'The Morris resignation'.

94 Ibid.

95 Krishna Guha, 'Blair believes government owes its health to strong heart', *Financial Times*, 15 May 2003.

96 Committee on Standards in Public Life, Public Hearings, 27 June 2002.

97 Catherine Macleod, 'Blair adviser McFadden is by-election front-runner', *Herald*, 30 July 1997.

98 Committee on Standards in Public Life, Public Hearings, 1 July 2002.

99 Ibid.

100 Ibid.

101 Ibid.

102 'Statement from Pat McFadden' to Committee on Standards in Public Life.

103 HC Written Answers, 24 July 2000, cols 442–3.

104 HC Written Answers, 10 Dec. 2002, col. 281.

105 HC Written Answers, 25 Oct. 2001, cols 313–4.

106 David Walker, 'Birt scans blue skies in Blair's strategy unit', *Guardian*, 11 Aug. 2001.

107 Rachel Sylvester, 'Dissent in Civil Service ranks as Blair bring in businessmen', *Daily Telegraph*, 9 Jan. 2002.

108 Public Administration Committee, Minutes of Evidence, 23 June 1998.

109 Interview with Lord Butler.

110 Public Administration Committee, Minutes of Evidence, 23 June 1998.

111 Ibid., 1 Nov. 2000.

112 'Big time for Howard', *Financial Times*, 21 May 1997;

P.H.S., 'Flight plan', *The Times*, 2 May 1997; 'Labour holds its head up in muddy waters', *Financial Times*, 4 June 1997.

113 Jill Sherman, 'School standards chief to beef up Whitehall', *The Times*, 22 June 2001.

114 HC Written Answers, 12 Nov. 2001, col. 547.

115 Public Administration Committee, Minutes of Evidence, 1 Nov. 2000.

116 Committee on Standards in Public Life, Public Hearings, 5 July 2002.

117 Ibid., 9 July 2002.

118 Ibid.

119 'Memorandum', Alastair Campbell to Foreign Affairs Select Committee, 24 June 2003.

120 'Ministers, Special Advisers and the Permanent Civil Service', Memorandum by Lord Armstrong of Ilminster to the Committee on Standards in Public Life, 11 July 2002.

121 Committee on Standards in Public Life, Public Hearings, 28 June 2002.

122 Ibid., 9 July 2002.

123 Ibid., 1 July 2002.

124 Rawnsley, *Servants of the People*, p. 27.

125 Ibid., p. 225.

126 John Deans, 'Assault on the Blair bunker', *Daily Mail*, 11 Aug. 1995.

127 Gould, *The Unfinished Revolution*, p. 177.

128 Rawnsley, *Servants of the People*, p. 27.

129 Rentoul, *Tony Blair*, p. 537.

130 Kavanagh and Seldon, *The Powers behind the Prime Minister*, pp. 255, 252.

131 Andrew Grice, 'All power to the kitchen cabinet', *Sunday Times*, 4 May 1997.

132 Rawnsley, *Servants of the People*, pp. 169–70, 137.

133 Interview with Lord Butler.

134 Public Administration Committee, Minutes of Evidence, 9 Feb. 2000, annex A.

135 Ibid., 1 Nov. 2000.

136 Ibid., 'Organisation Chart for No. 10'.

137 Public Administration Committee, Minutes of Evidence, 1 Nov. 2000.

138 Gould, *The Unfinished Revolution*, p. 219.

139 Rawnsley, *Servants of the People*, p. 61.

140 Oborne, *Alastair Campbell*, pp. 10, 4.

141 Stothard, *30 Days*, pp. 18–19.

142 Bill Hagerty, 'More spinned against?', *The Times*, 12 June 2000.

143 Hennessy, *The Prime Minister*, p. 488.

144 Oborne, *Alastair Campbell*, pp. 65–84.

145 Gould, *The Unfinished Revolution*, pp. 221–2.

146 Barratt Brown and Coates, *The Blair Revelation*, p. 6.

147 Public Administration Committee, Minutes of Evidence, 23 June 1998.

148 N. Jones, *Sultans of Spin*, pp. 208–10.

149 Public Administration Committee, Minutes of Evidence, 23 June 1998.

150 Campbell, 'Why it is foolish to forget about loyalty'.

151 Public Administration Committee, Minutes of Evidence, 23 June 1998.

152 Ibid.

153 Rawnsley, *Servants of the People*, p. 150.

154 Public Administration Committee, Minutes of Evidence, 23 June 1998.

155 Campbell, 'Why it is foolish to forget about loyalty'.

156 Public Administration Committee, Minutes of Evidence, 16 June 1998.

157 Ibid.

158 Public Administration Committee, Minutes of Evidence, 23 June 1998.

159 Hagerty, 'More spinned against?'

160 N. Jones, *The Control Freaks*, pp. 99–109, 267–8, 110–15.

161 Oborne, *Alastair Campbell*, p. 204.

162 Public Administration Committee, Minutes of Evidence, 16 June 1998.

163 Ibid., 23 June 1998.

164 Hagerty, 'More spinned against?'

165 Public Administration Committee, Minutes of Evidence, 23 June 1998.

166 Ibid., 1 Nov. 2000.

167 Michael White, 'No. 10 to challenge Tory media's funeral jibes', *Guardian*, 17 April 2002.

168 Committee on Standards in Public Life, Public Hearings, 9 July 2002.

169 Hennessy, *The Prime Minister*, pp. 477, 480, 479, 487.

170 Robinson, *The Unconventional Minister*, pp. 32–3.

171 Routledge, *Gordon Brown*, pp. 183, 207, 286.

172 Naughtie, *The Rivals*, p. 247.

173 See Balls, 'Open Macroeconomics in an Open Economy', pp. 188–9.

174 Rawnsley, *Servants of the People*, p. 46.

175 Robert Chote, 'A Chancellor in a hurry', *Financial Times*, 24 May 1997.

176 Michael White, 'Blair acts on "cronyism" culture', *Guardian*, 13 July 1998.

177 Committee on Standards in Public Life, Public Hearings, 9 July 2002.

178 Oborne, *Alastair Campbell*, p. 162.

179 Rawnsley, *Servants of the People*, p. 165.

180 Oborne, *Alastair Campbell*, p. 164.

181 Kevin Maguire and Will Woodward, 'They spun it, they wun it', *Mirror*, 3 May 1997.

182 N. Jones, *Sultans of Spin*, pp. 261, 273–5.

183 Ibid., p. 278.

184 Charlie Whelan, 'Time No. 10 cleaned up old pals act', *Mirror*, 3 July 2000.

185 'Mammon: Super-brain with keen eye for the puzzle of power', *Observer*, 11 May 1997.

186 Interview with David Clark.

187 Paul Routledge, 'Ed Balls – Brown's young egghead', *Independent on Sunday*, 8 March 1998.

188 'Mammon: Super-brain with keen eye for the puzzle of power'.

189 David Wighton and Christopher Adams, 'Brown aide elevated to top economic position', *Financial Times*, 23 Oct. 1999.

190 Balls, 'Open Macroeconomics in an Open Economy', pp. 118, 113–32, 115, 118, 116.

191 Balls, *Euro-Monetarism*, p. 16.

192 Balls, 'Open Macroeconomics in an Open Economy', p. 116.

193 Routledge, 'Ed Balls – Brown's young egghead'.

194 Robinson, *The Unconventional Minister*, pp. 59, 131.

195 For Brown's exposition of this, see *Hansard, House of Commons Debates*, 20 May 1997, cols 508–12.

196 Balls, *Euro-Monetarism*, p. 18.

197 Robinson, *The Unconventional Minister*, pp. 37–8.

198 Balls, 'Open Macroeconomics in an Open Economy', pp. 129–30.

199 Thomas, 'UK Economic Policy', pp. 65–6.

200 Treasury press notices; Committee on Standards in Public Life, Public Hearings, 5 July 2002.

Chapter 10

1 Pimlott, *Harold Wilson*, p. 338.

2 See e.g. Smith, *The Core Executive in Britain*.

3 For a full exposition of the theory, see Foley, *The Rise of the British Presidency*.

4 *Government Response to the Public Administration Select Committee's Eighth Report of the 2001–02 Session, 'These Unfortunate Events'*.

5 *Defining the Boundaries within the Executive*, Committee on Standards in Public Life, Ninth Report.

6 Marie Woolf, 'Powers of Blair aides "should be reduced"', *Independent*, 9 April 2003.

7 Andrew Sparrow, 'Whitehall watchdogs calls for curbs on Campbell', *Daily Telegraph*, 9 April 2003.

8 Peter Riddell, 'Prime Minister must accept proposals or continue to be mired in sleaze', *The Times*, 9 April 2003.

9 *Hansard, House of Commons Debates*, 12 May 2003, col. 38.

10 http://www.davidicke.net/newsroom/europe/england-/092201a.html.

11 'Ministers, Special Advisers and the Permanent Civil Service', Memorandum by Lord Armstrong of Ilminster to the Committee on Standards in Public Life, 11 July 2002.

12 Committee on Standards in Public Life, Public Hearings, 9 July 2002.

13 S. B. Chrimes, *English Constitutional History* (Oxford University Press, Oxford, 1965), pp. 10, 34.

Note on historiography and sources

1 George Jones, 'Harold Wilson's Policy-Makers', *Spectator*, 6 July 1974.

2 Donoughue, *The Heat of the Kitchen*, pp. 220–1.

3 See e.g. G. W. Jones, 'The Prime Minister's Aides'.

4 Klein and Lewis, 'Advice and Dissent in British Government', pp. 1–25, 2–3.

5 Mitchell, 'Special Advisers: A Personal View', pp. 87–98, 89, 97.

6 Willetts, 'The Role of the Prime Minister's Policy Unit'.

7 Donoughue, 'The Conduct of Economic Policy 1974–79'.

Bibliography

Unpublished primary sources

Public Record Office, Kew

CAB128	Cabinet minutes
CAB129	Cabinet memoranda
CAB130	Ad hoc Cabinet Committees, General and Miscellaneous Series
CAB134	Cabinet Committees: General Series from 1945
CAB147	Cabinet Office, Economic Adviser to the Prime Minister, Records
CAB152	Cabinet Office: Social Services Co-ordinating Staff: Files
CAB160	Cabinet Office: Personal Files
CAB 184	Central Policy Review Staff: Files
EW 3	Department of Economic Affairs: Private Office: Registered Files
EW28	Department of Economic Affairs: First Secretary of State and Secretary of State for Economic Affairs
MH104	Committee of Inquiry into the Pharmaceutical Industry (Sainsbury Committee): Minutes, Papers and Reports
MH166	Ministry of Health and Department of Health and Social Security: Hospital Construction, Registered Files
MT160	Ministry of Transport, Transport Policy General Division: Registered Files
PIN 13	Ministry of National Insurance, predecessors and successors: Determinations under the National Insurance Acts
PREM 5	Prime Minister's Office Ministerial Appointments
PREM 11	Prime Minister's Office
PREM 13	Prime Minister's Office
PREM 15	Prime Minister's Office
T160	Treasury Finance Department
T171	Chancellor of the Exchequer's Office: Budget and Finance Bill Papers
T199	Treasury: Establishment Officer's Branch: Registered Files
T230	Treasury Economic Section
T247	Treasury, Papers of Lord Keynes
T312	Treasury Overseas Finance Division
T320	Treasury: Public Income/Outlay Division: Registered Files
T328	Treasury: Fiscal and Incomes Policy Division and successors: Registered Files

Institutional papers

Co-efficients Collection, LSE, London
Fabian Society Collection, LSE, London
Centre for Policy Studies Collection, LSE, London

Private papers

Abel-Smith, Brian, LSE, London
Beveridge, William, LSE, London
Brittan, Samuel, LSE, London

Crosland, Anthony, LSE, London
Dalton, Hugh, LSE, London
Durbin, Evan, LSE, London
Holland, Stuart, private papers, selection supplied to author
Holland, S. 'Britain and Europe since 1945', paper presented to Institute of Contemporary British History Seminar, Institute of Historical Research, 26 March 1997, updated version
Holland, S. 'Special Advisers and Security', written statement to author, 16 July 2002
Kaldor, Nicholas, King's College, Cambridge
Titmuss, Richard, LSE, London
Wigg, George, LSE, London

Interviews

Lord Armstrong, 27 March 2003
Beckerman, Wilfred, 15 June 2001
Berrill, Sir Kenneth, 21 June 2001
Brittan, Sir Samuel, 10 August 2000
Lord Butler, 5 June 2003
Clark, David, 11 March 2003
Lord Croham, 5 July 2001
Lord Donoughue, 16 July 2002
Field, Frank, 25 March 2003
Foster, Sir Christopher, 3 April 2001
Graham, Andrew, 13 June 2003
Lord Griffiths, 9 October 2003
Lord Harris, 6 March 2001
Holland, Stuart, 15 March 2001
Lord Howell, 25 June 2003
Jackson, Robert, 10 April 2003
MacDougall, Sir Donald, 9 March 2001
Lord McNally, 5 July 2002
Lord Marlesford, 10 March 2003
Lord Marsh, 3 July 2001
Mitchell, Sir Derek, 19 April 2001
Morris, June, 31 May 2001
Neild, Robert, 16 July 2001
Palliser, Sir Michael, 12 July 2001
Posner, Michael, 2 July 2001
Redwood, John, 7 April 2003
Ridley, Sir Adam, 12 August 2003
Lord Sheldon, 12 March 2003
Lord Shore, 13 December 2000
Thirlwall, Anthony, 12 July 2002
Tyrie, Andrew, 10 April 2003
Wass, Sir Douglas, 18 June 2001
Lord Young, 23 June 2003

Published primary sources

Official

Civil Servants and Ministers: Duties and Responsibilities, Treasury and Civil Service Select Committee, HC 92 (HMSO, London, 1986)
The Civil Service, Expenditure Committee, HC 535 (HMSO, London, 1977)
The Civil Service, vol. 1, *Report of the Committee 1966–68*, Cmnd 3638 (HMSO, London, 1968)
Civil Service Yearbook (HMSO, London), various editions from 1973

The Decision to Go to War in Iraq, Foreign Affairs Select Committee (HMSO, London, 2003), HC813–I.

Defining the Boundaries within the Executive: Ministers, Special Advisers and the permanent Civil Service, Committee on Standards in Public Life, Ninth Report, Cm 5775 (HMSO, London, 2003)

Draft Model Letter of Appointment for Special Advisers (House of Commons Library, 1995)

First Report of the Committee on Standards in Public Life (HMSO, London, 1995) Cm 2850

The Government Information and Communication Service, Public Administration Committee, HC 770 (HMSO, London, 1998)

Government Response to the Public Administration Select Committee's Eighth Report of the 2001–02 Session, 'These Unfortunate Events', Cm 5756 (Cabinet Office, London, 2003)

The Government's Response to the Sixth Report from the Committee on Standards in Public Life, Cm 4817 (Stationery Office, London, 2000)

Guidance on the Work of the Government Information Service (Cabinet Office, London, 1997)

Hansard, House of Commons Debates, various

Imperial Calendar (HMSO, London), various editions 1965–72

Improving Management in Government: The Next Steps, Efficiency Unit, Report to the Prime Minister (HMSO, London, 1988)

Ministerial Code (Cabinet Office, London, 1997)

Ministerial Code: A Code of Conduct and Guidance on Procedures for Ministers (Cabinet Office, London, 2001)

Model Contract for Special Advisers (Cabinet Office, London, 1997)

Model Contract for Special Advisers (Cabinet Office, London, 2001)

National Superannuation and Social Insurance, Cmnd 3883 (HMSO, London, 1969)

Principal Memoranda of Evidence Submitted to the Committee on the Working of the Monetary System (HMSO, London, 1960)

Questions of Procedure for Ministers (Cabinet Office, London, 1992)

The Reorganisation of Central Government, Cmnd 4506 (HMSO, London, 1970)

Reinforcing Standards: Review of the First Report of the Committee on Standards in Public Life, Sixth Report of the Committee on Standards in Public Life, Cmnd 4557–1 (HMSO, London, January 2000)

Report of the Working Group on the Government Information Service (Cabinet Office, London, 1997)

Special Advisers: Boon or Bane?, Public Administration Committee, HC 293 (HMSO, London, 2001)

'These Unfortunate Events': Lessons of Recent Events at the Former DTLR, Public Administration Committee, HC 303 (HMSO, London, 2002)

Books and pamphlets

Abel-Smith, B. and Townsend, P. *New Pensions for the Old* (Fabian Society, London, 1955)

The Administrators (Fabian Society, London, 1964)

Balogh, T. *Fact and Fancy in International Economic Relations* (Pergamon, Oxford, 1973)

Balogh, T. *Planning for Progress: A Strategy for Labour* (Fabian Society, London, 1963)

Balogh, T. *Unequal Partners*, 2 vols (Basil Blackwell, Oxford, 1963)

Barber, M. *The Learning Game: Arguments for an Education Revolution* (Victor Gollancz, London, 1996)

Beckerman, W. *Growth, the Environment and the Distribution of Incomes* (Edward Elgar, Aldershot, 1995)

Bridges, E. *Portrait of a Profession: The Civil Service Tradition* (Cambridge University Press, Cambridge, 1950)

Bridges, E. *The Treasury* (Allen & Unwin, London, 1964)

Bridges, E. *Treasury Control* (Athlone, London, 1950)

Brittan, S. *The Treasury under the Tories, 1951–1964* (Penguin, Harmondsworth, 1964)

Brittenden, F. *A Guide to the Selective Employment Tax* (Butterworths, London, 1966)

Chapman, B. *British Government Observed* (Allen & Unwin, London, 1963)

Chester, D. N. (ed.), *Lessons of the British War Economy* (Cambridge University Press, Cambridge, 1951)

Crossman, R. *Inside View* (Jonathan Cape, London, 1972)

Crossman, R. *Planning for Freedom* (Hamish Hamilton, London, 1965)

George, C. and Bewlay, S. *Advice – and Dissent, Two Men of Influence: A New Look at Professor Kaldor and Professor Balogh* (Aims of Industry, London, 1964)

Kaldor, N. *Essays on Economic Policy*, vol. 2 (Gerald Duckworth, London, 1964)

Laski, H. *A Grammar of Politics* (Allen & Unwin, London, 1925)

Laski, H. *The Limitations of the Expert* (Fabian Society, London, 1931)

Laski, H. *Parliamentary Government in England* (Allen & Unwin, London, 1938)

Lipsey, D. (ed.) *Making Government Work* (Fabian Society, London, 1982)

Mandelson, P. and Liddle, R. *The Blair Revolution: Can New Labour Deliver?* (Faber, London and Boston, 1996)

Miliband, D. (ed.) *Reinventing the Left* (Polity, Cambridge, 1994)

National Superannuation (Labour Party, London, 1957)

The Reform of the Higher Civil Service (Fabian Society, London, 1947)

Sampson, A. *Anatomy of Britain* (Hodder & Stoughton, London, 1962)

Sampson, A. *The New Europeans* (Hodder & Stoughton, London, 1968)

Schacht, H. *My First Seventy-Six Years* (Allan & Wingate, London, 1955)

Sewill, B. 'A View from the Inside: In Place of Strikes', in *British Economic Policy 1970–74* (Institute of Economic Affairs, London, 1975)

Targetti, F. and Thirlwall, A. (eds) *The Essential Kaldor* (Duckworth, London, 1989)

Thomas, H. (ed.) *The Establishment: A Symposium* (Anthony Blond, London, 1959)

Webb, S. *Twentieth Century Politics: A Policy of National Efficiency* (Fabian Society, London, 1901)

Webb, S. and Webb, B. *A Constitution for the Socialist Commonwealth of Great Britain* (London School of Economics and Political Science, London, 1975)

Wells, H. *The Shape of Things to Come: The Ultimate Revolution* (J. M. Dent, London, 1993)

Whitehall and Beyond (BBC, London, 1964)

Memoirs and diaries

Attlee, C. *As It Happened* (London: Odhams, 1956)

Baker, B. *The Turbulent Years: My Life in Politics* (Faber, London, 1993)

Benn, T. *Against the Tide: Diaries 1973–76* (Arrow, London, 1989)

Benn, T. *Conflicts of Interest: Diaries 1977–80* (Arrow, London, 1990)

Benn, T. *Office without Power: Diaries 1968–72* (Arrow, London, 1989)

Benn, T. *Out of the Wilderness: Diaries, 1963–1967* (Arrow, London, 1988)

Benn, T. *Years of Hope, Diaries 1940–1962* (Hutchinson, London, 1994)

Blunkett, D. *On a Clear Day* (Michael O'Mara, London, 2002)

Brown, G. *In My Way: The Political Memoirs of Lord George-Brown* (Pelican, Harmondsworth, 1972)

Cairncross, A. *The Wilson Years: A Treasury Diary, 1964–1969* (Historians' Press, London, 1997)

Callaghan, J. *Time and Chance* (Collins, London, 1987)

Castle, B. *The Castle Diaries, 1964–1970* (Weidenfeld & Nicolson, London, 1984)

Castle, B. *The Castle Diaries, 1974–1976* (Weidenfeld & Nicolson, London, 1980)

Castle, B. *Fighting All the Way* (Macmillan, London and Basingstoke, 1993)

Churchill, W. *The Second World War*, vol. 1: *The Gathering Storm* (London: Folio Society, 2000)

Crossman, R. *The Backbench Diaries of Richard Crossman*, ed. J. Morgan (Hamish Hamilton and Jonathan Cape, London, 1981)

Crossman, R. *The Diaries of a Cabinet Minister*, vol. 1: *Minister of Housing, 1964–1966* (Hamish Hamilton and Jonathan Cape, London, 1975)

Crossman, R. *The Diaries of a Cabinet Minister*, vol. 2, *Lord President of the Council and Leader of the House of Commons, 1966–1968* (Hamish Hamilton and Jonathan Cape, London, 1976)

Crossman, R. *The Diaries of a Cabinet Minister*, vol. 3: *Secretary of State for Social Services 1968–70* (Hamish Hamilton and Jonathan Cape, London, 1977)

Dalton, H. *The Fateful Years, 1931–1945* (Frederick Muller, London, 1957)

Dalton, H. *The Political Diary of Hugh Dalton, 1918–40, 1945–60*, ed. Ben Pimlott (Jonathan Cape, London, 1986)

Donoughue, B. *The Heat of the Kitchen* (Politico's, London, 2003)

Falkender, M. *Downing Street in Perspective* (Weidenfeld & Nicolson, London, 1983)

Fowler, N. *Ministers Decide* (Chapmans, London, 1991)

Gaitskell, H. *The Diary of Hugh Gaitskell, 1945–1956*, ed. Philip M. Williams (Jonathan Cape, London, 1983)

Gordon Walker, P. *Political Diaries*, ed. R. Pearce (Historians' Press, London, 1991)

Gould, P. *The Unfinished Revolution* (Little, Brown, London, 1998)

Haines, J. *The Politics of Power*, (Jonathan Cape, London, 1977)

Hall, R. *The Robert Hall Diaries, 1954–61*, ed. Alec Cairncross (Unwin Hyman, London, 1991)

Healey, D. *The Time of My Life* (Penguin, Harmondsworth, 1990)

Heseltine, M. *Life in the Jungle* (Hodder & Stoughton, London, 2000)

Hoskyns, J. *Just in Time: Inside the Thatcher Revolution* (Aurum, London, 2000)

Howe, G. *Conflict of Loyalty* (Macmillan, London, 1994)

Howell, D. *The Edge of Now* (Macmillan, London, 2000)

Hurd, D. *An End to Promises: Sketch of a Government 1970–74* (Collins, London, 1979)

Jay, D. *Change and Fortune: A Political Record* (Hutchinson, London, 1980)

Jenkins, R. *A Life at the Centre* (Papermac, London, 1994)

Lamont, N. *In Office* (Little, Brown, London, 1999)

Lansbury, G. *My England* (Selwyn & Blount, London, 1934)

Lawson, N. *The View From No. 11* (Corgi, London, 1993)

MacDougall, D. *Don and Mandarin: Memoirs of an Economist* (John Murray, London, 1987)

Macmillan, H. *Riding the Storm, 1956–59* (Macmillan, London, 1971)

Major, J. *The Autobiography* (HarperCollins, London, 2000)

Owen, D. *Face the Future* (Jonathan Cape, London, 1981)

Owen, D. *Time to Declare* (Penguin, Harmondsworth, 1992)

Plowden, E. *An Industrialist in the Treasury: The Post-War Years* (Andre Deutsch, London, 1989)

Rothschild, Lord, *Meditations of a Broomstick* (Collins, London, 1977)

Tebbit, N. *Upwardly Mobile* (Futura, London and Sydney, 1989)

Thatcher, M. *The Downing Street Years, 1979–90: First Volume of the Memoirs of Margaret Thatcher* (HarperCollins, London, 1993)

Thatcher, M. *The Path to Power* (HarperCollins, London, 1995)

Whitlam, G. *The Whitlam Government, 1972–1975* (Viking, Ringwood, 1985)

Wigg, G. *George Wigg* (Michael Joseph, London, 1972)

Williams, H. *Guilty Men: Conservative Decline and Fall* (Aurum, London, 1998)

Williams, M. *Inside Number 10* (Weidenfeld & Nicolson, London, 1972)

Wilson, H. *Final Term* (Weidenfeld & Nicolson and Michael Joseph, London, 1979)

Wilson, H., *The Governance of Britain* (Sphere, London, 1977)

Wilson, H., *The Labour Government 1964–1970: A Personal Record* (Weidenfeld & Nicolson, London, 1974)

Wilson, H. *Memoirs: The Making of a Prime Minister 1916–64* (Weidenfeld & Nicolson and Michael Joseph, London, 1986)

Wilson, H., *Purpose in Politics: Selected Speeches by Rt Hon Harold Wilson* (Weidenfeld & Nicolson, London, 1964)

Lord Young, *The Enterprise Years: A Businessman in the Cabinet* (Headline, London, 1991)

Secondary works

Addison, P. *British Historians and the Debate over the 'Post-War Consensus'* (Harry Ransom Humanities Research Centre, Austin, 1996)

Addison, P. *The Road to 1945* (Pimlico, London, 1994)

Allen, G. *The Last Prime Minister* (Graham Allen, London, 2001)

Andrew, C. and Mitrokhin, V. *The Mitrokhin Archive: The KGB in Europe and the West* (Allen Lane, London, 1999)

Annan, N. *Leslie Stephen, The Godless Victorian* (Weidenfeld & Nicolson, London, 1984)

Baker, A. *Prime Ministers and the Rule Book* (Politico's, London, 2000)

Balen, B. *Kenneth Clarke* (Fourth Estate, London, 1994)

Balls, E. *Euro-Monetarism: Why Britain was Ensnared and How it Should Escape* (Fabian Society, London, 1992)

Balls, 'Open Macroeconomics in an Open Economy', *Scottish Journal of Political Economy*, vol. 45, 1998

Balogh, T. 'The Apotheosis of the Dilettante', in H. Thomas (ed.), *The Establishment: A Symposium* (Anthony Blond, London, 1959)

Balogh, T. 'Keynes and the International Monetary Fund', in A. Thirlwall (ed.), *Keynes and International Monetary Relations* (Macmillan, London and Basingstoke, 1976)

Barberis, P. *The Elite of the Elite: Permanent Secretaries in the British Higher Civil Service* (Dartmouth, Aldershot, 1996)

Barratt Brown, M. and Coates, K. *The Blair Revelation* (Spokesman, Nottingham, 1996)

Beckerman, W. *Growth, the Environment and the Distribution of Incomes* (Aldershot: Edward Elgar, 1995)

Blackstone, T. and Plowden, W. *Inside the Think Tank: Advising the Cabinet 1971–1983* (Mandarin, London, 1990)

Booker, C. *The Neophiliacs* (Pimlico, London, 1992)

Booth, A. *The British Economy in the Twentieth Century* (Palgrave, Basingstoke, 2001)

Brittan, S. 'The Irregulars', in Richard Rose (ed.), *Policy Making in Britain: A Reader in Government* (Macmillan, London, 1969)

Butler, D., Adonis, A. and Travers, T. *Failure in British Government* (Oxford University Press, Oxford, 1994)

Butler D. and Pinto-Duschinsky, M. *The British General Election of 1970* (Macmillan, London, 1971)

Cairncross, A. *The British Economy since 1945* (Blackwell, Oxford, 1992)

Cairncross, A. 'Economic Advisers in the United Kingdom', *Contemporary British History*, vol. 13, no. 2, Summer 1999

Cairncross, A. *Managing the Economy in the 1960s: A Treasury Perspective* (Macmillan, London, 1996)

Cairncross, A. *Years of Recovery, British Economic Policy 1945–51* (Methuen, London, 1985)

Cairncross, A. and Watts, N., *The Economic Section 1939–1961* (Routledge, London and New York, 1989)

Callaghan, J. 'The Left and the "Unfinished Revolution": Bevanites and Soviet Russia in the 1950s', *Contemporary British History*, vol. 15, no. 3, Autumn 2001

Callaghan, J. 'Rise and Fall of the Alternative Economic Strategy: From Internationalisation of Capital to "Globalisation"', *Contemporary British History*, vol. 14, no. 3, Autumn 2000

Campbell, J. *Edward Heath, A Biography* (Pimlico, London, 1994)

Carr, F. 'Foreign and Defence Policy', in Stephen P. Savage and Rob Atkinson (eds), *Public Policy under Blair* (Palgrave, Basingstoke, 2001)

Chapman, R. and Greenaway, J., *The Dynamics of Administrative Reform* (Croom Helm, London, 1980)

Cockett, R. *Thinking the Unthinkable: Think Tanks and the Economic Counter-Revolution, 1931–1983* (Fontana, London, 1995)

Coopey, R., Fielding, S. and Tiratsoo, N. (eds) *The Wilson Governments 1964–70* (Pinter, London, 1993)

Crick, B. *George Orwell: A Life* (Penguin, London, 1992)

Crick, M. *Michael Heseltine, A Biography* (Penguin, London, 1997)

Crosland, S. *Tony Crosland* (Coronet, Sevenoaks, 1983)

Crozier, B. *Free Agent: The Unseen War 1941–1991* (HarperCollins, London, 1994)s

Dell, E. *The Chancellors: A History of the Chancellors of the Exchequer, 1945–1990* (HarperCollins, London, 1996)

Dell, E. *A Strange Eventful History* (HarperCollins, London, 1999)

Donajgrodzki, A. P. 'New Roles for Old: The Northcote–Trevelyan Report and the clerks of the Home Office 1822–48' in G. Sutherland (ed.), *Studies in the Growth of Nineteenth Century Government* (Routledge & Kegan Paul, London, 1972)

Donoughue, B. 'The Conduct of Economic Policy 1974–79', in A. King (ed.), *The British Prime Minister* (Macmillan, Basingstoke and London, 1985)

Donoughue, B. *Prime Minister* (Jonathan Cape, London, 1987)

Elton, G. R. *England under the Tudors* (Methuen, London, 1974)

Favretto, I. '"Wilsonism" Reconsidered: Labour Party Revisionism 1952–64', *Contemporary British History*, vol. 14, no. 4, Winter 2000

Foley, M., *The Rise of the British Presidency* (Manchester University Press, Manchester, 1993)

Freedman, D. 'Modernising the BBC: Wilson's Government and Television 1964–66', *Contemporary British History*, vol. 15, no. 1, Spring 2001

Fry, G. *Reforming the Civil Service* (Edinburgh University Press, Edinburgh, 1993)

Fry, G. *Statesmen in Disguise* (Macmillan, London, 1969)

Glennerster, H. *British Social Policy since 1945* (Blackwell, Oxford, 1995)

Graham, A. 'Impartiality and Bias in Economics' in A Montefiore, (ed.), *Neutrality and Impartiality: The University and Political Commitment* (Cambridge University Press, Cambridge, 1975)

Graham, A. 'Thomas Balogh (1905–1985)', *Contemporary Record*, vol. 6, no. 1, Summer 1992

Harris, J., *William Beveridge: A Biography* (Clarendon Press, Oxford, 1977)

Harrod, R. *The Life of John Maynard Keynes* (Norton, New York and London, 1982)

Harrod, R. F. *The Prof: A Personal Memoir of Lord Cherwell* (Macmillan, London, 1959)

Heath, E. *The Course of My Life: My Autobiography* (Hodder & Stoughton, London, 1998)

Hennessy, P. 'The Attlee Governments, 1945–1951' in P. Hennessy and A. Seldon (eds), *Ruling Performance: British Governments from Attlee to Thatcher* (Blackwell, Oxford, 1989)

Hennessy, P. *Cabinet* (Blackwell, Oxford, 1986)

Hennessy, P. *The Great and the Good: An Inquiry into the British Establishment* (Policy Studies Institute, London, 1986)

Hennessy, P. *Muddling Through: Power, Politics and the Quality of Government in Post-War Britain* (Victor Gollancz, London, 1996)

Hennessy, P. *The Prime Minister: The Office and its Holders since 1945* (Penguin, London, 2001)

Hennessy, P. *Whitehall* (Pimlico, London, 2001)

Hicks, J., 'The Assumption of Constant Returns to Scale' in T. Lawson, J. Palma and J. Sender (eds), *Kaldor's Political Economy* (Academic Press, London, 1989)

Hogg, S. and Hill, J. *Too Close to Call* (Warner, London, 1996)

Hollingsworth, M. *The Ultimate Spin Doctor: The Life and Fast Times of Tim Bell* (Coronet, London, 1997)

Howard, A. and West, R. *The Making of the Prime Minister* (Jonathan Cape, London, 1965)

Howson. S. and Winch, D. *The Economic Advisory Council, 1930–1939: A Study in Economic Advice during Depression and Recovery* (Cambridge University Press, Cambridge, 1977)

James, S. *British Cabinet Government* (Routledge, London, 1999)

Jones, G. 'Harold Wilson's Policy-Makers', *Spectator*, 6 July 1974

Jones, G. W. 'The Downfall of Margaret Thatcher', in R. A. W. Rhodes and Patrick Dunleavy (eds), *Prime Minister, Cabinet and Core Executive* (Macmillan, Basingstoke, 1995)

Jones, G. W. 'The Prime Ministers's Aides', in Anthony King (ed.), *The British Prime Minister* (Macmillan, Basingstoke and London, 1985)

Jones, N. *The Control Freaks* (London, Politico's, 2002)

Jones, N. *Sultans of Spin: The Media and the New Labour Government* (Orion, London, 1999)

Jones, T. '"Taking Genesis Out of the Bible": Hugh Gaitskell, Clause IV and the Socialist Myth', *Contemporary British History*, vol. 11, no. 2, Summer 1997

Kaldor, N. 'The Case for Regional Policies', in F. Targetti and A. Thirlwall (eds) *The Essential Kaldor* (Duckworth, London, 1989)

Kaldor, N. 'Causes of the Slow Rate of Growth in the UK' in F. Targetti and A. Thirlwall (eds) *The Essential Kaldor* (Duckworth, London, 1989)

Kaldor, N. 'Foreign Trade and the Balance of Payments', in *Essays on Economic Policy*, vol. 2 (Duckworth, London, 1964)

Kavanagh, D. 'A Major Agenda?', in Dennis Kavanagh and Anthony Seldon, *The Major Effect* (Macmillan, London, 1994)

Kavanagh, D. and Seldon, A. *The Powers behind the Prime Minister* (HarperCollins, London, 1999)

Kendall, I. and Holloway, D. 'Education Policy', in Stephen P. Savage and Rob Atkinson (eds), *Public Policy under Blair* (Palgrave, Basingstoke, 2001)

Klein, R. and Lewis, J. 'Advice and Dissent in British Government: The Case of the Special Advisers', *Policy and Politics*, vol. 6, Autumn 1977

Lawson, T., Palma, J. and Sender, J. 'Kaldor's Contribution to Economics: An Introduction' in *Kaldor's Political Economy* (Academic Press, London, 1989)

Lee, J., Jones, G. and Burnham, J. *At the Centre of Whitehall* (Macmillan, London, 1998)

Lloyd George, F. *The Years that are Past* (Hutchinson, London, 1967)

MacDougall, D. 'The Prime Minister's Statistical Section' in D. N. Chester (ed.), *Lessons of the British War Economy* (Cambridge University Press, Cambridge, 1951)

McKenna, J. 'The Labour Party and the Second Application', paper presented to Contemporary British History Seminar, Institute of Historical Research, 20 May 2001

McLaine, I. *Ministry of Morale* (Allen & Unwin, London, 1979)

McSmith, A. *Kenneth Clarke: A Political Biography* (Verso, London and New York, 1994)

Marquand, D. *Ramsay MacDonald*, (Richard Cohen, London, 1997)

Matthew, H. C. G. *Gladstone, 1809–1874* (Oxford University Press, Oxford, 1988)

Miliband, R. *Parliamentary Socialism: A Study in the Politics of Labour* (Merlin, London, 1972)

Milward, A. S. *War, Economy and Society, 1939–1945* (Penguin, Harmondsworth, 1987)

Mitchell, J. 'Special Advisers: A Personal View', *Public Administration*, vol. 56, 1978

Morgan, K. *Callaghan: A Life* (Oxford University Press, Oxford, 1997)

Morgan, K. O. *Labour in Power, 1945–1951* (Clarendon, Oxford, 1984)

Morgan, K. O. *The People's Peace: British History since 1945* (Oxford University Press, Oxford, 1999)

Morris, J. 'Thomas Balogh and the Fight for North Sea Revenue', *Contemporary British History*, vol. 12, no. 2, Summer 1998

Naughtie, J. *The Rivals* (Fourth Estate, London, 2001)

Oborne, P. *Alastair Campbell: New Labour and the Rise of the Media Class* (Aurum, London, 1999)

Parris, H. *Constitutional Bureaucracy: The Development of British Central Administration since the Eighteenth Century* (Allen & Unwin, London, 1969)

Peden, G. C. *Keynes, the Treasury and British Economic Policy* (Macmillan, Basingstoke, 1988)

Pimlott, B. *Harold Wilson* (HarperCollins, London, 1992)

Plowden, W. (ed.) *Advising the Rulers* (Blackwell, London, 1987)

Porter, D. 'Downhill All the Way: Thirteen Tory Years 1951–64', in R. Coopey, S. Fielding and N. Tiratsoo (eds) *The Wilson Governments, 1964–1970* (Pinter, London, 1993)

Pryke, R. *Though Cowards Flinch: An Alternative Economic Policy* (MacGibbon & Kee, London, 1967)

Radice, G. *Friends and Rivals* (Little, Brown, London, 2002)

Ramsay, R. 'Wilson and the Security Services', in R. Coopey, S. Fielding and N. Tiratsoo (eds) *The Wilson Governments, 1964–1970* (Pinter, London, 1993)

Ramsden, J. *The Age of Balfour and Baldwin, 1902–1940* (Longman, London and New York, 1978)

Ramsden, J. *The Winds of Change: Macmillan to Heath, 1957–1975* (Longman, London, 1996)

Rawnsley, A. *Servants of the People: The Inside Story of New Labour* (Penguin, London, 2001)

Rentoul, J. *Tony Blair, Prime Minister* (Warner, London, 2001)

Robinson, G. *The Unconventional Minister: My Life Inside New Labour* (Penguin, London, 2001)

Rosebery, Earl of, 'Foreword' to Alfred Stead, *Great Japan: A Study of National Efficiency* (John Lane, London, 1906)

Roseveare, H. *The Treasury: The Evolution of a British Institution* (Allen Lane, London, 1969)

Routledge, P. *Gordon Brown* (Simon and Schuster, London, 1998)

Rowland, P. *Lloyd George* (Barrie & Jenkins, London, 1975)

Scally, R. J. *The Origins of the Lloyd George Coalition: The Politics of Social-Imperialism, 1900–1918* (Princeton University Press, Princeton and London, 1975)

Searle, G. *The Quest for National Efficiency* (Ashfield, London, 1990)

Searle, G. R. *Country before Party: Coalition and the Idea of 'National Government' in Modern Britain, 1885–1987* (Longman, London and New York, 1995)

Seldon, A. with Baston, L. *Major: A Political Life* (Phoenix, London, 1997)

Sinclair, P. 'The Economy: a Study in Failure', in D. McKie and C. Cook (eds) *The Decade of Disillusion: British Politics in the Sixties* (Macmillan, London and Basingstoke, 1972)

Skidelsky, R. *John Maynard Keynes*, vol. 1: *Hopes Betrayed, 1883–1920* (Macmillan, London and Basingstoke, 1983)

Skidelsky, R. *John Maynard Keynes*, vol. 2: *The Economist as Saviour, 1920–1937* (Macmillan, London, 1992)

Skidelsky, R. *John Maynard Keynes*, vol. 3: *Fighting for Britain, 1937–1946* (Macmillan, London, 2000)

Skidelsky, R. *Politicians and the Slump: The Labour Government of 1929–1931* (Macmillan, London, 1994)

Smith, M. *The Core Executive in Britain* (Macmillan, Basingstoke, 1999)

Stewart, M. *Politics and Economic Policy since 1964* (Pergamon, Oxford, 1978)

Stone, R. 'The Use and Development of National Income and Expenditure Estimates', in D. N. Chester (ed.) *Lessons of the British War Economy* (Cambridge University Press, Cambridge, 1951)

Stothard, P. *30 Days* (HarperCollins, London, 2003)

Theakston, K. *The Labour Party and Whitehall* (Routledge, London and New York, 1992)

Theakston, K. *Leadership in Whitehall* (Macmillan, Basingstoke, 1999)

Thirlwall, A. 'Kaldor as Policy Adviser' in T. Lawson, J. Palma and J. Sender (eds), *Kaldor's Political Economy* (Academic Press, London, 1989)

Thirlwall, A. (ed.) *Keynes and International Monetary Relations* (Macmillan, London and Basingstoke, 1976)

Thirlwall, A. (ed.), *Keynes as a Policy Adviser* (Macmillan, Basingstoke, 1982)

Thirlwall, A. *Nicholas Kaldor* (Wheatsheaf, Brighton, 1987)

Thomas, H. 'The Establishment and Society' in Hugh Thomas (ed.), *The Establishment: A Symposium* (Anthony Blond, London, 1959)

Thomas, R. 'UK Economic Policy: The Conservative Legacy and New Labour's Third Way', in Stephen P. Savage and Rob Atkinson (eds), *Public Policy under Blair* (Palgrave, Basingstoke, 2001)

Thorpe, K., 'The Missing Pillar: Economic Planning and the Machinery of Government During the Labour Administrations of 1945–51', PhD thesis, University of London, 1998

Tiratsoo, N. and Tomlinson, J. *The Conservatives and Industrial Efficiency, 1951–64: Thirteen Wasted Years?* (Routledge, London, 1998)

Tomlinson, J. 'Labour and the International Economy in the 1960s', paper presented to the Twentieth Century British History Seminar, Institute of Historical Research, 2 May 2001

Turner, J. *Lloyd George's Secretariat* (Cambridge University Press, Cambridge, 1980)

Walter, J. *The Ministers' Minders* (Oxford University Press, Melbourne, 1986)

Walters, A. 'My Deviationist Economics', *Independent*, 26 October 1989

Whiting, R. *The Labour Party and Taxation: Party Identity and Political Purpose in Twentieth Century Britain* (Cambridge University Press, Cambridge, 2000)

Willetts, D. 'The Role of the Prime Minister's Policy Unit', *Public Administration*, vol. 65, 1987

Wright, M. 'Treasury Control 1854–1914', in G. Sutherland (ed.), *Studies in the Growth of Nineteenth Century Government* (Routledge & Kegan Paul, London, 1972)

Wright, M. *Treasury Control of the Civil Service* (Clarendon, Oxford, 1969)

Young, H. *One of Us: A Biography of Margaret Thatcher* (Pan, London, 1993)

Young, J. W. *Britain and European Unity 1945–1999* (Macmillan, Basingstoke, 2000)

Young, J. W. *Britain and the World in the Twentieth Century* (London: Arnold, 1997)

Young, J. W. *Cold War Europe 1945–1989: A Political History* (London: Edward Arnold, 1991)

Zaleski, E. *Stalinist Planning for Economic Growth* (Macmillan, London, 1980)

Ziegler, P. *Wilson: The Authorised Life of Lord Wilson of Rievaulx* (HarperCollins, London, 1995)

Index

Abel-Smith, Brian 90, 117–119, 122, 148, 160, 165, 305

Adonis, Andrew 274, 275, 276

Alexander, Wendy 259, 260

Allen. Douglas; *see* Croham

Allen, Graham 11

Allen, John 59, 63, 66, 70, 72, 85, 88, 90, 91–2, 103, 122

Allsop, Christopher 108

Anstee, Margaret Joan 1034

Armstrong, Robert 127–9, 130, 131, 136, 1856, 209, 252, 310

Armstrong William 65, 67, 71–2, 76, 82, 84, 95, 126, 127, 135, 147, 163

Asquith, Herbert 35

Atlee, Clement 38, 44

Balls, Edward 251–2, 255, 289–90, 291–3, 304

Balogh, Thomas 33, 40, 45, 49, 50–3, 58–9, 61, 62, 63, 68, 69, 70–75, 78–88, 90, 91, 97–104, 105–6, 122, 164, 183, 298, 301, 304, 305, 311; government wages of 65–7; vetting of 70

Bank of England 82–3, 145–6, 293

Banks, Tony 164, 252

Barber, Anthony 139, 141

Barber, Michael 255, 263–5, 300

Baron, Tom 194

Beckerman, Wilfred 79–80, 121–2

Benn, Tony 84, 85, 86, 91, 114, 148, 151, 153, 155, 164–5, 168–9, 170, 173, 174, 176, 179, 182, 184, 297

Bercow, John 229–30

Beveridge, William 41; Beveridge Report 41, 119

Bevin, Ernest 38, 54

Biffen, John 196, 203

Birt, Lord John 251, 255, 279

Blackwell, Norman 223, 241–2

Blair, Tony; Prime Minister 268, 269, 298, 302; special advisers of 5, 8, 9, 133, 251, 257, 263, 265, 276, 278–9, 282, 283, 284, 295, 302, 311, 312; defence of special advisers 20; preparation for government 252–4, 268, 294–5

Blunkett, David; special advisers of 263–4, 265

Bridges, Sir Edward 46–7, 61

British Rail; privatisation of 231–2

Brown, George 78, 79

Brown, Gordon 220, 254, 283; special advisers of 251, 255–7, 265, 267, 289–94, 295–6, 302

Burke, Tom 223, 229, 232–5, 298

Burnham, Andy 261–2

Burns, Terry 290–1

Bush, George W.; policy of loyalty to 263

Byers, Stephen 279; Jo Moore affair 13–14; resignation of 15

Cairncross, Alec 65, 71, 73, 81, 82, 83, 84, 88, 93, 96, 121, 215

Callaghan, James 65, 71–2, 79, 83, 84, 86, 92, 93, 94, 95, 113, 151, 153, 163, 171, 173, 174, 178, 179, 183, 302

Campbell, Alastair 9, 10, 22, 246, 251, 256, 265, 268, 269, 271, 279, 280–1, 284–9; growing profile of 272, 288, 300, 308, 309, 312

Campbell-Bannerman, Henry 35

Cardona, George 196–7, 207

Carmichael, Kay 171

Castle, Barbara 84, 85, 92, 114, 116, 117, 119–21, 163–5, 176

Channel 4 News 237

Chaplin, Judith 237

Churchill, Winston 36, 39–40, 53

Citizen's Charter 240–1

Civil Service, perceived weakness of 5, 156; traditional career in 7, 32–3, 49; treasury dominance of 7, 34, 37, 76, 130, 151, 304; politicisation of 7, 11, 17, 19, 20, 68, 135, 220–1, 267; Civil Service Act 13, 22; Civil Service Code 23–28; Victorian reform of 31–5, 46, 61, 311; unification of Home Civil Service 37–8; French 50–1, 52, 77, 181; Fulton report 63, 75–8, 88, 150; opposition to special advisers 71, 73, 79, 88, 104, 129–30, 136, 166, 171, 188, 195, 197, 207, 267, 314; Civil Service Order 1978 154

Clark, Alan 246

Clark, David 262–3, 291

Clarke Charles 257, 261, 267

Clarke, Greg 229

Clarke, Kenneth 223, 229–30, 246

Clinton, Bil 270, 282

Cook, Robin 253, 262, 283

Cooper, Theo 103

Cope, John 124, 125, 127

Corry, Dan 260, 276, 304; checks following Paddington rail crash 17–18

CPRS, Central Policy Review Staff 133–6, 146, 147, 151, 156, 172, 183, 187, 209

CPS; Centre for Policy Studies 189–90

CRD; Conservative Research Department 125–7, 136, 138, 189–90, 209, 219–20

Cripps, Francis 148, 167, 169, 179

Cripps, Sir Stafford 44

Croham, Lord; prev. Douglas Allen 68, 96, 113, 115, 152

Cropper, Peter 186, 196–7

Crosland, Anthony 114, 121, 160, 161–2, 184

Crossman, Richard 56, 59, 69, 85, 86, 87, 96, 101, 102, 111, 114, 115, 117–8, 122, 174

Cryer, Bob 220

currency, devaluation 79–84 , 103; great train robbery reissue 86; integration with EEC 144–5, 199, 211, 216; (exit from ERM 238–9; (membership of single European 263(Howe's strategy for 196

Dalton, Hugh 43–4, 117

Daily Express 14, 74

Daily Mail 10, 14, 198, 246, 282

Daily Mirror 14, 114, 284, 285, 286

Daily Star 13

Daily Telegraph 237, 279, 308

Davies, Gavyn 171

Demos 260

Dewar, Donald 259, 278

Dobbs, Michael 195, 207

Donoughue, Bernard 135, 151–5, 171–2, 173, 174, 175, 176–80, 182, 210, 252, 298, 300, 311

Duguid, Andrew 188

Duncan Smith, Iain 16–17

Economist 18, 125, 130, 166, 176, 237

Eden, Anthony 48

EEC 105–7, 143–5, 164, 173

Evening Standard 136, 237, 249, 288

Fabian Society 35, 47, 50–1, 54–8, 60, 182, 260, 293

Falklands War 216

Field, Frank 268, 285

Financial Times 9, 75, 100, 217–8, 273, 274, 275, 276, 289

Finkelstein, Danny 229

Follett, Ken; on negative press briefing by aides 12

Forever Unmentionable Committee 82–4

Foster, Christopher 90, 110, 119–21, 122, 159, 208, 229, 231–2

Fowler, Norman 195

Fulton Report; see Civil Service

Gaitskell, Hugh 75, 93, 110

Gladstone, William 32–3

Gordon Walker, Patrick 111, 115–6

Gow, Ian 180

Graham, Andrew 102, 103, 104, 171, 177, 229

Granatt, Mike 265–6, 269, 280–1

Griffiths, Brian 199–200, 201, 202, 203, 213, 219, 221–2

Guardian 9, 120, 187, 191, 202, 279

Hague, Douglas 210

Haines, Joe 18, 129, 177–8, 283

Hanley, Jeremy 227

Harman, Harriet 260, 285

Hart, David 235–6, 246

Hart, Judith 85, 164

Harris, John 59, 64, 65, 85, 90, 110–117, 122, 167, 170, 300, 302

Harris, Robin 219

Haslam, Jonathan 243–4

Hattersley, Roy 158

Healy, Denis 166–7, 169, 297

Heath, Edward 123, 126–7, 132, 135, 136, 138, 139, 141, 142, 145, 182, 313

Henderson, Hubert, influence on Balogh 98–9

Heseltine, Michael, on appointed aides 12, 194, 232–35

Hill, David 158

Hill, Jonathan 239–40

Hockley, Tony 229

Hogg, Sarah 223, 237–9, 246, 304

Holland, Stuart 90, 103, 104–110, 160

Hopson, Chris 229

Hoskyns, John 185, 186, 188–92, 199, 202, 203–11, 214–5, 221–2, 298, 299, 301, 302, 304, 305, 312

Howe, Geoffrey 185, 190, 196–7, 199, 202, 204, 206, 213, 215, 219

Hudson, Miles 124, 125

Hunt, John 171–2, 182, 189

Hurd, Douglas 124, 136, 154

Hunter, Anji 270, 280, 309

Independent 14, 189, 233, 306

Ingham, Bernard 12, 203

IPPR, Institute for Public Policy Research 260

Irvine, Derry 10

ITN news 243

Jackson, Robert 124, 125, 127

James, Henry 186

James, Howell 195

Jay, Douglas 44–5

Jenkins, Roy 90, 95–6, 110, 112–4, 115–7, 148, 149, 167, 169, 170, 302

Jones, Nicholas 11

Joseph, Keith 189, 190, 193–4, 204, 205, 206, 213–4

Jowell, Tessa 261

Kaldor, Nicholas 41, 57, 59, 61, 63, 65–75, 78, 80–4, 88, 90, 91, 92–7, 108, 110, 122, 148, 165–6, 167, 169, 293, 297, 300, 301, 305

Kaufman, Gerald 85, 115

Kelly, Lorraine 14

Keswick, Tessa 223, 224, 230–1, 245, 246, 304

Keynes, John Maynard 38, 40–3

Kitchen Cabinet 85, 91, 113–4

Labour Party, research funding 149

Lamont, Norman 210, 237–8

Lansbury, George 57

Laski, Harold 45, 54, 55

Lawson, Nigel 185, 186, 191, 196–9, 202–3, 210, 213, 216, 217–8

Lester, Anthony 148, 167, 170

Letwin, Oliver 198

Liddle, Roger 10, 170, 253–4, 274–5

Lilley, Peter 243

Lipsey, David 148, 160, 161–2, 169, 182, 184

Lloyd George, David 4, 36; Garden Suburb Secretariat 36–7, 41

Luff, Peter 195

Lyttle, John 170

MacDonald, Ramsay 38, 57, 98

MacDougall, Sir Donald 66, 70, 73–4, 80, 81, 83

MacGregor, John 219

Macmillian, Harold 53, 64, 75

Mail on Sunday 14, 18, 246, 288

Major, John 185, 225, 236–43, 244–5, 247, 302, 313; resignation of 246; as Chancellor 196; on cabinet government 11–12

Malone, Gerald 229

Mandelson, Peter 133, 236, 248–9, 253–4, 291
Maudling, Reginald 75
McFadden, Pat 277–8, 282
McManus, Michael 229
McNally, Tom 149, 160, 163, 170
Miliband, David 256, 260, 271, 273–4, 280, 304
Miliband, Ed 289, 304
Millar, Fiona 284
miners' strikes 208
Ministry of Information 41–2
Moore, Jo 9, 13–15, 312
Moore, John 201
Morrell, Frances 148, 153, 155, 164–5, 167–8, 169, 170, 179, 297
Morris, Charles 180
Mount, Ferdinand 191, 199, 200, 202, 219, 221–2
Mountfield, Sir Robin 252, 267, 269, 276, 279
Murdoch, Iris; affair with Balogh 97

Neild, Robert 63–8, 71, 73–4, 78, 80–3, 88, 92, 93, 101, 102, 121
Neuberger, Henry 108–9, 110
New Statesman 9, 159, 181
Nolan Committee; see Standards in Public Life Committee
Northcote–Trevelyan Report; see Civil Service – Victorian reform of
Nye, Sue 255, 256, 289

Oakeshott, Matthew 149, 170
Oborne, Peter 284; dislike of special advisers 15–16
Observer 101
Orwell, George 42
O'Sullivan, John 219
Owen, David 152, 161, 170, 174, 176, 182, 228–9
Owen, Ed 265, 267

Palliser, Sir Michael 102, 104
Parkinson, Cecil 210
Patten, Chris 236–7
pensions; national superannuation 118–9, 165
Piachaud, David 171
Policy Directorate 275, 279, 295, 312

Policy Unit 2, 302; under Wilson148, 150, 151, 170–2 175, 176, 177; under Callaghan 173–5, 179 ; under Thatcher 183, 185–9, 190–1, 214; under Major 224, 236–43, 250, 303; under Blair see also Policy Directorate 251, 253–4, 270–1, 272–3, 276, 277, 280, 284
Portillo, Michael 186, 191, 207, 208, 235, 243, 246
Posner, Michael 121
Powell, Charles 203, 282
Powell, Jonathan 22, 251, 256, 278, 279, 280–1, 282–4, 304, 306, 309, 312
Prescott, John 276, 283
Priestly, J.B. 40
Private Eye 180
Public Administration Committee 12, 26, 244, 285, 286, 287, 312; report on Special Advisers 13; on Jo Moore 15, 297, 305

Reading, Brian 123, 125, 127, 129, 130–1, 136, 138–9, 140–2, 143, 144–5, 146, 147, 303
Redwood, John 189, 191, 199–201, 222, 227–8, 243, 245–6
Rees, Peter 197
Ridley, Adam 136, 186, 190, 196–7, 206–7, 218–9
Rifkind, Malcolm 235–6
Rodgers, William 170
Ross-Goobie, Alistair 198
Rothschild, Victor 136, 146, 167
Rowntree Trust; chocolate soldiers 149
Ryan, Connor 265, 269
Rycroft, Tim 227, 229

Schreiber, Mark; also Lord Marlesford 124, 125, 127–9, 131–2, 134, 136, 137, 139–40, 141, 142, 143, 147, 299, 304
Scotland on Sunday 236
Scott, Derek 170, 274–5
SCU; strategic communications unit 271, 285
SET; selective employment tax 93–6
Sewill, Brendon 124, 125, 127, 128, 129, 136, 138, 141, 143, 145, 146
Shepherd, Robert 186
Sherman, Alfred 189, 190, 191, 202, 205, 213–4
Shipley, Peter 190–1
Shore, Peter 57, 72, 85, 91, 114, 161, 163, 164, 165

Short, Clare 9, 308–9

Sixsmith, Martin 14–15

Smith, Chris 261

Special advisers 265; in europe 6, 20, 56, 133, 159, 181; in USA 6, 20, 56, 63, 86, 87, 133 ; in Australia 158–9; appointment of 3, 6, 10, 17, 22–23, 76, 152, 181, 225–6; portrayal by press of 19, 241; historical examples of 30, 36, 39, 299; in Wilson Government 63–122, 148–173, 313; in Callaghan Government 174, 178–9; in Heath Government 123–148, 313; in Thatcher Government185–222, 313; in Major Government 223–250, 313; in Blair Government 251, 254–296, 310, 313; vetting of 70; dislike of permanent civil service by 92, 101, 130, 131, 166, 168, 207–8, 234; access to classified material by 154–5, 177; to stop Civil Service infighting 175; leaks to press from 180, 312; resentment by MPs of 180–1, 202, 220, 228, 244, 247, 257, 268, 276; regulation of 154, 223–7, 248, 249–50, 257, 306–7

Spectator 288

Sproat, Ian 180

Standards in Public Life Committee 12, 15, 29, 151, 157, 162, 172, 174, 197, 223, 224, 244, 247–8, 257, 261, 280, 306

Stephen, David 160, 170

Stepping Stones Report 205–6, 208

Stewart, Michael 63, 66, 70, 72, 86, 88, 94, 103, 104, 174

Strauss, Norman 189, 205, 210

Straw, Jack 148, 163–45, 169, 252; special advisers of 265

Sun 14, 269

Sunday Telegraph 16, 179, 237

Sunday Times 180, 229, 241, 260

Tebbit, Norman 195

Thatcher, Margaret 185, 190, 191, 193, 199, 201, 202, 203, 205–6, 208, 209, 210, 212, 215, 217–8, 221–2, 241, 242, 297, 298, 302; suspicion of career civil servants 186; urged to keep Policy Unit 180; establishment of administration of 4

Third Way 273

Times 9, 233, 269, 276

transport; Act 1968 120; Victoria tube line 119

Trend, Sir Burke 66–9, 70, 72, 85, 100, 101–2, 134, 136, 311

Trevelyan, Charles Edward; *see also* Civil Service 31–2, 34

True, Nicholas 195, 239, 240

Tyrie, Andrew 197–9

Waldegrave, William 136

Walters, Prof Alan 146–7, 185, 187, 192, 199, 202, 210, 212–8, 221–2, 297, 300, 311

Wells, H.G. 35, 55

Westwell Report 185, 210–2

Whelan, Charlie 251, 267, 289–91, 312

Whitelaw, William 126

Wicks Committee; see Standards in Public Life Committee

Wigg, George 84, 85, 95, 100, 177

Williams, Hywell 228, 240, 245, 246–7

Williams, Marcia 84, 85, 91, 92, 105, 111, 150, 176, 178

Williams Shirley 162–3, 170

Wilson, Harold 39, 41, 52, 54–6, 58–61, 63, 69, 71–3, 75, 78, 79, 83–7, 91, 100–7, 109, 111, 113, 115–6, 127, 129, 148–9, 153–5, 157–9, 169, 171–4, 176, 177, 182, 183, 298, 300

Wilson, Sir Richard; see also Standards in Public Life Committee 8, 19, 46, 157, 188, 189, 224, 280, 283–4, 286–7, 310–1

Wolff, Michael 123, 125, 127

Wolfson, David 209, 210

Wright, Tony; see also Public Administration Committee 9, 15, 19

Young, David 193–4, 195, 204, 221–2

Young, Hugo 16